THE TRUSTEES 193

1984
1980
1976
1972
1968
1964
1960
1956
1952
1948
1944
1940
1936

George Henry Hudson Lyall
Thomas Renton Elliott
Sir Henry Hallett Dale
Lancelot Claude Bullock
Martin Price
Lord Piercy of Burford
Sir John Boyd
Sir John McMichael
Robert Malleson Nesbitt
Lord Franks of Headington
Robert Thompson
Lord Murray of Newhaven
Henry Barcroft
Charles Gordon Smith
Lord Swann
Lord Armstrong
Sir Stanley Peart
Sir William Paton
Sir David Steel
Isabella Helen Muir
Roger Gibbs

Chairman
Scientific Trustee

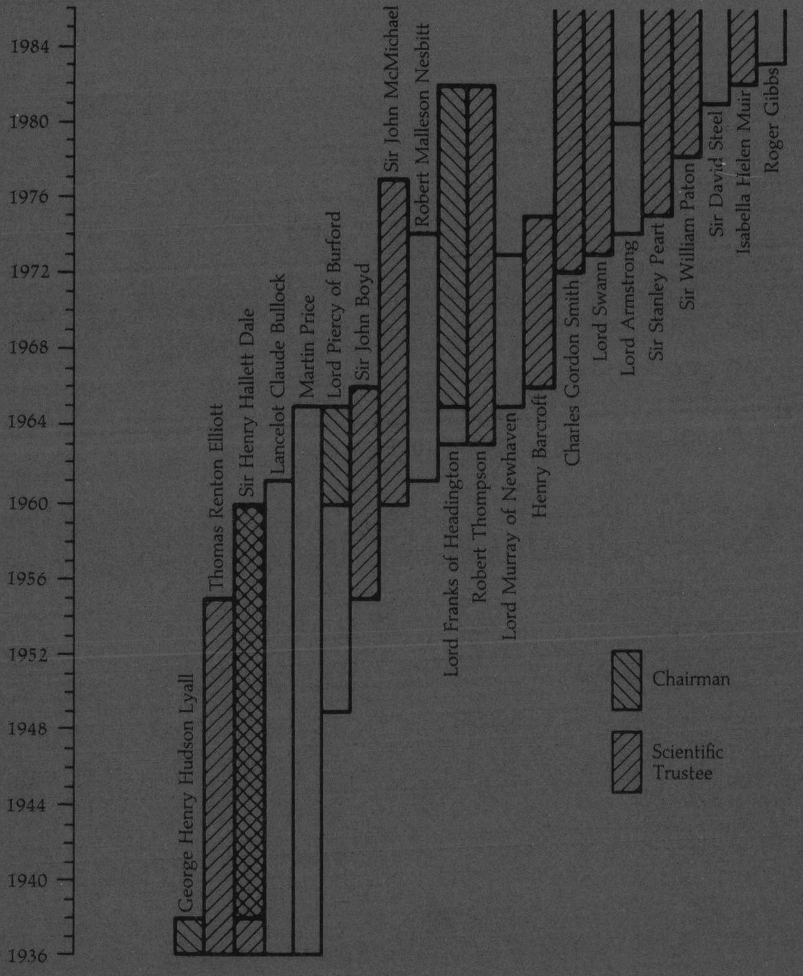

PHYSIC AND PHILANTHROPY

Sir Henry Solomon Wellcome (1853-1936)
Oil painting by Sir Hugh Goldwin Riviere, 1906
(Wellcome Institute Library, London)

Physic and philanthropy

A HISTORY OF THE WELLCOME TRUST 1936–1986

A. R. HALL AND B. A. BEMBRIDGE

With a Foreword by Sir David Steel

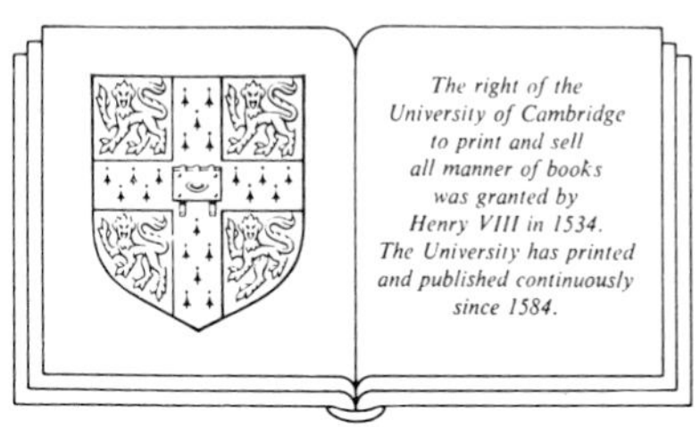

CAMBRIDGE UNIVERSITY PRESS

Cambridge

London New York New Rochelle

Melbourne Sydney

Published by the Press Syndicate of the University of Cambridge
The Pitt Building, Trumpington Street, Cambridge CB2 1RP
32 East 57th Street, New York, NY 10022, USA
10 Stamford Road, Oakleigh, Melbourne 3166, Australia

First published 1986

Printed in Great Britain at the University Press, Cambridge

British Library cataloguing in publication data

Hall, A. R.
Physic and philanthropy : a history of the
Wellcome Trust 1936–1986.
1. Wellcome Trust 2. Medicine – Research –
Great Britain – Finance
I. Title II. Bembridge, B. A.
610'.72041 R854.G7

Library of Congress cataloguing in publication data

Hall, A. Rupert (Alfred Rupert), 1920–
Physic and philanthropy.

Bibliography
Includes index.
1. Wellcome Trust (London, England) – History.
2. Medicine – Research – Endowments. 3. Veterinary
medicine – Research – Endowments. 4. Wellcome, Henry
Solomon, Sir, 1853–1936 I. Bembridge, B. A.
II. Title.
R854.G7H35 1986 610'720421 86–6888

ISBN 0 521 32639 7

CONTENTS

PART I
Origins and evolution of the Wellcome Trust

PART II
The impact of the Wellcome Trust on medical science

Appendices

ILLUSTRATIONS

ACKNOWLEDGEMENTS

The Trustees thank the following for photographs reproduced and permission to use them: The Museum and Laboratories of Ethnic Arts and Technology, University of California, Los Angeles (12); Westminster City Libraries (14); The Royal College of Surgeons of England (15); University College, London (30); The Manchester Museum (31); The Science Museum, London (40, 41); University of Melbourne (42); Christian Medical College Hospital, Vellore, India (47); Instituto Evandro Chagas, Belém, Brazil (49); Royal Society of Tropical Medicine and Hygiene (48, 50, 51, 52); London School of Hygiene and Tropical Medicine (54, 55); Mr N. Phelps Brown (58); Laboratory of Molecular Biology, Cambridge (61); St Mary's Hospital Medical School (62, 63); Australian National University (64).

THE TRUSTEES, 1936–86

FOREWORD

Sir Henry Wellcome was an astute businessman and a generous philanthropist. By his Will, he appointed Trustees who were both the shareholders of his Company and the heirs of his benevolent intentions. As Chairman of the present body of Sir Henry Wellcome's Trustees, I am proud to believe that Wellcome's Company and Wellcome's endowment of research in medical science have alike prospered far beyond any expectation he could have entertained. The credit for this belongs, of course, to my predecessors and their co-Trustees: to Sir Henry Dale, to Lord Piercy and to Lord Franks; perhaps most of all to Dale (the unique scientist to serve as a Chairman of the Trust) who did so much by wise decisions to save Wellcome's Company from wreck, and by deep foresight to set our support of medical science on the right lines.

Fifty eventful years have passed since Wellcome's death. During the first half of this time, under Dale's direction, the Trustees could do little better than lay sound foundations for future activity. The true worth of Wellcome's plan for medical research only began to be realised some 15 years ago. In this short period the Trust has become a large and powerful organisation with wide international responsibilities and a formidable body of scientific expertise at its disposal.

How these changes came about, how the functions of the Trust in its medical, veterinary and historical fields of research have developed, is told in the following history prepared by its officers. The whole has been edited by Professor A. Rupert Hall who wrote Part I and a portion of Part II. Dr. B. A. Bembridge is the principal author in Part II, where there are also contributions by the Director of the Trust, Dr P. O. Williams – who has served it for more than a quarter of a century – and other officers.

The Trustees wish to express their gratitude in particular to Professor

Hall and to Drs Bembridge and Williams who have all worked so hard to make this history possible. Our thanks are also due to the staffs of the Trust, of the Wellcome Institute for the History of Medicine and of the Wellcome Tropical Institute, the Archivist of the London School of Economics, and the many grant-holders (past and present) who have kindly responded to enquiries.

Sir David Steel

I am wondering whether our experience as Trustees
will eventually be more suitable for record
as a novel or a play.

Sir Henry Dale to Professor T. R. Elliott,
20 December 1943

Part I

ORIGINS AND EVOLUTION OF THE WELLCOME TRUST

1

A GREAT PURPOSE

Background

When Sir Henry Solomon Wellcome died in the London Clinic on 25 July 1936, just short of his 83rd birthday, he possessed one of the largest industrially-based incomes in Great Britain, comparable to that of the greatest landed aristocrats and with far fewer commitments. Naturalised in Great Britain for a quarter of a century and firmly settled in British life for much longer, he was never forgetful of his origins and family in the United States, whence indeed a large portion of his great wealth derived. Starting in an up-country drug-store owned by an uncle, becoming a travelling salesman for various manufacturers, Wellcome had in 1880 formed a partnership with Silas Burroughs with the object of introducing into Britain, where the drug industry was still primitive, the American wholesale manufacture of ready-made pills, christened 'Tabloids' by Henry Wellcome in 1884. The business prospered, and Burrough's death in 1895 allowed its sole ownership to pass to Wellcome.

Though his initial success owed much to showmanship and sales techniques, he remained always the puritanical son of a missionary father, deeply imbued with distrust of

> Youth at the helm, and Pleasure at the prow,

conscious always of moral responsibility and the serious import of all good intentions. It was in his power to do good, and good he must therefore do. It is surely no accident that Wellcome's disastrous marriage was to a daughter of Dr Barnardo. What is more strange is that Wellcome's wish to be benevolent assumed unusual forms. He did not, like his father-in-law, turn to the rescue of the poor and unfortunate, nor like Andrew Carnegie encourage learning and provide educational opportunities in conventional ways. Although the scientific foundations for

Wellcome's early success in the manufacture of pharmaceuticals – at first, wholly 'non-ethical' – were minimal, he had by his maturity developed a respectful understanding of the utility of medical research, and of its ability to change the treatment of disease. While Burroughs and Wellcome were creating that drug empire which Wellcome alone was to inherit, German chemical manufacturers were achieving a leadership in the preparation of the new, synthetic medicaments of which the best known is 'Aspirin' (1899), just as they had formerly achieved dominance in the dyestuffs industry. Whether or not Wellcome studied intently this example of his competitors' exploitation of an opportunity created by science, it is certain that he understood it and sought to pursue the same objective in his own company, through a creative combination of benevolence and profit in the true Victorian spirit. Even in his 60s Wellcome was closely enough in touch with the scientific pretensions of a rival firm, Parke Davis, to commend to Henry Dale a full investigation of the properties of ergot. His shrewdness could never be overestimated.

In the *Memorandum for the Guidance of my Trustees*, written when he was 79 but formalising principles he had long practised, Wellcome pointed out how splendid were the prospects for the future of the pharmaceutical industry:

> With the enormous possibility of developments in Chemistry, Bacteriology, Pharmacy and allied sciences if my desires and plans are carried out in the way of Research in co-operation with the several industrial organisations [of the Wellcome Foundation] there are likely to be vast fields opened for productive enterprise for centuries to come.

Wellcome's view of what 'Research' should be was not restricted to the laboratory search for new and effective drugs: it involved a broad and historical study of the human scene and of the ills that flesh is heir to. The bases of success in his business he defined as being 'original scientific research, historical study and practical experimentation' in the medical sciences, so that his Foundation might be 'always leading and first in the field' in developing improved methods for the treatment of disease and injury:

> The fruits of research work [he wrote] should constantly contribute to the effort to combat pain and disease and stay the hand of death, and thus the world at large [may] gain by added knowledge and by scientific discoveries and excellence and exactitude in production.

Bearing in mind the breadth of Wellcome's concept of research – embracing archaeological excavation and library investigation as well as laboratory experiment – it is evident that he had a vision of a vast medical culture, arising from a comprehensive study of the past and present experience of mankind, of which 'excellence and exactitude' in the production of substances able to improve the present lot of man were the useful, creative fruits. Wellcome made no attempt to work out the connections between the various elements of his ameliorist philosophy, for he surely took for granted the proposition that good intentions prudently and rationally executed must yield beneficial results as sanctified by the divine purpose if not by academic logic, but he assures his Trustees in plain terms that this is a philosophy that *works*; speaking of his huge collections illustrating the cultural history of man he wrote:

> I have found that the collection of these articles and the establishment of Museums and Libraries associated with the Research Work of my various Institutions has proved of the utmost value and has contributed greatly to the success of my industrial organisations as well as to the success of my various Research Institutions.

Hence, especially, it was important that his 'original Museums and Research Library should be made as complete as possible or practicable'.

Wellcome's contention, then, was that he had partially created, and would leave to his Trustees to perfect, a system in which rich comprehension of the medical culture in all its dimensions would inform industrial evolution as the immediate vehicle for the physical and psychological well-being of man in the future. Such a grand view, however naive in certain aspects, seems to have been unique to Wellcome. It certainly motivated his generosity and inspired the details of his Will (where the lawyers did their best to tie his philosophy into legal knots).

Inevitably the expression of this grand view in Wellcome's own lifetime was shaped by circumstance and his own particular tastes and preoccupations. His father's concern for the conversion and spiritual health of North American Indians may be reflected in his own long involvement with the Tsimshean Indians settled at Metlakahtla in British Columbia, about whom he wrote a book (1887), though this is no ethnographic study but rather a plea infused with sympathy for a primitive people, against the self-seeking severity of misguided missionaries and acquisitive settlers. Wellcome continued to finance these people to the end of his days, but made no provision for them in his Will. Similarly, Wellcome's enterprise in the Sudan was largely a product of circumstance – tropical medicine in all parts of the world cried out for investigation. The long-continued study of Lachish was inspired by an archaeologist, and was not Wellcome's own idea. What was his own was his receptivity and his enthusiasm.

The spirit in which Sir Henry Wellcome conceived of the realisation of his beneficent philosophy and of its continuance by his Trustees after his own death inevitably belonged to a now distant age of the past when the supremacy of private enterprise was unquestioned, when medical and scientific research depended for support rather on private benevolence than on the public purse, and when the underdeveloped three-quarters of the globe was very much the white man's burden. When, at the end of the century, Henry Wellcome found himself possessed of great wealth, far from seeking to associate his name with lavish cultural palaces in the manner of Frick, Mellon and Morgan (thereby incidentally enriching the Duveens and Rosenburgs of this world), he planned instead to ensure as far as possible the existence in perpetuity of the business organisation he had created, and to tie it to the advance of knowledge for the public good. He had no desire to found a dynasty, to acquire estates, or to build. He believed like most of his contemporaries in cultural, intellectual and economic progress and in the obligation incumbent upon those who had advanced furthest to assist their less fortunate brethren dwelling among Greenland's icy mountains, or where Africa's sunny fountains roll down their golden (but barren) strands. He believed also, as again many others from the late Prime Minister, W. E. Gladstone, downwards also believed, in the virtuous effect of the Reforming Hand. Some evil and misery in the world sprang from incapacity, which might be aided by those possessing greater strength; some came from ignorance, which the spread of knowledge might correct; some was fostered by vice, to be remedied by example and deterrence. A combination of intellectual, moral and monetary forces, suitably applied, could alleviate if not banish many ills, both in industrial and in primitive societies. Therefore he endeavoured to rule his empire as a model employer, or benevolent dictator; therefore too he endeavoured to encourage all who came under his influence to lead sober, prudent lives and fight the demon alcohol; therefore he relished for many years the opportunity to do good by research in one corner of the tropics. In doing good vicariously through Trustees he would perpetuate his great purpose.

Curiously, but surely of intent, Sir Henry Wellcome arranged to sign his last Will and Testament on 29 February 1932. The Will is a complex document in legal English, nominating the Trustees, defining their powers, and prescribing the manner in which they should dispose of the sums of money placed in their hands by the managers of the pharmaceutical business in support of archaeological, historical and medical research. The 'Memorandum of my Policy and Aims for the Guidance and Assistance of my Trustees' signed on the same day is, however, the work of Wellcome's own pen and though slightly more brief than the Will, and more discursive in style, is far more enlightening than the legal document as to the hopes, ambitions and visions of this elderly manufacturer.

The first essential was that the business should be profitable. Without funds, which had to be fought for as profits from the competitive, and indeed uncertain, battles of commerce, all philanthropic and learned intentions must fail. Hence Wellcome insisted like a military commander that in all departments at all levels 'the principle of the selection of the fittest must always prevail', and that any man found unfit for his duty must go. One measure of fitness for duty should be abstinence from alcohol, at any rate before the age of 26, and before the evening supper. The Directors and others in positions of authority in the business were to use precept and example in the avoidance of beery or vinous muzziness during the long afternoons. Another lesson that Wellcome had learned in his youth was that advertising multiplied sales, so he desired his successors to ensure that 'there shall be no material reductions in the proportional expenditure for publicity and other forms of propaganda' on behalf of Wellcome products, for this policy 'will ultimately result in greatly increased profits though the immediate results may be for a time to keep the profits within lower limits'. Wellcome foresaw that for so long as growth and change were occurring in the pharmaceutical industry, so long must the advertising battle for markets be waged. Besides advertising, Wellcome regarded the continued application of scientific discovery within the business as being crucial, but he was careful nevertheless to distinguish between its production and research aspects, arguing that the heads of the scientific laboratories he had organised and of his museums should not be expected to direct or supervise operations in the experimental or manufacturing departments. The lines of research work to be followed within the Foundation (under the authority of the Director of the Wellcome Bureau of Scientific Research) should be determined by the Trustees in consultation with the Directors of the Foundation, a 'frequent and harmonious exchange of views between all concerned' being strongly recommended in order to avoid the loss of opportunities and to ensure the swift exploitation of new knowledge. Much of this

Fig. 1. The Wellcome Building at Snow Hill in the City of London, destroyed in 1941.

intellectual fruit would doubtless constitute nothing more than an addition to the world's stock of information, yet also (Wellcome believed) a large part of it must prove of practical utility to mankind and the Wellcome business.

After the economic health of his enterprise, upon which all else depended, Wellcome's next most pressing advice to his Trustees turned on the health and comfort of the people who actually worked in it. Here, perhaps, some definitions are necessary. The Wellcome Foundation Ltd (constituted in 1924) was controlled by a Board consisting of a Governing Director (at the time of Sir Henry's death, Mr George E. Pearson) and four adjoint Directors, the sole shareholder being Wellcome himself and after his death, his Trustees, save that one share was allotted to each Director as a qualification for membership of the Board. The Foundation was composed of two parts: the pharmaceutical business, with offices at Snow Hill, London, designed by Wellcome and with factories at Dartford and elsewhere, and the Research Institution, established since 1932 in the Wellcome Building on Euston Road. The Research Institution in turn comprised the Wellcome Bureau of Scientific Research, the Chemical

Fig. 2. Two early directors of the Wellcome Bureau of Scientific Research; (*left*) Sir Andrew Balfour, F.R.S. (1873–1931) and (*right*) Dr C. M. Wenyon, F.R.S. (1878–1948).

Research Laboratory, the Physiological Research Laboratory and the Entomological Research Laboratory, together with the Museum of Medical Science and the Museum and Library of the History of Medicine. The Bureau had been the province of (Sir) Andrew Balfour (1873–1931), as it was later of Dr C. M. Wenyon; the heads of the Museums and Library were very much under Sir Henry Wellcome's own direction. As already noted, Wellcome was insistent that experimentation on and testing of drugs was no function of the Research Bureau; such work was properly part of the business.

Wellcome plainly recognised the hazards associated with research and with his business generally, and in some detail advised his Trustees on how fire risks and especially the dangers of toxicity might be avoided:

> I have always regarded it as one of our highest duties to enforce every possible measure to safeguard against the dangers of poisons of every kind and all other harmful substances, to protect all members of the staff and employees engaged in the production and handling of such harmful substances . . .

Nor was the protection of the consuming public by the maintenance of the highest standards of purity and control any less incumbent upon the managers of the Foundation.

As a model employer, Wellcome had provided for the welfare of his employees and research workers; there was a Pension Fund, there were works clubs and other provisions 'for the general welfare and development mentally, morally and physically of the staff and others employed' in the enterprise as well as a system of merit and long-service awards and a sick-benefit scheme; the necessity of continuing all this by a levy on the profits was to be firmly enforced by the terms of his Will. One of Wellcome's dearest wishes – with which he opens his 'Memoranda' – was for the laying out of a Model Town and Works in the style of Cadbury's Bournville or Levers' Port Sunlight, a project whose ideal characteristics he delineated in some detail.

> Among the essentials in selecting the site are healthfulness of locality, freedom from nuisances, practicability for transport and shipment for home and abroad, convenience, expedition and moderate cost of transport within the premises and to and from London and other railway stations and shipping ports, an abundant supply of good pure suitable water from various reliable sources including artesian wells and general cheerfulness of surroundings.

Neither Trustees nor Directors seem ever to have taken Wellcome's plan seriously, so that Dartford (which he thought to be unsuitable as a long-term base for his business) has remained the chief seat of manufacture; perhaps fortunately, in that the idea of the 'company town', however benevolently meant, seems alien to the spirit of the later 20th century.

After exploring briefly the vision of the founder of the Wellcome Trust, and noting the enormous importance he attached to the continuing and increasing vigour of the two aspects of his Foundation, Research and Production, which he entrusted to his Trustees, it remains to write something of the other interests and enterprises which he particularly commended to them by his Will.

Two institutions which Wellcome never forgot, where he had himself learned pharmacy, were the Philadelphia College of Pharmacy and Science and the University of Illinois School of Pharmacy. At both of these, as also at the Pharmaceutical Society of Great Britain, he wished 'the student most proficient in research' during each year to be rewarded by a Gold Medal. He had already provided a medal at Edinburgh for a student essay on the history of medicine, and financed cognate awards by the Association of Military Surgeons in the U.S.A. (for research), by the Africa Society (for distinguished service), and by the Royal Society of Anthropology. He wished his Trustees to continue these awards, and invited them to institute new ones of a similar nature.

Of a very different kind and of much weightier financial implication was Sir Henry Wellcome's double involvement in the Sudan, which (from 1898 to 1951) was an Anglo–Egyptian condominium, with Egypt itself very much in the British 'sphere of influence'. In the battle of 2 September 1898, near Omdurman, the Sirdar of the Egyptian army, Colonel Kitchener, had destroyed the forces of the insurgent Mahdi and opened the way for a new colonial regime. Kitchener soon handed over the Governor-Generalship to Sir Reginald Wingate (1861–1953). One of the first civilian groups to enter the region thus re-opened to Europeans, in 1900, included Henry Wellcome. The visit deeply impressed him: he saw the need and possibility of medical research in this now relatively accessible part of the interior of tropical Africa; he saw evidences of ancient history around him; and he found – as he had in the Americas on his travels – peoples in need of aid, guidance and benevolence. In the following year he equipped and financed the Wellcome Tropical Research Laboratories, directed by Andrew Balfour, then fresh from distinguished medical service in South Africa. These were associated with the recently founded Gordon College in Khartoum. After an extremely active decade, yielding four large volumes of reports, Balfour returned to England to create the Wellcome Bureau of Scientific Research, and it would seem that activity in the Khartoum Laboratories was less vigorous thereafter. Meanwhile Sir Henry had returned to the Sudan himself in 1910, in the process of convalescence from a long illness. Before leaving England he was invited by Kitchener – whom he must have met in the Sudan before – to a meeting in London at which he was urged by Kitchener to try to do something more for the Sudanese people.

The historian of Wellcome's intervention in Sudanese archaeology has written:

> it is important to realise that Mr Wellcome regarded his enterprise from its inception as one undertaken primarily for the benefit of the natives of the Sudan, and not solely as an archaeological expedition. He had embarked upon it in response to an appeal from Lord Kitchener, and his main preoccupation throughout was with welfare work and what

Fig. 3. Henry Wellcome at his excavations in the Sudan.

Fig. 4. Henry Wellcome with the staff of the Tropical Research Laboratory at Gordon College, Khartoum.

> may best be described as 'uplift' . . . Archaeology was the hand maid of philanthropy.
> (Frank Addison, *Jebel Moya*, Oxford University Press, 1949, 1–2.)

The philanthropy, of course, lay in the employment of the many hundred labourers whom Wellcome could afford to engage on large-scale earth-moving, and in his personal efforts for their welfare. Of these the most flamboyant was his institution of the Order of the Peacock; when a labourer had abstained from *merissa* (native beer) for eight weeks and had sworn on the Koran to drink it no more, he was admitted to the Order and solemnly awarded a peacock's feather to wear as its insignia. Further to employ, to impress and to create comfort Wellcome had constructed for himself a vast House of Boulders, the great stones being bonded by concrete and roofed with concrete and steel. For the more skilled parts of this work Italian and Greek masons were engaged, just as experienced Egyptian foremen were brought in to control the dig.

In opening up the site near Jebel Moya – conveniently only three kilometres from the railway crossing the Gezira plain that lies between the Blue and White Niles – Wellcome had at first only unskilled assistance, but within a month (that is, in February 1911) he had been joined by qualified men, including Europeans. Thus began a long task, whose completion in publication was to outlast Wellcome himself for many years. At the time of his death a vast quantity of material had been assembled, some already shipped to England but much still in Africa, and indeed undivided between the recipients of it.

The other major archaeological study which Wellcome supported began much later and in quite a different way. The initiative came in 1932 from a professional archaeologist, James Leslie Starkey (1895–1938), who had the ambition to tackle a major site in Palestine. He found three backers in Sir Henry Wellcome, Sir Charles Marston, and Sir Robert Mond, but the former soon took the lion's share of responsibility, so that the enterprise became known as the Wellcome Archaeological Research Expedition to the Near East. The decision was made to tackle a site at Tell-ed-Duweir, some 25 miles south-west of Jerusalem, believed by scholars to be the remains of the ancient city of Lachish, one of the five chief Amorite towns in Palestine. Work began in the autumn of 1932, with local labour under the direction of experienced workers, two of whom came from Egypt. It continued every season until Sir Henry Wellcome's death, and again thereafter as the Wellcome–Marston Expedition, Sir Charles taking on half the costs and the Trustees the rest. Again, nothing had been published when the Trust became effective.

Finds from Lachish were, nevertheless, to be published relatively early, in 1938, because of the peculiar interest attaching to the 'Lachish Letters', found early in 1935 by John Richmond when a room beneath a later Persian structure was cleared. The Hebrew 'letters' are inscribed potsherds, or ostraca, which had survived incineration; in contrast to the poverty of other very early material in Hebrew, they contain 'nearly 90 fully readable and some fragmentary lines of clear writing, beautiful language and highly important contents'. Now deposited in the British Museum, they probably represent the most important archaeological discovery associated with Wellcome's name, and it was fortunate that he lived to enjoy it. The double-page spread devoted to Lachish in *The Illustrated London News* for 6 July 1935 must have given him great satisfaction.

The foundation of the vast collections which Wellcome committed to his Trustees has been described elsewhere. (Helen Turner, *Henry Wellcome – The Man, his Collection and his Legacy*, Heinemann for the Wellcome Trust, 1980.) They represented an almost lifelong interest, since he

Fig. 5. The Anatomy section of the Wellcome History of Medicine Museum, at Wigmore Street in 1926.

already possessed a 'museum and library' in 1880 which could be exhibited at an American Medical Convention, and which he brought to England in 1882. He seems first to have been drawn to 'curiosities' of an anthropological character, reporting to the Royal Commission on National Museums and Galleries (1928) that

> my interest in anthropology came before the medical, but still they have both continued on parallel lines or have been merged.

In 1897, he engaged C. J. S. Thompson – who remained with him until retirement in 1925 – to develop his historical–medical material, though himself ardent in the pursuit of curiosities, much to the distress of his wife, Syrie. Many considerable coups were made, such as the acquisition of part of the Mockler Collection of Jenneriana in 1911 for £500 (the remainder was subsequently acquired at auction), and still more notable, that of Dr J. F. Payne's library in the following year, snatched from the hands of Sir William Osler for £2,300. After World War I Wellcome's collecting was organised on an even larger scale, employing several assistants. The first exhibition of his treasures in London (at 54A Wigmore

Street, June to September 1911) was arranged to coincide with the Seventeenth International Congress of Medicine and was open to medical men only. His Museum was first opened to public view in May 1914 and apart from short intervals remained open until August 1932, when it was transferred to the Wellcome Research Institution (now known simply as the Wellcome Building) in Euston Road. By then the bulk of materials was huge, much of it stored in a former factory at Willesden. Wellcome, always Director of his Museum, aided by his new Conservator Capt. P. Johnston Saint, now undertook a thorough re-working of the collections in preparation for a great new exhibition, until interrupted by death. Thus the grand building he had created had never actually served as a public Museum before the Trustees took office.

They found the Library too at Willesden where it had been since 1928 and, of course, quite inaccessible to scholars. Wellcome had insisted upon meticulous cataloguing but the Trustees found the state of the books confused.

At this stage, before considering the Will itself, the question must be asked: how *serious* and genuine was Wellcome's purpose? He may have spent, during his life, at least £1 million – golden sovereigns for the most part – on scientific research, on archaeology, and on his collections. As a result, a number of major technical discoveries were made, bringing profit to the firm of Burroughs Wellcome (for example, by the production of diphtheria antitoxin serum from horses); and four large volumes of reports came from Khartoum. Otherwise, the publication of Wellcome's archaeological excavations was to be wholly accomplished by his Trustees, and so was the institution of a Historical Museum and Library. The Research Laboratories too were rationally reorganised by them on a modern basis. In many ways, it could be argued, Wellcome had used his great wealth only to create a massive chaos which he then employed others to sort out. Wellcome had also been well aware of the indirect value of his 'hobbies', as Sir Henry Dale was to call them: all served to keep his name before the public. In the first year of the Trust's activity Dale noted of the Historical Medical Museum that

> It has apparently been accepted by the Inland Revenue Authorities as an advertisement, but the Trustees cannot fullfil their duty under the Will if they allow it, in reality, to fall below a proper standard of historical science and scholarship.

With admirable academic integrity, Dale here indicates a possible contrast between Sir Henry Wellcome, a frivolous dilettante for whom the 'cash value' of the Museum was its advertising draw, and the Trustees who had taken on the responsibility, to be literally discharged, of making it the learned institution which Wellcome had failed to create. Many would have thought such a contrast unfair to Wellcome.

Yet Dale spoke from knowledge: he had worked in Wellcome's Physiological Laboratory from 1904 to 1914, the first subject of his research having been suggested by his employer. With ability aided by good fortune, Dale had been launched on a great scientific career. Therefore, he knew the man of whom he spoke when he wrote (in 1941)

> Wellcome, in some respects, was a flamboyant poseur, who wasted on hobbies and a gigantic advertisement money which ought to have gone to assure the future of his business, and our Trust.

This was, of course, a private expression; Sir Henry Dale would not have uttered such an opinion in public. And it must be qualified as hasty and intemperate; the Trustees' early years had not been easy. It would have been far simpler if the Trustees' duties had been limited to spending money on medical research.

In 1941 Dale was annoyed because the business was not in the best of commercial health, provoked by the endless complexities involved in the Will, and frustrated by the inability of the Trustees to make progress in their prime object: the endowment of medical science. Hence his view of Wellcome's purpose cannot be read as a final, considered appreciation. Against it must be set Wellcome's own efforts to achieve his ends in a professional way. He engaged qualified assistants, such as O. G. S. Crawford and A. D. Lacaille in archaeology, the anthropologist Winifred Blackman, not to say such scientists as Andrew Balfour, Dale himself, and C. M. Wenyon (who, although not the recipient of Dale's unqualified approval, had been elected F.R.S. in 1927). The distinctions, including the F.R.S., awarded to Wellcome himself, also suggest that he was more than a rich poseur and hobbyist. The endless, and it may have seemed fruitless, excavations in the Sudan had been prolonged by factors outside their paymaster's control, first the War, then political unrest in the Sudan and Egypt: the Governor-General of the Sudan, Sir Lee Stack, had been assassinated by a nationalist in 1924. Moreover, the suggestions Wellcome passed on to his Trustees for winding up the dig and publishing its finds were perfectly sensible and professional. Whether the laboratories in the Wellcome Building on Euston Road, the Museum of Medical Science, and the Historical Museum and Library (as left by Wellcome to his Trustees) were as worthless in the war years as Dale – much pressed by national concerns of the greatest importance – seems to have been inclined to judge them, it is now hard to tell. Collecting was certainly Wellcome's hobby, and he certainly used the collections rather as a means of enhancing his own prestige than as bases for serious historical study. In this area his purposes were too large to admit of precise definition, and therefore of precise results, nor did he ever find a single authoritative scholar whose advice might have put his collecting on a more manageable, if more mundane basis.

The Will

Sir Henry Wellcome's Will, creating the Trust, is not, despite the excellence of the legal advice available to him, the clearest or most logical of documents, and resort has been had to the Courts on a number of occasions in search of clearer and more ample definitions. It deals with four principal matters: the formation of the Trust and its relation to the Foundation (that is, the business and the Research Institution); then, among the responsibilities enjoined upon or commended to the Trustees, there are personal bequests and honours to his family and American home, provision for Sir Henry's son, Henry Mounteney Wellcome, and for the employees of the business; the treatment of the scientific and archaeological work in the Sudan; and the encouragement of biomedical research and historical studies.

The Trustees named in the Will were: George Henry Hudson Lyall (1881–1938) and Lancelot Claude Bullock (1880–1969), partners in the firm of solicitors which advised him, the former initially acting as Chairman; Sir Henry Hallett Dale (1875–1968), Nobel Laureate, eminent physiologist, who was effectively to head the Trust until 1960, and Sir Walter Morley Fletcher (1873–1933), another great physiologist who, however, died before Wellcome; and finally Martin Price (d.1972), a chartered accountant who was to have considerable effect on the relations between the Trust and the Foundation. In addition to these five – the maximum number of Trustees, by Wellcome's wish – the Will prescribed that if Sir Walter Fletcher predeceased Wellcome (as happened) then Professor Thomas Renton Elliott F.R.S. (1877–1961) should take his place. Elliott, a close friend of Sir Henry Dale, occupied the chair of Clinical Medicine at University College, London.

The Trustees were to be sole shareholders, except for the single qualifying share allotted to each Director of the Foundation (of which an

Fig. 6. G. H. H. Lyall (1881–1938) and L. C. Bullock (1880–1969), Wellcome's solicitors whom he named as Trustees in his Will.

undated surrender was filed). However, the provisions of the Will leave the relationship between the two Boards indefinite. Wellcome's intention was that the Directors should run the business as a commercial enterprise, though final authority rested with the Trustees. Thus, the appointment and remuneration of the Directors was placed in the hands of the Trustees, who had the right to receive all the accounts of the Foundation, to attend meetings of the Board of Directors, and to receive all information about the operations of the Foundation that they might require. In the last resort (should the two Boards differ on some matter) the decision of the Trustees was to be final.

The clauses in the Will, dealing with the appointment of new Trustees as the original members of the Trust resigned or died, proved obscure, and had to be clarified by the Courts subsequently. The principles were, that the number of Trustees should be five (and not more), and that of these two 'shall be men who have had experience and be well qualified in medicine and allied sciences', two others 'shall be men of wide practical business experience one or both of whom should be of high standing and ability on the practice of law and with exceptional experience and qualifications in the conduct and administration of large and important estates'. Difficulty was also occasioned by a provision that the Trustees should abjure association with any company in rivalry with the Foundation – an act Wellcome required of all who entered into his employ. In fact, this clause was to render the Trust inoperative for some months after its founder's death.

What the Trustees did not possess was any executive authority, or really effective means of influencing the Directors' policy save by carrying through a *coup de main*. Moreover, Wellcome had deliberately placed a stumbling-block in the way of interference by the Trustees in the affairs of the Company: George Edward Pearson, named in the Will as Wellcome's faithful lieutenant, and lifelong Governing Director of the Foundation. One other Director was placed in an almost equally impregnable position: 'it is my express wish' declared the Will, 'that so long as they shall live and be able and willing to act the said George Edward Pearson and Gerald Leslie Moore shall continue Directors' of the Foundation. No way of determining 'ability' to serve as a Director was provided. It is thus obvious that though the Trustees ultimately had it in their power to change the Board of Directors, to exercise it would be a painful and perhaps publicly embarrassing process.

The next clauses of the Will make the Trustees responsible for the Foundation's Pension Fund (by the appointment of its separate body of Trustees) and its Welfare Fund, which was not only to serve the usual purposes of such a Fund but to furnish long-service and merit bonuses to employees. The arrangements of the separate settlement made for the benefits of Sir Henry's son, Henry Mounteney Wellcome, are confirmed, and a series of bequests and legacies donated to various members of the Wellcome family, all resident in the United States. There are others too, persons who had served him faithfully in life, including a pension for Major J. S. Uribe, 'my acting Camp Commandant at Gebel Moya in the Sudan'. There is an extraordinary story about this man, a Mexican, to the effect that Wellcome had purchased his life for £5 from a firing-squad.

There follow complex provisions for amenities to be financed by the Trustees at Garden City, Blue Earth County, Minnesota, a place to which Sir Henry's family had moved in his infancy, after his birth in the neighbouring state of Wisconsin. This was to take the form of 'a Library and Auditorium with Assembly Room, park and sports field and children's playground. . . a gift from and in the name of my brother the late Reverend George Theodore Wellcome and myself as a memorial to the memory of our Father and Mother . . .'. Sir Henry Wellcome had already engaged his friend George M. Palmer of Mankato, Minnesota, to act as his agent in this matter, to whom he had given $10,000 for the purchase of land. He instructs his Trustees, during the quarter-century after his death, to accumulate a total of $400,000 for the buildings at Garden City, which were preferably to be 'of strictly pure classical type of Greek or Ionic order of architecture' and for an endowment fund to make them useful, and 'to equip the library with works which while not excluding standard or other good works of fiction shall in the main consist of books of reference and books of [? *read* or] periodicals chosen with a view to the dissemination of scientific and practical knowledge in arts, natural and applied sciences and craftsmanship . . . and also books of history, research, exploration, travel and biography'.

Wellcome named other local trustees including Mr Palmer who were to undertake the project on the spot with the funds his principal Trustees should make available. He also directed that a Mausoleum should be built on the site to which the remains of members of his family should be transferred, but this onus was removed from the Trustees by the British Courts as not constituting a properly charitable purpose in law.

After these family concerns comes the long clause defining what was to be the perennial business of the Wellcome Trust. A Research Fund was to be formed from Wellcome's residuary estate and a percentage of the yearly profits of the Foundation, to be employed as

> a fund for the advancement of research work bearing upon medicine, surgery, chemistry, physiology, bacteriology, therapeutics, materia medica, pharmacy and allied subject(s) and any subject or subjects which have, or at any time may develop, an importance for scientific research which may conduce to the improvement of the physical conditions of mankind; and in particular for the discovery, invention and improvement of medical agents and methods for the prevention and cure of disorders and the control or extermination of insect and other pests which afflict human beings and animal and plant life in tropical and other regions and elsewhere, whether such researches are carried on in the existing institutions known as The Wellcome Bureau of Scientific Research, The Wellcome Entomological Research Laboratories, The Wellcome Physiological Research Laboratories, The Wellcome Chemical Research Laboratories, The Wellcome Museum of Medical Science including Tropical Medicine and Hygiene and The Wellcome Historical Medical Museum, or otherwise, or in any other research Laboratories or Museums which I or my Trustees may establish in any part of the world, or for grants to individuals and/or institutions for the purpose of research work in the directions above indicated or for the organisation,

> equipment and expenses of special research expeditions and commissions sent out from The Wellcome Bureau of Scientific Research or any other like institution or towards the funds of such research expeditions and commissions organised by others.[1]

The Research Fund might also be used for the publication of research, for the assistance of the China Medical Missionary Association (in accordance with a deed of trust executed by Sir Henry Wellcome in 1910), for the prizes and medals he had founded and for the support of the Wellcome Tropical Research Laboratories at Khartoum.

The same clause desires the Trustees to complete under the direction of a competent archaeologist the excavations at Gebel Moya in the Sudan 'which work is now temporarily suspended on account of after war conditions'. Wellcome suggested the name of Dr G. A. Reisner as a 'distinguished archaeologist who is familiar with my work and who has greatly assisted me by his advice and otherwise', or someone working in the field reporting to him; he also wished Dr Reisner and Sir Arthur Keith to jointly undertake the publication of the Sudanese finds, at the expense of his estate.

In a similar way the Foundation's Articles of Association also provided for a percentage of its yearly profits to be devoted to a fund denoted in the Will as 'The Research Museum and Library Fund', from which should be financed the Museums and Library already created by Wellcome, or others to be instituted by his Trustees 'and for the purchase and acquisition of books, manuscripts, documents, picture(s) and other works of art . . . and for conducting researches and collecting information connected with the history of medicine, surgery, chemistry, bacteriology, pharmacy and allied sciences'.

Both of these funds were to be registered as Charities.

Finally, a last proposal in the Will carries a long shadow extending into the highest levels of world affairs in a way Wellcome could not possibly have foreseen:

> for the purposes of my Will in America I SUGGEST to my Trustees the desirability of instructing John Foster Dulles (of New York City) Attorney-at-law.

Once again it may be noted that Sir Henry Wellcome possessed a good eye for the man with a future before him.

2

EARLIEST DAYS

Sir Henry Wellcome did not re-marry after his divorce from Syrie and had not for many years before making his Will anticipated that his only child, Henry Mounteney Wellcome, would assume control of his business. His name, said *The Times*, 'was known to everyone who has occasion to take his drugs in the tabloid form which has ousted the bottle of physic and the pill'. His coining of this (patented) term, his upbringing 'among the Dakota Indians', his 'great versatility and wide outlook' were remarked upon, as were his activities as 'anthropologist, field archaeologist, buyer of books, and collector on a large scale'. Little was known of his personality, save that Sir Henry Dale noted in correspondence his 'cautious loneliness', and Wellcome's sound plans to immortalise his name and family through a massive enterprise of benevolence were concealed until the Press got wind of the contents of his Will. Meanwhile, extensive tribute was paid to the contributions made by Wellcome to medicine, archaeology and 'his intense human qualities' – these were the words of Sir Reginald Wingate, who added that his loss would be felt throughout the world for 'he was truly a world benefactor'.

Wellcome's solicitor, George Hudson Lyall, himself a Trustee, at once conveyed the news of Wellcome's death to his colleagues. He, with the other two professional Trustees, his partner Lancelot Claude Bullock and Martin Price, was prepared to move straight ahead in his role of executor, to obtain probate (on 19 September 1936), pay taxes and so forth – as indeed he did, and six weeks after Wellcome's death a first sum of £968,700 in Estate Duty had already been deposited. But the two scientific Trustees, particularly Sir Henry Dale, were much concerned about the purity of their status and the fear of compromising it by even an indirect link with a manufacturing firm. A meeting with the other prospective Trustees and Mr George Pearson, nominated in the Will as Governing Director, helped to persuade Dale that 'the Trustees are not intended to take part in, or have any direct responsibility for, the conduct of the business, and are even prevented from interfering with its policy or that of its attached institutions, except under quite abnormal conditions'. He consequently felt able to assure the Secretary of the Medical Research Council, Dr Edward Mellanby, that he would only agree to serve as a Trustee if he 'should have no personal interest in or responsibility for the business or its conduct, and that my function would be limited to advising on the use of the proceeds in the best interests of medical research' (16 November 1936). Events were to thrust a great deal more responsibility than that upon Sir Henry Dale and his colleagues.

The autumn of 1936 was much taken up by correspondence between the prospective Trustees about this matter and the possibility that, when their names and the full terms of Wellcome's Will became known to the Press, the scientific Trustees should announce their acceptance of the Trusteeships as only 'provisional'. All five prospective Trustees had met on 28 July 1936 at the Foundation's Snow Hill offices, and again during the autumn, but only to consider the initiation of the Trust.

The two legal Trustees, L. C. Bullock and G. H. H. Lyall, were partners in the firm of Markby Stewart and Wadeson, which had acted for Sir Henry Wellcome during 40 years. Lyall, junior to Bullock in the firm, was named first in the Will and accordingly became the first Chairman of the Trustees. However, ill-health obstructed his activity and after his death (June 1938) Sir Henry Dale assumed the Chairmanship. Martin Price was senior partner in the firm of accountants, Viney, Price and Goodyear, which had long been employed by the Foundation and presumably by Sir Henry Wellcome in person. He was to be of great value to the group of Trustees in dealing with the business affairs of the Foundation. Another member of the same firm, Mr J. E. K. Clarke, was appointed Secretary to the Trustees at their first formal meeting on 13 January 1937.

The Scientific Trustees named in the Will had all been closely associated at earlier stages of their careers. Sir Walter Morley Fletcher, who did not live to take up the appointment, had been a distinguished investigator of respiratory physiology in the Department where both Henry Dale and Elliott had worked as young men. He had become (in 1914) first Secretary of the Government's Medical Research Committee, later of the Medical Research Council (1920). Fletcher died in 1933.

Henry Hallett Dale (1875–1968), the dominant figure in British biomedical research in the inter-war years, and the organiser of the Wellcome

Fig. 7. Sir Henry Dale, F.R.S. (1875–1968) on whom as Senior Trustee after Lyall's early death the Chairmanship of the Trust devolved.

Trust into an effective agency fostering such research, had received his scientific training at Cambridge, St Bartholomew's Hospital, and University College, London. After a brief and unrewarding experience of teaching histology there under Ernest Starling, Dale had in 1904 joined the staff of Henry Wellcome's Physiological Research Laboratories, then in a former private house at Herne Hill, London. He found Wellcome a generous but somewhat lackadaisical employer, who did not take the work of the laboratory as seriously as did the scientists he employed. Dale also acquired some distrust of the senior staff in the manufacturing company, and on at least one occasion appealed successfully to Wellcome himself against a ruling of George E. Pearson that he could not employ in a scientific paper the word 'adrenaline', copyrighted by the rival firm of Parke Davies. Nevertheless, and despite distractions caused by routine testing in connection with manufacture, Dale was able with excellent colleagues at Herne Hill to make discoveries of great importance, all stemming from Wellcome's off-hand suggestion that ergot ought to be investigated.

Dale left the Wellcome Laboratories in 1914, to become a departmental head of the National Institute for Medical Research (to use the later name), the major organ of the Medical Research Committee. Long recognised as its leading figure, Dale was to be appointed the first Director of the Institute in 1928.

After his move from Burroughs Wellcome to government service, the necessities of war and its aftermath kept Dale and his Department of the National Institute in temporary quarters at the Lister Institute from 1914 to 1920, when the former was established in the old Mount Vernon Hospital at Hampstead. Here Henry Dale spent the rest of his scientific career, from 1928 to 1942 as Director of the Institute and, at the end, much concerned with its move to its present headquarters in Mill Hill. Apart from his deep involvement with scientific research and many professional organisations – the most distinguished being his Presidency of the Royal Society from 1940 to 1945 – Sir Henry Dale (the knighthood was conferred in 1932) served as Chairman of the Scientific Advisory Committee to the Cabinet from 1942 to 1947. He was appointed to the Order of Merit in 1944. It is thus clear that Sir Henry Wellcome, in choosing Henry Dale as his second Trustee, had once again picked a winner, not only a man of the greatest scientific eminence and wisdom, but one whose conscientious discharge of all duties would ensure that the most careful and intelligent attention was devoted to Wellcome's concerns.

Thomas Renton Elliott (1877–1961) had put in six years of remarkable research in the Department of Physiology at Cambridge, in which among other things he enunciated (with great diffidence) the concept of the specific chemical transmitter acting at the synaptic junction in nerve fibres, before reading medicine at University College Hospital, London. After qualifying (1910) he was awarded one of the first Beit Research Fellowships. During the First World War he reached the rank of Colonel in the R.A.M.C. and was several times decorated; with peace, in 1918, he became the holder of the first of London's full-time Chairs of Clinical

Fig. 8. The two other Trustees, T. R. Elliott, F.R.S. (1877–1961), the second Scientific Trustee (*left*), and Martin Price (d.1972), an accountant (*right*).

Medicine, still at University College Hospital. He retired from this post, through increasing ill-health, in 1939 but continued his service as a Trustee until 1955. Sir Henry Dale wrote of him in this capacity:

> It was, to me, a matter for great personal rejoicing to find myself once more thus closely associated with my friend and greatly admired colleague of so many years. The early years involved the Trustees in much consideration of the proper interpretation of their functions, as the holders of an independent, charitable Trust. And in the discussions leading to agreed decisions on such matters, with the ultimate approval of the High Court, Elliott's wisdom, his high standards and his keen, generous vision, were of the greatest value to his colleagues.
>
> So too was the staunchness of his support through the difficult period, when the war brought the complete destruction, in one night's bombing, of the central offices of the business, and when the national need further demanded a bold policy of

> reconstruction, in some directions long overdue. And it was a cause of special satisfaction to his colleagues that Elliott was still able, in spite of his increasing disability, to retain his Trusteeship into a period in which the Trust was free to undertake a fuller discharge of its proper, charitable functions, and that he was still able to travel regularly from Scotland to attend the meetings of the Board, until 1955.

The first public announcement of Sir Henry Wellcome's generous intentions was made in the *Morning Post* of 19 November 1936. Under the heading 'All Profits Dedicated to Science' the newspaper printed a lengthy if not wholly accurate summary of the Will, named the Trustees, and gave such other information as anyone might have gained from visits to Somerset House and the Wellcome Building. It speculated that the Trustees would have 'the responsibility for the scientific direction of the income from not less than £1,000,000 of industrial capital' – this being, in fact, the nominal value of the share-capital of the Wellcome Foundation, all held by Sir Henry Wellcome during his lifetime. Whether the Trustees would ever be able freely to dispose of such a sum as (say) £100,000 per annum (£2 million in modern money) they certainly did not know, nor probably was anyone precisely aware of what Wellcome's personal income had been. As the *Morning Post* sagely added, no one could compute what the total value of the Wellcome empire might be. And the Trustees were conscious how great the obligations arising from the Will, not to say from taxation, might be: obligations which would have to be met before they began to think of making grants. The archaeological digs, the Research Laboratories, the Museums and Library, the Wellcome Building itself on Euston Road, the Welfare Fund, would all necessarily impose first charges upon whatever disposable income the Foundation might annually yield.

If nothing else, the newspaper column made the Trustees aware that some less rosy statement of the facts of the situation must be issued, though more than two months went by before it appeared. For the natural consequence of the publicity was that needy organisations at once solicited assistance. Applications had come in (by March 1937) from Australia and the U.S.A. as well as Britain, from bodies as various as the Bureau of Human Heredity, Guy's Hospital, and the Society for the Prevention of Asphyxial Death.

The cause of the Trustees' delay in responding to the *Morning Post*'s 'scoop' was the legal scruple which had troubled Sir Henry Dale from the moment he read the Will. The Will required all Trustees to enter into a covenant that they would assist no concern in rivalry with the Wellcome Foundation and, as Sir Henry Dale expressed it, the two medical and scientific Trustees (himself and Professor T. R. Elliott) felt that such a covenant might be held to restrict the free discharge 'of their more general duty to medical science, and to imply a particular concern with the business interests of the foundation'. If Sir Henry Dale's conscience seems almost too sensitive (as was, by implication, the opinion of the Counsel consulted), nevertheless, both Dale and Elliott were sincerely positive in their scruple. Both also, from their experience with the Medical Research Council, were conscious of the evils of patenting as practised by the pharmaceutical companies. The council had declared in 1928:

> Medical research is in general organised on a basis of free intercourse between workers: it is important that this should be preserved, but the introduction of rivalry in obtaining patents – even if only in defence against those who break the general tradition – would make this obviously difficult or impossible.[1]

Dale and Elliott clearly believed that it was necessary to make public their adhesion to this 'general tradition'. In the event the High Court upon application authorised a modified form of covenant safeguarding the Foundation's position while freeing the Trustees from any suggestion of being in its pocket. The inverse possibility – that the scientific wisdom and medical skill of the Trustees administering a charity might be of commercial benefit to the Foundation in a way that would endanger their charitable status – seems not to have been considered at this time. The Medical Research Council authorised Sir Henry Dale to assume the Trusteeship under the terms of the revised Covenant, and University College congratulated Professor Elliott on the distinction the Trusteeship conferred upon him and the College.

With the legal scruple removed, as it was by Mr Justice Bennett on 21 December 1936, the way was clear for Dale and Elliott to enter formally upon their Trusteeships on 13 January 1937, after which the first effective, minuted meeting of the Trustees was held. It was also possible for them to make their position known, their letter being published in *The Lancet*, *The British Medical Journal* and *Nature* (30 January 1937). The Trustees drew attention to the obligations incumbent upon them, *after* the payment of what must be a large demand for Death duties, to form a Welfare Fund for the employees of the Foundation, to pay annuities as specified in the Will, and to create the Wellcome Memorial at Garden City, Minnesota, though strictly speaking this had not been made a matter of priority in the Will. The Trustees then explained the dual nature of the Wellcome endowment: to provide for research and the Museums and Library, and ended with an account of the revision of the covenant demanded of them.

Behind-the-scenes contacts with the *B.M.J.* – as indeed with Sir Richard Gregory of *Nature* also – produced in the former journal a first leading article drawing heavily on the text of the Will (30 January 1937). It drew the obvious parallel with the Carlsberg Foundation in Copenhagen, with the difference that 'in the Wellcome bequest the machinery whereby the revenues are earned is in character with the purposes to which they will be devoted' and noted that industrial institutions, unlike those of the church and universities, depended for their continuance on continued commercial acumen. This, however, would have to come from the Directors of the Foundation, rather than the Trustees. The *B.M.J.* was confident that it would be forthcoming, and looked forward to the Trust 'being a big undertaking, perhaps bigger in the next generation than it can be in this'. The responsibility for ensuring a worthy achievement, in keeping with the philanthropic vision of the testator, would primarily fall on the medical trustees who, besides enjoying 'the confidence of all their scientific colleagues' might hope to 'add another noteworthy chapter to their own eminent services to medicine'.

While considering the actual establishment of the Trust as a legal entity, the Trustees must also in the early days have sought information on the magnitude of the sum they might expect to dispense year by year, and the nature of the payments to which, at least temporarily, they were already committed. Apart from Wellcome's personal bequests – not amounting to a large total – and the expense of the Memorial in Minnesota which was deferred to the future, they had to provide for taxation on the estate (after its valuation), for the various scientific laboratories and museums that Wellcome had created, for his archaeological enterprises, and the various minor causes specified in the Will.

Sir Henry Wellcome's gross income must regularly have been in excess of £150,000 per annum (say £3 million in the money of 1983). To be precise, the profit declared by the Foundation for the year August 1937 to August 1938 was £172,922, increasing to £198,568 for the following 12 months; this at a time when an important academic post, or a major medical practice, would be worth less than four figures.[2] The Estate Duty payable, however, would swallow the equivalent of this income for many years: as Sir Henry Dale wrote to the Editor of *The Lancet*, Sir Squire

Sprigge M.D., in very early days (23 January 1937), Wellcome's estate had been declared to the Inland Revenue as exceeding £2,000,000 in value, and duties up to this limit had been 'promptly paid'.

> It is obvious, however, that the full value of an estate of this size cannot be finally settled with Somerset House in a month or two, and that further duty will have to be paid on supplementary valuations, of which the dimensions are unknown.

The reason for promptness in payment lay in an interest charge of 10 per cent on indebtedness to the Inland Revenue. Since the Trustees had no resources, the payment was made by the Foundation, partly from reserves but partly also by borrowing money. Valuation, assessment and payment went on for five years after Wellcome's death, by April 1939 £1,198,254/19s/2d had been paid to the Inland Revenue, that is, the net profit for some five or six years. Until the process of valuation was complete, and indeed until all debts created by payment of the assessments on the estate had been discharged, the Trustees could hardly look beyond the expenditures which were forced upon them.

The process of reaching an agreed valuation with the Inland Revenue authorities was rendered the more lengthy by the complication of Wellcome's assets, not only on the manufacturing side but with respect to his vast collections. What was their worth in terms of money? For those parts of the collections which the Trustees from the first – it would appear before the end of 1936 – had decided not to retain, valuation must rest upon the process of sale, which would not be speedy. Furniture, model ships, ceramics and porcelain (apart from objects associated with pharmacy), arms and armour and much else (of possible interest to antiquarians and ethnologists but lacking in medical content) was to be purged. A collection of Patent Models in the U.S.A. was sold for $10,000.[3] The firm of Allsops was charged with the responsibility for the dispersals, and a long series of sales was advertised and held at Alford House in Kensington, with rather disappointing results, partly because the expenses charged by the firm might amount to 65 per cent of the gross proceeds. The first 12 sales (November 1937 to August 1938) brought in only £9,824 net, roughly £1 per lot sold. The many *inro* and *netsuke* sold would no doubt fetch far more in 1983 than in 1938, but 'Six various wax heads' and 'Twelve various Russian ornamental combs' would possibly never have commanded high prices. Numerous paintings (232 on 20 July 1938) and vast quantities of furniture were disposed of at knock-down prices. The

Fig. 9. Henry Wellcome and the Conservator of his collections, Capt. P. Johnston Saint.

Librarian (Mr S. A. J. Moorat) complained bitterly of Allsop's book-sales, where 18,000 volumes might be got rid of in one day, made up into large parcels containing early editions, rare pamphlets and fine bindings, for as little a 3½d per volume on average. When the book business was transferred to Hodgson's, specialists in that line, performance improved to the level of 10d per volume and a particular rare item like William Petty's *Art of Double-Writing* (1648) might fetch as much as £3. Not surprisingly, a great deal of non-scientific and non-medical material, not to say trash, was found among the libraries that Wellcome had acquired by the ton. It was estimated that 110,000 to 275,000 books could be disposed of. Dale and Elliott went to many personal pains in the task of sorting. In fact, the sculpturing of a coherent and practicable Historical Medical Museum and Library – something less than a gigantic Museum of Mankind – from the rich chaos left by Sir Henry Wellcome was, and has remained, a matter very much of direct interest to the Trustees, who in the early days exacted monthly reports from the Conservator (Capt. P. Johnston Saint) and the Librarian on the progress of the sorting, cataloguing and dispersal of the collections. The last book sale came in 1946.

From a modern point of view it may seem that the Trustees were a trifle unimaginative or timid in not at least offering to other museums a share of the huge mass accumulated by Wellcome that had little chance of exhibition in a medical museum, and this was certainly the opinion of the Conservator. Some of the non-medical material was nevertheless of great scholarly value, as was pointed out by Mr T. T. Paterson, Curator of the Museum of Archaeology and Ethnology at Cambridge after he had made an inspection at Willesden. 'You have one of the finest collections of prehistoric material in the world' he wrote in December 1939. 'There are individual collections which are unique, and could not be replaced under any circumstances should they be dispersed as the Trustees would like. For research students these collections are of inestimable value.' Paterson specifically indicated that should dispersal continue, the University would be pleased to receive gifts though it could not afford to buy, a proposal accepted in principle by Sir Henry Dale subject to the making of an arrangement about values with the Inland Revenue. Wartime pressure no doubt prevented any further steps being taken, but at least the scattering of the archaeological and ethnological collections through the salerooms was halted and they were, in time, to find homes in other museums.

The testator, had, in fact, created a curious situation which has only been finally resolved in the last few years, for by putting his Museums and Library in his Research Institution and incorporating the latter in his Foundation, he effectively placed both wings of the Research Institution under control of the Directors of the Foundation, a control which the Governing Director (in whom Wellcome had placed so much confidence), Mr George E. Pearson, was not at all inclined to surrender to the Trustees. And it was certainly the case (down to very recent days) that all the employees of the Museums, Library and Laboratories were on the Foundation's payroll and appointed by it. Although Pearson's position might seem consistent with the letter of the organisation created by Wellcome, it was (as Sir Henry Dale asserted in a memorandum of

November 1937) inconsistent with Wellcome's own practice and his designation of Trustees as an immortal self:

> He himself always maintained, both before and during my appointment (as Director of Wellcome's Physiological Research Laboratories), that the Laboratories and Museums were his personal property and interest, and unconnected with his business, except in so far as they served its interests at his request.

In Dale's view the Trustees, not George E. Pearson, were Wellcome's successors in these respects.

> The Trustees are clearly given power by the Will to spend the profits from the Foundation, their Property, on research in the Testator's existing Laboratories and on his existing Museums, as well as on outside enterprises. In their capacity they can claim a voice in the policy of these Institutions, even though the expenditure may, for accounting purposes, be regarded as a Foundation expense, and escape Income Tax.

Dale's view was that Dr C. M. Wenyon, as Head of the Research Institution (or Bureau), should report directly to the Trustees and not to the Governing-Director. Here was a potent source of conflict.

The tensions of these early days, when Dale began to impose a sense of scientific responsibility upon the Trust (but was as yet uncertain whether he could carry his non-scientific colleagues with him) may be gathered from an amusing letter he wrote to Professor Elliott in November 1937 after, it seems for the first time, lunching with his co-Trustees and Pearson at Frascati's restaurant:

> Pearson, during lunch, opened in his usual style, assuming as beyond question his personal and unshared responsibility, as Governing-Director in succession to Wellcome for everything in the foundation including the Museum and everything connected therewith. I countered, as usual, with the responsibility of the Trustees, and especially the medical Trustees, to the medical and scientific public . . . and that we were not prepared to take such responsibility for what was done by him, or Johnston-Saint, without our knowledge or approval . . . They are on the run, and if we can help them to save their faces we can, I believe, get things on a better footing.

Sir Henry Dale was perfectly capable of speaking forcefully when the case merited it.

While relations between the Trust and the Foundation slowly became less amicable – to the point where the Trustees began to hold Special Meetings in the absence of Mr Pearson as adviser – the Trustees were taking steps to either wind up or develop other of Wellcome's interests.

One institution specifically mentioned in the Will, though not in mandatory terms, the Wellcome Laboratories in Khartoum, was never even considered by the Trustees, presumably because it had been taken over finally by the Sudanese Medical Service in 1935.

Under Balfour's successors – A. J. Chalmers (1913–29) and (Sir) R. G. Archibald (1920–35) – the scientific study of tropical diseases such as schistosomiasis had made great progress, inspiring in part the comment in the Milner Report (1919) that 'There is no better investment for the money of any colony than scientific research, both medical and economic . . .' However, the administrative and national development of the Sudan made the continuance of outside support inappropriate and, although a specific proposal was made to the Trustees that they should give support to the Khartoum laboratories, they decided not to do so (May 1938) as the Wellcome name had been allowed to disappear. Some years would pass before the Trustees returned to tropical medicine, in a different region of Africa.

The Trustees read the Will as virtually enjoining upon them the cessation of archaeological work in the Sudan, though that at Lachish in Palestine continued for a couple of years and it was not until 27 June 1938 that the Trustees formally resolved that they 'did not desire to continue their interest in Archaeology that had no close relation to medicine or its history', nor could they implement this negative decision until the obligation imposed upon them had been fully discharged: the task would take nearly 20 years. The Trustees' first move was to seek advice and administrative help from Dr G. A. Reisner and Major J. S. Uribe. The former had been named in the Will as a suitable scholar to complete and publish the work at Jebel Moya, while the latter – who came on an extended visit to England to assist the Trustees – had long been in Wellcome's service as the manager of his 'dig'. Like Sir Arthur Keith, whom Wellcome had wished to study the early human remains found in the Sudan, Dr Reisner was unable to accept the commission which, on his recommendation, was transferred to Dr Frank Addison who fully agreed that 'to dig up more acres of the Jebel Moya site would not be likely to increase the sum of scientific and historical knowledge to an extent at all commensurate with the effort and expense involved'. Accordingly, through Major Uribe, affairs in the Sudan were wound up, despite some problems such as the use of Wellcome's 'House of Boulders' as a dispensary for the local people by a Dr Corkhill, 'as a memorial to the welfare work done by the late Sir Henry Wellcome'. Dr Addison's task of publishing work performed long before was to continue for nearly 25 years, the first two volumes of 'The Wellcome Excavations in the Sudan', *Jebel Moya*, were published sumptuously by the Oxford University Press (at the Trustees' expense) in 1949. Of all the archaeologists who had actually dug with Wellcome in the Sudan only one, Dr O. G. S. Crawford, later founder of the journal *Archaeology*, who had been there in 1914, was still alive and was able to publish his own work in the third volume of the series, *Abu Geibi and Saqadi & Dar el Mek* (1951). The human material was, in the end, examined by two Indian scholars, Mr R. Mukherjee and Mr C. R. Rao, under the supervision of Dr J. C. Trevor of the Museum of Archaeology and Ethnology of the University of Cambridge. It is a curious feature of their report, published in 1955, that the impression of the field anthropologists that women had greatly outnumbered men in the population of Jebel Moya, was corrected to a ratio of near equality. When the present writer was at Cambridge he had the privilege of sharing a certain basement store beneath the Examination School with Wellcome's Sudanese skulls and ephemeral sheet music from the University Library. Altogether the support of these studies of the material and their publication cost the Trustees some £18,000.

To Professor J. L. Starkey, directing at Lachish, the cost was far greater. By his sixth season of work under the patronage of the Wellcome Trustees and Sir Charles Marston, the political situation in Palestine under the British Mandate was highly unstable. Arab 'bandits' or 'guerrillas', hostile to the Jewish incursion and the British authority which (they believed) protected it and energetically pursued by the British army under such officers as Bernard Law Montgomery and 'Jack' Evetts, were reduced to raid and murder. On 10 January 1938, while driving his car from Tell-ed-Duweir to Jerusalem, Starkey was stopped by a party of such guerrillas and shot dead, near Beit Kibrin. Nevertheless, work continued at the site under the direction of Mr Charles H. Inge and Miss Olga Tufnell until May 1938, and at another palaeontological site near Bethlehem, under Dr Stekelis, until 1940. During the last months of these digs their costs were wholly borne by the Trustees, as was the cost of publication. When Mr Inge vanished into the apparatus of war, this task fell wholly on to Miss Tufnell, who worked for 20 years on the Lachish material

THE WELLCOME ARCHAEOLOGICAL RESEARCH EXPEDITION
TO THE NEAR EAST

LACHISH I

(TELL ED DUWEIR)

THE LACHISH LETTERS

BY

HARRY TORCZYNER

BIALIK PROFESSOR OF HEBREW IN THE UNIVERSITY OF JERUSALEM

LANKESTER HARDING

ALKIN LEWIS

J. L. STARKEY

PUBLISHED FOR
THE TRUSTEES OF THE LATE SIR HENRY WELLCOME
BY THE
OXFORD UNIVERSITY PRESS
LONDON NEW YORK TORONTO
1938

Fig. 10. The first of the five volumes describing the work at Lachish which has been resumed in recent years by Israeli archaeologists.

assembled at the Institute of Archaeology of the University of London, then in Regent's Park. The Trustees have already expressed their gratitude to the University and to the Directors of the Institute, originally Dr V. Gordon Childe, for the invaluable assistance thus given.

As already mentioned, *The Lachish Letters* were published in 1938 in a scholarly edition by Professor Harry Torczyner of the University of Jerusalem, the fragments or *ostraca* being deposited in the British Museum. *Lachish II,* dealing with the 'Fosse Temple' (and edited by Miss Tufnell with Mr Inge and Mr Lankester Harding) followed in 1949; after the war Vols III and IV appeared in 1953 and 1958 respectively. After the series of reports was completed, material was presented to a great many Museums in Britain and overseas, among them the Louvre in Paris and the Metropolitan Museum of Fine Arts in New York.

The successful winding-up of Sir Henry Wellcome's archaeological enterprises in an impressive series of volumes was perhaps the most rewarding of the Trustee's concerns during the early years. Others were troublesome and unproductive, for example, a suit brought against the Wellcome Foundation on behalf of a certain child who had died at Cork, Ireland, on the grounds that serum used of Wellcome manufacture had been defective. The Trustees were not party to the action, but felt greatly concerned as shareholders in the defence since, if the allegations had proved just, the reputation of the Foundation would have been jeopardised, and the likelihood of profitability reduced. The Directors of the Foundation appealed to the Trustees for guidance on a number of matters of policy, and received it. Fortunately when the Kenneally Case came to trial in the High Court (more than two years after it began) the Foundation was found completely blameless.

Another matter of concern to the Trustees in the first years was the plight of Jewish scientists and medical men who, having sought refuge in Britain, found means of support difficult to come by. Sir Henry Dale was especially closely linked with Dr Otto Loewi (1873–1961) since the two men had shared the Nobel Prize for physiology or medicine for their work on chemical neuro-transmitters. Loewi was lucky to escape to England stripped of his prize-money and all else by the Nazis, in September 1938. The Wellcome Trustees maintained him for over a year, in part at the Nuffield Institute, Oxford, through the Society for the Protection of Science and Learning. Loewi later settled in the United States. Humanists were equally in trouble: one of those helped was Dr Richard Walzer, who was employed for a considerable time in cataloguing Wellcome's Arabic and Persian manuscripts, and was aided in his edition of Galen's text *On*

Medical Experience. Another was the eminent Viennese historian of medicine, Max Neuburger, rescued by the efforts of Sir D'Arcy Power and Charles Singer only a few days before the outbreak of war. Until his departure from England to join a physician son at Buffalo, New York (August 1948), this elderly scholar was maintained by the Trustees as a consultant on the development of the Historical Museum and Library. The Historical Museum had been formally closed at the outbreak of war, and a programme of re-arrangement embarked upon; thanks to Dr Neuburger's insistence, this adopted divisions by historical epochs rather than the topical sequences previously employed.

The collections and the concomitant sales were regularly before the Trustees as matters of business. It was difficult for them to know how best to proceed: the Museums and Library were structurally parallel to the Research Laboratories but, whereas the Scientific Trustees felt competent with respect to the latter, the former appeared unfamiliar. However, Dale particularly perceived that both wings of the Research Institution must be intellectually respectable, and for this reason among others could not resign responsibility for them wholly to the Directors of the Foundation. Mr George E. Pearson, Dale was certain, was quite unable to direct either historical or scientific research, indeed, he believed that Pearson had played down research so that Wellcome would have more free cash for his other 'hobbies'. On the scientific side this had already damaged the business:

> I know (Dale wrote in a memoir of November 1937) that there is a widespread impression that the business of Burroughs Wellcome & Co., at one time well in advance of similar enterprises in this country, is tending to exploit its past achievements and reputation, and failing to take its part in the new developments required to keep pace with the change in therapeutics.

On the historical side, the problem was to formulate a proper policy for the future to replace the disorganisation of the past and see that it was put into effect. Both Elliott and Dale felt that this scholarly responsibility fell particularly heavily on their shoulders. As the former wrote to Lyall, when the Trust was barely six months old:

> we seem to represent Sir Henry [Wellcome] in that particular Directorship to which he latterly gave all his personal attention rather than to the business, which he left to the care of Mr. Pearson.

Similarly Dale wrote to Elliott some weeks later (October 1937)

> Nobody, I think would question our proper concern with the main object and purpose of the Museum – whether it is to be used, in accordance with the apparent intentions of the Trust, for study and research in medical history, or whether it is to be planned as an extremely expensive and doubtfully effective advertisement.

The concern of the Scientific Trustees for the Museum and Library was enhanced by their certainty that Pearson, as head of the Foundation, could not guide it towards 'study and research' in history, and their doubts whether even Johnston Saint, the Conservator, or Moorat, the Librarian, was a fully competent and purposeful historical scholar. The Historical Medical Museum, Dale wrote (in the memoir previously cited):

> has apparently been accepted by the Inland Revenue Authorities as an advertisement, but the Trustees cannot fulfill their duty under the Will if they allow it, in reality, to fall below a proper standard of historical science and scholarship.

That the Museum's work, as conceived in 1937, did as yet fall below a 'proper standard' was forcibly made known to Sir Henry Dale in a memoir signed by most of its graduate staff and conveyed to him privately. The unsatisfactory outlook of its management was further revealed in the highly illiberal 'conditions of employment' – permitting no independent research or any publication whatever – imposed on these staff, of which Elliott remarked (October 1937): 'We seem to have been wrong in thinking that slavery had been abolished in England'. All this could not be amended at a stroke.

In the pre-War years the Conservator was continually urged to hasten the examination of the packing cases stored at Willesden so that non-medical material could be disposed of by Allsops, and the Librarian exhorted to abbreviate and hasten his cataloguing of the 'possible' books so that the unwanted could be sold. Slowly the Trustees began to form a policy. In February 1939 they agreed to the principle that they would assist the publication of works 'relating to Research Studies in Medical History'. Two early projects for *A History of Welsh Medicine* and Johnston Saint's *History of Spontaneous Generation* came to nothing. But Dr Charles Singer was much assisted by the Trustees (in the years 1944–7) in the production of notable works on Vesalius and Galen. Negatively, they also decided just one year after that no further drug-jars or pestles-and-mortars should be acquired, and turned down a deal with King's College Hospital for the acquisition of Lord Lister's operating table. It was in order to develop an idea of what a Historical Museum and Library might be like, as well as to assist a refugee scholar, that the Trustees engaged Professor Neuburger to inspect and report upon Wellcome's material legacy, as well as to give them a full account of all comparable institutions in Europe.

Very much in the spirit of Wellcome's own interventions into tropical medicine was the support given by the Trustees to anti-malaria research. Mr Henry Foy had been selected in 1932 by League of Nations' officials to investigate malaria and its control in Greece, using funds provided by a generous American (Mrs David Simmons). Mr Foy, a product of Oxford and Zürich, was a physiologist by training. He had become interested in tropical diseases while holding a post in Trinidad, working for some months in a leprosarium at Manaus on the Upper Amazon. In Greece he had established a small laboratory at the Refugee Hospital in Thessaloniki (Salonika), catering mainly for Greeks escaping from Asia Minor. Here the incidence of malaria was high. I owe to the late Col. H. W. Mulligan, former Director of the Wellcome Research Laboratories, the story that when Mr Foy was asked on one occasion to supply specimens of *Plasmodium falciparum*, the parasite transmitting malignant tertian malaria to man, for the London School of Tropical Medicine and Hygiene, he was for some time unable to do so, having ventured into a remote district in search of appropriately infected mosquitoes, where he was held captive by bandits. This laboratory was visited by many experts on malaria, as offering unusual opportunities for the study of the disease and its sequelae, such as blackwater fever.

When, in 1937, the funds administered by the League of Nations neared exhaustion, the British Medical Research Council appealed to the Wellcome Trustees (that is, to Sir Henry Dale) to make continuance of the work of Mr Foy's laboratory possible. An agreement was reached with the Greek Government, so that from the beginning of 1938 Mr Foy was placed in charge of 'The Wellcome Trust Research Laboratory, Thessaloniki', the Trustees having agreed to meet expenses up to a limit of £2,000 per annum. Soon after taking this on, the Trustees also approved a plan put forward by Mr Foy for an extension to the laboratory providing more working space and accommodation for ten beds, so that clinical studies could be made on patients suffering from malaria. There was a slight problem about this in that Mr Foy, whom Dale once described as a scientist of 'unusual and irregular training – a real Quaker Enthusiast!' was not medically qualified. Accordingly, Dr Athena Kondi, who was already employed at the Refugee Hospital, was appointed to take charge of the clinic. Both she and Mr Foy were supported by the Trustees for many years, though the German invasion – their forces reached Thessaloniki on 9 April 1941, the third day of their thrust from Bulgaria – entailed the displacement of the Wellcome Laboratory (with most of its equipment saved), to Johannesburg, where it joined the South African Institute for Medical Research. Subsequently, in the summer of 1941, the Trustees resolved (with extraordinary nonchalance) that if Dr Kondi could not be found useful work at their expense in Africa she should return to Greece – then under the ruthless oppression of the Nazis and undergoing terrible privations: starvation was soon universal there and mortality rose to appalling heights. Fortunately, Dr Kondi was indeed working productively with Mr Foy, whose proposals for his laboratory the Trustees found 'eminently satisfactory'. After a brief post-war return to Greece it was ultimately re-established in Nairobi in 1948; for the wartime development of insecticides had effectively exterminated malaria in Greece.

The sum total of all these small enterprises in the pre-war years, to which should be added the cost of medals and prizes of which awards were made in accordance with the terms of the Will, amounted to a negligible sum as compared with the Foundation's profits, for the reasons already given; the 'Thessaloniki' Laboratory, for example, over a period of 19 years, cost under £45,000.[4] But the Trustees were, as already indicated, far from complacent about the future outlook – quite apart from the possible effects of a war which everyone believed to be inevitable. They lacked conviction that the business was being energetically run, with that innovative, scientific look to the future which Wellcome himself had commended. All of them detected apathy in the direction of the firm, a feeling which apparently the appearance of Mr Pearson at their meetings did not remove. Sir Henry Wellcome had been 84 years old when he died, and Pearson had been his lieutenant for 40 of them; both before and after his appointment as General Manager of Burroughs Wellcome (1905) he had very largely built up the foreign business of the firm in North and South America, Australia, and China. In 1938 he was 70 years old, while the next most senior Director, the Supervising Accountant G. L. Moore, was 64. The head of the Bureau of Scientific Research, Dr C. M. Wenyon F.R.S., also a Director, was 60.[5] Of these only the last – who unfortunately did not command Sir Henry Dale's respect – could be expected to have competent knowledge of the latest developments in pharmacology and its clinical applications. Charles Morley Wenyon (1878–1948) had been in tropical medicine at the London School and elsewhere since 1905, and associated with Sir Henry Wellcome since 1907. A heart attack in 1932 had perhaps impaired his vigour. Was it not, in the circumstances, to be feared that Burroughs Wellcome had already fallen behind firms like Bayer and Glaxo? The latter firm, Professor Elliott learned from his physician brother, was active in pushing 'the biological products which doctors are using more and more', while Burroughs Wellcome 'seemed to deal chiefly in tabloids which were wanted in imperfectly settled countries but were of little use now in England'.

The implication of stagnation was somewhat unfair, in that the Company had shown itself to be innovative in various ways during the 1920s and 1930s. It had been the first in England to manufacture insulin on a large scale, in 1923, within one year of its discovery by Banting and Best; Dr Sidney Smith had isolated digoxin in 1930, and the Company's brand is still in use 50 years later; it had been active in pharmacological research, and had successfully penetrated the increasingly important veterinary market. But it had failed badly with the new chemotherapeutic agents such as sulphonilamide.

The view of the Foundation's historian, like that of Sir Henry Dale, is that Wellcome lost interest in his business after the building up of its many foreign branches and their organisation into the Foundation in 1924. Thereafter the iron discipline of the unimaginative and over-cautious George Pearson prevailed, his parsimonious views being strengthened by the Depression from 1929 onwards. The Company's business ceased to grow, and its relative share of markets tended to decline, even into the post-war years. When they first examined the business the Trustees inclined to attribute its stagnation to old-fashioned marketing and insufficiency of research. Should not the Company, in Professor Elliott's words, in trying to persuade medical men to prescribe its products, emphasise the Company's reliance, as a manufacturer, on medical research and its whole-hearted commitment to the support of research? Otherwise a contradiction arose. For, Professor Elliott pointed out in a letter to Mr Bullock (21 March 1938), the 'scientific men, and especially [Sir] Andrew Balfour were always eager to keep themselves and their Bureau [of Scientific Research] disassociated in the public eye from the commercial side' of Henry Wellcome's business, even though its profits made their work possible; the situation was now quite different because 'Man is to benefit, not the private shareholder'.

Gradually, pursuing the logic of these last reflections, the Trustees were compelled to press heavily upon the Directors of the Foundation, particularly the Governing-Director who was becoming isolated from his younger colleagues. In April 1938, when his scientific propriety as well as his practical acumen was touched, Dale spoke out sharply against 'certain sections of a pamphlet published by Messrs Burroughs Wellcome' which made some reference to the therapeutic use of animal substances which he could not countenance.

> In the course of a lengthy discussion [by the Trustees] Sir Henry Dale strongly recommended that the Directors of the Wellcome Foundation Ltd. should seriously consider their attitude towards the progressive development of modern therapeutics and also the nature of their advertisements.

Pearson promised to put these views before his Board and the offending pamphlet was withdrawn, but occasions still continued to arise where the Trustees felt that the Foundation was deficient in assuming leadership in its industry, even (after the outbreak of war) with respect to promoting the national cause.

At a more personal level, too, they were distressed to find that the Governing-Director had made a very large loan to the Company, on which he was receiving five per cent interest free of all tax. Dale fairly reminded them that Wellcome regularly extended this valuable privilege to his senior employees, and had done so to himself in the past; but it did not seem in accord with the new spirit of the Trust. Counsel's opinion was sought, and following Counsel's advice Pearson was asked to reduce his loan. Against him, other Directors claimed that their remuneration was inadequate, another matter that the Trustees had to settle.

Profits had risen during the last pre-war years; nevertheless the Trustees were not quite satisfied with what they saw in the accounts of the business, nor indeed with the form of the accounts themselves. Martin Price instituted a study of the course of Sales and Profits from 1925 to 1939 which 'prompted enquiry into the policy and administration of the Foundation'. One of the senior Directors, named by Wellcome in his Will, Mr G. L. Moore, agreed with 'the view of the Trustees that the information shown by the financial statements now available indicated that reorganisation of the business in certain respects was desirable . . . in particular the selling organisation and advertising departments should receive careful consideration'. It was observed that while the sale of 'General Goods' had improved slightly abroad over the years, the market for such goods at home had declined, though total home sales were kept well up by the success of Wellcome Sera and allied products. Examples of the trading figures causing concern are these for 1937:

Gross profits (£1000s)	Home	Abroad
Insulin and sera	196	32
General goods	202	180

If the ratio in foreign sales between the biologicals and the general goods was about 'normal', then the sale of general goods at home was clearly very depressed. At a joint meeting of the two Boards on 1 April 1940, George Pearson could only point to the overall economic recession since 1929 and a decline in interest in such commodities as cod-liver oil and malt, but his fellow Directors, Mr Moore and Mr Oakes,

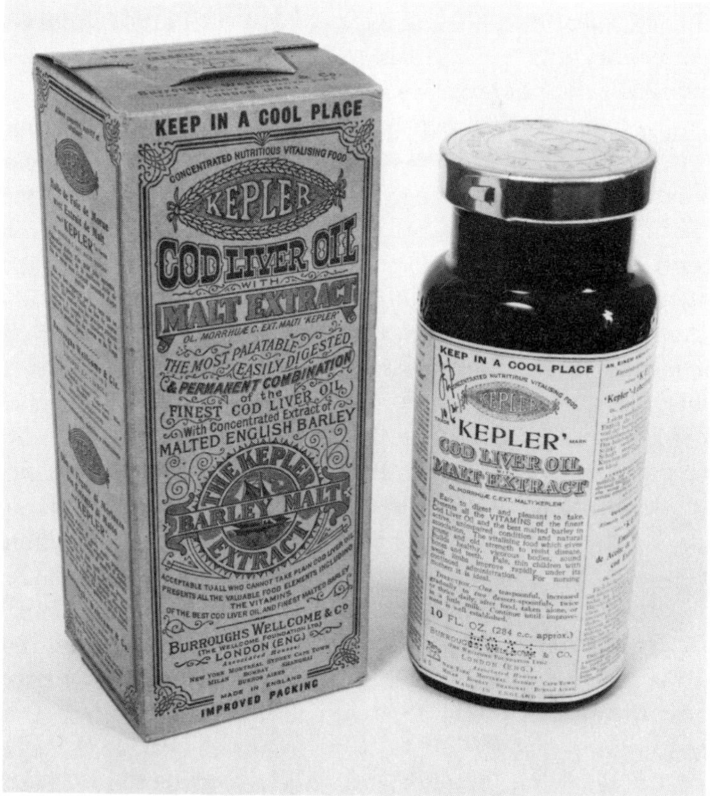

Fig. 11. 'Kepler' Brand cod-liver oil and malt, for many years a profitable commodity to Burroughs Wellcome.

> concurred in regarding the decline in trading results as reflecting a general loss of initiative and an unprogressive policy in the conduct of the business since 1929 . . . to lack of enterprise in the introduction of new products, to delay in the adoption of modern methods of advertising and marketing, and to the retention by the Foundation of a complicated and unpopular system of trading terms.

The same two Directors alleged that some departments of the firm were badly staffed and that there was a deficiency of younger men qualified for promotion, a point also noted in the Trustees' own deliberations. Dr Wenyon thought that more research of direct relevance to therapy could be carried out.

This meeting left Pearson in a minority of one defending the status quo. At a subsequent Trustees' Meeting, on the strong recommendation of Martin Price, it was decided to bring in Mr T. R. G. Bennett from outside, as a man 'possessing the necessary technical and executive qualifications and experience', to be Managing Director of the Foundation and General Manager of Burroughs Wellcome & Co. Pearson was to remain in an advisory capacity and as Chairman of the Board of Directors. When this resolution – justified by the Will – was privately communicated to Mr Pearson by Sir Henry Dale he declared his intention of resigning as Governing-Director at the end of the year. Mr Bennett was offered a 19-year contract from 1 May 1940 at a salary rising to the high maximum of £5,500; he had at one time been employed by the rival firm of Johnson & Johnson. By thus installing their own man in the seat of power, the Trustees had decisively asserted their ultimate control, as shareholders, of the Wellcome Foundation, and the fact that they would exercise in reality, as well as pro forma, their right to be satisfied with the management of the Company as regards both scientific and commercial policies. The four Trustees of 1940 had been absolutely at one (as their correspondence shows) in their analysis of the problem, and the only possible remedy for it, a reconstruction and revivification of the Company. In his first letter to Mellanby about the Trust (6 August 1936) Sir Henry Dale had foreseen the unwelcome possibility that such a situation as this might arise; now it had been effectively dealt with.

It was perhaps fortunate that this internal crisis had to be dealt with at a quiet time of the Phoney War; and for some little time to come the pressures of the war were to affect the Trust very little, save that the Trustees took a special interest in Air Raid Precautions as applied to the

Foundation buildings and staff in London. The collapse of France in May 1940 and the imminent sense of national disaster prompted Mr Bullock to the suggestion that Burroughs Wellcome, as a charity, should offer to the Government, free, a 'considerable part' of its annual production. Demand was indeed great; profits rose to about £400,000 in each of the years ending August 1940 and August 1941, though war taxation brought them down to the former level. Mr Bullock's proposal was not adopted, but the Trustees offered the Medical Research Council special aid in the production of blood plasma and serum at Dartford. In the end, this was transmuted into support for a freeze-drying plant for plasma and serum constructed at Cambridge under the direction of Dr Lansborough Thomson. The Trustees, bearing their sandwiches for the utility train, went to see it in operation with Admiral Dudley on 26 February 1942.

3

OUT OF THE DARKNESS

By chance, the start of the real war in Europe coincided with the ending, temporarily, of that concern about the leadership of the Foundation which had plagued the Trustees from the first. For the war years, and some little time thereafter, they were content to leave Mr Bennett in charge, indeed raising him to the very high salary (for those days) of £10,000 a year. In turn he was careful to consult frequently with the Trustees and keep them fully informed about the health of the business whose shares they held. With their approval some changes in the Board of Directors of the Foundation were made and in consequence a Memorandum of Agreement between the Trustees and the Directors was drawn up (August 1941) noting that Sir Henry Wellcome's Will had given

> to the Trustees a power and responsibility which are different from those normally held and exercised by the shareholders of a company. It makes them, in the last resort, responsible for the policy of the Foundation as framed and adopted by the Directorate . . .

Normally, the Memorandum continues, the relationship between the two parties would take effect by 'friendly consultation' between them, in order to ensure the Trustee's approval of the activities of the Foundation, of its plans for future development, and of its major decisions of policy; but the Trustees (it was recorded) had thought it right 'at this juncture' to secure a more formal recognition of their responsibilities and right to be consulted.

The five years of Britain's active warfare, 1940–5, must be regarded as a interregnum in the history of the Trust and the Foundation. The pharmaceutical industry was to all intents and purposes under governmental regulation, and in this period of national struggle for survival and heavy casualties there could be no thought of aiming to make large profits for charitable purposes from the sale of drugs. Moreover, the trade of the Foundation's overseas branches – except that in the United States – was disrupted by the war and its interruption of sea-borne traffic. It is true that the turnover of the Foundation increased greatly during the war years, to about £2 million per annum, but this was penalised by Excess Profits Tax; in any case, some of the new business like the manufacture of penicillin (abandoned later) brought in little or no net profit. Nor were the Trustees, under wartime conditions, minded to press on rapidly with the proper organisation of the Trust: Sir Henry Dale, in particular, was immensely busy as President of the Royal Society (1940–5), Director of the Royal Institution (1942–6), Chairman of the Scientific Advisory Committee of the War and Post-War Cabinet (1942–7), Member of the Medical Research Council, and member of a Special Mission to the United States (1942). Not surprisingly, he was sometimes compelled to miss meetings of the Wellcome Trustees.

One constant preoccupation of the Trustees was the management of the Historical Museum and Library, formally a component of the Scientific Research Institution and so under the direction of Dr Wenyon until 1944 (when he became a Director of the Foundation) and afterwards of Dr C. H. Kellaway (1889–1952) of whom Dale thought well. From September 1939 the Museum was officially declared to be closed; even before the outbreak of war it had been severely compressed by the incursion of Company staff to the Wellcome Building. Nevertheless, examination of the massive and diverse materials continued: indeed, in his monthly report for September 1939 the Conservator noted the completion of nine reconstructions of ancient pharmacies of various types.

> Further (wrote Capt. Saint) I propose to proceed as soon as possible with the creation of the reproductions of the Alchemist's Laboratory, the Indian Drugs Shop and the House of the Surgeon at Pompeii.

Cataloguing of the Prints and Drawing, of the Gallery of Egyptian Medicine, and of the Galleries of Indian and Religious Medicine was also continued. Conscription effected some reduction of the Museum's staff, but the war also brought in foreign experts, as previously noted. Dr Richard Walzer, formerly of the universities of Berlin and Rome and the first historical scholar to have a work published by the Trustees, examined the Oriental manuscripts, while Professor Max Neuburger was enrolled from February 1941 as a permanent adviser to the Museum and Library after several extensions of his temporary consultancy. Four years before the members of the Museum scientific staff had privately urged on Sir Henry Dale the need for a more scholarly and systematic approach to the planning of the Museum than that of Capt. Saint, a view supported in Professor Neuburger's reports; in March 1941 Dr S. H. Daukes, who had been appointed Director of the Historical Museum as well as of the Museum of Medical Science (also closed for the duration), prepared the first outline plan for the development of a coherent Museum arranged chronologically. The same plan was presented to the Trustees in more detail in April 1943, and shows the former 'Hall of Statuary' and Gallery occupied by the Library. At this time the staff of the Museum and Library numbered 45 persons, as compared with 74 in 1937.

All plans were destroyed by the necessity to stop all Museum operations in the autumn of 1946. This was a second disturbance, for in April 1945, owing to the closing of the store at Willesden, it had been necessary to deposit 1,300 cases of ethnographic material (some still unexamined) at the British Museum, whose Director (Sir John Forsdyke) happened to be a personal acquaintance of Mr Bennett. For this courtesy it was agreed that the British Museum should have first pick of material not of medical interest, the rest going to other museums. Distribution of this ethnographic material did not begin until 1949, or end until 1955, nor was it effected without certain rubs arising which required the personal intervention of Sir Henry Dale. After it was all over the Keeper of Ethnography at the British Museum recorded with satisfaction that the Trustees had made 'one of the greatest gifts from a single source which the Museum's Department of Ethnography had ever received'. Many other museums in Britain were enriched, as were the Auckland Institute in New Zealand and the Museum für Volkerkunde at Frankfurt-am-Main, and some materials were sold. Nevertheless, ten years later 15,000 items of ethnographic interest remained, including bronze masks from Benin, Ashanti gold weights and African royal regalia also in gold, and much other excellent material from Mexico, Peru and Polynesia, all of which was gratefully received in 1965 by the University of California at Los Angeles for its Center for Ethnic Arts and Technology.

The virtual suspension of Museum work from October 1946 arose because the Foundation's occupation of offices in Red Lion Square (since the destruction of its Snow Hill building during the raid of 10–11 May 1941) was to cease in May 1947. There had been talk for some time of putting up a new office block on the vacant site adjacent to the Wellcome

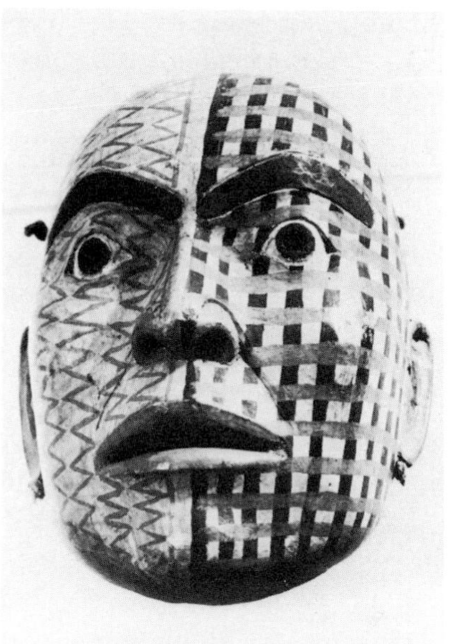

Fig. 12. Two pieces from the ethnic material presented to the University of California, Los Angeles: (*left*) Tsimshian Indian (N.W. U.S.A.) mask, painted in red and black; (*right*) from the Congo, female figure holding a bowl.

Building owned by the Foundation but this step (if ever feasible) offered no immediate solution to the problems of accommodation, nor was there better success with an attempt to lease premises in Theobald's Road. In fact the Company was at this time so desperately short of capital, and the Trustees – fearful still of the outbreak of another European war – so determined not to lock up their own resources in a building for the Foundation's benefit, that the Company found itself unable to resign to the Museum (still not open, of course) space essential for its own functioning which it could not afford to rack-rent elsewhere. Accordingly, Dr E. Ashworth Underwood, Director of the Historical Medical Museum from January 1946 onwards, was informed by Dr Kellaway that the Board of the Foundation had decided to occupy the Museum galleries and dismiss most of its staff. The Library, however, was to continue. The Trustees agreed only to a much less harsh restriction, believing that 'the Wellcome Research Institute should not be utilised as permanent offices but should be available for use for the purpose for which it was built by the late Sir Henry Wellcome'. They recommended that the Museum research work should continue, and that the closure should not last more than five or six years. To little avail: the Foundation commandeered all the Historical Museum's space and ceased to fund its staff. All the Trustees could do was to agree to devote £7,000 a year to the work of the Museum in a rented building, which (after fruitless attempts) proved to be 28 Portman Square (May 1947). Here once more specialist exhibitions of historical medical material were arranged and so some tiny fractions of the vast Wellcome Collections became freely accessible to the public from 1948 onwards. The exile was to last eight years: Dr Underwood was able to re-establish the Museum in the Wellcome Building at the end of 1954, with an exhibition of the work of Paul Ehrlich mounted in the Main Hall.

Although the Foundation was persuaded to contribute £1,000 per annum to the cost of the Museum (which remained its property until 1960, after the Trustees had accepted responsibility for it), the Trustees were deeply distressed at this further postponement of Wellcome's design for a historical institute, and when the Foundation produced a new threat to close the Library also, they were outraged. The Directors were summoned to meet the Trustees (January 1948) when Dale told them roundly that it was unreasonable to seek now to reverse the decision made only a few months before, at a moment when the new establishment of the Museum had 'only recently become effective, on the clear understanding that the Foundation would continue to support the Library'. The support of the Library 'should be considered a first charge on the surplus revenues of the Wellcome Foundation Limited in view of the expressed wishes of the Testator, and should not call for review in the same way as other overhead expenses'. The Trustees agreed, however, that some economies in the running of the Library would be proper. The Directors submitted.

This incident should not be read as a complete failure on the part of the Trustees to understand the Directors' problem in maintaining, in the heart of London, a large building which brought little commercial advantage. In particular Dale tended to regard the Wellcome Research Institution as something of a white elephant, and was critical of Dr Wenyon's attempts to sever himself from the Company, as a pure scientist. There was nothing in the least humiliating or undignified in carrying out researches for the benefit of industry (he wrote),

> The thing which I should find humiliating would be to be used as a sham facade of research. That is the real danger of the Wellcome Research outfit, and particularly of its Euston Road embodiment.

These expressions explain an earlier letter to Bullock (November, 1941) where Dale had written:

> It is useless to cry over the milk spilt in Euston Road but if Wellcome had had steady vision, we might now, and probably should, be in a position to carry out his largest dreams.

The problem of cash shortage had first become known to the Trustees in August 1944, when the Foundation was compelled to seek authorisation to extend its Bank loan up to £1 million, in order to pay Excess Profits Tax. They agreed, with the condition that the Directors must submit quarterly statements and reports to the Trustees on the state of the business so long as indebtedness to the Bank should exceed £½ million.

The ill-health of the Burroughs Wellcome Company was probably as old as the Trust itself; later analysis showed that even in 1939 the working capital of the Company had been less than its obligations. By the end of the war this deficit had increased to over £½ million, and the Directors had begun to borrow from the Midland Bank as early as 1942. This was largely because war pressures had compelled the Company to expand its production and to put up new buildings, for the manufacture of penicillin, for example: nearly £800,000 was invested during these six years in buildings and other capital items. Further, stocks of materials had increased from £330,000 in 1939 to £1½ million in 1946. Mr Bennett had hoped to achieve a 50 per cent increase in sales very soon after the restoration of peace, and had ordered re-equipping and extending of the plant at Dartford, and the purchase of stocks of raw materials, in order to satisfy sales amounting to £3,000,000. What was actually sold amounted to far less: stocks of manufactured goods and raw materials rapidly accumulated. In 1948 the then Chairman of the Foundation explained the situation to the Midland Bank in the words: 'the Management of the business had slipped and a rash financial policy had been pursued', aimed at larger sales than could ever be realised. The war years had taken the edge off competitive efficiency, had slowed down independent research for new products, and disrupted the Foundation as an international organisation. The companies in Australia and South Africa were being run at a loss, those in India and China had disappeared. The war years also left a legacy of import and export controls everywhere restricting the restoration of international trade.

The consequence was a swift run-down towards commercial disaster. On a number of products, due to high overheads and manufacturing costs, gross profits fell so low as to leave no net return, so that for the year

1947 the Burroughs Wellcome accounts went into the red. By November 1946 the Foundation Directors felt it necessary to borrow £400,000 more at once, raising the loan ceiling to £2¾ million. The Trustees – having cabled Dale in New York – agreed on the condition that 'an immediate independent investigation be made into the financial position of the Foundation' by Mr H. E. Sier, a former senior partner in Viney, Price and Goodyear, a man of acuity in dealing with figures and having a shrewd business head. His report dissected the economic anatomy of the Company to lay open the causes of its ill-health in inadequate saving of capital and over-expansion; though he fairly opined that the business had been well-run up to August 1945, he judged that the falling-off since then indicated a definite failure of managerial control: weakness on the accounting side, especially, was obvious. Sier's complete, detailed and damning analysis both urged the Trustees to strong action and justified it. Mr Sier himself was invited to join the Board of Directors of the Foundation, strengthened also by the addition of Mr W. N. Creasy (1908–74) the Manager of the highly successful American branch of Burroughs Wellcome. With the retirement of some Directors, the new Board was to lead the Company back to prosperity five years later, without structural change, which the Trustees always resisted. In 1947 Mr Bennett, its Chairman, was convinced that the structure was woefully at fault, and ascribed all the trouble to that cause. Defects existed he wrote,

> because Wellcome had little or no conception of the kind of organisational form that would be required either before or after World War II to enable an international business to be directed, managed, and developed.

Bennett particularly resented the incorporation within the Foundation – 'a facade, really amounting to misrepresentation' – of the Wellcome Research Institution, as a direct charge upon the Company's profits constituting an 'internal Trust'. He wished to put the Institution and its building directly under the Trustees, and to organise in place of the Foundation a new company, Burroughs Wellcome (Holdings) Ltd, responsible for the general policy of the whole group, under which the various national companies would be gathered together with the useful research laboratories and stations. The Trustees in the autumn of 1947 refused to adopt this plan, and by March 1948 had come to the conclusion that Bennett must be replaced as Managing Director and Chairman. The other Directors of the Foundation did not dissent, and (with compensation for the termination of his contract) Bennett was retired in May.

Dr D. E. Wheeler and Mr C. G. Oakes, who was brought back from the Australian Company, were appointed joint Managing Directors while Mr Sier took over, in effect, as Chairman. Soon the Trustees were so pleased with the recovery of the Company that they increased his salary by £1,000 per annum.

However, the maximum bank loan of £2,640,000 – more than one year's turnover – was reached at the time of this management crisis. The Trustees had rejected the proposal that Burroughs Wellcome should 'go public' by an issue of preference shares, though Bullock favoured this step at one time, and the Midland Bank, as the Company's creditor, also favoured the raising of new capital in this way or by recourse to one or other of the Finance Reconstruction Corporations. But as Sier pointed out, the profitability of the Company in 1946 and 1947 was so poor that a Preference Share issue would have been unlikely to succeed. At the end of 1947 it was estimated that for the current year, on a likely turnover of £2.2 million, the gross profit would be some £700,000, and the overheads £736,000. Research cost £185,000 but 'This expense is considered essential if we are to recover our place. . .. New products will bring profit and prestige if exploited quickly'. The Board was sensitive to the Company's continued lag in the field of chemotherapy, and for similar reasons, when the disposal of the Veterinary Research Station at Frant was considered, the Board decided that it should be retained.

Improvement soon came from attention to detail: improved control and accounting procedures, increased profit margins, and reduction of stocks. A number of properties were sold, including the sites in Euston Road and at Snow Hill and an office at East 41st Street in New York. A small toilet-preparations factory that had been acquired in Woking was sold again for £36,000. By September 1948 the Bank loan had been reduced by nearly £200,000, by March 1949 it had been pushed to the right side of £2 million. As the Dartford works improved its productivity the debt was reduced faster; in December 1950 the mortgage which the Midland Bank had acquired in July 1947 was torn up, and in August 1951 the last of the loan was paid off. Through these years it was the American branch that really saved the Foundation and the Trust, as the Board recognised:

> There can be no doubt that the fact that we own this asset gives the Bank a very great sense of security, and that, undoubtedly, is the reason why they have been less onerous in their demands than might have been expected.

From 1948 onwards the American subsidiary, having ably built up its manufacturing and distribution resources, was making very large profits; the Bank of England, seeking dollars for the national purse, leaned heavily on the Foundation to have high dividends brought over, which of course suited the Board's policies also. Another outside factor was the introduction of the British National Health Service, which rapidly stimulated the trade in pharmaceuticals.

Nevertheless, while the Bank loan was in being the Foundation was formally prohibited from declaring any dividends to the Trustees, whose income thus vanished for five more years while every penny went back to the Bank.

Through the first ten penurious and frustrating years of its existence the Wellcome Trust had been dependent on four men; one frequently ill in Scotland, two heavily burdened professionals, and the fourth doing three men's work in other capacities. Both Sir Henry Dale and Professor Elliott found that their Wellcome responsibilities spilled over into other activities, as with the Animal Health Trust; Dale wrote that besides his work directly for Wellcome,

> There is additionally a good deal of work which I do, by direct contacts with a number of medical and scientific bodies, which is not strictly work for the Trust, but has, I think, nevertheless a real value from the Trustee's point of view.

To relieve the burden, at a time when Elliott's health was particularly bad, the appointment of a new Trustee was considered and the legal position confirmed. Bullock and Price wanted another businessman; the two Scientific Trustees both felt that the development of the Foundation required 'rather more scientific judgment of the probable future developments of therapeutic practice than financial judgment as to the proper means of obtaining or reserving capital'. Although Elliott made a tentative approach to Sir Wilson Jameson, Chief Medical Officer at the Ministry of Health – who was not free to take up the Trusteeship immediately – nothing more was done, perhaps because of the lack of unanimity between the Trustees.

It may seem strange that Dale should put relation to the Foundation in the first place when speaking of a new Trustee (noting also the value of Jameson's administrative experience). The fact is that Dale, at any rate, through all these years was oppressed by a sense of the commercial uncertainty of the business; carelessness, incompetence or negligence among the Directors of the Foundation could ruin all the beneficent prospects that Wellcome had laid open – as indeed all but happened in the black and bitter year of 1947. So his ultimate objects must be the development of a rational, properly directed programme of scientific research within the Company in order to enable it to progress, and (at a much lower level) the transfer of the Museum and Library to the Trustees to be properly managed as 'genuine educational charities'. In the words of a letter to Elliott (26 March 1941):

> I entirely agree with you that, at some time or other, we shall have to have a very much clearer definition of our present and future functions. . . . [T]he line of least resistance would be for us to sit back, and to say that our only further function would be to receive revenues and to spend them outside the Foundation . . . leaving the Foundation thus to make what arrangements its Directorate think fit, with regard to their own provision for research. It would be an easy attitude, but I think a wrong one. It would relieve me, in particular, from embarrassments of more than one kind. . . . I am wholeheartedly of your opinion, however, that if we continue to hold these Trusteeships, we have got to do our duty by the Foundation and its own scientific and educational plans.

Holding these opinions before the critical years of 1946–9, Dale was unlikely to change them thereafter; even though in sober truth the crisis had been brought about by commercial misjudgment and was relieved by commercial acumen, it showed how unreliable the merely commercial mind might be.

Curiously enough, the first addition to the body of Trustees named in the Will arose from their decision to look for a first-class man to add to the Directorate of the Foundation. Bullock was a co-trustee with Lord Piercy (1886–1966) in a quite separate Trust; he was asked by the Trustees to seek from Piercy the name of a suitable eminent, and appropriate Director. Lord Piercy, Chairman of the Industrial and Commercial Finance Corporation and a Director of the Bank of England, held a number of other important positions in finance and education. Lord Piercy, after a talk with Mr Sier about the structure and business of the Foundation, proposed privately that Lord Inman (1892–1979) might be sounded out; he too was an experienced company director and Chairman, an underwriting member of Lloyd's and also a man interested in hospitals. This suggestion did not appeal to Sir Henry Dale who characteristically preferred a Director with experience of the pharmaceutical industry, but

Fig. 13. Lord Piercy of Burford (1886–1966), Chairman of the Trustees from 1960 to 1965.

Dale was rapidly attracted to the idea of inviting Lord Piercy himself to become a Trustee, as he appeared to be willing to take on an additional commitment. On 13 December 1948 Piercy met the whole body of the Trustees for the first time at a luncheon, and on the 17th Dale wrote to invite him formally to become one of their number. Before the end of 1948 the necessary steps had been taken, Lord Piercy making no difficulties about undertaking the covenant required of Trustees in the Will.

Fig. 14. The Trust's first independent office, established with the Museum of Medical History at 28 Portman Square, London, W1. The house was demolished in 1961.
Photograph courtesy of Westminster City Libraries, Archives Department, Marylebone Library

In its first years the Wellcome Trust had no office. The Trustees met at the Wellcome Research Institution, which was convenient for meeting members of the Foundation. The two professional men and Mr Clarke, the secretary, worked from their firms, Sir Henry Dale from Hampstead and (later) the Royal Institution, the Trust contributing part of his secretary's salary. Professor Elliott managed without assistance and wrote from one or other of his private residences. By 1941 Dale was conscious of the need for an office, a place to keep files and meet people, but nothing was done before 1946. When Dale lost his home and office in

Albermarle Street on his retirement from the Royal Institution, the Foundation rented him space in Dilke House, Malet Street, which he shared with Elliott and his secretary, Miss Cutts. This too was lost in the following year, and subsequently the Trust office was established, along with the Museum, at 28 Portman Square (a house since demolished). Propinquity tended to strengthen the relationship between Dr Underwood and the two Scientific Trustees, and to increase their interest in the Historical Medical Museum.

With the final settlement of tax claims upon the Wellcome Estate and the recognition of the Trust's charitable status by the Inland Revenue authorities in October 1944, the possibility of important action appeared at last. The lawyers had back-dated the charitable tax-exemption to July 1937 – admittedly, almost a year after Sir Henry Wellcome's death – and for the years up to April 1945 the Inland Revenue returned to the Trustees £552,000 of previously paid tax, an enormous sum compared with the petty expenditures of so many previous years. Originally the Trustees had hoped so to arrange matters with the Foundation that a single comprehensive operation for tax relief would cover both the Trust and the Wellcome Research Institute, but this proved impossible to obtain as did other efforts to secure charitable status for the entire Wellcome Foundation as a body devoted wholly to charitable ends. However, Mr Justice Morton did (January 1944) resolve certain legal scruples touching the Articles of Association, and at the same time declared that Wellcome's wish to have his family re-interred in a mausoleum at Garden City could not be considered as a charitable object in law. In fact, action upon the clauses in the Will relating to Garden City, Blue Earth County, Minnesota was again deferred (September 1945) when local enquiries revealed that the place was still too underdeveloped to benefit from Sir Henry's ambitious improvements.

With this large sum suddenly in hand, the Trustees formulated a financial policy based on the following considerations.

1. The probability that dividends receivable from The Wellcome Foundation Limited would not for some time be as large as the Company's earnings justified, in view of the Company's need to finance post-war reconstruction and development.
2. The contingency that in any year the income of the Trust from The Wellcome Foundation Limited might fall below the level anticipated by the Trustees, and on which they had based their plans for charitable disbursements.

3. The necessity of ensuring that income be available in any year sufficient to cover annuity payments.

£100,000 was to be set aside for the future Memorial in Minnesota, and £140,000 invested so as to constitute a Fund for the satisfaction of the annuities created by the Will, for as long as these should last. Thirdly, £200,000 was also to be invested to form an Equalisation Fund, into which the Trustees might dip if necessary should the dividend from the Foundation fall below average, which was expected for the future to give the Trustees a disposable income of some £120,000 per annum. Accordingly, by September 1945, £383,000 had been invested in gilt-edged stocks whose yield at that time was so low (2½ per cent or less) that the Trustees could expect little income from this large capital – less than £10,000 per annum – in comparison with their expected dividends; and for the time being there remained about £100,000 available for possible disposal.

No doubt the sense of relief from fear and oppression produced by the successful invasion of Europe in the summer of 1944 combined with the imminence of commercial profitability to create in the Trustees a spirit approaching euphoria, and for the first time a variety of projects came up for consideration and even received support.

Friendly contact was made with both the Medical Research Council (of which Sir Henry Dale was a member until 1946, and Chairman of one of its Committees until 1949) and the Nuffield Foundation. There was talk of adopting a Universities Fellowships Scheme like that put up by I.C.I., which Dr F. A. Freeth explained in detail to the Trustees. Dale, however, preferred (August 1944) the idea (in the ripeness of time) of the Trustees themselves selecting Fellows, with the aid of expert advisers, from candidates nominated by the universities – in this writing with the support of his son-in-law, Professor A. R. Todd. The sums actually awarded at this time, after careful deliberation, were still very small, such as the £1,700 to assist the extension of the Department of Pharmacology at Oxford (November, 1944) or the £830 received by Dr F. McFarlane Burnet for the library at the Walter and Eliza Hall Institute of Research in Pathology and Medicine at Melbourne, Australia. (The Canterbury Medical Library at Christchurch, New Zealand, had been similarly aided by a tiny annual sum for a number of years.) The Trustees were willing to look even further afield: not forgetting Wellcome's interest in China, and after taking the advice of Dr Joseph Needham and others, they awarded £6,000 to aid students of pharmacy at Chungking (then still the capital of China) and at the West China Union University, Chengtu, during a period of three years. Other proposals carefully considered came to nothing. Lord Killearn, then British Ambassador to Egypt, was eager to establish a British non-governmental research laboratory in that country to study health matters in relation to both the local civil population and the British forces in Egypt. There was already a considerable American effort, which Elliott was reluctant to attempt to rival, and Dale doubted if anything could usefully be done. Similarly the Trustees did not rush to take over a closing military health-research laboratory at Accra in West Africa; here a factor was advice from Col. Walter Elliott that the development of academic studies at Ibadan would be likely, in the future, to render that place – subsequently the seat of a University – a more suitable locus for the Trustee's benevolence. In the case of the University of Oxford, an offer by the Trustees of a considerable grant for the purchase of a house to be used as an Institute of Human Nutrition fell through early in 1947 because it proved impossible to find a suitable building.

With considerable resources available in the summer of 1945 the Trustees were able to respond to an appeal from the President of the Royal College of Surgeons, Sir Alfred Webb-Johnson, with a handsome gift of £80,000. This was to be used for that part of the extension to their building which was to house their Museum, and which was to bear the name of Sir Henry Wellcome (who had in his time been an Honorary Fellow of the College). By July the Trustees had received the thanks of the College for their 'tribute to the service which the Royal College renders to surgery and to medical and scientific knowledge by the maintenance of museums of human and comparative anatomy and physiology'. A little later the Trustees readily agreed to give important assistance to medicine in the University of London. At the School of Hygiene and Tropical Medicine the Dean (Dr J. M. Mackintosh) was eager to inaugurate a half-time Professorship of Clinical Tropical Medicine to be held by Brigadier (later Sir) Neil Hamilton Fairley F.R.S. (1891–1966), an Australian physician with a most distinguished career in this field both before and during the war, when he had directed the anti-malarial measures of the Australian forces engaged in jungle warfare. It was proposed that the other half of his time would be given to the Wellcome Research Institution. This proposal pleased both the Trustees and the Foundation, and £44,000 in 3 per cent government stock was accordingly given to the University as a semi-endowment. The other Chair, that of Pharmacology tenable at the Pharmaceutical Society, was already in being but the funds available from the University of London and the Society jointly were inadequate for the proper provision of stipend and laboratories. On this

Fig. 15. The new building of the Royal College of Surgeons, replacing wartime destruction, was the first major benefaction of this kind made by the Trustees. It houses the College's Museum and bears Sir Henry Wellcome's name.

occasion the approach was made by the Society's Secretary, Mr (later Sir) Hugh Linstead M.P., who had previously advised the Trustees about other matters.[1] The Trustees accepted his argument that maintenance of active research at the Pharmaceutical Society's laboratories was important, and agreed to furnish a sum of £74,000 in order to endow a research professorship.

Another 'first' of this eventful summer of 1945 was the institution of two Research Fellowships in order to enable two young Australian scientists, Dr Hugh Ennor and Mr John W. Legge, to spend two years in Britain pursuing advanced research in biochemistry, the former with Professor Rudolf Peters at Oxford, the latter with Professor David Keilin at Cambridge. In the month following this double grant – made on the recommendation of Dr Kellaway, now Director of the Research Institute – a third Fellowship was awarded to Dr E. W. Todd for work at the Rockefeller Institute at New York, but this grant (rather curiously, as it seems today) was made through the M.R.C. and at the request of its Second Secretary, Dr A. Landsborough Thomson. Early in the next year (April 1946) work in bacterial cytology at the private Strangeways Laboratory at Cambridge by Dr Carl Robinow was also supported by a Fellowship for three years.

Strictly, these *ad hoc* awards were not the first Research Fellowships provided by the Trustees, since they had given such assistance to the Veterinary Educational Trust (later the Animal Health Trust) from its inception in 1943. In this case the Fellows were selected by a joint committee consisting of the two Scientific Trustees and representatives of the Veterinarians. This scheme continued for a number of years, though not without administrative problems, and provided useful support for young biological researchers. It survived an extension from 'small' (that is, largely companion) animals to farm animals of which Dale and Elliott were initially dubious because of possible rivalry with the Agricultural Research Council's well-established research laboratories.

The Trustees were already aware that it was not necessarily very useful to attract a young researcher from a temporary state, or university-financed post to a better-paid Wellcome Fellowship of equally limited duration, even though such a side-step might release funds to support another scientist. A Travel Fellowship, bringing promising men and women to outstanding centres of research activity, should promote the individual skill and fecundity of the recipient, a result much less likely to follow from a mere side-step when the Wellcome Fellow might even remain at the same bench under the same laboratory head. Dale was eager for the participation of Trustees in the choice of Fellows, and took part energetically in the interviewing process. He recognised also the need not to be too much swayed by the accident of personal contact with himself or Elliott, noting Kellaway's natural eagerness to advance the research careers of young Australians. Even in the 1940s he saw the need for the Trustees to develop positive strategies for the disposal of their funds, though none had taken firm shape before the Foundation's return to prosperity in 1950. In general, appeals to the Wellcome Trustees from societies and other bodies devoted to a cause were refused. On the other hand, the need to rebuild, to extend and re-equip the scientific laboratories in British universities was urgent and real, and it is hardly surprising that a large expenditure went into such objects – particularly in the early 1950s when £320,000 was devoted to building projects in Leeds, London, Oxford, the Strangeways Laboratory at Cambridge and other places, and £52,000 was spent on seven items of equipment, especially electron microscopes: the new technology of scientific research placed unprecedented demands on laboratory budgets.

4

CHANGING CHARACTER

Sir Henry Dale's retirement after 23 years as a Trustee came, by his own wish, in July 1960 although he was to continue as a Scientific Consultant to the Trustees until the end of his days. Lord Piercy, who succeeded him in the Chair, continued to lead the Trust for five years, up to his 79th birthday. His tenure of office saw many changes in the Trust, which at last acquired a fully professional character. In the first place, it acquired an elegant abode; after leaving Portman Square (together with the Museum) in December 1954 Sir Henry Dale had cramped accommodation for nearly two years at 24 Harley Street until, during the autumn of 1956, it was possible to occupy a handsome town-house at 52 Queen Anne Street, which offered all the space the Trustees could desire at that stage.

By this time an administration consisting of more than Sir Henry's secretary had been created, while the number and complexity of grants was steadily increasing. Moreover, the Trustee's ultimate responsibility for the Foundation continued to impose burdens upon them, further increased by the direct involvement of the Scientific Trustees with Mr Creasy and the affairs of Burroughs Wellcome (U.S.A.) Inc. There was a great deal for elderly men to contend with, and when a new Scientific Trustee was at last chosen, in 1955, he too was already 63 years old. The decision, shortly before Lord Piercy's retirement, to enlarge the number of Trustees from five to seven, was really very necessary.

Not the least of the changes in the Trust was in the personality of the new Chairman. Lord Piercy and Sir Henry Dale shared the good fortune to maintain vigour and mental alertness into extreme old age; they were alike in being men of strong opinions and determination, and each in a different way was an altruist. But temperament and career made their styles of leadership of the Trust very different. Dale applied the scientific

Fig. 16. The elegant entrance to the offices of the Wellcome Trust at 52 Queen Anne Street.

method to non-scientific problems of management and commerce; Piercy was much more the political animal, at home among the grey figures populating the corridors of power whom Dale, at heart, distrusted. Piercy's ultimate object was to make the Trust and Foundation a single, unitary machine for generating and dispensing vast funds, though he was never passionately concerned about the precise employment of the

Trust's wealth; neither biochemistry, nor clinical science, nor tropical medicine, ever spoke strongly to his imagination. Dale in the last resort was more sentimental; though seeing all Henry Wellcome's weaknesses of character and intellect clearly, he wished *his* dream to be realised, not that of Lord Piercy or of any other organisational genius of the new kind.

Sir Henry Dale's awareness of the difficulties left by Wellcome to his Trustees is well brought out in a paper he wrote for his colleagues in April 1951, at a time when they were much disturbed by the introduction of a 50 per cent Distributed Profits Tax imposed on companies, irretrievable by the shareholders to whom the profits were distributed even if these enjoyed charitable status. This measure would, in Dale's words, 'deprive the Trustees of a large part of the tax-free revenues which they expected to have for use'. It was their duty to seek to avoid this frustration of the testator's intentions by any lawful means. The root of the trouble, he agreed, was in Wellcome's separation of the Foundation – meaning the Burroughs Wellcome companies – from the Trust, as a purely commercial firm. If he had proceeded otherwise, the whole could have been considered a charitable concern, that it 'would have been a matter only of friendly agreement with the Directors of our business, how much of the realised profit was required for extension of capital equipment and trading activities, and how much was properly available for expenditure on the charitable objects of the Trust'. Furthermore, he went on, the distinction between spending on in-house and outside research would have become 'merely formal', all alike would have been a charitable expense. Such an arrangement 'would produce a healthier relation between the Trustees and the Directorate with regard to the scientific activities supported by both' for it would avoid 'a certain feeling of competition – good-humoured but none the less deleterious' between them whose result had been, he suspected:

> to create a tendency in the Research Department (or Institution) of the Foundation to spend an unduly large share of the resources available for such purposes on researches immediately under their own control and within their own structure.

Dale instanced as a happier example – from the point of view of the Profits Tax at any rate – the Lister Institute, whose profits from the manufacture of vaccines and sera helped to maintain, without mulct, the integral research programmes.

The Trustees went so far (June 1951) as to seek Counsel's opinion on the question whether or not the whole Foundation could acquire charitable status, and so exemption from Profits Tax and Income Tax together. Mr Buckley's advice (November) shaded from the non-committal to the dubious. Indeed, Dale's argument, even to a layman, seems somewhat naive. The deep distinction between the processes of making money and spending money seems to resist such easy smoothing over. Mr Buckley noted that the manufacturing activities of Burroughs Wellcome could hardly be regarded as secondary or incidental to the benevolent work of the Trustees, as could be argued in the case of the Lister Institute. His procedural recommendation was that the Trustees should put their case informally to the highest level of the Inland Revenue, and, accordingly, Lord Piercy agreed to make a personal approach to Sir Eric Bamford, chairman of the Board of the Inland Revenue (February 1952).

Apparently no such meeting ever took place, because the different idea was taken up of a direct approach to the Treasury, with the object of promoting legislation to relieve all Charities of the effects of the Distributed Profits Tax. For it had now been realised that because its incidence fell as heavily on some other large Charities (not least, the Nuffield Foundation) as upon the Wellcome Trustees, any steps must be taken in concert with them. (Could one envisage a large fraction of Morris Motors being classed as a charitable enterprise?) When the matter was pursued, however, it emerged (in a letter from the Hon. Geoffrey Gibbs, June 1952) that Lord Nuffield 'thought it unwise' for Charities having a manufacturing base to push their luck by seeking such an exemption. There the matter ended: in October 1951 the Labour government had suffered defeat, Churchill resumed office, and a new era of economic liberalism appeared to have dawned, though Profits Taxes were not abolished.

Nevertheless, the restoration of the Foundation to commercial health occasioned a steady increase in the disposable dividends received by the Trustees from it. 1952 was a year in which a number of steps had to be taken with respect to the higher direction of both. The first was the extension, by Court order, of the Trusteeship of Dale and Elliott, who were both running out of time. The non-scientific Trustees were all of the opinion that both should continue; as Elliott wrote to Bullock concerning the Chairman of the Trustees at this time:

> Dale seems untouched by the years and should be retained as long as possible. There can never again be found a chairman equal to Dale, with his eminence in the scientific world and also his personal knowledge of the business in which he once

> held a senior post, years further back than any of the present Directorate.

The legal business duly went through, prolonging Dales' tenure to the age of 80 and Elliott's to that of 78 (in 1955) but not without the advice expressed by Mr Justice Roxburgh that steps should be taken to bring in a younger Trustee.

Much more perplexing was the question of the Chairman of the Foundation. Mr H. E. Sier was about to reach the retiring age, after effecting a splendid recovery of the business. He was an accountant and a business man, who had served the Foundation part-time because of his responsibilities to other companies. As the time for the appointment of a successor approached it became clear that he and the other Directors thought this was an ideal arrangement, to be perpetuated, while the Trustees (realising from the first that a part-time Chairman might well turn out to be a puppet in the hands of the other Directors) favoured a strong full-time appointment. In the early summer of 1952 Sir Henry Dale and Lord Piercy began actively to look about for a possible man, seeking the advice of Lord McGowan, the great mogul of Imperial Chemical Industries. Through his brother Hugh Gaitskell, the distinguished Labour politician, Lord Piercy sounded out Mr Arthur Gaitskell, lately Chairman of the Sudan Gezira Board. He was soon to be at liberty, was the right age, and had experience of important managerial posts as well as of government service overseas at the highest level. But he was not scientifically trained. Mr Michael Perrin, on the other hand, five years younger and equally a product of Winchester and New College, Oxford, who was put up by Sir Wallace Akers, the extremely able Research Director of I.C.I., had read science, and acquired research experience before joining the Company. Not only had he done well in I.C.I. (in the development of polythene) but he had made a great reputation for himself in atomic energy during the war. In 1952 he was General Research Advisor to I.C.I.. Dale had met and liked him during the war years, and his strong feeling that he was 'by far the best man for the purpose we were likely to get' was reinforced by a long talk with Perrin on 21 August 1952. On the other hand, Piercy after meeting Perrin thought him 'not the precise article' – too much the scientist, too unfamiliar with the problems of marketing and business microeconomics. His rather weak preference for Arthur Gaitskell, whose 'line of experience' Dale thought 'not so directly related to the special demands of the positions in view' was rapidly overcome by Sir Henry Dale, partly because of some lack of enthusiasm for entering industry on Mr Gaitskell's part, and by the end of September the Trustees were unanimous in their choice of Mr Perrin as next Chairman of the Foundation.

A difference of view between the Trustees and the Directors, if a friendly one, appeared as soon as the two names, and the Trustees' preference, were communicated to Mr Sier. The Directors rejected both men, Mr Sier adding his view that a scientific background was not essential in the Chairman. What they were really opposing, however, was the idea of a full-time head, a post they thought 'not in the best interests of the Foundation'. Both Dale and Piercy thought that the Directors had been induced by weak arguments to adopt an untenable position, and the Trustees found no difficulty in resolving not to flinch, in the last resort, from their ultimate responsibility as shareholders, formally minuting (24 November 1952) their resolution that the Chairman of the Foundation should be a full-time officer having:

> a wide experience with the scientific, administrative and commercial problems involved in an industrial enterprise based on progressive scientific research, and such experience of and contacts with scientific, industrial, official and governmental circles as would qualify him to consider and plan for the future development of the Foundation on a broad basis and at the highest level.

Experience of commerce and finance in the Chairman was desirable, the minute continued, but less important than the qualities just defined. It was written and introduced by Dale himself, who used similar language in writing to Bullock – absent through illness – to explain the course of events.

The Trustees now 'requested' the Directors directly to appoint Mr Perrin, and after some further argument they capitulated. As Lord Piercy put it, when the Trustees made it quite clear that they 'meant to have their way' as regards a full-time Chairman – the real sticking-point for the Directors rather than the choice of individual – 'the whole thing collapsed'.

The handover of power took place in February 1953. This change followed by just a few months the death in harness of Dr Kellaway, 'my very dear friend of many years' as Dale wrote of him, who for a decade had directed the Wellcome Research Institution.

Thus, for the third time, the Trustees had changed the headship of the Foundation. To clear themselves from the last legacy of Sir Henry

Wellcome's personal management of his business they had installed an experienced business man – of whom they had rightly thought well for a number of years – then they had replaced him by an accountant in order to correct a chaotic situation in which informed direction of the company had become impossible – and now they had selected a scientific mandarin. Each time the type of Chairman chosen by the Trustees had matched the real needs of the situation. Evidently, in insisting upon Michael Perrin, the Trustees had a view to the increasingly sophisticated nature of the pharmaceutical industry, and to the extent to which it was becoming a highly specialised branch of chemical engineering. Certainly their appreciation of the man and of the situation for which they chose him were correct, if one may judge by the success of the Foundation under his Chairmanship.

Exceptional as these circumstances were, the Trustees have been constantly called on not only exceptionally but regularly in order to keep the business of the Foundation at its higher level moving, and to confirm or modify decision of the Directors. It is not surprising, for example, that the Trustees were consulted during the 1950s about more than one attempt of United States manufacturers to buy either the whole Foundation or its American subsidiaries. Not that these approaches were ever considered very seriously on the British side, for both Trustees and Directors were far too conscious of Sir Henry Wellcome's pride in his business ever to be tempted to surrender it; but it would have been neither polite nor commercially prudent to ignore such offers. When in 1953, soon after Michael Perrin's appointment as Chairman of the Foundation, he decided upon certain reorganisations including the appointment of Dr Adamson as Research Director, Sir Henry Dale wrote two-and-a-half pages of observations upon the memorandum submitted by the Foundation to the Trustees, in broad approval of the new scheme. Similarly, it was Dale who supplied 'copy' about the policies and activities of the Trustees for a special *Supplement* on Sir Henry Wellcome, the Trust, and the Foundation which was issued with *The Times* of 17 April 1953, in celebration of the anniversary of Wellcome's birth. Also in the same busy year the Trustees had to consider complex representations from Mr Perrin about the provision of capital for the future development of the Foundation; if the Company was to expand, modernise, and market new products, then capital had to be invested in buildings and plant for both research and production; estimates showed that about £½ million of new capital would be required for each of the next four years. Unless a decision should be taken to raise new capital on the market on the prevailing terms, the capital could only be provided by the Trustees' continuing to accept a less than normal percentage of gross profit as their dividend. This they decided to do, and the increase in assets of the Company under Mr Perrin was accordingly very large.

Another issue constantly before the Trustees at this time was the search for a legal method of relieving the Foundation of a burden of taxation which pressed heavily upon the charitable funds of the Trust. Dale was himself the 'chief instigator . . . of the exploration of the reconstruction of the Foundation and Trust as a single charity' which came to nothing in 1952. An approach was made to Mr John Boyd-Carpenter, Financial Secretary to the Treasury, to secure an amendment to the law in terms favourable to a business with profits devoted to charity, but the Minister felt unable to recommend such a change. In 1954 the Trustees took up a scheme proposed by the Foundation for the setting up of a Company, Burroughs Wellcome (Overseas) Ltd, to which the Foundation would lend several millions of capital; with this fund the new company would acquire all the foreign holdings belonging to the Foundation. The profits of these foreign companies would then be accrued and returned to the Foundation as repayment of the capital originally borrowed, thus not falling into the category of 'income from foreign investments'. The opinion of Counsel (Mr F. Heyworth Talbot) was in favour of the legality of such a scheme, which was put into effect by an incorporation on 26 January 1955. It was calculated that this would enable the Trustees to recover large amounts of tax at the rate of eight shillings in the pound, rather than three shillings and fourpence.

On other occasions the Trustees examined such matters as the incidence of double taxation relief, and appeals were sometimes made for the intervention of the Trustees as persons well connected with Ministers and other people in high places. When for example, Mr Oakes (joint Managing Director) was irate because of the pirating of Wellcome Foundation preparations in Italy (where no adequate patent protection was given by the government to foreign manufacturers), notably as regards the drug 'Daraprim' (pyrimethamine), he appealed to Lord Piercy to make the facts known – and, as was claimed, the general annoyance of British and American businessmen at this state of affairs – to Mr Peter Thorneycroft, President of the Board of Trade. Not only did the Trustees receive many papers from the Foundation, as well as other sources, in addition to their attendance at meetings as shareholders, but the affairs of the Foundation constantly demanded consideration of expert advice and learned opinion, and the taking of decisions on which much depended.

Although Sir Henry Dale's fellow-Trustees were further to prolong his Chairmanship to 1960, they began long before this time to feel that the increasing volume of business connected with the making of grants, the selection of Research Fellows and so forth, imposed too heavy a burden on the Chairman. 'Far too great a burden is, and has been for some time past cast upon you in connection with the affairs of the Trust' wrote Bullock to Dale (September 1954); could not someone with scientific and medical knowledge be appointed to assist him in the review and appraisal of applications for grants? Dale agreed that some administrative machinery was now necessary, to which 'the experience which I have accumulated through what I have been able to do for some years in that direction will still have some value'. A proper administration would permit the pursuit of 'a stable and organised spending policy, which is the real and proper function of our Trust'. He noted that the Nuffield Trust had a staff of about 60, and now that the Wellcome Foundation's profits were becoming stabilised, the sums at the Wellcome Trustee's disposal should not be altogether beyond comparison with those of the Nuffield.

> If we were to do our duty to the proper function of our Trust, we ought to be prepared to spend something of the order of £10,000 per annum on administration, instead of a good deal less than £1,000 as at present. I have been able to deal, on an opportunist basis, with such applications as have come to us unprompted. To do the job properly, we ought to take the initiative in constructing a scheme of expenditure. For that we must have a whole-time administrative staff, and I think that, for a year or two more, I could help them, and the Trustees, in consultation on such schemes as may be produced.

Dale noted that, besides preparing proposals for submission to the Trustees, a Scientific Secretary should be able to arrange for them to receive the opinions of expert advisers upon projects, and form advisory committees for the more important fields; he would also travel on their behalf 'to Australia, for example, or to India, and report on projects there'.

Naturally enough Dale consulted Sir Harold Himsworth, the Secretary of the Medical Research Council, who suggested that the Trustees take on a member of his own staff. Although Dale's first preference lay elsewhere this was finally done, and Dr F. H. K. Green was engaged as Scientific Secretary from October 1955, Mr Clarke remaining Secretary. Dr Green had been with the M.R.C. since 1929. Within less than a year of Dr

Fig. 17. Sir John Boyd, F.R.S. (1891–1981), appointed a Trustee in succession to Professor T. R. Elliott.

Green's engagement, as it became clear that a larger scientific staff was necessary, Lt-Col. H. J. Bensted R.A.M.C. who had directed the Central Laboratory of the Public Health Service in England and Wales came in as his Deputy (November 1956 to July 1958) and from April 1958 Dr Edwin Clarke, a neurologist, was brought in as Assistant Scientific Secretary.

By that time, in October 1955, Professor Elliott had retired. He was replaced as a Scientific Trustee by Brigadier J. S. K. Boyd, R.A.M.C. (retd) – 'one so eminently qualified for the work of the Trust, and with so intimate a knowledge of the research activities of the Foundation' in the commendation of Sir Henry Dale. The reason for Dale's encomium was that Boyd had been Director of the Wellcome Laboratories of Tropical Medicine since 1946, where he had directed and personally conducted research of great distinction. John Boyd had become an army doctor in 1914 soon after qualifying; in Salonika he had worked on dysentery with C. M. Wenyon, and later continued his investigations of dysentery-causing organisms in India and at Millbank. In the Second World War he had much to do with the same disease, with malaria, and with the organisation of blood-transfusion. He had retired from the R.A.M.C. as Director of Pathology at the War Office.

Boyd withdrew a year early from his position at the Wellcome Research Institution in order to take up the Trusteeship, but continued his own laboratory work until 1963. He had been connected with the Burroughs Wellcome firm long before, during Sir Henry Wellcome's lifetime, and he was devoted to the perpetuation of the strange combination of philanthropy, science, museumship and business that Wellcome represented. For many years he was the Trustee especially concerned for the Historical Museum and Library and he was greatly to encourage Dr Noel Poynter in his long struggle to enhance and develop both as instruments of medical history.

When Sir Henry Dale retired he had reached 85 years of age, and it is hardly surprising that both his physique and his health were less robust than in the past. His successor, though not so many years his junior, always referred to him as 'Dear old Dale'. After Mr Bullock's departure, in September 1961, only Mr Price remained active of the original five Trustees. Dale's place was taken (October 1960) by Professor John McMichael, of the London Postgraduate Medical School, well known to both Dale and Elliott since before the war, when he had been first a Beit Memorial Fellow and then a Royal Society Fellow. Professionally a cardiologist, Sir John (as he became in 1965) had considerable administrative experience in the University of London and close academic connections with the U.S.A. and Canada, where he had received many appointments and awards for his distinguished scientific work. Sir Henry Dale had always given him the firmest support in the development of his career. Thirteen years younger than his senior in the Trust, Sir John Boyd, McMichael represented a different scientific generation and, in many ways, a different world of science; Boyd represented the bacteriology and pathology of the late nineteenth century, McMichael the experimental

Fig. 18. Sir John McMichael, F.R.S. (b.1904), appointed a Trustee in succession to Sir Henry Dale.

physiology of the 1920s and 1930s, and the tradition of clinical research created by Sir Thomas Lewis.

In the succession to Mr Bullock the connection with the firm of Markby Stewart and Wadesons was maintained by the choice of Mr R. M. Nesbitt, now senior partner in the firm, an office held by his father before him when solicitor to Sir Henry Wellcome. He was already acquainted with Lord Piercy in the City, and experienced in the kind of business that the

Fig. 19. Mr R. M. Nesbitt, Mr Bullock's former partner, was chosen to succeed him as a Trustee.

Wellcome Trustees encountered. During the 13 years of his Trusteeship (1961–74) Mr Nesbitt was much concerned with the development of the Historical Museum and Library, and with the establishment of The Wellcome Custodian Trustees Ltd, which was formed in 1958 to take corporate possession of the Trust's own investments, constituting its reserve fund.

The professional status of the Trustees was on two separate occasions the subject of appeal to the Courts. On the first occasion a series of actions was fought to establish the right of the Trustees to regard their personal remuneration under Sir Henry Wellcome's Will as being earned income, taxed accordingly, and especially free from the Special Contribution imposed by Sir Stafford Cripps as Chancellor of the Exchequer in 1946–7. The Commissioners of the Inland Revenue held, on the contrary (29 November, 1950), that the Trustees were in receipt of an 'investment income'. From their decision the Trustees (in the name of Sir Henry Dale) appealed by case stated to the High Court, which (in the person of Mr Justice Harman) decided in July 1951 that the Commissioners were wrong. Dale's Counsel had argued that the Trustees not only controlled two research funds and the Wellcome Foundation (a large concern), but took part in fortnightly business meetings; Dale himself needed an office and secretary for his Trust work, which regularly occupied him for two hours every day. Mr Justice Harman could not see how Dale might be said not to work for his pay; however, the Court of Appeal – to which the Commissioners at once elevated the decision – was less clear-sighted and favoured the Appellants. It took a final remove to the House of Lords (June 1953) before Dale was finally vindicated in his staunch refusal, Hampden-like, to pay unjust taxes.

It is not very clear why the Trustees persisted. After their defeat in the Court of Appeal, they were inclined to give up, for a lot of money had been spent already and the saving to individuals or to the Trust, through success, would be minimal. It seems to have been the conviction of Counsel that the reading of the law by the Commissioners and the Court of Appeal was bad, and ought as a matter of principle to be altered, which persuaded them to go on. It is possible also that the Trustees were perceptive of a certain hostility in law to charitable trusts in general, and especially to those founded on industrial profits; they knew, for example, that tax law in the United States was much more generous in its provisions covering industrial donations to charities than were the British authorities, and so they may have been the more readily induced to fight on for a point which, if gained, would enhance the position of trusteeship in general by one small step.

For (as we have seen) at this time they were also seriously considering various schemes for so reorganising the Wellcome Foundation that it would be taken out of the tax realm altogether, or at any rate to the greatest possible extent.

The second important reason for recourse to the High Court was the need to increase the number of Trustees from five to seven; a re-writing of a very precise limitation in the Will which the Trustees regarded in the most serious light. The increase was, it seems, first proposed by Mr Bullock, whom Lord Piercy once described as 'the father and mother of our present set-up'. The unspoken motive for seeking this change was perhaps the considerable age of the existing body of five Trustees (not to say Sir Henry Dale, still an important force even in retirement): Mr Price was 79, Lord Piercy (now Chairman) was 76, Sir John Boyd 69. The only way in which a younger man could be brought in and given experience before any of these three retired (or died suddenly) was by adding to the number of Trustees. Ostensibly, the plea to the High Court (which the Trustees resolved to make on 31 May 1962) to alter the terms of Wellcome's Will was based on the growth of the Foundation for which they were responsible (assets valued at £8 million in 1955 had become worth £20 million in 1962) and the corresponding increase in magnitude of the dividends available to the Trustees for their charitable objects (to £613,000 in 1962). The statement of case also pointed to the enhanced complexity of science since the 1930s with the expansion of such new subjects as 'biochemistry, biophysics, chemotherapy, antibiotics, molecular biology, virology, genetics, experimental surgery to mention only a few new and expanding fields of research'. Two Trustees expert in science could not be expected to cover adequately the vast field of modern scientific medicine. Further, the pressure on the Trustees reduced the qualitative value of the benefactions they made:

> In addition to the detailed consideration of applications for assistance, the Trustees must, even more now than in the past, devote time to thought on and discussion of the basic aims and policies of the Trust . . . it may well be that the time has come for a more active policy in order to increase the efficiency of the work the Trust sets out to do . . . it may be better in some fields that the Trustees should themselves initiate and promote projects.

So to do they needed time for reflection free from administrative care and the weighing of grant applications.

The Chairman himself thought that the plea to the High Court stressed excessively the scientific component of the Trustees' business: the Trustees 'would never have made this application', he wrote, 'in order to get one' more medical scientist added to their number. The need, in his view, was 'for an additional Trustee who really understands finance and the workings of the City' (January 1963). Once again, the possibility that the Foundation might go to the money market for extra capital – rather than build up capital slowly by accretion, to the disadvantage of the Trust – was under serious consideration. And that, as Lord Piercy remarked in a telephone conversation 'that's like handling dynamite; that's going to give a lot of worry and trouble and you can't rely on much help on that from the medical trustees'. Accordingly, despite the preference of Sir Henry Dale and the serving Scientific Trustees for the immediate election of a third scientist, probably a biochemist, the Affidavit submitted by the Trustees to the High Court in April 1963[1] emphasised

> that the present need for additional Trustees is felt not only on the medical scientific side of the Trustees' work, but also on the financial and commercial side, where the problems of the Foundation become daily more numerous and complex. The Trustees must be able to act with as much authority and conviction in the commercial sphere as the scientific. It would be advantageous to give more flexibility to the constitution of the Trusteeship, and to enable the particular qualifications required at any time in a newly-appointed Trustee to be selected to fit the position of the Trust at the time and the expected retirement of existing Trustees.

On this issue the Chairman won. An order was duly made, without opposition from the Attorney-General, by Mr Justice Pennyquick on 13 May 1963 raising the number of Trustees to seven, and freeing them from any stipulations as to their special competence.[2] But almost a year earlier Lord Piercy had begun to sound Sir Oliver Franks with the hope of bringing him into the Wellcome Trust, and indeed of putting him into the Chair as his own successor. He was a friend of Piercy's, already a Beit Trustee, and (as recently elected Provost of Worcester College, Oxford) it was hoped relatively free of other engagements.

It is hardly surprising that Lord Piercy was extremely anxious to secure the services of Lord Franks (as he was soon to become); few if any could have been better qualified for the future Chairmanship in every respect save medical expertise. After a brilliant career in academic philosophy followed by no less marked success in the wartime Civil Service, in the Ministry of Supply, Mr Attlee had sent him to Washington as Ambassador to the United States; then, in 1952, he had begun yet another eminent career in the City as Director and Chairman of Lloyd's Bank (from which office he had retired in 1962) and in other roles; even medicine had already claimed his attention as Chairman of the Governors of the Oxford Hospitals. In October 1962 Lord Piercy explained the work

Fig. 20. Lord Franks, who took over the Chairmanship of the Trustees from Lord Piercy in 1965.

of the Wellcome Trust in detail to his friend, stressing the possibility of developing new policies and fields for work and the informal division of support for medical science between the Trust and the Medical Research Council; he also mentioned the possibility of obtaining such distinguished scientific colleagues as Sir Cyril Hinshelwood O.M. or Lord Todd. Lord Franks, however, was uncertain of the path his future activity would take and declined committing himself at this stage. Piercy believed that the recently-created Peer was tempted to begin another career in the House of Lords, and discreetly advised him against it. When, in the following spring, appointment of a sixth Trustee became possible, Lord

Piercy again appealed to him and this time, after a period of reflection, Lord Franks accepted his offer (5 August 1963). In order to provide a reasonable time for his induction to the Trust before his assumption of the Chairmanship, appeal was once more made successfully to the High Court, in order to extend Piercy's Chairmanship for twelve months to 7 February 1965, when Lord Franks took over.

As to the seventh Trustee, the Chairman in 1963 already had his eye on Sir Keith Murray, retiring Chairman of the University Grants Committee (see below, p. 109), rightly aiming at men moving in the highest academic and governmental circles: 'he's the sort of chap we'd like to get'. Lord Murray was in fact to be his own successor. Immediately, however, it was necessary to strengthen the technical scientific side of the Board of Trustees, and this time the choice was made of another Londoner, Professor R. H. S. Thompson, who became a Trustee two months after Lord Franks on 1 December 1963, 'one of the leading biochemists in the country' as Sir Henry Dale called him.

Professor Robert Henry Stewart Thompson, aged 51, was an Oxford biochemist who had been a Fellow and tutor at University College, Oxford, and who had worked with Sir Rudolph Peters. During the war he had been largely responsible for the discovery of British Anti-Lewisite and had been awarded the Radcliffe Prize for Medical Research by the University of Oxford. He became Dean of the Medical School at Oxford, before moving in 1947 to the newly established Chair of Chemical Pathology at Guy's Hospital Medical School, London. In 1955 he became the first Secretary-General of the International Union of Biochemistry, and served as a member of the Medical Research Council from 1958–62. Two years after his appointment as a Trustee he was appointed Courtauld Professor of Biochemistry and Director of the Courtauld Institute of Biochemistry at the Middlesex Hospital Medical School, and was later to serve as a member of the Defence Scientific Advisory Council.

An unexpected development, just before Professor Elliott's withdrawal from the Trusteeship, arose from Sir Henry Dale's visit to the Foundation at Tuckahoe, New York State, in the autumn of 1953. There Mr Creasy, the head of Burroughs Wellcome (U.S.A.) Inc. explained to him for the first time the standard provision of United States tax law whereby a tax-payer, such as a corporation, could make tax-exempt contributions to recognised charities up to a certain proportion of his income or its profits. (In writing a memoir for the benefit of his co-Trustees on this matter, Dale erroneously gave the proportion as 15 per cent; in fact it was, and is, five per cent.) Where a corporation like Burroughs Wellcome was paying a

Fig. 21. Professor R. H. S. Thompson, F.R.S. (b.1912) who completed the number of seven Trustees in 1963.

proportion of tax at a rate higher than 50 per cent, the effect of taking advantage of this provision would be that of every $10,000 given to charity – up to the 5 per cent limit – less than $5,000 would come out of its taxed profits. Creasy pointed out that Sir Henry Wellcome's intention to promote medical science could, within the United States, and up to the legal limit, be implemented by the American Company independently and on a tax-free basis. The dividends remitted to the Foundation in London would be slightly reduced, but the sums available for charitable purposes, of the kind Wellcome would have approved, would be greatly increased, largely at the cost of the Internal Revenue Service.

Dale saw the advantage at once, and was eager to grasp it. The easiest and least challengeable way to implement the scheme would be to establish a separate body to administer a Fund, to which the American Company would regularly transfer a proportion of its profits, the managers of the Fund would then finance proper charitable projects in medical science. The (American) legal aspects of this were fully reviewed by Mr Dowling of the American Company in March 1954, the proposal was formally accepted at an Extraordinary Meeting of the Directors of the Wellcome Foundation Ltd, in October (at which the Trustees were represented by Sir Henry Dale), and on 24 May 1955 the Burroughs Wellcome Fund was incorporated in the State of New York. The first meeting of the Members took place the next day at Tuckahoe, Sir Henry Dale being one of those present, having just come down from Canada, where he had passed his 80th birthday 'at the Seignory Club, a delightful sporting residence and estate at Montebello, between Montreal and Ottawa'.

All this was of course done with the consent of the Trustees and, on the British side, besides Dale and Elliott (as Scientific Trustees), Michael Perrin (Chairman), Drs Wheeler and Adamson (Managing and Research Directors of the Foundation respectively) were appointed Directors of the new Fund. The principle first adumbrated by Mr Creasy was always approved in London, but the Trustees were naturally cautious to preserve the final authority of the Foundation and the Trust in their respective roles, while not overlooking the normal prerogative of the Directors of the American Company to make donations to philanthropic causes, as the Foundation also did independently in London. For this reason they were anxious that the British participation in the Burroughs Wellcome Fund should not be merely nominal; apart from regular correspondence, they have from time to time attended meetings of the Fund in the U.S.A. with their American colleagues.

The Directors of the Fund were free to proceed on a somewhat different basis from the Trustees, by building up, from the annual contributions put in by Burroughs Wellcome (U.S.A.) Inc. a large capital to re-invest, distributing charitably the income received from this capital. Following the advice of Dale's colleague and friend Dr A. McGehee Harvey of the Johns Hopkins Medical School they chose Clinical Pharmacology as an important and needy field, close in interest to the business of the Company, upon which support should be concentrated. Again striking out on a new line, the Directors instituted a competitive Clinical Pharmacology Award, to be made by an Advisory Committee of which Professor Harvey was chairman, composed of distinguished American medical scientists from a number of institutions. Up to 1983, 36 Awards have been made to 'Burroughs Wellcome Scholars in Clinical Pharmacology' in 27 different medical schools in the U.S.A., at a total cost of $5.4 million.

After the death of William N. Creasy, his name was commemorated in 1975 by the institution of Creasy Visiting Professorships in Clinical Pharmacology, which have already brought over 50 distinguished foreigners to teach and discuss their work in the U.S.A. In later years too, the Fund, as its resources grew, has made competitive awards in many other fields of science such as toxicology and molecular parasitology, opened up programmes of Research Travel grants and so forth. To date (1983) the total granted by the Fund since its inception amounts to nearly $15½ million.

During the 1950s the Trustees were not unmindful of another obligation in addition to their support of medical research and history imposed upon them in Sir Henry Wellcome's Will, but not yet discharged, nor indeed were they allowed to forget it. After the war they were able to receive further information about Garden City, Blue Earth County, in Minnesota, to which Wellcome had wished to devote $400,000 from his estate. Two advisers in particular were able to help them with local knowledge: Professor Wallace D. Armstrong of the University of Minnesota at Minneapolis, and Dr Charles F. Code of the Mayo Clinic at Rochester, Minn. There was an old association between Wellcome himself and the Mayo brothers – who may in part have inspired his own charitable designs – and Dr Code was a friend of Sir Henry Dale's. The Trustees learned that Garden City still lived up to its name (as it does to this day), as a lightly populated residential area with agriculture the only important economic interest. Mankato, 11 miles away, had become a commercial and industrial centre to which many of the inhabitants of Garden City commuted. As early as 1952 the Trustees recognised that (in Bullock's words) it would benefit this community more not to adhere strictly to the terms of Wellcome's Will. Sir Henry Dale, too, was concerned lest, by creating an inappropriate Memorial – another 'white elephant' – the Trustees should 'make the memory of the benefactor a source of proverbial merriment and mockery in the United States'; his concern perhaps reveals some underestimation of the inviolable American respect for the wealthy dead. Dale wrote already of going out to get a 'first hand idea of what the memorial might mean and what interests it might serve'. The Trustees now knew that the new Consolidated School of the township provided an excellent auditorium for meetings, and facilities for sports; while a public park, which Wellcome had intended to provide, already existed in the wooded 'Fairgrounds' where picnic tables and space for games existed. Sensing the disproportion between Wellcome's plans and the local situation, Dale felt that 'we are hitherto completely at sea, with no proper ground even for speculation concerning the kind of community that Garden City is, or is likely to be'.

However, steps were taken that summer (1952) to obtain better information about the precise distribution of Wellcome's land-holdings in the township, and its (very slight) business development. In September a careful descriptive report was submitted by a Mr Mathes of New York, who advised that the Trustees should consolidate the lots they owned and concentrate on the provision of a Library, as a really useful benefaction to the citizens.

Because no obvious sign of action appeared, and because there was public knowledge in Minnesota of Wellcome's generous intentions towards Garden City, inquiries came to the firm of lawyers representing the Trustees there from time to time, and in August 1953, it appears, the editor of the *St Paul Dispatch* wrote to the American Ambassador in London making some complaint of the Trustees' dilatory conduct. They were, of course, well within the time-limit of 25 years stated by Wellcome as a 'desire' for the completion of the Memorial and they had by this time set aside, invested in sterling funds, the sum of $400,000 named in the Will for the building and endowment of the Memorial. (The Mausoleum for the reinterment of Sir Henry Wellcome's parents had already been abandoned.)

Before this could be spent in Garden City, however, permission of the Treasury for the transfer into dollars had to be sought (and was duly obtained); certain difficulties as to the legal title of the land bought by Wellcome through nominees had to be removed and, moreover, it was necessary to choose and appoint Special Trustees in Minnesota to carry out whatever scheme seemed best, to whom this large capital could be conveyed. With all this in mind Sir Henry Dale flew out especially in May 1956, despite his great age, to explain the Trustee's actions and to settle matters for the future. At Garden City he met (in his own words) 'a set of really fine people, full of a proper patriotism for their local community and its best interests, but friendly and ready to understand all the anomalies and difficulties of the Memorial problem'. From among those whom he met, and with the aid of local advice, the Trustees in London were able to appoint five Special Trustees who were to bring the Memorial into existence (27 November 1956). It became clear that a certain 'tidying-up' of landownership was necessary, and also that powers would have to be taken to vary in detail the terms of the Will. These legal steps were in time safely accomplished, though they involved yet another appeal to the High Court.

By the spring of 1958 a definite plan for the construction of an ample building, adjacent to the School, of which the chief features would be the Library and a Hall, capable of seating over 1,000 people and of conversion to sporting use, had been agreed by all parties concerned. Construction was rapid. For the official opening Sir Henry and Lady Dale were accompanied to Minnesota by Mr Bullock and the two Secretaries of the Trust; there they were joined by Mr Creasy of Burroughs Wellcome (U.S.A.) and his scientific chief, General Wood. Dale's aeroplane post-card to Lord Piercy (5 October 1959) records a 'Very successful and enthusiastic opening ceremony yesterday of the really noble Wellcome Memorial. Everybody delighted. Fine speech by (Orville) Freeman, State Governor of Minn'. Sir Henry himself, of course, had made the principal speech of presentation to the people of Garden City, while Bullock handed to the Special Trustees the cheque for $150,000 representing the endowment fund for the Memorial.

5

THE FORMATION OF POLICY TO 1964

For many years it would have been futile for the Trustees to take decisions of a general character about their support of the objects specified in Sir Henry Wellcome's Will, except perhaps with respect to medical research libraries and history of medicine where the field of action was limited both by definition and circumstance. The Trustees' *First Report*, extending to 1956, makes it plain that on the scientific side almost every kind of support had already been attempted: both small and massive grants had been made towards new buildings, towards the provision of costly apparatus, and towards the expenses of arranging or attending scientific meetings. Scholarships and Fellowships had been awarded to scientific research workers. One independent research unit was regularly financed. Many travel grants had been awarded to enable scientists to study, to investigate, or to improve their technique in appropriate places. Most of the recipients were British, and most of the money was spent in Britain, a natural imbalance necessarily strengthened by the close monetary controls on the export of sterling imposed by government in these post-war years, but there was always a proportion of money going overseas and a good deal to the countries of what would soon be called the New Commonwealth. The range of scientific activity covered was equally inclusive, from anaesthesia to virology and X-rays; some bias towards pharmacology was only to be expected. Animal and tropical medical research was supported on a small scale, as well as research potentially benefiting Europeans. One might say that virtually every legitimate object of expenditure received some benefit during the early years of the Trust, though many applications had to be refused as falling outside the scope of its charity.

Since many first approaches were no doubt informal, it would be impossible now to determine how many legitimate and possibly meritorious applications were discouraged or refused because of a lack of money in the Trustees' pockets. One has the impression that even as recently as 30 years ago the business of research institutes and university departments systematically pursuing foundations and industry for support was far less commonplace and organised than it is today. The Trustees took no open steps to invite applications for particular purposes, and consequently the number of applications received was not large; probably as many were addressed to the Wellcome Foundation – perhaps because of the ever-running confusion of names – as to the Wellcome Trust. What the Trustees might and could do in aid of scientific research seems to have been diffused rather by word of mouth and personal contact than by formal announcement: news of the Trustees' activities tended to stress the limitation of their resources, a note still struck in Sir Henry Dale's first Press Conference about the work of the Trust (5 October 1955), though this event may be taken as a first public declaration by the Trust that it was open for business. Inevitably those London Institutions whose senior officers were in almost daily contact with Sir Henry Dale had far more opportunity for making their aspirations and needs known to him than did individuals to whom the name of Wellcome was barely known. As in all human affairs, personal acquaintance was of vital importance; too much should not be made of this point, however, since after all London has long been the centre of English medical life, as it has been the seat of the Medical Research Council.

Just as an approach to Sir Henry Dale was the most obvious way of initiating a negotiation with the Wellcome Trustees, so Dale was the final arbiter of the scientific merit of applications. Professor Elliott, living in Scotland, and largely withdrawn from the scientific world, gave him most valuable counsel but can hardly be judged to have been a potent force in either beginning or deciding grants, except in relation to the Animal Health Trust where he was the more active Trustee. The 'lay' Trustees were perfectly content to leave all questions of scientific choice to these two, at least until the late 1950s when Lord Piercy became an increasingly prominent figure in the Trust's affairs, who found a certain fellow-feeling on some points with Sir John Boyd. Not, of course, that there was ever the least hint of dissension between these two and Sir Henry Dale, whose scientific authority to the end remained decisive, but it is clear that some matters were at this stage thoroughly gone into, if only for their financial aspects, which might formerly have passed on the nod. The businessman's appreciation of a particular proposal may well differ markedly from that of the scientist, even when the businessman was once an academic teacher of history. Thus Lord Piercy privately pencilled the words 'No intelligible scheme here' on a request from Professor J. T. Randall, F.R.S. (now Sir John) for a grant of £120,000 in December 1959, not long before Dale's retirement. Professor Randall, a physicist (indeed, co-discoverer of the cavity magnetron which was crucial to the development of centimetric-radar during the war) had become deeply and effectively interested in biophysics, and was to become Director of an M.R.C. Biophysics Unit. He sought the grant to enable King's College, London, to acquire the lease of a commercial property in Drury Lane, a few minutes walk from his College, and to convert it to house a new department of biophysics under his direction. Remembering the crowded King's site on the Strand, and the notable achievements already of Randall's group, it is hardly surprising that his application was strongly backed by his College, by the University of London, and by the M.R.C.. Scientifically the proposition could hardly be more assured: the fly in the ointment was the relative brevity of the lease for disposal.

Fortunately it proved possible to secure some adjustment of the terms, everyone was happy, and the grant was approved. The Department of Biophysics of King's College, London can be seen, rather incongruously opposite the New London Theatre, in Drury Lane to this day (see p. 308).

In the early days grants were invariably responses to *ad hoc* situations, responses which the Trustees could rationally feel were in many cases meeting national needs, as with the Royal Society, the Royal College of Surgeons of England, the Royal Society of Medicine, and even the University of London. Certainly the considerable sums of money devoted, at the request of Sir Harold Himsworth, to various projects and needs of the Medical Research Council were supplying the wants of the nation. Apart from the relatively small amount of money granted to private institutions – among which the Strangeways Laboratory, the most richly endowed by the Trustees, stood in a peculiar relation to the University of Cambridge – most of the rest of the grant money went to university people through perfectly orthodox if informal academic channels. There was as yet no such thing as a 'programme'. The nearest approximation to it was in the provision of funds for an annual scholarship or fellowship, over a period of years, to departments or bodies such as the Animal Health Trust. The share of the Trustees in the actual running of these schemes was small. The first step along a new path that was to lead a long way was taken with the inauguration of the Carlsberg–Wellcome Travelling Research Fellowships in the spring of 1957. Mr

Michael Perrin, in the first year of his Chairmanship of the Wellcome Foundation, had made contact with the Carlsberg Foundation in Copenhagen and drew Dale's attention to analogies between its relation to the Carlsberg Brewery and that between the Wellcome Trustees and the Wellcome Foundation, suggesting the possibility of useful international cooperation in promoting common objectives. Danish representatives were entertained in the Apothecaries' Hall in London, and the result was a scheme for year-long exchange visits – a Danish researcher would come to England, and an Englishman go to Denmark – of a kind that has continued happily since.

In this case, it seems, Mr Perrin provided a modest opportunity which the Trustees eagerly grasped. In other cases they could reasonably hand over the day-to-day work to better equipped bodies, simply offering the necessary finance. This happened with the Publications Grant made to the Royal Society to assist suitable biological journals (March 1953). Inflation had fallen as a particular evil upon the smaller learned societies, each struggling to maintain a journal; Dale had received a number of appeals for help, but (as he wrote to Sir Edward Salisbury, Biological Secretary of the Royal Society) 'we had no mechanism for examining and scrutinising these appeals'. The Royal Society was already administering government money to subsidise publications, so the Trust could, and did, usefully increase the sum available.

It is obviously important that a body possessing the power to decide whether resources shall be devoted to this project for scientific research or that shall reserve sums sufficient to cope with tactical situations such as that just described. It is also obvious that it is subject to moral imperatives limiting its perfect freedom of action. For example, it would have been disobliging, to say the least, in the Trustees to refuse the modest and infrequent calls for help from the Medical Research Council, normally occasioned by the sheer inadequacy of its own grants to match its heavy responsibilities. Again, there was a moral pressure to give large sums for buildings, in that the University Grants Committee (following the scriptural injunction to give to them that have, only too often present in the minds of some civil servants) insisted that a university should raise money from its own sources and private benefactors for a building project, before providing the bulk of the finance itself. The Trustees' refusal to contribute, say, one quarter the cost of a new laboratory might mean that the laboratory would not be built at all. And, again, the Trustees did not possess until after 1960 the professional staff capable of

Fig. 22. The *Lady Dale*, presented to the Medical Research Council in 1958 for service on the Gambia River in West Africa. Ironically, the vessel proved rather too grand for her purpose.

running extensive programmes, involving (for example), the process of selection of Fellows out of a large number of candidates.

In each of their first three biennial *Reports* the Trustees under the general heading of policy declared that 'their policy in making grants within the terms of their Trust had advisedly been one of opportunism' – 'eclectic opportunism' in the words of the *Third Report* (1961) – by which was meant giving support to enterprises 'of which the merits were endorsed by the best scientific opinion, but which, for one reason or another, had not hitherto received the help they needed'. Or, to use another expression, the Trustees made it their aim 'to identify and to fill important gaps in the existing facilities for promoting and assisting investigations, rather than merely to duplicate the activities of other grant-making bodies'. Though the *Reports* do not specifically say so, the gaps in question were created by the insufficiency of the funds available to the National Health Service, the Medical Research Council, the Universities, and other bodies for the support of research to be carried out by organisations which these bodies had themselves called into existence.

As the *Second Report* duly notes, the filling of the gap might entail the provision of an exceptional piece of equipment, such as the motor-cruiser on the Gambia river (p. 226) or the diagnostic motor-van asked for by Professor J. H. Kellgren, of the University of Manchester, in order that he could carry out field research on rheumatoid and industrial diseases. Very often it entailed the provision of new research laboratories, since 'official' building programmes were always decades in arrears of the ambitious programmes of energetic research workers all over the country. The *Fourth Report* (1962) drew attention to the large proportion of expenditure ('more than half of the total funds provided') devoted to the buildings and equipment, because of the 'present relative poverty of the Universities', and the failure of university treasurers to budget adequately for the needs of medical science.

The acceptance of the fortuitous in the Trustees' choice of investments in research is well illustrated by a memorandum recorded by Dr Green, the Scientific Secretary, after the tour of the eastern United States that followed his participation in the ceremonies at Garden City (October 1959). Dr Green noted that among other visits he had called at McGill University and at the University of Pennsylvania 'to explore the possibility of finding other projects within the United States and Canada which might be worthy of support from the Trust if and when definitive applications were in due course submitted'. A later sentence states a truth no less significant than trite: 'The sources of the new applications to be expected after our travels will probably be determined mainly by our itinerary and contacts'; of course, Dr Green sought out those informants who were likely to be most knowledgeable and helpful, including Dr McGehee Harvey of the Johns Hopkins University, Drs Walter Bauer and F. Schmitt of Boston and Cambridge in Massachusetts, Professor C. H. Best of Toronto and Dr Wilder Penfield of Montreal, but he had no time to visit the many and rising institutions of the central and western States. Finally, there is a sense of an almost desperate trawl in a further record that 'Two other tentative proposals [were received] one through Mr Creasy, the other through personal contacts on board the R.M.S. "Caronia" '. Among the positive results of Dr Green's tour were grants for the Best Institute in Toronto to build two new floors, and to the Johns Hopkins Hospital for a laboratory specially designed for the study of the human circulation (total cost, £85,000). At McGill University in Montreal the Wellcome Research Chair in Anaesthesia was extended for five more years; a Professorship (attached to a Chair at Harvard) was established at the Massachusetts General Hospital, and an Associate Professorship also for research in anaesthesiology at the University of Pennsylvania was extended (total cost, £113,000). No doubt all these were highly meritorious and important objects, but in view particularly of the vast sums devoted to medical research in the United States by the Federal Government, the universities, and private foundations, one may wonder whether this relatively minute intervention by the Wellcome Trustees was really of the highest priority, and usefulness.

At this point, near the end of Sir Henry Dale's long Chairmanship, the Trustees could in each year (if they chose) provide four or five universities with considerable laboratories, meet all their own regular commitments, and still have very large sums available for the direct support of research in a variety of ways. The steady growth of the Trustee's activity during the first 20 years after the Second World War was made possible only by the steady increase in Company profits in real terms, of which the American branch contributed an ever-greater proportion. As we have seen (p. 54) the three immediately post-War years had resulted in a gross loss of some £400,000; for the year 1949–50, under the continued drive of the new Board of Directors, this had been converted into a gross profit of £1½ million. By 1960 this figure had been doubled again and by 1965 it had trebled. Of course this gross profit was reduced by the sums required for re-investment, by taxation, and by other deductions; the sum disposable by the Trustees was far less, about £400,000 in 1956. Nevertheless, in measuring the activity of the Trustees, some comparative figures are illuminating. In the year 1949–50 their charitable outgoings amounted to some £25,000 only, as follows:

	£
Annuities	5,000
Archaeology (publication)	3,100
Thessaloniki Laboratory	3,000
Animal Health Trust	1,000
Museum of the History of Medicine	12,000
Fellowship (Dr S. F. MacDonald)	800
	24,900

At this point, the *total* expenditure chargeable to the Research Fund (1936–50) amounted to £242,000, while that chargeable to the 'Museums and Libraries Fund' came to only £36,000. Only a few years later the sums being disposed of were of a quite different order. Taking successive three-year intervals, the value of grants authorised increased in spectacular fashion:

		£
1954–6	–	651,100
1957–9	–	1,537,000
1960–2	–	2,793,000[a]

[a] The accounting figure for the grants of this period is £5,832,000. I have for comparative purposes deducted the £3,039,000 paid to the Foundation by the Trustees for the Historical Museum and Library. The vast purchase was made possible by the Directors declaring a dividend of £3 million, on which the Trustees recovered tax paid of £1,900,000, making the Trustees' receipts for this year £4.9 million (see p. 125).

By 1962 the assets of the Foundation were valued at almost £21 million and its pre-tax profits were put at £3.8 million. It will be obvious that the Trustees were matching their generosity to the rapid magnification of the resources available to them.

To take again a single year, 1959–60, the Trustees' charitable expenditure may be analysed as follows:

	£
Buildings	358,000
Special equipment	113,000
Senior research appointments	98,000
Miscellaneous	166,000
	735,000

In addition, their own recurrent expenses amounted to £42,000, a figure whose size is another measure of the changing scale of operations. The *total* sum granted by the Trustees up to August 1960 exceeded £2.3 million, of which sum, owing to the recent growth in the size of grants, only about £800,000 had actually been claimed by the recipients.

If the Trustees were to avoid spending such large sums as were now becoming available to a disproportionate extent upon building grants, or in assisting the M.R.C., it was necessary that they should carefully consider:

(a) whether they particularly wished to support one or more branches of medical science in particular, besides tropical medicine, veterinary medicine and pharmacology; and
(b) how to initiate methods for choosing between possibly large numbers of applicants for Fellowships, if Fellowship schemes should be instituted.

Because, by 1960 the total number of grants to institutions and individuals was already very large, it happened that without any specific design the coverage of places and topics was very wide. Thus, when Lord Piercy's attention was drawn to a rather unusual ailment – Hashimoto's disease – so that he asked Dale whether the Trust had ever given any thought to it, Sir Henry could promptly reply (January 1958):

> I think we can properly say that we have already done more to promote the investigation of this one rather rare disease, than any other organisation which would be in a position to support it.

He pointed out that a worker on this disease was occupying a place in the Wellcome Extension to the Middlesex Hospital, that a special centrifuge had been given to another at University College Hospital Medical School, and that three relevant Travel Grants to the U.S.A. had been made. Of course, one would nowhere find a decision of the Trustees' to take a special interest in Hashimoto's disease: the interest was a product of the pattern of applications received and approved.

Similarly, when in 1957 a grant of £4,000 was made to Dame Kathleen Lonsdale (Department of Chemistry, University College, London) so that she could buy time on the Ferranti 'Pegasus' computer at the Northampton College of Advanced Technology (now the City University) the use of computers was still so rare that this special machine was controlled by the National Research Development Corporation. Dame Kathleen required electronic computing time 'for the programme of research by herself and her colleagues on the crystal structure of organic molecules'. But there is no evidence that the Trustees had any awareness of taking a decision of historical moment, or of deliberately encouraging a new and sophisticated technique. The move towards electronic computation came from the applicant, and was approved and facilitated by the Trustees.

In the earlier days of its rise to wealth and influence the Trust was naturally overshadowed by the Medical Research Council, where both Dr

Green and Dr Williams gained their first experience of the endowment of research. Any form of rivalry between the two agencies was obviously out of the question, but the designation of 'spheres of interest' was not easy, particularly with regard to Fellowship schemes. The Council maintained research institutes, which the Trust supported only on a small scale; the Trust gave money to universities and societies for buildings in a way not practised by the M.R.C. Such distinctions were obvious enough; but in other types of grant-giving it might be that all the really first-class projects would be funded by the Council, and that only those who had failed with the Council would turn to the Wellcome Trust. At the very beginning of the Trust's pre-history, in 1936, Sir Henry Dale had pointed out to Dr Mellanby, the Secretary of the M.R.C., that Wellcome by his very nomination of his scientifically expert Trustees seemed to envisage close links between the Council and the Trust he meant to create, with the Council clearly the dominant body. Similarly, a secondary role for the Trust seems to be implicit in Green's note of a lunch-time conversation with Sir Harold Himsworth (the then successor to Mellanby) at the Athenaeum Club on 30 May 1961. Himsworth judged (in Green's words) that the M.R.C. 'in general now had adequate funds to meet most of the legitimate demands made upon them (*sic*) in the United Kingdom, though occasionally they would be glad to refer to us a request for some major item of research equipment'. He also hinted that M.R.C. funds were not so rich but that the Council would be happy to leave tropical medicine more or less entirely to the Wellcome Trustees.

Later in their discussion the two Secretaries touched on new fields of research, and especially on that of organ transplantation in man (the kidney was in question). The Medical Research Council was organising a conference on this topic in the following July, and Green fell in with Sir Harold's view that the Trust should not ask for the right to send an observer of its own, but should ask Professor Peter Medawar to make a report of the conference's proceedings to the Trustees. Green seems also to have fully accepted Himsworth's opinion that the time for heavy investment in this form of clinical research was not yet ripe, and that (indeed) the carrying out of organ transplants was still so hazardous as to make the clinical practice verge on the unethical. There is no hint in his notes that on such a matter he might have thought it proper to investigate independently the possibility of taking a different and perhaps more energetic line. He was content to let the Council call the tune, even though the Trustees might later agree to join in paying the pipers.

A very pleasant and appropriate initiative which the Trustees were also able to join in forwarding led to the establishment in 1961 of the Henry Dale Professorship of the Royal Society, as announced on Sir Henry Dale's 86th birthday (9 June 1961). In this case the first suggestion for a joint commemoration of a long association with both bodies came from the President of the Royal Society, Sir Howard Florey, who managed to overcome Dale's modest reluctance to see his name thus honoured. The Wellcome Trustees provided a permanent endowment for this research chair, to which was first appointed Dr J. L. Gowans of the University of Oxford. After Sir James Gowans (to give him his present title) was appointed Secretary to the Medical Research Council in 1977, he was succeeded by another Oxford scientist, Dr R. L. Gardner, as Henry Dale Professor.

One of Sir Henry Dale's last forward-looking recommendations to his co-Trustees, argued in a memoir dated 29 February 1960, was to recommend the introduction of a committee structure for the grant-making process. He pointed out, not for the first time, the increasing burden of work that fell upon the two Scientific Trustees – himself and John Boyd (and especially indeed on Dale). Rather than increase the total number of Trustees – a step to be taken five years later – he proposed that they should appoint for 'short but renewable periods of service . . . experts qualified to be made members of one or more Advisory Committees'. The work of these Committees would be serviced by enlarging the Scientific Secretariat (now consisting only of Dr Green and Dr P. O. Williams, who had replaced Dr Edwin Clarke as Assistant Scientific Secretary from February 1960). Green further suggested that the first Advisory Committee might consist of Dale himself who, after his retirement in July 1960, was still consulted on many matters, Brigadier Boyd, Col. Bensted, Professor John McMichael (Dale's successor as Trustee), Professor A. F. Huxley and Sir Charles Harington, the Director of the National Institute for Medical Research and a former member of the Medical Research Council. Informally, it seems, Professor Huxley had already assisted the Trust people at an interviewing board, where his participation had been found extremely useful. At this time, however, Lord Piercy would hear nothing of any such scheme. He wrote rather firmly that he disliked the whole idea of a categoric distinction between 'scientific' and 'lay' Trustees, and (by implication) the hint that the essential process of grant-making might be done by subsidiary groups on which the 'lay' Trustees would have no voice. Equally, it is clear, Piercy disliked any attempt of the 'scientific' Trustees to shrug off non-scientific business as not being their concern. So the idea of committee structure, did not, at this time, proceed.

Nor did it fare better when Green revived it a couple of years later. In his proposal the Scientific Advisory Committee would have consisted of Sir Henry Dale and the two Scientific Trustees with four appointed members, to be offered honoraria for their services. He thought the Committee would do most of its business by correspondence and that two formal meetings a year would suffice. It would help with the processing of applications, and especially with 'the more important and interesting function of planning a strategy for the Trust's future grant-making activities, by deciding in which particular territories of medical science the Trustees should concentrate a substantial part of their effort at any given time'. Green also pointed out that the mass of business at Trustees' meetings inhibited proper long-term consideration of its functioning.

As before, Lord Piercy (on 27 February 1962) replied: 'I am not convinced that the answer is a Scientific Advisory Committee on the lines you have sketched. Nor do I feel that the time is ripe, for bringing forward this project for discussion by the Trustees', though (perhaps to soften his refusal) he indicated that he was himself trying to think out a better organisation for the Trust.

While the form and operations of the Trust remained unaltered, steps were being taken towards the development of a varied programme of personal awards. The first scheme to be organised was that for Travel Grants; the Trustees had always believed in the necessity for travel to ensure the communication of the methods and results of research; in the ten years up to 1955 they spent nearly £8,000 in this way. Dr Green put up a systematic treatment of Research Travel Grants to the Trustees in August 1955, which they approved and settled regulations for it in October. Grants were to be limited to medical scientists of Great Britain and the Commonwealth, and a maximum expenditure of £10,000 was permitted. The *First Report*, in fact, enumerates an expenditure of £11,400 on 46 recipients; the *Second Report* records a vast expansion of activity in that nearly £38,000 was expended upon 167 grants. Geographical restriction has been removed, too, in that Research Travel Grants were awarded to scientists from European countries, Japan and the U.S.A. (at least a dozen). In the *Third report*, noting the steadily increasing pressure of applications for Travel Grants (269 awards were made in the biennium 1958–60), the Trustees noted a decision to fix the total sum granted annually in this way at £30,000. They commented that there had been 'no diminution in the strictness with which the Trustees' advisers have considered the merits of the different applications, in their relevance to the general object of the grants, or in their dimensions in relation to each particular need'. In fact, it was becoming harder to get a travel grant, and there was a steady tendency for the average value of each individual award to decline, as the total sum awarded increased.

By this time also (1960) the Trustees were making a few larger awards to enable Research Fellows to spend longer periods abroad than was possible with the £200 or so of the ordinary Travel Grants. The object was to enable 'candidates with good academic qualifications' to obtain further training for research overseas and especially in the United States. A special variant of these awards was worked out with the Medical Research Council, which discovered that the pressure on its own travelling fellowships was too great. The Trustees agreed in 1960 to give the sum of £12,000 p.a. (for five years initially) to the Council, 'so as to enable the Council to award five Sir Henry Wellcome Travelling Fellowships under conditions similar to those of the Rockefeller Medical Fellowships'. This is another example of the collaboration between the Trustees and the M.R.C. previously noted and evidence (on the part of the Trustees' officers) of a certain reluctance to extend further their involvement in personal selection.

In this connection the rapid multiplicity of Travel Grant applications had, in fact, forced the Trustees to a considerable measure of delegation in the process of selecting recipients of these small awards. A Sub-Committee consisting of the Scientific Trustees, the Scientific Secretary and his Assistant with, for some years, Col. Bensted, effectively disposed of the business.

The idea of travel of course appeared in the scheme for Carlsberg–Wellcome Research Fellowships (p. 91), first implemented in 1957 when Mr J. Burger, a chemist at the Danish Pharmaceutical College, went to Birmingham University and Dr S. P. Lepage, then a trainee member of the British Public Health Laboratory Service, travelled to the State Serum Institute in Copenhagen, in each case for one year. A similar scheme applicable to Sweden, with the Swedish Medical Research Council acting as the counterpart body to the Trust, was approved by the Trustees in November 1961 with the initial exchanges made in the year 1962–3, the first Fellows chosen being from Edinburgh and London. This joint scheme was introduced because Professor McMichael, when visiting Sweden, had discovered that the Swedes thought only of sending their better postgraduate students to the U.S.A. for advanced training, not supposing that the United Kingdom would have any facilities to offer for their benefit.

Earlier in the same year, in June 1961, Professor McMichael had also broached to his co-Trustees a plan for Senior Research Fellowships in Clinical Science. Its formal origin was in the recognition that the once highly prestigious Beit Memorial Fellowships in Medicine could no longer provide a sufficient stipend to attract the best men and women at the right age. An unstated premise was that, besides inflation, the National Health Service had rendered the professional structure of British medicine different from what it had been before the war. 'A service would be rendered to medical science by establishing a type of research Fellowship of sufficient standing to enlist the interest of workers of first-class research potential in the clinical field,' wrote Professor McMichael. Both the Health Service and the University Medical Schools, he thought, kept people too long at a 'trainee' level, making it impossible to acquire clinical responsibility before the age of 35 or so. Hence, if he (or she) wanted to get on quickly a doctor either had to emigrate or to give up research and become a Consultant as rapidly as possible. Appointments Boards at non-teaching hospitals – where a responsible post might be given to a younger man or woman – 'have too often taken the view that a keen interest in research is undesirable in someone who has to undertake general consultative work on large numbers of sick people'.

What was needed, in McMichael's opinion, was an alternative road offering a dedicated researcher a proper reward for his merits. Those chosen for it should have had the status of Lecturer in their institutions, so as to gain both freedom and responsibility in their clinical research. The Fellowships would be tenable at Teaching Hospitals only, and the Fellow would be responsible for a certain number of appropriate patients under the nominal supervision of the Professor of Medicine. Professors would be asked to nominate plausible candidates for the Fellowships, which would be of five years' duration (age 30 to 35) and would be asked to give certain pledges about the future career development of any Fellow selected. It was reckoned that the average annual cost of each Fellowship would be about £3,375.

Since, in each of the two years 1960–1, 1961–2 the total of grants made for new buildings extended to nearly £½ million, it is evident that the plan for Senior Research Fellowships in Clinical Science was on the small scale, and in the first round only one such Fellow was chosen. In 1971 a review of the scheme through its first years encouraged a decision to continue it, and in that biennium six new Fellowships were awarded. Nine such Fellowships were awarded in the biennium 1980–2, and it is clear that this particular scheme continues to fulfil an important function (see Appendix IX). Even so, it was a long time before anything parallel could be set beside it.

This was by no means because the Trustees were unaware of the difficulty in discovering how to make the *best* use of the large sums now available to them. When Mr Perrin informed the Chairman of the Trust that, for the first time, the dividend paid to them by the Wellcome Foundation would touch £1 million for the year 1962–3, Lord Piercy

> did not express any great cheerfulness over this, as I told him that on its present policy there was no great demand at this moment for the money, and (that) my hope was to get the policy on a different line.

What this 'line' was to be is not clear, but inference from Lord Piercy's remarks in recorded telephone conversations suggests that he hoped for a definition of positive objectives from the Trustees, the pursuit of which might be continued over some length of time and with massive support. He did not think it was enough to choose among the initiatives proposed by others. Particularly he was conscious that the handing out of buildings and equipment in an almost automatic way to one university after another was a somewhat uncritical procedure. As Dr Williams, by now Scientific Secretary,[1] pointed out in the first broad memorandum on the policy options open to the Trustees – which they had asked him to draw up in December 1963 and with which, it seems their Chairman was in general agreement – out of the £5½ million given away up to August 1962, 60 per cent had been on buildings and equipment, and only about one-third of this amount on the combined programmes for Fellowships, Scholarships and Travel Grants. In geographical terms London had been the great beneficiary, with Oxford and Cambridge coming second. The Trustees had strengthened the existing medical–scientific establishment without in any way reshaping it, and had largely done what the Universities Grants Committee and the Medical Research Council ought to have had the funds to do themselves. Projecting the same Trustee's policy over the next ten years, without allowing at all for an increase of Company profits in real terms, they could look forward to creating and equipping over the next ten years nearly half a million more square feet of laboratory space – a total building half a mile long by 50 yards wide. Such generosity might improve and extend the conditions of scientific research, but no

Fig. 23. The Trust in 1962. *From left to right*: Sir Henry Dale (Scientific Adviser), Sir John Boyd, Sir John McMichael, Lord Piercy (*Chairman*), Mr Price, Mr Nesbitt, Mr Clarke (*Secretary*). *Standing*, Dr Green, Dr Williams (*Scientific Secretaries*).

Fig. 24. The two Wellcome Chairmen – Lord Piercy (*right*) and Sir Michael Perrin.

one could describe it as highly imaginative and its innovative fruits were at best indirect. It was a policy of adding cupfuls to a basket already almost full; although there were always arguments against 'frittering away' the Trustees' resources in a multitude of small grants, or alternatively committing them indefinitely to the maintenance of particular units or institutions, were there not perhaps other, more creative ways of using them than had been found hitherto?

For if the Trustees committed themselves too firmly to the practices of the establishment would they not sacrifice what Dr Williams had even earlier (1961) referred to as 'The particular value of private funds . . . their use to break ground neglected by the policy of fairness and uniformity inherent in large Exchequer financial organisations'? What was meant, of course, was that a really exceptional talent for innovation deserves a specially strong degree of support at an early stage. There is no point (as Samuel Johnson noted long ago) in overwhelming with assistance the swimmer who has safely struggled ashore. The Trustees ought to pick special fields for emphasis, not forgetting the history of medicine 'in which we have an obligation to take a lead in framing a national policy'. In making such decisions the Trustees should be guided by experts who might be asked 'to help us frame a policy in selected fields', and by the 'field work' which the Secretariat ought to be able to carry out, especially to assess the needs and capabilities of the developing countries.

There were those who did not mince words in making known their opinion of current practice, not least Michael Perrin, the Chairman of the Foundation (who may well have thought, as others have been inclined to think, that the most useful practical research was done in the Foundation's own laboratories). According to Lord Piercy's record (January 1963):

> He had some cynical remarks to make on the way we (the Trustees) hand around electron microscopes and other items, and in effect encourage every Tom, Dick and Harry to come along and get one of these things, so that in the upshot we disbursed the whole of our funds without doing anything of real magnitude or significance anywhere.

Perrin 'believed that in the long run it would make a much larger impact, and it would certainly do much good' if the Trustees were to resolve to support each year, after due investigation, 'two or three projects to which they would contribute a really substantial sum, say £200,000 in a lump'. It might be well to spread the enterprises thus supported or begun around different countries, year by year. He particularly mentioned India as a country deserving the Trustee's long-term investment, the existing commitment at Vellore being, he thought, too petty.

Perhaps remembering this conversation and certainly reflecting the same line of thought, Lord Piercy in his speech opening the new Biochemistry building at Cambridge (to which the Trust had been a major benefactor) remarked (27 September 1963):

> It is nowadays in a position to consider important complete projects for research if they come along.

However, this hint did not produce any very rapid alteration in the pattern of grants made by the Trustees. Soon after taking over from Dr Green, Dr Williams noted 'We are beginning to get in a position where there are a lot of applications coming and we've no strict policy. It's very hard to say no to anybody,' as Mr Perrin had complained before. It was due to the pressure of their new Secretary that the Trustees began to focus their minds on abstract issues of policy formation. In his policy paper of January 1964 Dr Williams outlined the four classes of grant that it was possible for the Trustees to adopt. These were:

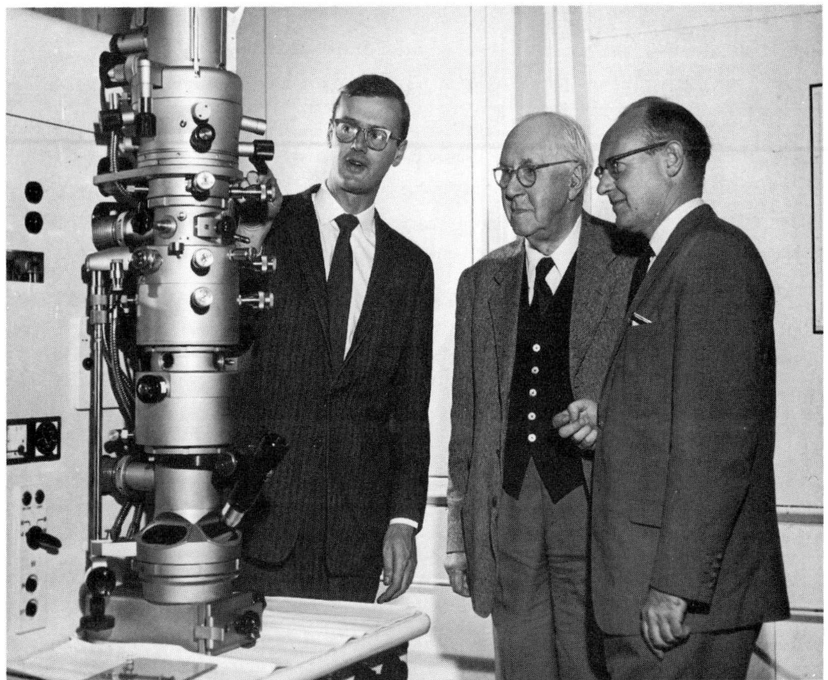

Fig. 25. Sir Henry Dale (*centre*) examines an electron microscope presented to McGill University in 1960.

1. maintenance of its own research institutes;
2. development of research in selected geographical regions or countries such as India;
3. development of research in selected topics;
4. development of research of selected individuals.

All of these classes of support had been adopted by the Trustees though (as already noted) they had in general supported the strong rather than the weak; and they had not, nor were ever to be, strongly inclined to develop research institutes of their own. As Dr Williams wrote – and few would disagree – 'University medical centres provide the ideal environment in which research can be best pursued'. The universities themselves were very ready to accept the help that the Wellcome Trust could offer, and (at this period, at any rate) the derivation of the operating costs of new buildings and equipment from U.G.C. sources was not a severe problem.

There were indeed excellent reasons for adhering to the opportunist policy of making grants. Applications came from the most active and forceful researchers in each field. They could, in principle, be weighed against the putative claims for equivalent support from other individuals or centres in the same field. No grant in any one year was so large as to limit the Trustees' freedom of action in subsequent years. The definition of the need for assistance – for example, the purchase of a particular piece of apparatus – came from the individuals best qualified to know what was necessary to advance their work. Could the Trustees and their officers perceive the needs of medical science, the weak places that needed additional strength, better than the working scientists themselves? Moreover, intelligent and prudent opportunism could not be other than a fail-safe policy: no one could ever blame the Trustees for putting their money into research laboratories, and generally backing the scientific establishment. When grants were made to such bodies as the Royal Society of Medicine or the Royal Society itself, though the money made no direct contribution to research, the grants were still well within the terms of Wellcome's Will, and were received with favour by the scientific community. Had the Trustees instead chosen, for example, to endow a splendid Institute for Research into Acupuncture – quite within their powers – their action would have been received with amazement and perhaps derision. The greater the power of choice exercised by the Trustees, the more independently they took the initiative in the use of their resources, the more open to criticism they might be. If there was to be any shift from the prevailing policy, so as to permit greater continuity and coherence in the pursuit of carefully formulated objectives (without, of course, approaching the narrowness of purpose characteristic of bodies devoted to the 'conquest' or alleviation of a single disease) then it would be necessary to move with discretion.

Through the 1960s the Trustees approached closer to the acceptance of positive policies and a number of special meetings were held for the exploration, with outside experts, of particular ideas. In his first paper Dr Williams had indicated the possibility that the Trustees might specially favour certain chosen areas of research, instancing veterinary medicine, virology and especially clinical research. 'In recent years the possibilities for physiological and biochemical studies of man in health and disease have increased so greatly that provision of increased opportunities [for clinical research] should be very productive.' Hitherto the distribution of grants had rather favoured the basic sciences: pharmacology, physiology and biochemistry had received a total exceeding £400,000 in each case, followed (in order of magnitude) by surgery, biophysics, virology and general medicine. A new balance could only be effected cautiously.

Fig. 26. Lord Murray of Newhaven (b.1903) who was appointed a Trustee in 1965.

In May 1964 the Trustees invited Lord Murray of Newhaven (to anticipate the title he was shortly to assume), the recently retired Chairman of the University Grants Committee, and Mr Perrin to join them at a dinner at the Charing Cross Hotel at which the strategic development of the Trust was to be discussed, taking as the basis for discussion the policy paper by Dr Williams already mentioned, which was generally thought to be, 'on the right lines'. Because of his long and broad academic experience

Lord Murray played a leading role at the meeting, suggesting that when the Trustees helped new building starts at Universities, they might reasonably ask for a partial refund from U.G.C. sources after a lapse of time,[2] and supporting the importance of equipment grants because of the delays imposed by official channels. A couple of weeks after the dinner he circulated a memorandum setting out his ideas more formally. All the Trustees, he noted, ruled out the idea of their founding a major Research Institute of their own, and he echoed, no doubt, their own view again in holding that their 'major effort' should be 'on projects initiated and put forward by individuals', in accordance with current practice. He pointed out that the total sum now available to the Trustees for the support of medical research was about equal to that expended by the Medical Research Council – whose flexibility, however, was limited precisely by their maintenance of their own laboratories or units – the two together being equal to nearly one-quarter of the whole expenditure of the Universities of Britain on medical research (funded by the U.G.C.), that is, slightly over £7 million per annum. The significance of this help, mainly given by the Trustees to British Universities, was obvious, and Lord Murray remarked that 'In general, the price paid for university autonomy is not a heavy one'. In the context of the Robbins Report, and the programme of university and college expansion approved by the government in 1964, Lord Murray believed that non-U.G.C. support for medical research might be crucially significant. He made another suggestion which has, over the years, brought about important changes in the Trustees' administration of their funds, by proposing that

> it might be worth the Trustees' trouble to convene a small conference of top-level researchers and ask them to guess what fields are undeveloped in relation to the health needs of ten to fifteen years from now, and which are likely to stand in greatest need of outside support.

That approach to 'futurology' seems perhaps a little crude – no physicist in the world, it is safe to say, would in 1935 have predicted a nuclear explosion a decade later – but the spirit behind Lord Murray's words has been exemplified in the development of far more widely ramified and varied relations between the Scientific Officers of the Trust and all aspects of the scientific, medical and veterinary professions than was possible in 1964.

6

THE GRAND DESIGN, 1961–4

One form of a reconstruction of the Trust–Foundation duality, which would have taken it (at least to the satisfaction of the Charity Commissioners) out of the hurly-burly of commerce altogether required much consideration in the 1950s; during Lord Piercy's Chairmanship another kind of reconstruction, aimed now at giving the Directors of the Foundation greater commercial freedom, rather than relieving them of the stigma of profit-seeking, was deeply thought upon and, like the former, made the subject of legal advice. On this occasion both the Trustees and the members of the Board were much more divided among themselves than they had been a decade before.

The question at issue was capital growth, whose counterpart was that of dividend restriction. Every penny put into new plant at Dartford, or into starting overseas branches, was a penny diverted from the Trustees' account, and a penny (moreover) at risk, for it might be long (if ever) before the invested penny in turn yielded profits. If, on the other hand, the Foundation had access to the capital market, by the sale of shares, there would be the less (immediate) need to restrict dividends, and the risks would be shared by the Trustees with outside shareholders. If the question be asked – as it was: why could not the necessary capital be raised by borrowing from the Banks or by the issue of debentures, the answer was that such methods were good enough for short-term loans, but not suitable for the long-term growth of an enterprise, not least because of high interest charges. As businessmen, the Directors of the Foundation felt themselves hampered in carrying out the best plans they could formulate for the benefit of their Companies by their inability to go to the market for fresh supplies of capital. They felt this as a handicap which was not imposed on their competitors.

The appointment of Lord Piercy as Chairman of the Trustees indicated the promise that it might be removed. Lord Piercy understood the problem of 'capital starvation' – it had been his job to help British industry overcome it – and he had no fears of those financial manoeuvres and commercial–legal arguments that puzzle the timid layman. He had no personal feelings going back to Wellcome's lifetime, and could see the objectives of growth and profit without sentimental embarrassment. It seems likely that Mr Perrin had appraised the significance of the change of Chairmanship before making his first move early in 1961. The initial suggestion put up by Mr Dudley Robinson, the Finance Director, was that ownership of the Foundation be transferred to a new Company, Burroughs Wellcome (Holdings) Ltd, of which the Trustees would hold 51 per cent of the shares. The remainder would be available for issue in the acquisition of other firms. Alternatively, according to Lord Piercy, he thought Burroughs Wellcome (Overseas) might be floated as a public company 'without any legal obstacle from the Will . . . but some Trustees might feel it to be a bit near the bone'. In January 1961 the other business Trustees, Mr Bullock and Mr Price, did not oppose some such step to help the Foundation expand. Mr Robinson's second idea was seriously investigated; the specific proposal was to increase the nominal capital of Burroughs Wellcome (International)[1] to £6 million in £1 shares, of which 1,200,000 would be placed on the market; £4.8 million being the estimated asset-value of the company. But the Foundation was not unanimous in advocating this step, albeit none of the original shares would have been disposed of. Led by the formidable Mr Creasy, and distrustful of the whole English policy, the American company wrote powerfully against the change, not without an emotional appeal to tradition. To consider selling shares in Burroughs Wellcome to the public 'would be taking a step that would be irreversible and in contravention to [*sic*] Henry Wellcome's intentions'. The Company's 'image' as an essentially charitable concern – marketing the best products for the endowment of further medical research – would be ruined (as would some useful advertising copy), further,

> To my mind, it would also be breaking faith with those of us in the Company, and for that matter outside it too, who believe and have faith in the unique character, traditions and high aims of the Company.

Nevertheless, and despite some internal misgivings, the Trustees resolved to seek Counsel's opinion of such a sale. In April 1961 Sir Milner

Holland returned a cautious statement advising that the Will did not preclude the sale of shares, saying nothing of Wellcome's use of the word 'unavoidable' to categorize the circumstances in which the business might be sold, and adding the opinion that the Trustees had no valid reason for asking leave of the High Court to offer shares for sale.

He added: 'There is no ground of which I am aware for thinking that the Trustees ought to oppose the proposal. On the contrary – the clear indications are, that it is for the benefit of the Foundation.' However, the Directors decided not to press on with it as they had more immediately pressing matters to deal with. Over a year later Lord Piercy told Mr Perrin in conversation that he had never liked the 'Overseas' scheme.

There the matter rested until Mr Robinson revived it in May 1963. Lord Piercy, who had already put to him the idea of selling Ordinary 'A' (non-voting) shares in the Foundation early in the year, made it clear that he was opposed to floating the Overseas Company on the market. In the autumn the Chairman communicated this new plan to his fellow-Trustees. On 28 November they assembled at the Athenaeum Club, after preliminary rounds, to give 'decisive consideration of this problem, which has now been simmering for some time', in Lord Piercy's words. They again decided to appeal to Counsel, but more than one Trustee was eager to note that this decision did not commit him to authorising the sale of shares, should Counsel's opinion favour its legality.

By this time the matter, revived in May in its old form, had taken a new and even more serious turn.

The root of the problem was in the desire to expand the Company. Mr Perrin's paper of June 1963 makes this very clear, as do the supporting documents from senior members of the Foundation. These record that negotiations with other drug-houses, which would have enabled the Company to enter fields (such as the manufacture of hormones and vitamins) in which it was unrepresented, had failed either because the exchange of shares between commercial partners could not be effected by the Foundation, or because the Foundation could not raise, from its own internal resources, sufficient capital for a 'take-over' of the other firm. When the private veterinary products firm of Cooper McDougall and Robertson Ltd had been acquired in 1959 for a price of £1.75 million this was precisely what had happened: a much bigger deal could not be financed in the same way, even with the willing aid of the bankers.

In accordance with the spirit of the times, the Foundation Directors sought expansion as the alternative to death; indeed, it is difficult, perhaps impossible, for a large commercial firm to maintain stability, neither expanding nor contracting, and certainly impossible for one that intends to exploit scientific research to do so. Only if the Company should be able to profit from the chance windfall of a major therapeutic discovery in its own laboratories would such an expansion be possible without a major input of fresh capital, either for the acquisition of rival or complementary businesses, or for starting up in new fields. Mr Perrin also underlined the importance of collaboration in some field of medical production with governmental organisations in non-European countries, where success might turn on local investment, and equally of the development everywhere of non-ethical and veterinary products. Other Directors noted that Burroughs Wellcome was no longer such a relatively large unit in its field of business as it had been formerly.

The method of raising capital and acquiring greater freedom that commended itself to the Directors of the Foundation and to Lord Piercy was that of the creation of new shares in the Company. The existing ten million shares, worth (say) £3 each if marketable, were of course to all intents the sole property of the Trustees. The proposal was to split them into two equal parts: five million voting shares would be permanently retained by the Trustees who would thus maintain their undisputed control as shareholders. Five million 'A' shares would have no voting rights, but would rank for dividends with the voting shares. The Trustees could retain these, and receive the total dividend distribution as before, or sell a fraction of them on the Stock Exchange to increase their own capital fund for investment outside the Company. Indeed, they would have to sell a parcel of the 'A' shares in order to establish their monetary value in the market. Further, the 'A' shares would be available for exchange with another company, or for issue in payment for another company in a 'take-over'. Such an issue, creating a class of shareholder entitled to dividends but to no say in the management of the company in which he had invested, was not unknown in British business but was understood to be viewed with some suspicion by both the Stock Exchange and the Treasury.

The advantages of this manipulation to the Foundation have been stated; its Directors were not slow to note that it would confer benefits on the Trustees also. If the Company were in a position to borrow capital in the market by the issue of shares, it would have less need to create internal capital by saving from profits. Therefore dividends would increase. Further, capital accruing to the Trustees from the sale of 'A' shares would probably bring a larger return than that which they were at present receiving (this argument, of course, makes some assumptions about the mentality of the putative market purchasers of 'A' shares). Finally, the 'A' share device would permit the Trustees to distribute fewer eggs among more baskets. Not only would the nightmare of the unlamented Distributed Profits Tax (p. 68) be soothed, but any fears about the future of Burroughs Wellcome & Co. arising from the possibility of nationalisation, or economic collapse, would be calmed too. This was an important point. Prudent Trustees must consider the need for diversification in the sources of income committed to their care. If Lord Nuffield had not in good time withdrawn his earlier veto, and if the Trustees of the Nuffield Foundation had lacked the power or the opportunity to recover a large capital sum by the sale of British Leyland shares (as the company had then become) in 1971, the future before Lord Nuffield's great charity would have been bleak indeed.[2] Sensitive to this need, the Wellcome Trustees organised a separate holding Company, the Wellcome Custodian Trustees, and have through the years built up a portfolio of investments guaranteeing an income independent of, though much less than, that received from the Foundation.

The Directors did not, however, stress the point that some of the advantages laid before the Trustees were mutually contradictory; the proceeds from the sale of 'A' shares could not be employed both to expand the Company and to endow the Trust with independent capital; nor could diversification be obtained without net reduction in the Trustee's share of the Company's profits.

The Directors' recommendations were by no means well received in every quarter. Lord Piercy was firmly on their side, and developed their arguments in favour of expansion in various ways. He recognised that there could be no question of the Trustees' surrendering any *control* of Burroughs Wellcome, but thought the new scheme would remove the 'inhibitions which cramp [the] policy and [the] future' of the Foundation and mitigate 'an antimony between the interests of the Trust (as promoters of the scientific charitable object) and the interests of the Company (visualized as committed to competition and expansion)'. On the other side several Trustees, like Mr Creasy (who objected as forcibly and in more or less the same words as before), stuck at the adjective 'unavoidable' applied by Wellcome in the Will to the circumstances in which a sale of his creation by his Trustees might be contemplated. To a lay reader, the relevant paragraph suggests that Wellcome only contemplated the sale of his Company in a situation of disaster, when it might be the only way of salvaging something from a wreck. Sale was permissible only as the worst thing that could ever happen. Mr Bullock, from retirement took precisely this view:

> [Sir Henry Wellcome] was particularly emphatic that he wanted his Trustees for all time to occupy the same position of absolute control of the Foundation as he then held, and that in no circumstances were his Trustees to let the public in as shareholders *except in the case of dire necessity*, and even then the Trustees were not to do so without laying all the facts before a Judge of the Chancery division of the High Court, and getting the necessary order.

Neither the Directors of the Foundation nor the Trustees were unanimously in favour of the creation of saleable 'A' shares. Sir John Boyd was clearly opposed to it, should the step prove to be lawful. So was Sir Henry Dale – like Mr Bullock, no longer a Trustee. He noted Wellcome's virtually absolute prohibition of sale, in preservation of a long-held personal ideal, and though he did not (like Mr Creasy) speak of a 'breach of faith' in the Trustees, the thought runs through his submission. Dale also stated – somewhat in contradiction of his view in 1951 (p. 68) – that the clear separation of the charitable work of the Trustees from the commercial production of the Company was necessary and inevitable; for example, Trustee-funded research for the benefit of all mankind must be clearly set off from Company-funded research for the benefit of Burroughs Wellcome.

Learned Counsel (Mr C. A. Settle, Q.C. and P. W. E. Taylor jointly) took a very different view from these. They argued that in law Wellcome's Will could not prevent the Trustees as shareholders exercising the normal legal powers of shareholders in a limited company, therefore (they wrote on 24 March 1964):

> In our view the Trustees are free to exercise their voting rights as the holders of shares in the Foundation for the purpose of enabling the Foundation to issue new shares in any manner which the Articles of Association of the Foundation for the time being in force shall permit . . . notwithstanding the terms of Clause 17 of the Testator's Will and without any application to the Court.

Since Counsel opined that, on the other hand, circumstances were not such as to render a sale of shares 'unavoidable' in the terms of Clause 17, their argument threw the burden on the Articles of Association, which they examined with great care. In particular, the Articles would have to be altered so as specifically to allow the public sale of shares (those in force prohibiting such sale) and the Trustees would have to give up their rights in Article 104 finally to determine the manner of the distribution of profits.

Thus, Lord Piercy's insistence (November 1963) in going a second time to Counsel was largely justified; for the Foundation to 'go public' *was* lawful (in Counsel's view): should the Trustees conclude that

> it is expedient to achieve these ends [diversification of assets, enhanced income] by a sale of a part of their holdings of shares in the Foundation the Court has power to approve such a sale

as part of a suitable scheme first approved by the Charity Commissioners. All was not quite plain sailing, however, for there was food for thought in the rider:

> A Judge of the Chancery Division would in our view only differ from the unanimous views of seven eminent trustees on a matter of practical administration of the Trust if there were some very cogent reason for him to do so.

In his copy of this opinion Sir John Boyd underscored the word *unanimous* several times. The Trustees were not unanimously in favour of the reconstruction of the Foundation, nor likely to be so. Mr Bullock wrote privately: 'I cannot imagine anything more contrary to the wishes and instructions of Wellcome than the scheme which Settle advises.' Boyd himself had written to Mr Perrin, shortly before:

> I still have the conviction that the changes under consideration, if they were implemented, would destroy an intangible something the importance of which would be fully appreciated only when it was irrevocably gone.

Counsels' opinion did not change his position. Mr Price also was against; Lord Franks and Professor Thompson at least dubious.

The Trustees held a number of meetings to try to resolve the issue in April, May and October 1964, of which no minutes remain. Lord Piercy warned:

> If the Trustees decline to allow this [the Foundation plan] they would take upon themselves a very great responsibility as a very large invested capital is at stake.

And Mr Nesbitt said darkly that 'a wrong decision now might well affect the whole future of the business'. Mr Perrin returned to the charge with another strong paper, noting the hefty profits received from Cooper McDougall and Robertson after reorganisation, and the expenditure of nearly £3 million by the Foundation on the acquisition of new companies, or pieces of them, during 1963. He could see no course as promising for the Foundation in the future, as that of buying new technology, new products, and new markets by appropriate take-overs and swaps. (Yet still 60 per cent of the profits came from the American subsidiary.) This, really, was his answer to Lord Franks' question about what the Foundation intended to do, if the new shares were created. It is, of course, often more profitable to buy other people's research and other people's markets than to create either from scratch.

The last stages of the Grand Design were complicated by a take-over manoeuvre on the part of the Wellcome Foundation which splashed into the national Press on the third and fourth of July 1963. The proposal came from an American businessman, Mead Johnson, who owned a one-third interest in British Drug Houses Ltd, a firm controlled by Mr Geoffrey Eley. Mr Johnson proposed to try to acquire the other half, at a cost estimated at about £7 million. The share value of B.D.H. had previously been high, but had latterly fallen despite its marketing of a contraceptive pill, and the last dividend had not been covered by the firm's profits. Mr Perrin and his co-Directors were at first extremely eager to pursue the negotiations as fast as possible; Lord Piercy and his co-Trustees, on the other hand, were alarmed at the magnitude of the proposed deal in relation to the low dividend record and as time went on also by uncertainty concerning the management of the reformed company. They acted as a salutary brake on the Directors' enthusiasm which itself, as matters went forward, cooled considerably. In the end it was the Directors who decided, while Lord Piercy was attending a dinner of the University of London, that satisfactory terms could not be arranged so that, to the astonishment of the financial Press on 11 July, the take-over bid came to nothing.

Shortly afterwards, however, a proposal for the Foundation to acquire an interest in the much smaller firm of Calmic Ltd went through without a hitch and with the Trustees' full and rapid approval.

Who can now judge whether the policy of buying markets and innovations would have succeeded better than that of creating them by successful research? After the many discussions that took place in 1964 it became clear that the Trustees were not going to come to that unanimous positive decision which could have been taken to the High Court. Perceiving this, it seems, Mr Perrin stood down and agreed to let the whole question drop, as it had in 1961. Already on 27 April 1964 Sir Henry Dale had expressed the view to Lord Piercy that 'any further discussion of the practical application of Settle's opinion should be postponed *sine die*'. There was no point in effecting an open breach between the Trustees, and Lord Piercy's time was almost run out. Mr Perrin suggested that the matter be left in limbo for a year or two. Lord Piercy must, one feels, have been disappointed by the Trustees' failure to carry through, under his confident leadership, an elegant business manoeuvre which would have released all the Foundation's force for commercial battle, not left it to continue its struggle with one arm tied up in a charitable sling. He had long sought some such freedom. He had long feared that his medical co-Trustees would be too timid to grasp it, to play for the highest stakes on the Stock Exchange. Perhaps both he and they were right.

The 'year or two' proved to be 20 years. During the long and fruitful Chairmanship of Lord Franks the Trustees tended to leave the Foundation's affairs very much to the Directors, and while the value of the firm greatly increased (though it has never been the *largest* pharmaceutical concern in Britain) the Trustees did not attempt to influence its business management and commercial policy. Structural changes within the Foundation have been effected without the Trustees' intervention. In the Spring of 1985, however, the Foundation again made financial-page headlines with the Trustees' announcement that they proposed to market one-fifth of their total shareholding, valued at some £200 million (see below, pp. 209–11).

This is a smaller operation than that countenanced by Lord Piercy, and for different reasons. 'Going public' in 1985 is thought of primarily as bringing free capital to the Trustees, not to the Foundation. Very often, over the years, they have considered the 'all eggs in one basket' question without resolving upon any positive change, partly because of Sir Henry Wellcome's wish that his firm should remain privately owned, partly because of uncertainty whether alternative investment would increase dividends and security alike. Now a positive decision has been taken. There can hardly be argument – since it is the universal practice of investors to hold a mixed portfolio – that for a Trust to have some diversification of its property is prudent; constant vigilance, constant adaptation to circumstance, alone enable immortal corporations to survive.

Further, an elementary calculation suggests that the Trustees could very easily receive, on an investment of £200 million, dividends which would handsomely increase those which they at present receive from the Foundation on their whole property. If their primary obligation is to support medical research in general, and not pharmaceutical research within the Wellcome Foundation in particular, then they have a duty both to maximise the yearly dividends available for that purpose, and to maintain a high degree of adaptability in face of changing future circumstances.

7

RECASTING MEDICAL HISTORY

The Wellcome Institute

As has been mentioned before, the Wellcome Museum of the History of Medicine shared 28 Portman Square with the Trust offices from 1947 to 1954. Dr Underwood was Director of the Library as well as of the Museum, but as the Library had remained in the Wellcome Building (so named, officially, from 1955) it secured a considerable measure of independence under successive active librarians, Mr W. J. Bishop and Dr Noel Poynter (from January 1954). Dr Underwood was personally much concerned with the Museum exhibitions at Portman Square and his heavy editorial responsibilities. The Library was the more costly partner, it occupied much of the Trustees' interest, and as it developed with pace and vigour, free from upheavals, it tended to become the dominant partner also.

Because the Museum and Library were, in formal terms, organs of the Foundation no mention of them appears in the Trustees' first three published Reports, though of the Trustees' interest in both and active intervention in their affairs much evidence has been provided already. Support of studies in the history of medicine outside the Museum and Library was, however, directly enjoined upon the Trustees in the Will, and after the early period whose chief characteristic was the publication of the historical works of Jewish refugee scholars, other studies were assisted, not least those of Dr Charles Singer (Dr Underwood's father-in-law). Indirectly also this was done by grants to the Libraries of the Royal College of Physicians of London and of the Royal Faculty of Physicians and Surgeons of Glasgow, in order to make historical works in medicine more readily available. Directly, the Trustees made grants from 1954 onwards to promote the writing by Surgeon-Commander J. J. Keevil R.N. (Retd.) of a four-volume history of *Medicine and the Navy, 1200–1900*.

Although Commander Keevil died at the end of 1957, having reached the Peace of Utrecht in his story, the Trustees encouraged Professor Christopher Lloyd and Surgeon-Captain J. L. S. Coulter R.N. to complete what has now long been established as a standard work. It would be out of the question to mention here all the historical projects and publications assisted by the Trustees, but one cannot omit a reference to Joseph Needham's magisterial *Science and Civilization in China*, recognised as one of the fundamental, and most extraordinary, historical achievements of our century.

Another enterprise very dear to the heart of Sir Henry Dale was the publication of the collected scientific writings of Paul Ehrlich (1854–1915), who had contributed so richly to the development of modern medical knowledge. Miss Martha Marquardt, Ehrlich's secretary during his last thirteen years, was another who had sought refuge in London; she was (Dale wrote to Elliott in September 1946):

> a very charming old German lady, who was the devoted personal secretary of Paul Ehrlich for many years. At present she is devoted almost as completely to the interests of [Sir] Almroth Wright

at St Mary's Hospital, Paddington. A fraction of Miss Marquardt's salary was paid by the Trustees so that she could transcribe the Ehrlich material – which she alone was able to decipher; part of this material she had brought from Germany, part (including laboratory notebooks) was lent by Ehrlich's family, and part was collected by Miss Marquardt from Frankfurt-am-Main. After her death in 1956 the three volumes of papers she had prepared were edited for publication by Dr F. Himmelweit. In 1978, at the request of Ehrlich's heirs, the original papers (including some that were the Trustees' property) were deposited in the Rockefeller University, New York City.

A rather different historical exercise was the first re-make of the film 'William Harvey and the Circulation of the Blood', originally shot for the silent screen, in 1928, by Sir Thomas Lewis and Sir Henry Dale. With the aid of a grant from the Trustees to the Royal College of Physicians of London, a sound-track colour film was made with the commentary spoken by Sir Henry Dale himself. As time for reading of printed captions was unnecessary, the action could be considerably speeded up and this new film, presented to the Harvey Tercentenary Meeting in London in 1957, was a very much more professional and scientifically elaborate production than the first. It has deservedly interested and pleased many and diverse audiences. A third version of the same theme was made in 1972, also with the support of the Trustees.

From these relatively small and informal beginnings the Trustees were to develop in the 1970s a considerable programme of encouragement for scholarship on the history of medicine, as will be seen (p. 135), but always the Museum and Library, or Institute for the History of Medicine as it became later, has been their chief and most expensive concern. Even today its budget exceeds by three or four times over all other expenditure on the history of medicine.

A revival of interest in the Library and Museum on the part of the Wellcome Foundation – for whatever reasons – thoroughly restored their fortunes as the commercial picture improved. In the autumn of 1949 Dr Charles Kellaway as head of the Research Institute strongly admonished Dr Underwood for hiding the Library (in Euston Road) under a bushel, while putting the Museum (in Portman Square) in the limelight. To do justice to the Library, now open for public use, Mr Sier gave a lunch at the Russell Hotel (2 December 1949) to a distinguished party of librarians and scholars. In the following year the Foundation agreed to resume full responsibility for both Museum and Library, which it did from 1 September 1950. The return of the former to the Wellcome Building did not take place, however, until the end of 1954. Now the prospects for future development were bright. Dr Underwood had prepared, by April 1955, a detailed report on what should be done in the future. The Library, he thought, was still 'in a very good state' though in need of additional storage space within the Building (as remains true to this day). The existing Museum, however, was no more than 'a place in which small temporary exhibitions are held'. Underwood proposed that eight galleries in the Building should be allotted to the Museum: four of these, on the first floor, should constitute the main public exhibition, divided temporally and physically into four sections (Pre-history to the Middle Ages; Renaissance to the Nineteenth Century; The Nineteenth Century, with emphasis on the evolution of medical instrumentation; Primitive and Exotic Medicine). The other four galleries should be closely packed with appropriate cases containing a study collection for the use of scholars, divided into 29 groups by period and topic. For the staffing of this new Museum he estimated that two members must be added to the existing scientific staff, and that he would have to recruit more technicians, typists, and attendants.

Through Dr Charles Singer, Underwood must have known a good deal of what had happened in the teaching of the History of Science and

Medicine at University College, London, where Singer had held for some years an Honorary Professorship of the History of Medicine. Though this had disappeared before the war, Underwood himself held an honorary appointment in the College from 1946 onwards, and was for many years a co-opted member of the University's Board of Studies in History and Philosophy of Science. He was properly eager to establish a link between the Wellcome Historical Medical Museum and Library and the University of London. As he wrote in his report:

> The full use of the available facilities for [historical] research purposes can only be achieved when there is a close association with the research and teaching staff of a university.

If such an association could be formed – and no institution in the country was more appropriate, at that time, than University College, London – and if proper building space could be provided for the Museum and Library the possibility would exist

> of establishing an Institute of the History of Medicine such as no other city or university anywhere would be likely to surpass.

The object would be further promoted by the granting from time to time of up to three Historical Research Fellowships for appropriate topics.

Dr Underwood's proposals were clear, professional and far-sighted. All of them have been realised, though not all simultaneously. The Trustees respected their Director, and invariably followed his advice (or Dr Poynter's) on matters submitted for their opinion. They were prepared to spend money on the *History of the Society of Apothecaries*, revised and extended by Dr Underwood, and to award a Fellowship to their former Assistant Scientific Secretary, Dr Edwin Clarke, in order that he might devote his whole time to the history of medicine. Another Fellowship was granted to Mr R. S. Roberts, in the Faculty of the History of Medicine of the Society of Apothecaries. The scholarly staff of the Library was further strengthened by the Fellowship awarded to Dr A. Z. Iskandar, who continues his studies of Arabic medical manuscripts in the Institute for the History of Medicine to the present day (1985). These grants were all made in 1959, and perhaps – with the numerous grants in aid of publication recorded in the *Fourth Report* – indicate, together with the subsidy allowed to the journal *Medical History*, an increasing concern for the subject. It is interesting too, that the ancient pharmacies (prepared long before, and still an attraction for the visitor to the Wellcome Building) were erected on the Upper Ground Floor in this same year. However, the Trustees were not yet prepared to expand the Museum on the large scale, nor to contemplate a coherent research-and-teaching organisation attached to it. They would have been reluctant particularly to press the Foundation further on the question of space in the Wellcome Building. And at least one Trustee opposed the creation of an 'academic empire' in Euston Road.

Hence, through the second half of the 1950s, while Library organisation and resources were steadily improved under the energetic management of Dr Poynter, the Museum persisted quietly in organising a series of topical exhibitions which did not, perhaps, attract very widespread attention. A vast proportion of Sir Henry Wellcome's collections still remained virtually unexamined, certainly unused and indeed (in their packing cases) unusable. Despite much devoted labour through the years no printed catalogue of any section of the Museum's holdings was to appear before the late nineteen sixties.[1]

The Trustees had long felt some hesitancy about making grants from their own funds to the Museum and Library because they were organisationally included in the Wellcome Foundation along with the Burroughs Wellcome Company, 'in which situation the Trustees, as the administrators of an independent charity, considered it impossible to provide for their support or development'. As we have seen, these words of the *Third Report*, though reflecting the feeling of the Trustees at that time, are not strictly accurate as to facts, since the Trustees had wholly maintained the Museum from 1946 to 1950, and had from time to time made special grants to enable costly purchases to be made by the Library. Their historical Fellowships also contributed to the 'development' of the institution. One of the most sizeable of the special grants permitted the Library to purchase, in 1962, 'the important collection of books and manuscripts relating to the early history of medicine in the Americas' formed by Dr Francisco Guerra, formerly Professor of Pharmacology in the National University of Mexico, 'undoubtedly one of the finest of its kind in the world' (*Fourth Report*). By this time, however, the Museum and Library had become the Trustees' own property (p. 96), though the staff continued to be employed and administered by the Foundation until 1981.

It seems that the first suggestion that the Trustees should take over formal responsibility for the Museum and Library from the Foundation was made by Professor Elliott to Sir Henry Dale in 1952; as the latter transmitted it to Mr Perrin (January 1953) he had

> suggested some kind of understanding between the Trustees and the Foundation, which would give the Trustees a right of more direct interest in policy with regard to the Museum and Library, but leave the financial provision in the hands of the Foundation

Elliott was indeed much concerned at this time with the progress of the Library catalogue, whose publication the Trustees were prepared to finance themselves.

The basis for the Trustees' purchase, in 1960, of Sir Henry Wellcome's collections was a favourable opinion obtained from the learned Counsel, Sir Milner Holland Q.C. of Lincoln's Inn. In briefing him, the Trustees had explained that although the Museum and Library

> according to the Will, must be regarded as Assets of the Foundation, the Trustees feel bound to interest themselves more closely in them, in order to ensure that the Testator's wishes are, and will continue to be, carried out

This formula expresses a certain scruple about the attitude of the business men in the Foundation to these scholarly facilities, a scruple worrying the Trustees from the beginning. They further pointed out that their legal ownership of the Museum and Library would ensure the permanence of the collections, and permit them to be developed without endangering the charitable status of the Trust. Perhaps a little extravagantly, the brief further argues that a nationalisation of the pharmaceutical industry in the future might deprive the Trustees of the Museum and Library altogether as organs of Burroughs Wellcome, thus frustrating the clear intention of Sir Henry Wellcome 'that the Trustees would be responsible for this unique museum and library'.

When the purchase was completed and a formal agreement concluded between the Trustees and the Directors of the Foundation about the administration of the Museum and Library, the Trustees set up in February 1961 a Committee over which a Trustee normally presided, including representatives of the Foundation, to advise them on its affairs. This body, now known as the Institute Committee, deals with the budgeting, staffing, and broad policy of the historical institution under the Trustees' control and (since 1981) direct management.

With the Library now their own, the Trustees lost little time in considering how to make its arrangement worthy of its contents and to improve its usefulness to scholars. They approved a plan first submitted

Fig. 27. The Reading Room of the History of Medicine Library, opened in 1962, as it was in 1982.

Fig. 28. The Oriental Room of the History of Medicine Library, also opened in 1962. This was one of the new rooms provided for special collections.

by Dr Poynter on 1 January 1961. At this time only the gallery of the present reading-room was available for readers, the main floor below serving as a bookstore and offices. The Librarian proposed that new bookstores, using mechanical shelving and air-conditioning, should be made in the basement capable (at that time) of housing all the books published before 1850. The reading-room as it is today and annexed offices could then be formed. Further, rooms would be provided at the east end of the north gallery on the third floor (that is, on the same level as the reading-room gallery) to house the Oriental manuscripts (still in packing-cases) and the Americana, including the large collection bought from Dr Guerra. All this work of reconstruction and furnishing, at the direct cost of the Foundation, was completed by the summer of 1962; the much beautified and enlarged Library was solemnly opened by Lord Brain on 25 September 1962.

It was at last possible to set the riches of the Library before the wider public. The first catalogue to be printed was that of the Incunabula,

Fig. 29. The entrance to the American Room of the Library, showing display cases.

prepared by Noel Poynter and published in 1954. In 1962 the catalogue of western scientific and medical manuscripts which had long engaged the former Librarian, Mr Moorat, began to appear in a first volume covering the manuscripts written before 1650 (the work was completed, in two further volumes, in 1973). The first volume of an author-catalogue of printed books also came out in 1962. This essential tool had long worried the Trustees. Ten years before they had called in the Assistant Keeper of Printed Books in the British Museum Library to give them advice on the cataloguing procedure in use by Mr Bishop and his assistants, and upon his report more steps had been taken to speed up the long toil, which is still (1985) not concluded.

Only a couple of years afterwards considerable heart-burning was caused by the decision of the Directors to move their Research Laboratory in Tropical Medicine from the Wellcome Building to join the considerable research facilities of other kinds that they were creating, on a suitably spacious estate, at Beckenham in the South London suburbs. There is no possible legal doubt that this Laboratory, like others founded by Sir Henry Wellcome and his Museums and Library, was under the administrative control of the Directors, who also 'owned' the Wellcome

Building itself. Though the Trustees had never been totally happy about the situation, they had not yet insistently opposed the Directors on such issues. The questions that now arose were (1) was it right to move tropical medical research out of its 'historic' home and (2) what should be the disposition of the space formerly occupied by the Laboratory in the Wellcome Building, should this be released? All the Trustees, and Sir Henry Dale also, favoured the move with the sole exception of Sir John Boyd, former head of the Wellcome Laboratory of Tropical Medicine. On 16 June 1962 Lord Piercy succeeded in 'bludgeoning', (his own word) his co-Trustees into approving the Directors' decision. However, all the Trustees equally disliked the Foundation's plan to move into the former laboratory-space office staff at present working in rented accommodation in Tottenham Court Road. Such a move would only strengthen the occupation of a building intended for learning and research by a 'cuckoo' – the business. Lord Piercy constantly urged upon Mr Perrin the construction of a large modern office block at either Beckenham or Dartford, so that the whole of the Wellcome Building could pass under the Trustees' direct control and be used for the development of the Museum and Library and the accommodation of their own staff, with the possibility of leasing out any spare room. But this goal has not yet been attained.

Accidentally, the removal of the Tropical Medicine Laboratory to Beckenham nearly coincided with the retirement of Dr Underwood from the Directorship of the Museum. When Noel Poynter had been appointed Chief Librarian in December 1953, the Foundation – in close consultation with the Trustees – had instructed him to report directly to the Research Director, Dr Adamson, rather than to Dr Underwood: the Museum and Library had thus become separate organisations as they were, at that time, also in different buildings. This separation had, in part, been justified by the argument that very different talents and experience were required in the two departments, each of which was better run separately. A decade later Lord Piercy still adhered to this view: he greatly admired Dr Poynter's abilities in his own field, and saw no reason why the Museum section should not remain comparatively a sideshow. Nevertheless, it was decided to make Dr Poynter Director of the Museum as well as Chief Librarian (from 1 April 1964) with the idea of bringing in a Curator to serve under him. Some time passed, however, before the scale of Museum activities was fixed. The first issue of principle was whether or not an attempt should be made to display the non-medical materials remaining in the Wellcome collections. Underwood had always taken it for granted that the Museum should be inclusive – although he tended to view a great deal of the medical material as unsuitable for display to the general public. The last paper he laid before the Trustees on the future of the Museum (March 1963) carries a note of despair: vast parts of the collection in packing cases at Dartford were unexplored and unexplorable; no part had been finally catalogued; the Wellcome Building itself was as inadequate as were the crowded and damp Dartford stores for the 'ideal' Museum he had in mind. Underwood seems to have been crushed by the task upon which almost 20 years of labour had made so little impact. Some measure of it may be gauged from the fact that the (untouched) ethnological material at Dartford occupied nearly 7,000 cubic feet of crates; if transferred to accessible storage cupboards, as he proposed, he reckoned it would occupy 27,000 cubic feet – a range well over a quarter mile long if the cupboards were seven feet high and two deep! Then, as he knew, time, heat, damp and removals had had their effect upon the collections; he had to ask for a large programme of conservation. Underwood could see no way to cut his problems down to manageable size. Perhaps he showed the Trustees for the first time what an incubus upon their shoulders the collections could still be.

Not surprisingly, they took up with more enthusiasm the positive suggestions of the buoyant Noel Poynter. It had become clear that the 'large' Museum which Dr Underwood had taken for granted would deprive the Trustees of an important fraction of their resources for the support of medical research. Hence the question arose, in Dr Williams's words:

> Should Wellcome's collection guide the policy of the Trust, or should the Trust define its policy and fit the use of the collection to it?

In the end, the Trustees have strongly preferred the second alternative and Dr Williams already foresaw that it would be prudent to seek the advice and opinions of outside experts in framing an appropriate policy.

Meanwhile, it was evident that any steps towards meting out justice to the Collections would require the Foundation to surrender space in the Wellcome Building. Nothing else was decided before the appointment of the new Director: Dr Poynter. His views were firmly antipathetic to Dr Underwood's:

> The Museum must be strictly confined to its specialised field of the History of Medicine. At present non-medical materials form a larger proportion of the whole than the purely medical. They should be removed.

What need had a medical museum for 100,000 stone-age implements, occupying some of the best shelving at Dartford, which Mr Lacaille had been cataloguing for twenty years past, and would be cataloguing for ten years to come? Poynter suggested that these, and the thousand cases of ethnography, should go to other Museums. He demanded a decision *now*.

Since December 1963 the Trustees had been aware that Mr Perrin would release a good deal of space for the use of the Museum within the next two years. Poynter now offered (10 April 1964) a clear and strongly argued plan for exploiting it. His plan started from the assumption that improved education had rendered the old broad and diffuse plan outmoded; the new Museum should be small, professional and devoted to research. It was essential therefore that everything worthwhile should be on site at Euston Road, for the rest there should be a ruthless purge. In the then small Museum space in the Wellcome Building 'the general atmosphere is one of dirt and disorder and decay'; the stores at Dartford contained perhaps 30 per cent of rubbish: broken furniture 'thrown out of Wigmore Street in 1931', useless showcases, 'and models made for former exhibitions and "world's fairs", cheap 19th century plaster casts, chipped and otherwise imperfect'. Besides this very necessary clean-up (which might have been embarked upon long before) Poynter proposed, positively, that at Euston Road there should be, as space became available, three permanent galleries: one devoted to Medicine in Art, the second to a Synoptic View of the History of Medicine, and the third to Medicine in Non-Western Cultures. Each gallery would contain its own extensive reserve collections. Two further galleries would be assigned alternately to current exhibitions beginning with *Medicine and Health in Shakespeare's England* to celebrate the quater-centenary of the Bard's birth.

All this pleased the Trustees, though the scheme as later realised was modified in many ways by Poynter himself. During the next two years the main accomplishment was the presentation of 20,000 objects to the Centre for Ethnic Art and Technology at the University of California at Los Angeles (p. 50), the transfer of some 300 cases containing Egyptian antiquities to University College, London, and the similar transfer of stone implements to the British Museum. These movements permitted both a reduction of the storage at Dartford and an improvement in its condition. Meanwhile, Dr Poynter had perfected detailed plans and costings which were accepted by the Trustees in the autumn of 1966, and permitted the present 'reception area', seminar room, picture store and offices to be created on the second floor, communicating with the main floor of the Library.

The new Director's plans for the staffing of the Museum were less well received. Most of those who had soldiered on with Dr Underwood through the 1950s were approaching retiring age, and he was eager to bring in or create a larger and rather different group of experts. The Trustees fully endorsed Poynter's objectives: (1) that the Museum should be a centre of research, and (2) that the first necessity was to prepare printed catalogues of the collections. However, they were still eager to receive advice about future developments from a wider independent group of scholars and dubious of the necessity for the Museum and Library to carry posts for 'academic research in specialist fields'. Two and a half years before, in May 1964, Lord Piercy (in conversation with Mr Perrin) had expressed frank distaste for any plan to 'roll-up the Museum into an Institute of History' with an array of researchers:

> all these ideas are so utterly repulsive to me, also I think they call up the question of images which, I am sure, would make Wellcome turn in his grave.

He had been reinforced, it seems, in these conservative opinions by Sir Ifor Evans, the Provost of University College, London, who had (in effect) torpedoed in 1962 an attempt by one of his own professors to annex the Museum and Library to University College. Others – notably Sir John Boyd, Dr Williams (who already envisaged the creation of a historical Institute) and, later, Lord Murray took a very different view.

With Dr Underwood's retirement impending, Dr Edwin Clarke (who had returned from Yale University) was brought in to join the staff in late 1963, with a principal interest in the history of neurology. Dr Guerra had been given a Research Fellowship to pursue his Spanish-American expertise, Mr J. W. Barber-Lomax represented veterinary history as well as helping administer the re-united institution, and a number of younger recruits were soon to refresh its staff. Meanwhile, following the public announcement (November 1964) of the considerable enlargement of the Museum that was planned, new possibilities arose for the introduction of the history of medicine within the framework of Professor J. Z. Young's Department of Anatomy at University College, London. Dr Edwin Clarke led this new sub-Department of the History of Medicine from September 1966; temporarily, until the building work in Gower Street had been completed, it was housed in the Wellcome Building, where Dr Clarke had been conducting lecture courses since his first appointment. After this change, Dr K. D. Keele accepted a part-time post as consultant to the Museum.

With firm provision made for the teaching of medical students and other undergraduates at University College, which has continued and expanded to the present day, the Trustees took the firm line that the Museum and Library should serve advanced study only. In October 1966 they approved the terms of a memorandum defining general policy in this respect under three heads:

1. 'The primary object [of the historical institution] should be to provide facilities and materials for senior students of medical history'.
2. The space available to it in the Wellcome Building should be used only for 'the promotion of research and education in medical history, and its use for subjects of peripheral interest, merely because the material is available, is contrary to the Trustees' policy'.
3. Permanent appointments should not be made solely to promote academic research in specialist fields.

The last proviso – which was never applied to the letter – was presumably intended to ensure that all staff members should fulfill definite museum, library, or educational functions.

In order to assist the Trustees in forming their policy with respect to medical history, the Symposium of experts was at last arranged to assemble in July 1967: it was in fact the first meeting to be held in the newly-fashioned Seminar Room of the Library, which Dr Poynter intended to dedicate jointly to the memory of Sir Henry Wellcome and Sir William Osler.

The Symposium devoted to the Museum and Library, as often with such assemblies, produced a good many opinions, some facts, few strong lines for future action. The North American historians of medicine – Richard Shryock and Lloyd Stevenson among them – spoke very highly of the facilities offered by the Library to foreign scholars. All members welcomed the expansion of the Museum and urged the Trustees to devote more money to the history of medicine and its own institution especially. There was some opinion that more might be done to set the treasures of the Museum and Library before both scholars and public, but no clear idea of how the two kinds of activity (with objects and books) might be firmly integrated; Dr Frank Greenaway made what may have been a pregnant suggestion in pleading for closer co-operation between the Wellcome Museum of the History of Medicine and the Science Museum, his own institution, where thoughts were turning towards the biological sciences. Strong enthusiasm for the wider introduction of the history of medicine into courses for medical students went with hesitancy about how the Trustees' institution might be fitted into the university system, if it was prudent so to do. Some participants in the Symposium thought it preferable that the Museum and Library should remain an independent institution of the highest calibre.

At least the Trustees were left in no doubt that their institution was highly esteemed in many parts of the world. In summing up, Lord Murray explained the general framework within which the Trustees worked, as determined by the Will and the ever-uncertain business conditions affecting the Foundation. Figures quoted by him suggested that about one-sixth of the Trustees' budget had recently been devoted to the Institute,[2] and he hinted that as the Trustees were thinking of giving some support to the academic history of medicine outside London, this proportion could not easily be much increased. He drew attention also to the Trustees' principal preoccupation with *research*, from which education flowed as a proper and natural consequence. (In line with this view, the Trustees a few months later recorded an official minute that their Institute for the History of Medicine should not engage in the teaching of undergraduates.) Lord Murray also made it clear that the minor, technical recommendations of the Symposium – for a continued reduction of the collections to essentials, for the extension of acquisitions up to the recent period, and for the greatest degree of flexibility of physical arrangements for the Museum – would receive the endorsement of the Trustees.

Other decisions made as a result of what they heard at the Symposium led to changes and enlargement in their commitment to medical history. An early change was that of name, from Museum and Library to Institute, an elevation often canvassed before (February 1968). To assist the Trustees in academic matters and general policy planning on the historical side, they appointed an Advisory Panel with Lord Cohen of Birkenhead as Chairman; Professor W. C. Gibson (Vancouver) and J. S. Steudel (Bonn), both members of the Symposium, brought international expertise to its early meetings. This Panel (now under the Chairmanship of Professor Peter Mathias) has continued to advise the Trustees in this way, and in relation to grant applications, ever since.

Most important of all, the Trustees decided with the encouragement of the History of Medicine Advisory Panel, during the post-Symposium years, to fund Units for the study of the history of medicine at Oxford and Cambridge. Enquiries had been made of a number of universities having Medical Schools (outside London) about the acceptability of such studies;

the two ancient universities were chosen as the most natural and appropriate places for the new activity. Both universities have provided space and other support for the History of Medicine Units, and both have, in the course of time, accepted the Heads of the Units as university teachers, so that the cost of neither is wholly borne by the Trust. Substantial and long-continuing support for study and teaching in the history of medicine, without the formal organisation of a Unit, has also been given in more recent years by the Trustees to other universities, notably Edinburgh and Manchester.

The construction of the enlarged Museum of four display galleries, with offices, lecture-room and air-conditioned picture-store inevitably proceeded somewhat slowly as the Foundation was able to release space and contractors moved in. A technical account of its plan and arrangements was contributed by its first and sole Curator, Mr Colin Sizer, to the *Museums Journal* in June 1970. Not all the plans for showcases, temperature and humidity control and so forth worked out well at first, and problems relating to the admission of the public into the Wellcome Building, fire-precautions, and security were not easy to solve. As the scheme developed, certain differences in outlook between Dr Poynter and the Trustees appeared, notably with respect to the use of the Institute for teaching rather than research. Further, the cost of the preparatory Museum operations continued to mount: by November 1969 this had risen to a total of £267,000, considerably more than the annual budget for the institution at that time. The cost of the works was divided between the Trust (£115,000) and the Foundation (£152,000) which under its engineer, Mr D. G. Cox, undertook the building operations. At one point Dr Poynter felt impelled to remark (27 April 1969)

> it is still my understanding that the Trustees are agreed that I should bring the Museum to the same level of professional organisation and competence as I achieved in the Library. Only then can it serve efficiently the research aims of the Institute.

This was partly because the Trustees wished to move cautiously with respect to the appointment of specialist Museum staff: the first of these, Mr Sizer, took up his post from 1 January 1969. The Trustees did not dissent from Dr Poynter's view that at least one assistant curator, a conservation expert, a picture expert and so on were necessary for the proper exploitation of the collections, but they wished to take each step separately and seriatim, especially so long as the galleries and work-room were unfurnished. Nevertheless, if somewhat too slowly for its Director's wishes, a nucleus of expert staff was built up and proper, professional work on the collections, including the conservation of pictures and books, was resumed on a higher level than before.

While the reconstruction proceeded, special exhibitions continued to be mounted, including 'Medicine and Surgery in the Great War, 1914–18', 'Vision and the eye', and 'Dickens and Medicine' (Dickens being a special interest of the Librarian, Mr E. Gaskell). In 1972 the work was at last done with the completion of a general exhibition of the history of medicine 'on the lines proposed by the founder', despite the necessity to remove the reserve stores from the Company's warehouses at Dartford to a new storehouse at Enfield. Since this was the high point in the fortunes of the Museum in the Wellcome Building, it is worthwhile to quote the sentences devoted to this display in the *Ninth Report*:

> All the main periods and trends are illustrated by carefully selected objects ranging from the fossil bones of dinosaurs and mammoths of remote antiquity to important examples of modern medical technology. These include the first electron microscope to be used in the United Kingdom dating from 1941 and presented by the Animal Virus Research Institute at Pirbright, the prototype model of an electronic red cell counter presented by the Atomic Energy Authority at Harwell, the original blood transfusion apparatus used in France by Sir Geoffrey Keynes in 1916, presented by the Welsh Regional Transfusion Service at Cardiff through the good offices of Professor Maycock of the Lister Institute, and an early model of the Melrose 'heart–lung machine' designed for use in cardiac surgery, presented by the Royal Postgraduate Medical School at Hammersmith.

It is impossible to say what might have come from this endeavour. It seems, with hindsight, that Dr Poynter's incursion from the fields of books into that of objects, carried out with his typical energy, determination, industry and instinctive sense of how to make an impact, was carried out with insufficient resources and (still) with inadequate study of the collections, in many departments. Much more no doubt could and would have been achieved in future years, but Dr Poynter himself was due to retire in 1973, and the Trustees, guided by their Medical History Advisory Panel, were turning their thoughts to new paths. The same *Ninth Report* recording the fulfilment of Dr Poynter's Museum dream, also stated the Trustee's decision to place their emphasis on 'further development of academic scholarship' in the history of medicine: 'To make this possible it will be necessary to reduce the space, time and funds at present being used in the Wellcome Institute for the portrayal of the subject to the public. Arrangements are being made so that this function can continue elsewhere.'

Two main sets of considerations underlay this sharp, yet long-maturing change of policy. The first was the propriety of the line taken by Dr Poynter as Director of the Institute for the History of Medicine, tending strongly to popularisation of the subject both among doctors and among the lay public. There had been Saturday morning teaching at the Institute, for the benefit of candidates for the Diploma in the History of Medicine offered by the Society of Apothecaries, and other vigorous proselytising endeavours reluctantly tolerated by the Trustees. They were conscious always of the insistence in Wellcome's Will on research, though his own practice had been to open his Museum to the general public. The Trustees became increasingly troubled by a realisation that the Museum would not be primarily a place of research in the history of medicine, but a popular spectacle chiefly made the resort, as the national museums are, of school children. Not that they thought such an appeal to children and citizens unworthy, but it was not one which it was incumbent upon the Wellcome Trust to support. The Will did not enjoin upon them the task of creating a public, national Museum of Medicine, which necessarily (if it was not to become merely antiquarian) would have to grow and seek continuity with recent developments in every field. Thus, for several years before his retirement, the Trustees began to suspect that their Director was steering their Institute in the wrong direction, for the best of reasons, and admittedly fulfilling a sound social purpose.

Secondly, and as a consequence of this line of thought, the Museum began to loom as potentially a vast financial commitment. If an adequate staff with proper resources were to be provided, if the extension of interest to the mid-20th century were undertaken, if the object were a national museum even on a small scale, then inroads might well be made on the Trustee's developing programme of medical research, their prime purpose. And this would happen without realising Wellcome's desire for the advance of *research* in medical history (save in a very specialised sense). The Trustees began to see the prospect of the Museum world, as opened before them by Dr Poynter, as vastly spacious and costly, and strange to them; it is not surprising that they preferred the academic world which most of them knew intimately, and whose methods and objects they understood and supported.

Units and collections

Various factors combined, from the time of the Symposium in July 1967, to incline the Trustees towards a more broadly-based support for the history of medicine than had been possible before. The first was their own re-affirmation of a constant policy to encourage only post-graduate level research studies at the Museum and Library (or, from February 1968, the Institute for the History of Medicine). Though the Trustees had long disliked, and continued to dislike the idea that the Institute might in any way be absorbed by the University of London, they saw in the end the wisdom of tying such studies by younger scholars to the university system. Secondly, the History Advisory Panel – which one or more Trustees have always attended – introduced new interests and new ideas. Thirdly, with increasing frequency and ingenuity, scholars in universities other than London began to interest themselves in historical projects for which Wellcome support seemed appropriate. Thus, in one year (1967) Dr A. C. Crombie, Senior Lecturer in the History of Science at Oxford, then at All Souls College, received a grant of £15,000 spread over five years to finance a Research Fellowship in the History of the Medical Sciences and was also awarded a second grant to enable Dr Joseph Schiller to study at Oxford the development of physiology in France, particularly the work of Claude Bernard. Of course, historical work outside London had been supported before, but now the scale of interest was increasing and, further, Ph.D. candidates began to come forward. Fourthly, the Sub-Department of the History of Medicine under Dr Edwin Clarke (established in the Department of Anatomy at University College London from October 1968) quickly became a lively nucleus of activity. A number of scholars, some with considerable experience, were happy to attach themselves to it while carrying out historical researches in London; Dr Clarke was called upon to advise a growing number of students preparing Ph.D. theses, and he was invited to give short courses of lectures at the Royal Postgraduate Medical School and the Royal Free Hospital Medical School, as well as in University College. The U.C.L. Unit was thus from the first breaking into the University system, and points of entry were being found elsewhere too.

As early as November 1968, the Trustees had accepted the principle of

University Academic Units in History of Medicine, at an annual cost then estimated at about £10,000 each, accepting the fact that this might to some extent curtail activities at the Institute for the History of Medicine if the total history budget was kept to £250,000. Further, they had accepted the Cambridge plan (at just under £14,000) in October 1970, and the Oxford plan (at about £13,000) in March 1971. However, consultations, visits, and bureaucratic processes required further time so that formal acceptances of the Trustees' assistance for organised studies in the history of medicine in the ancient Universities did not take place without more delays. At Cambridge Dr Mary B. Hesse was actively interested in promoting this new branch of study, which could (in part) be embraced within the new Medical Sciences Tripos. The scheme, providing for an Assistant Director of Research and junior staff, was approved by Grace in May 1971. Dr Robert M. Young was the first holder of the new post, the Unit being at first established in Bene't Place, later joined with the Department of History and Philosophy of Science. Dr Young's vigorous and unconventional scholarship soon attracted a lively group of students.

Events at Oxford advanced a little more slowly, partly because of difficulty in finding a suitable home for the Unit, which ultimately established itself at 47 Banbury Road. Dr Charles Webster, F.B.A., the present head of the Oxford Unit, who had (like Dr Young) formerly received support as a Wellcome Research Fellow, was appointed to his post in July 1972 and simultaneously to a Readership in the University of Oxford.

In the course of the negotiations with the universities, of which the outcome was to be the creation of three history Units with a combined original annual budget of some £37,000 representing a considerable commitment to academic history of medicine, both the Trustees and the Advisory Panel were thinking about the future of the Institute for the History of Medicine after Dr Poynter's retirement. The Trustees were anxious not to slip along a path of gradually increasing cost so far as the Institute was concerned, and therefore decided to limit its budget to £250,000 per annum having already questioned the economics of some of its activities, such as the publication of monographs on the history of medicine. As the expenses of the Institute already approached the limiting figure it was clear that no further recruitment of staff on its Museum side would be possible, that therefore the continuance of the collection of recent material and its presentation must become problematic, and that consequently there was a danger that the Museum itself would tend to stagnate. On the other hand, the Trustees and Panel (after careful evaluation of the forward policy for the Museum advanced by Dr Poynter) were inclined to believe that a more cost-effective way of helping research in medical history was to support scholars and students in the academic context, with the Library as their principal resource.

Early in 1971 the Trustees asked the History of Medicine Advisory Panel to consider a future strategy for the Institute, in view of Dr Poynter's impending retirement; this document was finally presented in January 1972. Already, however, in November, Dr Frank Greenaway – a member of the Panel and a senior member of the staff of the Science Museum – wrote to the Trustees pointing out that plans for enlarging that Museum gave hope for the extension of its exhibitions into new areas, such as the history of biology and medicine, not hitherto represented at South Kensington, and that thus Sir Henry Wellcome's Museum might, by transfer, become the core of a national collection of the history of medicine, displayed with the highest expertise and backed by the most professional curatorial skills. The Trustees deputed Sir John McMichael and Dr Williams to consider the suggestion further with Sir David Follett, Director of the Science Museum, and Dr Greenaway. It became clear that the Department of Education and Science would be likely to give the Science Museum the finance for this new role, and that the Museum collections alone were in question. All parties agreed that the Library should remain in the Wellcome Building, and be developed as a centre of academic excellence. Such a division of Museum and Library had, of course, long been practised by Sir Henry Wellcome himself, though with him, objects, rather than books, had taken first priority.

The History Panel had already, before these negotiations began, committed itself to the view that

> the most important need for the future development of the study of the History of Medicine is the training of, and provision of career opportunities for, scholars who can advance the subject by working on the collections of books and materials available in many parts of the world and in uniquely high concentration in the Wellcome Institute,

treating the Museum function of providing permanent and opportunist exhibitions as essentially educational, and therefore less central. It put the point very cogently that

> unless the Institute becomes a centre of professional historians of medicine and medical science, it cannot be expected to

> achieve university recognition or to sustain its internal position other than as a unique depository of books and objects.

No one, presumably, would deny the proposition that museums may be, and sometimes are, major centres of historical research; the point at issue was rather whether *this* Museum of the History of Medicine could or should develop both a research and an educational function. The Panel took the view, and recommended to the Trustees, that the research function in the history of medicine was best pursued in other ways, and that it would be a deviation away from the most important purpose of the Institute – to be a major world centre for the creation of new knowledge about the development of medicine – 'to devote time and effort to portraying what is already known for education purposes'. Another, more general way of looking at the issue, of which the Panel was also conscious, was that the creation of a national Museum of Medicine, with proportionate staff and resources, fully capable (as the national museums in this country are) of embarking on major and protracted research programmes, was beyond the capabilities of the Wellcome Trustees without their gravely curtailing their support of medical research.

It is hardly surprising, therefore, that the Panel, when again consulted by the Trustees in December 1971, resolved that 'the library should be the main concern of the Trustees and should if necessary be developed at the expense of the museum in its role as an educational tool', and that while recognising the importance of objects as well as literary materials for the historian of medicine 'the expense of running and adding to a professional Museum up to modern standards was hardly warranted by its educational or research utility, in relation to the principal objects of the Wellcome Trust', that is, to *research* into the science and history of medicine. Rather than that the museum collections should become a lifeless adjunct to an active Library, the Panel preferred transfer to 'a national museum where facilities for display and study of them could be provided'. The Library, on the other hand, was 'the keystone to the academic future of the Institute'. The Panel made various other proposals for the advancement of this academic future, not least for an association between the Institute Library and that of the Royal Society of Medicine, the most important medical library in England. Such an association has indeed been worked out through the years, so that the historian of medicine in London has no difficulty in pursuing his topic from the oldest to the most recent researches.

Thus advised, the Trustees

> agreed that their policy for the Institute should aim at developing an international postgraduate research institute based on the Library, which should if possible be integrated with an up-to-date library of [Medical Science] such as that of the Royal Society of Medicine. They agreed that the educational function at present undertaken by the Institute through its Museum exhibitions should be greatly reduced in scope, or preferably, that the museum collections should be transferred to the care of the Science Museum with a view to its being kept up-to-date and exhibited to the public on a scale which would not be possible with the Trustees' financial resources.
> (Minute, 10 January 1972).

While an agreement was slowly worked out in detail, with a joint committee appointed to advise the Trustees consisting of Dr Williams, Dr Margaret Weston (the new Director of the Science Museum), Dr Greenaway, Dr Edwin Clarke and – until his retirement – Dr Poynter, rumours of the Trustees' intention to close the Museum of the History of Medicine in the Wellcome Building began to circulate. A reporter from *The Times* sought information, and a cautious statement about the negotiations was issued to the newspaper in March 1973 and in the course of the following month Mr St John-Stevas, on behalf of the Department of Education and Science, replied in similar terms to a question in the House of Commons. Later in the year the Trustees took the exceptional step of issuing an *Interim Report* for 1972–3 of which the Museum story formed a principal part. This emphasised that the

> Trustees would continue to exercise their ultimate responsibility for the preservation and welfare of the Collection

and presciently observed that it was likely that

> as a department in the Science Museum devoted exclusively to the history of medicine, the collection would be seen by many more of the public than at present.

The *Interim Report* further explained that the Trust was to expend at least £150,000 over five years on sorting and cataloguing the collection, three chief categories being chosen: material of use to the new Medical History Gallery of the Science Museum, scientific material useful to other Departments of the Museum, and the rest – all of which, so far as it possessed real value, was to be disposed of to other Museums. There were, indeed, objects of first-rate importance.

The next biennial *Report* (for 1972–4) was able to print verbatim the agreement reached between the Department of Education and Science and the Wellcome Trustees, with respect to the transfer to the Science Museum, which was subsequently blessed by the High Court (March 1977). But before all the legal issues had been finally settled, public concern about the future of Sir Henry Wellcome's collections had been quieted by a meeting arranged by the Standing Commission on Museums and Galleries at the end of 1974, at which the new plans were explained in detail and professional critics fully satisfied of their appropriateness. The first exhibition employing Wellcome material, called 'The Breath of Life', was opened at South Kensington in July 1974. However, the reconstruction at the Science Museum, and the sorting and cataloguing at Euston Road, were to take many years yet and require the work of many hands. At the end of 1976 Dr Brian Bracegirdle was appointed first Keeper of the new Department of the Science Museum. Mr Sizer resigned in June 1977 to become Director of Reading Museum and Art Gallery.

Quite in the early days of the History of Medicine Advisory Panel it had been asked by the Trustees to consider the relationship of the Institute for the History of Medicine to the universities. Among its recommendations for future policy (January 1972) the Panel included the formation of an academic group at the Institute, that is, a team of scholars (with the Director as their leader) employed neither as museum curators nor as librarians, possessing qualifications and abilities respected in the academic world generally, whose lives should be devoted to research and advanced teaching in the history of medicine. This group, not to be overburdened by routine duties or outside demands, would have the knowledge and leisure to advance the subject dramatically. This policy was acceptable to the Trustees. A few months after he had succeeded Dr Poynter as Director of the Institute (1 October 1973) – and was himself followed in the Sub-Department at University College, London by Dr W. F. Bynum – Dr Edwin Clarke submitted to the Trustees two papers about the reshaping of the Institute, not least the formation of an academic group. Dr Clarke, who had experience of the Graduate Schools of the History of Medicine at Johns Hopkins and Yale Universities, was eager to make the Wellcome Institute a centre of at least equal calibre and influence. In the former paper (January 1974) Dr Clarke roundly declared that under his direction 'the scholar and the serious student should take precedence . . . the prime purpose of the Institute is to advance the history of medicine as a scholarly discipline, defined as that part of intellectual history which concerns the evolution of scientific and social concepts in medicine'. This purpose was to be served by a team of scholars, including a classicist, an Arabist, and specialists on the medieval, early modern and recent periods. These historians should be qualified and empowered to supervise the work of research students, candidates for higher degrees, which (Dr Clarke argued) made 'an association of the Institute with a University, presumably the University of London', a most important and necessary development.

In a second paper Dr Clarke considered the composition of the proposed Academic Unit more closely, noting the names of several scholars who might be invited to join it, and pointing out that as the museum side of the Institute was being run down, the opportunity existed to bring in new staff. This course of action was, of course, broadly in accord with the Trustees' policy for the development of the Institute. As first constituted, in 1976–7, the Academic Unit consisted of The Director, Dr Bynum (as head of this Unit, and of the Sub-Department of the History of Medicine at University College, London), Dr A. Z. Iskandar (an historian of Arabic medicine, formerly a Research Fellow), Dr Vivian Nutton (a Cambridge classical scholar with a special interest in ancient medicine) and Dr Christopher Lawrence, who was given a special responsibility for research on the Wellcome Collections. In 1979 Dr Roy Porter, also of Cambridge, joined this group as an historian of social medicine. University College, London, which has for many years generously supported, through its Anatomy Department, the history of medicine, has arranged for appropriate members of the Academic Unit of the Institute to receive recognition as teachers by the University of London, so that they can accept all university duties and responsibilities.

This group, and its younger assistants, has indeed (as was hoped) greatly improved the volume and quality of work in medical history during the last ten years and, by its activity in publication and energetic reformation of the periodical *Medical History* – whose original success was created by Mr Bishop and Dr Poynter – has put the Institute firmly in the scholarly picture. There have been some matters for regret, particularly in that some momentum was lost in capturing the interest of the practising physician as an amateur medical historian. But the gains have been greater. A large body of research workers in history is now firmly linked with the Institute: its inner circle consists of candidates for higher degrees, most of whose studies are under the direction of the Institute staff and of 'resident' Research Fellows and visiting scholars; the middle circle consists of students and teachers primarily associated with London University and other academic institutions in the metropolis; the outer circle consists of people working in the provinces who attend for symposia, seminars and lectures arranged at the Institute. The majority of these scholars are professionals, not all of course medical historians in the classical sense, for the Institute circles now include besides medical men, demographers, social historians, historians of science, and that breed who can only be described as 'general historians'. Naturally good working relations have been established with cognate bodies in London and elsewhere.

This success has justified Dr Underwood's plea for academic affiliations long ago (p. 124) and the efforts in the same direction of others since, and it has finally been effected through that friendly co-operation with University College, London which has endured through many decades. In 1974, at the suggestion of Professor A. G. Dickens (then Director of the Institute of Historical Research, and a member of the History of Medicine Advisory Panel) the possibility of obtaining for the Institute for the History of Medicine the status of a 'Senate Institute' of the University of London was explored. As such, the Trustees' institution would have become an organic part of the University, on the same footing as the London School of Hygiene and Tropical Medicine, the Warburg Institute, or the Institute of Historical Research, though responsibility for financing it would have remained with the Wellcome Trustees. Its staff would have been university teachers, and it would have been integrated into the university teaching structure. However, events proved that the university was unwilling to proceed along this path, perhaps because the spirit of the times seemed somewhat hostile to such specialised bodies as the Senate Institutes of London University, perhaps because it feared the addition of a new potential burden. The alternative line of a looser association with University College was therefore pursued by the Trustees, leading to the creation of a joint Academic Committee of the College and Trustees, to monitor academic appointments financed by the latter and indeed participate in the process of appointment. With the seal of College approval the academic staff of the Institute, as well as that of the Sub-Department of the History of Medicine within the College, are able to exercise the responsibilities of university teachers.

Under Dr Clarke's direction of the Institute, other changes took place. Space in the Wellcome Building was lost to the Foundation, perhaps inevitably, when the newly-made Museum galleries were closed; another part has been redeveloped as a lecture-room. As in the past, the Directors of the Wellcome Foundation have from time to time found their part occupation of the Wellcome Building as their business headquarters unsatisfactory. Like the cuckoo in nature, they have on occasions entertained the ambition to expel the Institute from the building altogether; while on other occasions they have considered the opposite policy of withdrawal, leaving the whole of the Wellcome Building to the Trustees. Because of strongly competing demands for space, when the Trustees had the opportunity in 1981 to acquire the former Bentley House – the London office and warehouse of the Cambridge University Press – they seized it, and new developments are taking place there (p. 201). The Wellcome Foundation is at present (1985), on the contrary, seeking to reduce its office space in central London, and the Trustees' have accepted the transfer of the Wellcome Building to their ownership.

Another reduction effected by Dr Clarke was in publication, which had become a considerable and doubtful investment, besides creating recurrent costs in storage space, loss of interest, and wages in dealing with stock and sales. At the end of 1973 the 20,000 copies of books in stock were valued at £90,000 and the *net* cost of publishing, during the previous five years, had amounted to £50,000. Dr Clarke felt that though it was proper for the Institute to publish *Medical History* at a loss, as its house journal, and also *Current Work in the History of Medicine,* the Trustees should not continue to act as a non-profit-making publishing house, and they have since taken this view.

Meanwhile, the very large task of sorting and distributing the Wellcome collections continued. The Science Museum devoted some of its own staff to the task, and transferred material catalogued (by machine-readable methods) to their own store from July 1977 onwards. Over 26,000 objects were dealt with in this category. The Trustees had agreed that in addition to the material intended for the new medical galleries, scientific objects of other kinds might be deposited on loan with appropriate Science Museum Departments. 650 instruments or objects were transferred in this way. Other young museum experts employed on a temporary basis by the Trustees organised the distribution of material falling into neither of these categories to other museums, some of which gratefully accepted many major accessions as permanent loans: for example, the Koptos Lions went to the Petrie Museum at University College, London, and the Lachish Collection with many fine Egyptian pieces, to Manchester University Museum. This task was at last completed and the Museum store finally cleared only in 1983. However, visitors to the Wellcome Building in Euston Road will find the reconstruc-

Fig. 30. One of two large limestone figures of lions, excavated by Sir Flinders Petrie at Koptos in Upper Egypt (1894) and acquired by Sir Henry Wellcome in 1927. Dating from at least 3,000 BC they were highly polished and perhaps painted red. This lion, reconstructed from thousands of fragments, weighs about half a ton. The two lions were presented to the Petrie Museum of Egyptian Archaeology at University College, London in 1980
Photograph by courtesy of the Petrie Museum

ted historic pharmacies on view there, and the iconographic collections of oils, water-colours, prints and photographs still the subject of important historical researches by Dr Burgess, Mr Schupbach and outside scholars. Other evidence of Sir Henry Wellcome's collecting enthusiasm can be found in the Trust headquarters, in the Foundation offices, and in Cambridge at Addenbrooke's Hospital and the Whipple Museum, where the staff of the Unit for the History of Medicine arrange rotating exhibitions with material chosen from the Wellcome collections in the Science Museum stores.

The first-fruits of the Trustees' policy were seen by the public in December 1980 when Sir William Paton F.R.S., a Trustee, opened the first Wellcome Gallery, a series of 'shop windows' displaying full-size scenes of medicine in the past, but the true richness and range of Wellcome's

Fig. 31. School children in the Manchester Museum with a figure of the Egyptian god BES, presented by the Wellcome Trustees. BES was associated with music, dance, marriage and family. Photograph courtesy of the Manchester Museum

legacy were only disclosed with the opening of the second Gallery by H.R.H. Princess Alexandra just a year later, in December 1981. Both galleries are splendid testimonies to the teaching and technical skill of the Science Museum staff who prepared them.

8

THE EXPANSION OF THE ORGANISATION

For many years, as has been repeatedly emphasised, the Trust operated on the most modest scale and with the simplest of machinery, everything in the first period depending upon the scientific experience and managerial acumen of Sir Henry Dale. Later, a good deal of the professional burden was assumed by the two Scientific Secretaries with their small staff, while much administrative work was undertaken by Lord Piercy, as Chairman, and Mr J. E. K. Clarke, in their City offices. As the retirement of the latter after more than 35 years of service approached, the Trustees in 1973 again considered their situation. They adhered to the opinion that seven was the best number, divided between four medical Trustees, and three with a broad knowledge of affairs. Medical Trustees should have wide experience, and not merely be experts in a specialist field; and because of the Trustees' ultimate responsibility for the running of the Foundation, two at least of the 'lay' Trustees 'should have considered experience in the world of business and finance'. Subsequent programmes have tended to increase the work of the Scientific Trustees, however, and in recent years as many as five of them have fallen into that category, although the Chairman (since Sir Henry Dale's time) has always been a 'lay' Trustee.

In the absence of a Trustee qualified in the Law, it was felt necessary to appoint formally a Legal Adviser to the Trustees, so that 'there should be new and clearer arrangements to ensure that full consideration of legal matters should be given at an early stage of the business to which they were relevant'. (At this time the chief point of such business was the transfer of the medical-history collections to the Science Museum, p. 141.) Mr Francis Tufton, who had long acted as solicitor to the Trustees in the firm of Markby Stewart and Wadesons, agreeed to act in this capacity.

Fig. 32. Professor Henry Barcroft F.R.S. (*left*) was appointed a Trustee in 1966 and Dr C. E. Gordon Smith (*right*) in 1972. Both are distinguished biologists.

Five years later (1978) he was succeeded by his partner, Mr K. M. Miller. The Trustees also resolved to organise a Financial Section in their office to undertake the work for which Mr Clarke had formerly been responsible; Mr K. C. Stephenson was appointed as the first Finance Officer from 1 September 1974, and commenced the organisation of this new Section. For the management of their investment portfolio the Trustees continued to rely on the advice of Messrs Lazards Ltd.

The autumn of 1974 was also a time of change in that the Trust offices moved from 52 Queen Anne Street to 1 Park Square West, much closer to the Wellcome Building and with the Medical Research Council facing across Marylebone Road (see below). About this time too the composition of the Board of Trustees changed considerably. The senior of the Trustees still in office is Dr C. E. Gordon Smith (January 1972), who had been appointed Scientific Adviser to the Trustees in 1969 when Sir John Boyd – who had gone on under that title after retiring as a Trustee in 1966 – finally severed his connection with the Trust. In October 1966 Sir John's place had been filled by the appointment as a Trustee of Dr Henry Barcroft F.R.S., Professor of Physiology at St Thomas's Hospital Medical School, and like his father before him an eminent research scientist, who was also qualified in medicine. However, the Trustees evidently felt the need for continued advice in Boyd's field. Like Sir John, Dr Gordon Smith has an expert knowledge of microbiology and tropical medicine, which has been of the highest value to the Trust in the development of its programme in tropical medicine. In 1969 he was Director of the Microbiological Research Establishment at Porton Down, but soon became Dean of the London School of Hygiene and Tropical Medicine, an office he still holds.

When Lord Murray of Newhaven retired from the Trusteeship in October 1973, the opportunity was taken to bring in a man distinguished alike in pure science, university administration, and public life. Sir Michael Swann, F.R.S., a zoologist, had lately retired from being Principal and Vice-Chancellor of the University of Edinburgh in order to become Chairman of the B.B.C., a post he held for the long term of seven years. He has great experience of governmental committees and governing bodies. Lord Swann (as he became in 1981) is still a Trustee. The connection with the Trust of the next appointee was unfortunately of brief duration. When Mr R. M. Nesbitt retired a year after Lord Murray, in October 1974, his place was filled by Sir William Armstrong who had had a long and distinguished career in the Civil Service, becoming in 1968 Head of the Home Civil Service and Permanent Secretary to the Civil Service Department. Shortly after becoming a Trustee he too was raised to the peerage and appointed Chairman of the Midland Bank, of which he was already a Director. The hope that Lord Armstrong might succeed Lord Franks as Chairman of the Trustees was destroyed by his sudden death on 12 July 1980.

The fourth of the new Trustees of the 1970s was Dr (now Sir) Stanley Peart, F.R.S. Professor of Medicine at St Mary's Hospital Medical School, Paddington, appointed from 1 January 1975 in succession to Professor Henry Barcroft. Professor Peart continues the tradition that one Trustee is active in clinical medicine as well as in medical sciences, in his case biochemistry and physiology.

In the first years of the Trust the points of contact between it and the medical–scientific world were necessarily few in number: in the persons of two Scientific Trustees and one Secretary (with, later, an Assistant). At this stage it would have been impossible, clearly, for the Trust to manage schemes of its own or to deal properly with large numbers of individual grantees. Meanwhile the size and complexity of the scientific world was rapidly growing. The increase in the number of Trustees (p. 80) – and the reduction of their average age – were the first steps toward an improvement of communication between potential donor and potential recipient.

Fig. 33. Lord Armstrong (1915–80) was a Trustee for only six years.

Like Dr Williams, Sir John McMichael, Professor Thompson, and Professor Barcroft were able and willing to travel more frequently and extensively than their predecessors had done, a matter of particular importance with regard to medicine in the developing countries. The scientific secretariat of the Trust too, by becoming stronger, was able to undertake more functions. A year after Dr Edda Hanington joined the Trust as Assistant to Dr Williams (1965) there was a change of nomen-

Fig. 34. The scientific strength of the Board of Trustees was increased by the choice as Trustees of Lord Swann (*left*) a zoologist, and Sir Stanley Peart (*right*), a clinician. They were appointed in 1973 and 1975 respectively.

clature in that he became Secretary to the Trustees, Mr Clarke taking the title of Financial Secretary. Dr Hanington, a graduate of the Royal Free Hospital and Royal Postgraduate Medical Schools, had a special interest in migraine, and more generally in mental health. She was thus well qualified to open up new phases of the Trust's active support of medical research.

To provide stronger administrative support for the scientific staff and handle the increasing volume of paper-work involved in controlling grants and Fellowships, the Trust took advantage of the experience of the Medical Research Council. Both Mr M. A. F. Barren, who was appointed Administrative Officer in 1967, and Mr D. G. Metcalfe who came with him as Fellowships Officer, had previously served the Council.

In the next few years, as disposable income hastened past the £2 million mark, the management of the Trust's affairs assumed very much its modern shape. In accordance with the Trustee's express intention to invest more heavily in research in tropical medicine, Dr B. E. C. Hopwood was recruited to the medical staff in June 1969, starting work the following

October. At this time too Dr Williams became Director of the Trust, with Dr Hanington as Assistant Director and Deputy Secretary, while Drs Hopwood and Bembridge, who joined the group in the following Spring, were known as Assistant Directors. The former, a medical graduate who had also been called to the Bar, had considerable experience of the health problems of both Ethiopia and Uganda, where he had been Deputy Chief Medical Officer in the Ministry of Health. He took immediate charge of the tropical field, one of his first tasks being to organise a Symposium in London on 'Cassava, Cyanide and Nutritional Neuropathy' which met in October 1969. To Dr B. A. Bembridge, a specialist in ophthalmology with experience in Edinburgh and Oxford, was assigned the rapidly developing European Programme. For some years after the institution of the Carlsberg and Swedish Fellowship schemes (p. 91) there had been little fresh development, but from 1969 onwards links were forged with many countries. During a visit to Germany in that year Dr Williams made a contact with the Deutsche Forschungsgemeinschaft, leading to a meeting of representatives from the Wellcome Trust and the German organisation in October 1969, and then, six months later, to the appointment of a joint Anglo–German Committee with the object of prompting co-operation and exchanges in medical research between the two countries. This Committee met for the first time, in London, at the end of October 1970.[1] As Sir John McMichael pointed out at this meeting, the Trust had financed so far 26 European Research Fellows to work in Britain – not perhaps a large number compared, say, with the activities of the Humboldt Foundation – but the significant point was that two-thirds of these Fellows had come from Eastern Europe, and only one-third from the West. With the European Economic Community effectively operating, and Britain's future membership of it in prospect, it was important to break down procedural and financial barriers to scientific collaboration, the more so as English had effectively become a lingua franca of science. As Dr Williams was fond of pointing out, Europe could be at least as great a power in research as the U.S.A. if its physical and human resources were combined and deployed to the best advantage. Particularism entailed duplication and waste, while denying the finest opportunities to the creative talent of the poorer countries in Europe. Meanwhile, the U.S.A. acted as a greater magnet: both British and Germans preferred to visit (and remain) there, rather than work in each other's countries.

While these negotiations with the D.F.G. were going forward, the Trustees had already agreed to devote a small sum to the European Society for Clinical Investigation, whose case had been urged by Professor C. T. Dollery of the Royal Postgraduate Medical School. This Society had been 'established to foster clinical research in Europe and to provide a forum where good work could be presented by younger research workers. . .. Many members have been both surprised and delighted to find out how much good research work has been done in other European countries with which they had hitherto few contacts'. The Trustees financed up to three Fellowships a year, selected from a short list of nominations by the Society, to enable denizens of any European country to work in another. However, after four years this scheme was given up, partly through lack of interest in the scientific community, partly because it seemed to duplicate other Fellowship programmes, and partly because the Trustees felt, as a principle, that exchanges ought to be to or from Britain if financed by them.

The specifically German scheme put into effect for the first time in 1971 aimed at a larger effect, by an annual exchange of three Fellows each way – but it seems all the offers were never taken up. The object was

> to encourage candidates who are already experienced in research, and especially in clinical science, to spend a year in Britain or Germany working at a research institution of their choice, to develop their research by the acquisition of new techniques or expansion of experience.

It was hoped that the Anglo–German Committee might, together with the mutual Fellowship agreements made with Denmark and Sweden, form the basis for a European Medical Research Organisation, which the Foundations of other countries such as the Volkswagen Stiftung in Germany, the Carlsberg, and the Agnelli in Italy might also be able to support, so that medical research might be given a pan-European framework. This ideal was not to be realised. Meanwhile, other ideas were explored, for inter-laboratory exchanges, 'working-parties' and short-visit schemes, for the Trustees were quite prepared to devote up to £300,000 per annum to their European programme, if suitable schemes could be worked out. Two examples where support was given by the Trust were a 'workshop meeting' on the standardisation of the mediators of cellular immunity and their bioassay, held at Schloss Reisensberg near Ulm in Germany in June 1972, arranged by Professor Fliedner, and a co-operative research project arranged between the laboratories of Professors Fleischhauer at Bonn and of Sir Francis Knowles F.R.S. of King's College, London. The difference in economic level and standard of living between West Germany and England did, however, present a crippling difficulty. The Trustees were willing to offer 'displacement allowances' and other unusual benefits to European Fellows, but found that the stipends regarded as normal in the Bundes Republik were totally out of line with British practice, and were not willing to depart so far from it as would satisfy the German scientists. The result was that, though the British showed a modest interest in the scheme, the Germans soon ceased to apply for the Wellcome Fellowships as they could obtain much better awards in their own country.

In this initiative, the Trustees developed a close association with the British Council (which commissioned a report on universities in Germany at this time). A second meeting of the full Committee was held at Bad Godesberg in May 1973.

Although the idea of a European Medical Research Organisation to coordinate and stimulate scientific and clinical investigation so that the Wellcome Trust could 'provide the focus for the cooperative development of European medical research' – not to be realised, unfortunately – was new, encouraged by the new unity of Western Europe, the Trust had long awarded Fellowships to Europeans wishing to work in Britain; as Sir John McMichael had reminded the first meeting of the Anglo–German Fellowships Committee, 36 such Fellowships had been financed in the years up to 1970. However, their distribution argued against the usefulness of a common *west* European scheme. Again, though Sweden was a non-E.E.C. country, the Anglo–Swedish exchange scheme had gone very well so that by 1971 up to five awards were made in a single year instead of the single Fellowship each way originally envisaged. In fact, of course, medical relationships had very little to do with political arrangements, and the Trust continued to look with a benevolent eye upon the problems and impoverishment of the Soviet bloc. In 1971 a Fellowship Exchange agreement was negotiated with the Hungarian Institute of Cultural Relations and in 1976 (after a visit to Sofia by Drs Bembridge and Williams) a similar arrangement was made with the Bulgarian Academies of Sciences and of Medical Sciences, at a cost to the Trust of £7,500. The needs of Polish medical scientists were relieved by an agreement whereby equipment was bought on their behalf by the Trust in Britain, and shipped to their laboratories, negotiated in 1973.

In 1972 the Wellcome Trust initiated a collaboration with the Ciba Foundation of London in organising a Symposium to which participants came from 21 countries, devoted to a study of their respective systems for providing medical care and research. The proceedings of this meeting were published by Ciba in the following year as *Medical Research Systems in Europe*.

In the absence of sound, workable international schemes, the Trustees perforce continued with the policy of bilateral agreements, which by 1973 included Finland, The Netherlands, and France.

The French case is particularly interesting because a keen enthusiasm was expressed by parties on both sides of the Channel for the strengthening of associations between medical research workers in the two countries, between which cultural links are generally strong, and between which existing exchange agreements had proved less than fully effective. Goodwill was not lacking, money was not lacking, the language barrier was not serious: the problem was to find the right mechanism.

So far as the Wellcome Trust was concerned, the issue was opened up by a conversation between Dr D. W. Adamson, Research and Development Director of the Wellcome Foundation, and Dr Elie Wollman of the Institut Pasteur in Paris, in July 1969. It was taken further by Dr Gordon Smith, also on a visit to the French capital, and thus the way was prepared for discussions by Dr Williams with the heads of the Institut Pasteur, the Institut National de la Santé et de la Recherche Médicale (I.N.S.E.R.M.), and the Fondation pour la Recherche Médicale Française (F.R.M.F.). To improve the Trust's familiarity with French medical research, moreover, Dr Cornelius Medvei – an endocrinologist trained in Vienna but long settled in England – was commissioned to make a series of visits in 1971–2 to French universities (Paris, Strasbourg, Bordeaux, Montpellier and several others).

Dr Medvei was favourably impressed by the modernity and vigour of the French scene, and argued forcibly that the British should not always think of Paris and France as equivalent. Arrangements for collaboration in research would be welcome and justifiable. At last, after much correspondence, representatives from the two countries met in London in November 1972 to consider detailed arrangements; it had already been decided that I.N.S.E.R.M. and the Trust would finance a Fellowship exchange in the field of prenatal physiology. It was thought that five or six exchanges each way in every year might be profitable. Despite all the preparatory effort, no precise proposals emerged, and when the Travelling Research Fellowships were advertised for 1973–4, no special mention was made of a French scheme, and the somewhat ominous phrase was added: 'The candidate must make his own arrangements with the department in which he proposes to work' putting all the onus for planning the details of an exchange upon the putative candidate, or his Head of Department. Although three grants were made in 1973–4 to enable French research workers to come to Britain for research, and three other grants facilitating inter-laboratory collaboration, the exchange scheme never took off. Apparently no awards were made in 1975, though there were two in 1976. Thereafter applications from France were dealt with under the broad scheme for European Exchange Fellowships, with some foreign support arranged *ad hoc*. It seems that I.N.S.E.R.M. sent, and the M.R.C. brought over, more French medical scientists to Britain during the 1970s than did the Wellcome Trust. In 1981, however, there was an improvement in that seven Fellowships were awarded, and two inter-laboratory collaborations financed, at a total annual cost of £58,000.

From 1980 onwards, the Wellcome Trust has participated in meetings of a Joint Franco–British Medical Interchange Committee organised by the British Council in collaboration with I.N.S.E.R.M.

These matters have been related in some detail to illustrate the point that the new initiatives approved by the Trustees demanded a great deal of staff work and the special attention of qualified officers. As time went on, and the sums expended increased in real terms, the Trustees also began to look for more detailed and thorough examination of projects before support was given to them, and a more scrupulous monitoring of their progress and final results. As the experience of years accumulated, they began to think about assessment of their generosity to medical science. Had they tended to pick the right people, who became leaders in their fields? Had they backed the universities where innovations were made? Had they, by putting money into neglected subjects, brought them into prominence? Again, knowledge and study were required if such questions were to be answered. By 1969 despite piecemeal additions to the space originally available for the Trust's offices at 52 Queen Anne Street it had become clear that a move to larger premises must be made; the prospective change in the financial administration by itself enforced the step. The Trustees learned of a block of property, on lease from the Crown, stretching from Upper Harley Street to Park Square West along Marylebone Road, that was to become available for redevelopment. (In fact, though the stucco façades were preserved, the interior was to be completely reconstructed in modern office form.) The Trustees acquired this lease, and appointed Louis de Soissons and Partners as architects (March 1970). Possession of the site was taken in November 1971. There followed four and a half years of the problems and inflations inevitably associated with a building project, the main burden falling upon Mr

Fig. 35. The present offices of the Wellcome Trust at Park Square West, London NW1.

Maurice Barren. Price estimates rose from £550,000 to £730,000 before completion. The new offices were occupied in September 1974, and are generally agreed to constitute a highly successful example of a small high-quality office suite, practical and well equipped but with real internal and external elegance reminiscent of the original architecture of Regency London. The remaining lease at Queen Anne Street was successfully sold about a year later, making a very considerable contribution to the cost of the new offices. Since they were completed, opportunity has been taken to provide a handsome group of rooms in which symposia and conferences can be held, appropriately named after Lord Franks who had just retired from the Chairmanship of the Trust at the time when this modification was accomplished.

The Trustees signalised their occupation of their new offices by mounting in 1975 an exhibition giving a view of their activities over almost forty years, during which about £27 million has been dispersed. The exhibition presented an account of Sir Henry Wellcome himself and of the Foundation he had created, as well as of the development of the Trust, and described numerous examples of the medical research the Trustees had supported, into such diseases as schistosomiasis and leishmaniasis in the

Fig. 36. Sir David Steel (*left*) has been Chairman of the Trustees since 1982; Mr Roger G. Gibbs (1983) (*right*) supports him on the business side.

tropical field, into comparative neurology and ophthalmology in veterinary science and into many other specialised topics of which some 50 examples were displayed, ranging from radio immunoassay for microbial antigens to the physiology of calcitonin. Nor was the history of medicine forgotten, material on the Units and the Institute for the History of Medicine being included. This was the first attempt to make the work of the Trust widely known since the centenary of Sir Henry Wellcome's birth in 1953 and the only extensive pictorial record so far assembled in illustration of its multifarious activities.

Lord Franks was succeeded as Chairman from March 1982 by Sir David Steel, who had been appointed a Trustee at the end of the previous year. He is also a Director of the Bank of England and a Trustee of *The Economist*. Sir David, after a distinguished career in the Second World War, took the Law Society examinations and entered the oil industry, serving as Chairman of British Petroleum Ltd from 1975 to 1981.

On Professor Sir John McMichael's retirement as a Trustee at the end of 1977 his place was filled by the appointment of Sir William Paton F.R.S. (to use the title conferred upon him in 1979), Professor of Pharmacology

Fig. 37. Two scientifically-distinguished Trustees were appointed in 1977 and 1982: Professor Sir William Paton, F.R.S. a pharmacologist (*left*) and Dr Helen Muir, F.R.S., a biochemist (*right*).

in the University of Oxford. A member of a family distinguished in the Church, Professor Paton qualified in medicine (1942) and has devoted his whole life to research into physiology and the action of drugs. Before returning to Oxford he had worked at University College Hospital and the National Institute for Medical Research. He has a long and deep interest in the history of science and medicine, and took office as Honorary Director of the Wellcome Institute for the History of Medicine from October 1983.

The next change in the composition of the Board of Trustees came with the retirement of Professor Thompson, Deputy Chairman, in August 1982. His long service of nearly 20 years had seen the whole growth of the Wellcome Trust to influence and authority. In succession to him, the choice of a woman Trustee marked another progressive step. Dr Helen Muir is Director of the Kennedy Institute of Rheumatology and head of its Division of Biochemistry. She was a colleague of Sir William Paton's at the National Institute for Medical Research and has had a long connection with St Mary's Hospital, Paddington. Dr Muir is also unique as a Trustee with a declared interest in horses and hunting.

For the period of a year only six Trustees were in office, of whom the Chairman alone was eminent in the worlds of finance and affairs, all the remainder being scientists. The balance was adjusted by the selection as a Trustee of Mr Roger Gibbs, Chairman of the Gerrard and National plc, a financial discount house. Since Mr Gibbs is much the youngest of the present Board he can look forward to guaranteeing its financial acumen for many years.

Lord Franks was Chairman for seventeen years. As Sir Henry Dale brought the Trust into existence and directed it upon a path of useful activity which it has followed ever since, so Lord Franks presided over its growth into a major financial power in the world of medical research. Perhaps the greatest significance of Lord Franks' tenure of office was the changes in this world, and the adjustment of the Trust's activity to cope with them. Dale had been brought up in a period when medical research was dominated by Germany, Britain and the United States (in that order); when the role of the state in all aspects of medicine was still minor; and when the globe was still divided between imperial and colonial peoples. Medical research – of varying qualities and volumes, it is true – is now far more widely diffused than it was 50 years ago, and if in tropical countries especially problems of starvation, disease and over-population remain essentially the same, the context within which such a body as the Wellcome Trust has to work has been profoundly altered in terms of the modern division between the Developed and the Developing (terms which are themselves merely convenient euphemisms). Within the narrower compass of Britain, where the Trust does most of its work, the shift in the situation realised in the time of Lord Franks' chairmanship is no less large though prepared by such major earlier events as the 1944 Education Act and the 1948 creation of the Health Service. These and other major measures intended to open prospects of physical health and intellectual development for all the inhabitants of these islands such as had never before existed, came at the beginning of what proved to be Britain's economic and political decline. Constantly pressed for resources, the state has time and again been forced to aim for equality and fairness not by encouraging growth at the bottom, but by cutting off at the top. As the butter has been spread more evenly the layer has become thinner. From the first, Sir Henry Dale committed the Trust to the support of academic medical research in the universities which (in the peculiar British system) are also integrally linked with great public hospitals and their research departments. The Trustees have consistently decided against a policy of 'going it alone' in private institutes, or of seeking to solve a single health problem. Even their collaboration with the Medical Research Council has tended to become less significant: the Council's scheme for electing Sir Henry Wellcome Research Fellows was wound up, at the Trustees' request in 1976, after 71 awards had been made. But in this period university research became more and more impoverished as, in a time of high inflation, governmental support for the universities decreased steadily in real terms. The chief issue, therefore, continually pressing upon the Trustees through all these years was: how could they best employ their resources to maintain the force and quality of a research system which was, as they saw it, in danger of gradual and slow disintegration. Sir Henry Dale had seen the slender means at the Trustee's disposal in his day as an encouragement and a lever; in Lord Franks' time the question became rather that of using much larger resources to reinforce the increasing number of weaknesses in the official structure of medical research.

9

CHARTING A NEW COURSE, 1965–82

A major event in the evolution of the Trustees' manner of working was the beginning in the 1960s of the series of two-day meetings – usually held at a suitable conference centre – at which the Trustees discuss the general policy to be followed during the next 12 months, deciding what their objectives should be, and how the sums likely to be available for distribution should be provisionally allocated between them. Some of the new or strengthened lines of activity thus opened up – for example, the fields of veterinary and tropical medicine – are discussed elsewhere. This chapter will be concerned with the changing strategy of the Trustees with respect to Britain, that is to the support of scientific and clinical medicine in British universities.

Throughout the years, through many changes in detail, the Trustees have felt it appropriate that in this country, particularly, their funds should be channelled into university departments. They have not judged it necessary to fortify the 'campaigns' against particular diseases – which tend, in fact, to receive from the public as much money as they can usefully employ in research – nor to establish research establishments of their own in Britain. Without any impairment of friendly relations, they have ceased offering finance for schemes of the Medical Research Council. However, the ways in which the Trust has assisted university medical research have changed considerably through the last two decades. Notably, with the object in part of maximising their freedom of action but also in part to detach themselves more clearly from the agencies of governmental finance, the Trustees under Lord Franks's Chairmanship deliberately resolved to reduce their investment in bricks and mortar (compare p. 103). In the years 1960–2 £883,000 had been spent on new laboratories, including grants of £174,000 to the London Postgraduate

Fig. 38. Dr Kondi at work in the field.

Medical School at Hammersmith and £120,000 to the University of Otago at Dunedin in New Zealand. Large sums had also been given to other London Medical Schools and two Children's Hospitals (Great Ormond Street and Westminster) for research accommodation – in one instance, to house an M.R.C. Unit. Outside London, Birmingham, Glasgow and Edinburgh had also benefited. In the following two years the buildings total was slightly less (£785,000) and included only one grant exceeding £60,000, for the Department of Pharmacology at Yale University. In their *Fifth Report* covering these years, the Trustees hinted at a future change of outlook, noting that though

> they have been able to do good service to the advancement of medical science by expending nearly half of their funds on buildings required for medical researches in University departments, it would obviously not be suitable for them to regard so extensive an allocation for this purpose as a permanent feature of their policy.

In their *Sixth Report*, for the years 1964–66, pp. 14–20, the Trustees put the point more strongly; it was 'inappropriate as a policy' that so large a proportion as almost one-half of their funds should be used to provide accommodation; future requests of this sort would be submitted to a 'stricter view' and they would normally only be approved if 'a building proposed is to accommodate a programme of research which the Trustees in any case desire to support'. The laboratories required for their research by scientists maintained by government funds should, the Trustees affirmed, also be provided from the same funds. Almost £1 million had, in fact, been given to building programmes in these two years, University College, London and the University of British Columbia being recipients of the largest grants from the Wellcome Trustees.

This policy was re-affirmed in April 1966 when, responding to approaches for assistance with extensive future building programmes at the two ancient English universities, the Trustees once more recorded 'that it is the purpose of the Trust to pioneer new developments and not to act as a substitute for the government in providing funds for normal university building', normal including the replacement of obsolete laboratories, and the construction of laboratories for new subjects that a university had decided to support. Henceforward, aid would be given only for the construction of laboratories where the work to be done could be 'considered to be new and requiring special facilities'. Lord Franks wrote in April 1966 to explain the Trustees' policy to the Vice-Chancellors of Oxford and Cambridge, again defining their objective as 'support for medical research to make it possible for men of appropriate calibre to develop projects which might languish without this extra assistance'. The corporate state could not be allowed to have it both ways – it could not demand the total control of medicine, scientific research and education and then expect from private institutions the supplementary finance which alone would make the state machine work adequately. In fact, if private bodies made that machine work, the state would gladly absorb their resources, while retaining control of policies.

It will be understood that, where the case put up has seemed strong enough, the Trustees have continued to give large sums for buildings. In 1978 Professor D. K. Peters (of the Royal Postgraduate Medical School) was awarded £140,000 for new laboratories and improvements intended to further a research programme linking basic science with clinical medicine. This, the Trustees noted, was a special case because the strong clinical research at the Royal Postgraduate Medical School has been an important element in British Medicine.

In the next year £38,000 was added to this gift, the cost of Professor Peter's works having by then risen to a total of £433,000. Similarly, a grant to Dr P. F. Baker (King's College, London) of £97,000 in 1978, for building conversions to facilitate inter-departmental collaboration in studies of the biochemistry of the development of erythrocytes, the pharmacology and physiology of blood platelets and the mechanisms of calcium homeostatis had to be increased by £32,000 in the following year. The Trustees subsequently introduced a clause into their awards of this sort disclaiming ability to entertain inflationary increases. Nevertheless, another large grant (£180,000) was made in 1979 to Professor J. Vallance-Owen, of the Queens' University, Belfast, to make possible 'studies on the biological and chemical characteristics of gastroenteropancreatic hormones', and three grants for building conversion works were made in the 1980–2 biennum, relating to the 'selected subjects' ophthalmology, pharmacology, and tropical medicine.

The major gifts made by the Wellcome Trustees for the construction or renovation of laboratories, and for the provision of equipment and apparatus, are summarised in Appendix V, which also shows succinctly the quantitative effect of the Trustees' new line of policy, as put into effect during the late 1960s.

By this time the Trustees had fairly definitely decided that they should make serious efforts to aid 'neglected subjects' such as dermatology, neurology, mental health and tropical medicine. The root cause of the relatively slow progress made in such fields as these seemed to be the isolation of the clinicians and the few researchers working in them, combined with the 'band-wagon' effect drawing the best minds and most money to those other fields where rapid progress was occurring and reputations were being made. There seemed no reason why the basic methods that had worked so well elsewhere should not also work, if applied properly, in relation to the diseases of the skin, the mind, and the tropics. The biochemistry of mental disease was just opening up with promise, but psychiatrists in general were 'not trained for the biochemical approach that is needed'. Obviously much more was required than building programmes and Fellowships: positive encouragement and a better career structure for research workers were needed and planning was really more important than money.

Some part in the gradual shift of view about the functions of the Trust must certainly be attributed to its changing composition. Lord Franks had taken over the Chairmanship early in 1965. In the following October Lord Murray of Newhaven (who had already, as we have seen, been advising the Trustees) joined their number. Lord Murray's background was in agricultural science. He began a long association with Lincoln College, Oxford, in 1932, becoming Rector of the College in 1944. From this post he went on to become Chairman of the University Grants Committee (U.G.C.), retiring after ten years in 1963, whereupon his connection with the Wellcome Trust began. No one of his generation has had a wider experience of university affairs in Britain and elsewhere, or possessed a more statesman-like view of their changing course. Lord Murray was appointed Director of the Leverhulme Trust in the same year that he became a Wellcome Trustee. Thirdly, Dr P. O. Williams, Scientific Secretary since 1964 (p. 153) took over from Mr Clarke as Secretary to the Trustees on 1 January 1966, Mr Clarke continuing as Financial Secretary. This meant that the officer in charge of the day-to-day business about the making and administration of grants was placed immediately in contact with the Trustees, and became in all respects their chief executive. To assist Dr Williams, Dr Edda Hanington was appointed, also from 1966, Assistant Secretary.

All these new appointments added vigour, fresh imagination and extra experience to the work and planning of the Trust. It seems to be the case that all shared the ideal that the Trust should grasp the initiative more firmly, and determine lines of action of its own. For example, Lord Murray argued (October 1966) that the existing preponderance of support given for academic buildings was unwise because it would really be more useful if the deficiency in the finance that each university received in the form of its U.G.C. grant, as compared with its aspirations, were to be (at least partially) compensated by Wellcome grants for research projects, thus extending the so-called 'dual-support' (U.G.C. plus Research Councils) system to 'triple-support'. Further provision of scientific buildings might only create space without also creating the means to pay people to work in it – as was soon to happen in the hospitals. Moreover, he pointed out, if the Wellcome Trust gave large sums for medical research laboratories the U.G.C. would tend to switch its grants to other building projects. And, thirdly, he noted that in so far as the Trustees provided funds for new projects or buildings at the request of the Medical Research Council, in cases where the Council's own resources proved inadequate, it was resigning the process of selection between the favoured and the unfavoured research programme wholly to the M.R.C.

In October 1966 the Trustees re-affirmed their wish to support in appropriate ways 'neglected subjects' (p. 173) and also to improve the basic scientific training of young medically-qualified scientists, in order that they should be fitted and equipped to embark upon a career of research. With the emphasis taken off buildings and equipment, it became possible to think rather in terms of developing the human potential upon which Britain has always prided herself.

This new thinking on the part of the Trustees received expression in a formal statement of general policy and chosen objectives published in their *Sixth Report, 1964–6* pp. 14–20 (reproduced in Appendix I). This reaffirmed their intention to reduce relatively their involvement in building projects, and to cease to 'make up for the deficiencies created in regular budgets by inadequate allocation from public funds'. Rather, the Trustees 'would support promising new advances or inadequately supported or interdisciplinary subjects which offer opportunities for development'. Further, they would give preference in making awards to certain kinds of investigation over other kinds.

With these aims, a choice had still to be made between two chief routes to their achievement. One route was by enabling leading scientists of proven ability to organise larger research teams, so that they could either tackle a greater number of problems or make swifter progress with those under attack. This method had the merit also of multiplying employment opportunities for recent graduates and increasing their research experience. By the mid-1970s the Trustees were spending some £2¾ million each year in this way on the provision of research assistance to Heads of Departments and other senior scientists. Alternatively, programmes could be introduced to increase the number of posts available in the Universities for men and women at a middle level, of great promise in research, who might otherwise find that the development of their careers would entail the sacrifice of their research time. Such posts might be stepping-stones to Chairs for some, or permanent positions for others. A division of resources between these routes was a difficult and delicate one, as Lord Franks pointed out in 1976. And, in fact, one cannot be followed to the exclusion of the other, since the multiplication of qualified and able research assistants automatically increases the population of young researchers, aged from (say) 28 upwards, who will be looking for further career prospects. It will be obvious too that the cost of each senior post for five years is very much greater than that of a post-graduate studentship – the former now amounting to about £100,000.

During the 20 years the Trustees have at their annual policy meeting agreed on an approximate division of the resources they expect to receive from the Wellcome Foundation during the coming year, between their various programmes. For example, in 1966 they anticipated sharing out a disposable income of £1½ million in the following way:

	£
Ad hoc grants	650,000
History of Medicine (including the Institute)	250,000
Fellows from overseas	200,000
'Neglected subjects'	150,000
Tropical Medicine	150,000
Veterinary Medicine	100,000
	1,500,000

In 1972 the proposed allocations to definite programmes were both more numerous and more generous:

*Selected subjects**	(£000s)		
Dermatology	75		
Neurology	50		
Surgery	50		
Obstetrics and reproduction	100		
Veterinary	200		
Tropical	450		
		£ 925,000	(43%)
Fellowship and lectureship programmes			
Senior Clinical Fellowships	60		
European programme	100		
		£ 160,000	(8%)
Ad hoc *grants, medical sciences*			
Basic	400		
Clinical	250		
		£ 650,000	(30%)
Recurring commitments			
History of medicine	359		
Developed countries	10		
Travel grants	40		
		£ 409,000	(19%)
		£2,144,000	(100%)

* Usually known earlier as 'neglected'.

In 1966 the Trustees had proposed to devote just over one-half of their resources to '*ad hoc*' grants – those made in response to spontaneous appeals from the scientific community rather than in fulfilling a planned programme – whereas by 1972 such *'ad hoc'* grants had fallen to less than one-third of total expenditure. By the time the allocation for 1976–7 was made, the *'ad hoc'* proportion had diminished even further, but in subsequent years it has tended to increase once more:

	1976–7	(%)	1980–2 (2 years)	(%)
	£		£	
Selected subjects	1,725,000	(35)	7,200,000	(31)
Fellowships and lectureships	1,525,000	(31)	4,500,000	(18)
Ad hoc grants	800,000	(16)	6,400,000	(26)
Recurring commitments*	885,000	(18)	6,400,000	(26)
	4,935,000		24,500,000	

* Including inflationary increases of former awards.

The reason for this reversal of the earlier trend may well be the increasing poverty of the Universities in Britain.

Meanwhile, the funds allotted to Fellowships and Lectureship programmes – including the various European Fellowship Exchange programmes – have steadily increased. The oldest such programme is that introduced in 1962 by Sir John McMichael, for Wellcome Senior Research Fellowships in Clinical Science (p. 102), for which about 150 applications were considered during the first 20 years to 1982, more than one-third of them successful. The cost of each of the five or so new appointments made in each year is now about £100,000. In 1971 Dr Hanington reported on the operation of the first nine years of the Fellowships scheme, recommending strongly that it should be maintained. The Trustees have continued to regard this programme as extremely successful, since the Fellows have invariably gone forward to Professorships of Medicine or other positions of high responsibility. In 1977 a cognate scheme in Basic Biomedical Sciences was introduced, with an initial allocation of £250,000, 12 awards being made in the first year with biochemistry and physiology departments in the universities as the principal beneficiaries. The idea was to remedy 'the paucity of suitable openings' which would enable 'extremely able scientists in the basic biomedical field to develop their talents to the full'. Demand seemed to fall off rapidly, however, and this offer was withdrawn after only three years when the Medical Research Council introduced a similar programme of awards.

Through the middle years of the 1970s the Trustees became particularly concerned to identify both medical topics, and even particular medical problems, to which more research input was needed, and to know how best to offer this input, conscious always of the desirability of 'ensuring that men of the highest quality should continue to develop their ideas in the setting of a university that might be tending to be levelled down'. On the principle that two heads (or two laboratories) are better than one they strongly favoured *interdisciplinary research,* and, in general, the Trustees 'wished their new policy to develop in such a way as to make it possible for the universities to help themselves to redeploy their resources into a pattern more appropriate for the future'. This involved familiarity with the thinking of the university medical scientists themselves, or in other words required close contact between the Trust staff and these scientists – another reason for the growth in the number of medical officers (p. 187 below). Therefore, in 1974, the Trustees asked for an extension of the Senior Research Fellowships in Clinical Science, and continued support for 'neglected subjects', among which Mental Health, it was thought, might be helped by two special awards calling for the application of pharmacological and biochemical skills. The special areas of the Trustees' interest remained, as before, tropical medicine (Chapter 11), veterinary medicine (Chapter 12) and, in human medicine, clinical pharmacology, dermatology and surgery, besides mental health.

Two years later, in May 1976, the Trustees undertook a searching review of their policies based on a thorough compilation of information about awards made in previous years and the results that already seemed to be flowing from them. Two meetings with representative professors from all the universities in Britain maintaining medical schools had allowed outside opinion of the Trust's activities to be sampled, meetings which elicited much commendation and little criticism. The flexibility of the Trust's system as compared with the more cumbrous machinery of the State was praised. As regards the division of resources between basic and clinical sciences the professors do not seem to have been of much help, and the body of Trustees itself contained partisans favouring one or the other: indeed, it is impossible to make in the abstract a perfectly just in-principle distribution of resources between long-term and short-term programmes of advancing medical science. It is only possible to proceed empirically and opportunistically, as the Trustees have always done, backing the best possibilities that arise.

As regard tropical medicine, the Trustees noted with interest the increasing intervention of the World Health Organisation (p. 224), whose effects upon their own policies could not yet be defined, and decided to offer a small number of training Fellowships in this field. They judged the level of their support (at about 16 per cent of the budget) to be correct. Their support for Veterinary Medicine at £300,000 per annum in total (6 per cent of the budget) they recognised as far too small, but the Trustees were reluctant to increase this proportion until it could profitably be taken up by the Universities through their development of a greater interest in veterinary research. The Trustees also reconsidered thoroughly their financing of human medicine, deciding now that after eight years of support at the rate of almost £100,000 per annum dermatology could no longer be called a 'neglected subject' in medicine; it had established itself as a field of research and valuable studies were now being carried on at a number of centres (see below, Chapter 13). Pathology now suggested itself as another speciality deserving of encouragement, which should take the form of the offer of at least two Research Fellowships, at a cost of about £60,000 per annum.

The Pathology Fellowships, first awarded in the autumn of 1976, were parallel to the Fellowships for research in Surgery first offered four years before – originally it was thought that as many as six of these might be offered in any one year, but in the first round (1972) only two awards were made (both to Scots' surgeons) at a cost of £17,000. By 1976 the number of Surgery Fellowships on offer was put at four. The surgeons themselves were clearly conscious of the need for more research in their subject, including such topics as trauma, a step which would have the additional merit of tending to reduce the professional barriers between surgeons and physicians. In April 1971 Professor R. Shields (Liverpool University) had written:

> what is lacking is support for men who have the Fellowship [of the Royal College of Surgeons of England] and who now wish to have experience of research work. Usually the right sort of men have had, by this time, some fleeting knowledge of research. . . All are potential recruits for academic surgery and it is by encouraging this group that the Wellcome Trust, I feel, could do the greatest good for British surgery.

Like other Professors of Surgery in the British Isles, Professor Shields was invited to a one-day conference on 6 May 1971, to consider the optimum method by which the Wellcome Trust could encourage research in surgery, and the recruitment of the best young surgeons to the academic side of the profession. It was reported at this meeting that, to that date, the Trustees had given £336,500 for buildings in connection with surgery, but only £18,000 for Fellowships. At their meeting in June following, the

Trustees approved the Fellowships scheme in terms suggested by the meeting.

In both cases, the Trustees had endeavoured to divert some of the best young professionals from career patterns that, normally, fail to encourage research. In surgery, the discouragement arises from the length of the normal period of training before full professional qualification is reached – eight to ten years – and the infrequency of opportunities to obtain a post, in the normal sequence, giving time for research. In the case of pathology, the problem was a certain decline of interest in the field among young doctors, and the inevitable direction of those entering it to the National Health Service and the provision of the services it requires, again without the availability, at any stage, of posts where research might be the principal activity. In both cases, it seems, an improvement in university recruitment has resulted from the Trust's schemes. In the four years 1978–82 £535,000 was spent on 15 Fellowships in Pathology and £450,000 on 25 Fellowships in Surgery.

In order to further the direct application of the Trust's resources in the fields selected for special encouragement, fresh administrative moves were made, that is, the establishment of two more Advisory Panels and the advertisement of Competitive Awards for relatively large sums. The Advisory Panels established by the Trustees in July 1976, for Tropical Medicine and Mental Health, will be discussed in Chapters 11 and 13. The fields to be encouraged by major Competitive Awards were at first loosely denoted in October 1976 as Infection, Neurology and the Senses, the Eye, and Trauma. At their next meeting the Trustees narrowed these further, to:

1. Interdisciplinary studies of the vascular system of the human brain in relation to disease;
2. Interdisciplinary studies of the metabolic effects of infection in man;
3. Fields linking ophthalmology to general medicine.

In June 1977 (3) was again modified to 'Ocular Disorders related to Systemic Disease'. It was decided to devote up to £100,000 for an award in each of these topics, to which the Trustees later added a fourth option of similar magnitude for Mental Health.

This scheme, which as the *Twelfth Report* notes was a more effective implementation of a desire to stimulate interdisciplinary studies first expressed in 1974, was widely advertised in 1977 and several awards were made. For the Vascular System of the Human Brain 12 applications were received, grants of up to £100,000 being made to Dr A. Murray Harper and colleagues in Glasgow University and £60,000 being granted to Mr J. S. P. Lumley (St Bartholomew's Hospital Medical College). To study the metabolic effects of infection in man £83,000 approximately was granted to Professor J. C. Waterlow (London School of Hygiene and Tropical Medicine); however, the Trustees judged the overall response to this offer disappointing and decided not to repeat it in the same form. In the field of ophthalmology they had already supported successful collaborative research into diabetic retinal vascular disease carried out at the Institute of Ophthalmology and the Royal Postgraduate Medical School; now fresh awards of £46,000 were made to Dr A. J. Bron (Oxford) for a multidisciplinary study of diabetic retinopathy, a major cause of blindness. Nor was the pathology of trauma forgotten after being cited at the beginning of this programme. Traumatic events such as accidents, poisoning and physical violence are a common cause of death and also of hospitalisation; their effects spread widely through the whole body, in ways which are still insufficiently understood. As a result of the Trustees' specific offer, grants were made for collaborative work at the University of Manchester on the immunology of injury (£96,000), at the University of Glasgow to investigate the calorimetry of the metabolic response to injury (£30,000) and at the University of Oxford to study muscle metabolism after injury (£35,000).

The first Competitive Awards in Tropical Medicine were made (July 1977) for the study of the malarial parasites *Plasmodium falciparum* and *P. vivax*. The Institute of Animal Genetics at Edinburgh received £21,000 to aid work on the typing of these parasites, while Professor D. J. Weatherall (Oxford) received £51,000 to finance an investigation of the interaction of *P. falciparum* with human red cells and bone marrow. In the following year Dr S. R. Bloom and Dr J. Polak (Royal Postgraduate Medical School) were granted £93,000 for research into peptidergic innervation in Chagas's Disease (see also Chapter 11).

As already hinted, the Trustees have been constantly preoccupied since the 1970s with the welfare of medical research in British Universities and within the framework of the National Health Service. The trend followed by the State during the last decade and longer has been towards the provision of reduced funding (in absolute terms), with greater insistence upon obtaining 'value for money', which may in turn entail the pursuit of short-term objectives in preference to long-term, and of the more glamorous objective in preference to the more humdrum (but really useful to the community). The Trust has always been sensitive to the effects of national policies upon the work of the Medical Research

Council, as happened when the new principles introduced by Lord Rothschild were applied to it. In their *Ninth Report, 1970–2* the Trustees observed that the effect was 'to direct the activities of the Medical Research Council more towards the practical needs of the health service', and so in time it might bring about a situation where the Council ceased to be an 'independent government financed organisation' in order to become a 'contractor for medical research of special relevance to government activity'. A probable consequence would be a reduction of the M.R.C. funding of 'pure' research in the universities, already suffering on the other side from a reduction (in real terms) of their University Grants Committee budgets.

Again, in their *Tenth Report, 1972–4*, the Trustees drew attention to another way in which 'the overall trend of social change is to require more return of practical value from the activities of our various institutions'. Because of the undue dependence of the National Health Service on immigrant doctors, the university medical schools were under pressure to produce more doctors, a requirement which 'with increasing emphasis on more practical training [of British doctors], may well impair the academic depth of undergraduate education'.

It would not be correct to suppose that in their desire to maintain both the quantity and quality of medical research in British Universities, despite the effects of inflation, of relative national impoverishment, of administrative reorganisation and political vicissitudes, the Trustees have acted merely in a doggedly conservative spirit, or that they have believed the universities to constitute necessarily perfectly efficient organisations for medical research; for example, they recorded in July 1974 'the view that in the long term the universities would come to no harm if economies were to force them to improve their academic quality and efficiency'. At the same time, they could not but accept a responsibility for compensating, as far as possible, for deficiencies arising from the reduction of governmental funds through the usual agencies such as the University Grants Committee, the Medical Research Council, and the Agricultural Research Council.

Apart from the fairly straightforward issue of equipment for research – and it is a truism that its expense and complexity have steadily increased – the Trustees have seen the latent dangers to medical research in British Universities as lying principally in a shortage of research posts – tending to render a career in medical research, at least in this country, less attractive as compared with clinical practice; in a breakdown of the flow of information and technique from the research laboratory to the hospital;

and in a reluctance to undertake research in the less fashionable or obviously rewarding fields. The Trustees' support for 'neglected subjects' will be further considered in Chapter 13 (below); the remainder of this chapter will review their various policies for promoting university research in general, in accordance with the broad desire for

> The promotion of good men with good ideas in the broad field of medical science, so that these ideas can be developed (1974).

A first response by the Trustees to the increasing impoverishment of the universities took the form of a letter from Lord Franks to the Vice-Chancellors offering £2.5 million over five years in order to make possible the advancement of research workers of distinction who might otherwise be tempted, by the absence of clear prospects, to emigrate or to abandon research. As a consequence, three appointments were made rapidly in 1968, at the Royal Postgraduate Medical School, at the University of Birmingham, and at University College, London. In the next biennium (1968–70) the sum devoted to these University Awards, intended only as a measure affording temporary relief, multiplied by four times to £240,000; 12 awards were made, mostly to permit an increase of salary for an individual to Senior Lecturer level. During the period 1970–2 a number of University Awards were again made, without any special significance being attached to them, to a total value of £194,000. The *Tenth Report* of the Trustees announced the demise of this Scheme 'because the universities can no longer offer a guarantee of a future appointment'. Thus only a fraction of the funds originally set aside for the purpose was exploited, the Scheme being limited in usefulness by its essentially temporary character. The same purposes were to be more effectually served by the Senior Lecturers' programme a few years later, when the Trustees felt better able to embrace long commitments.

One of the most obvious measures having long-term benefits for research is the creation of new professorships, as the Trustees had done since the start of their active history. As recently as 1970 £88,000 were given in a single year towards the founding of two new Chairs – the Wellcome Chair of Experimental Pathology at University College Hospital Medical School, and a personal Chair in Geographical Pathology at St Thomas's Hospital. In general, however, the Trustees have not judged the endowment of new Chairs, which is not necessarily a very effective procedure unless a great deal of ancillary provision is undertaken by the recipient institution or otherwise, with its commitment of large capital sums, to be the procedure of choice. They have preferred more openly competitive schemes, and ones which more clearly fulfilled the 'pump-priming' function which, as the Trustees wrote to the Select Committee on Science and Technology in June 1976, they regarded, together with the encouragement of first-class research talent, as their principal purpose.

Thus (as stated also in 1974) the Trustees have tended to see it as less important to have their funds available to permit large-scale, once-for-all capital expenditures by universities (as in creating a new professorship or a new building) than to have funds to enable universities to solve temporary problems, to turn a corner, or to move from one line of research to another. For example, by financing a proleptic appointment for a short period, a grant could cover the period before a professorship or other senior position could be released by retirement for a particular scientist. Again, Research Leave Fellowships permitted a man or woman to accelerate a particular piece of work, or to embark with full power on a new one; usually in such cases the provision of research assistance would also be necessary.

> In general [the Trustees agreed] they wished their new policy [1974] to develop in such a way as to make it possible for the universities to help themselves to re-deploy their resources into a pattern more appropriate for the future. . . . It would be particularly important in developing the details of his overall policy that the staff of the Trust should tap university ideas for assisting the developments envisaged and where possible seek the views of the younger members of university staff.

From this time (1974) the Trustees have continually emphasised the value of interdisciplinary collaboration, particularly in joint research carried out by clinicians and basic scientists. Thus in their report to the Select Committee of 1976 they defined the merit of the Linked Fellowships scheme introduced in 1971 as being that it enabled

> a non-medical scientist to work on a clinical problem while still retaining a foot-hold in the department of his basic discipline.

The first five awards under this scheme, at a cost of £97,000, were made in the years 1972–4; they permitted, for example, a scientist working in the Departments of Chemistry and Biological Sciences of the University of Birmingham to carry out an investigation on the human jejunum at the Birmingham General Hospital. In the next four years, 1974–8, 26 awards were made (£355,000), continued into 1979, but after 1980 the Linked Fellowships were merged into the general fund for Basic Science.

The Competitive Awards scheme (p. 175) also served to encourage university research in directions which the Trustees thought particularly likely to be valuable. As they noted in 1977:

> These awards have proved very successful in drawing attention to a particular field and have shown that a number of research workers are willing to modify their programmes if there is a possibility of obtaining a special grant.

Furthermore, the Trustees found that the Competitive Awards promoted interdisciplinary linkages between institutions:

> Where a large number of good applications are received, they can act as catalysts in linking good centres in a collaborative programme. This has been so in two cases: the first Schizophrenia award linked Imperial College and the Clinical Research Centre, and the second the Veterinary award which linked the Royal Veterinary College, London, with Imperial College. The Trustees thought that this linkage was a valuable element and had proved a more successful way of promoting interdisciplinary research than had been the case when they simply tried to encourage universities to put forward projects of this type.

However, the volume and merit of the response to the offer of such an Award in a particular field were found to depend greatly upon an accurate definition of the Trustees' intentions and a thorough previous knowledge of the state of the field and of what was practicable within it.

Two other Special Fellowship programmes begun in 1977 but, after three years, re-absorbed into the general programme of *ad hoc* grants were the Senior Research Fellowships in Basic Biomedical Sciences and Research Leave Fellowships. The former, announced in the *Eleventh Report*, were available 'for any basic science problem relevant to medicine', candidates being qualified either in medicine or in the basic sciences, the object being 'to provide opportunities for research for particularly promising scientists at a time when University posts are scarce' and at the same time fulfilling the Trustees' intention to devote a larger proportion of their resources to basic research. In 1974–7 this proportion was raised to 30 per cent (= £1,666,000) but decreased again in the next biennium. Research Leave Fellowships were intended to enable university staff to take unpaid leave for a year from their normal duties in order to accelerate their progress in research. The Trust paid the cost of a temporary substitute. Fourteen awards of this kind were made at a total cost of £357,000 while 15 Basic Biomedical Sciences Fellowships were granted at a total cost of £1,269,000.

The withdrawal of the two Fellowship schemes, partly because of new offers made by the Medical Research Council, by no means indicated a decline in awareness of the Trustees' part of the universities' continuing difficulties. In 1980 they drew attention in their *Thirteenth Report* to the 'especially deleterious' consequences for medical research of the general reduction (in real terms) of university funding and of other policy changes such as the charging of economic fees to overseas students. The shortage of university posts in particular 'has caused a deep depression among junior Fellows and other staff who could see little prospect of developing a research career', demoralisation actually producing a decline, rather than an increase, of high-quality applications to the Trust for research support. Initiative had been stifled by the gloom prevailing in the academic world. Again, in 1982, the financial cut-back which had 'led to soul searching in the London medical schools and had such damaging effects upon such institutions as the Royal Postgraduate Medical School, have been regarded with great dismay by the Trust'. Once more, the effect was measurable in a reduced interest in seeking research grants among university staff.

One clear result of the academic financial shortage, the efficiency drive, and the quest for value-for-money, has been to compel the Trustees to contemplate longer-term ventures. Pump-priming and quick injections of finance were inadequate measures to relieve an ailing situation, particularly in relation to fields of research that required special, and therefore prolonged, development; or where the Trustees' desire for greater effort was more than counterbalanced by government's desire to opt out. This was brought out plainly at the Trustees' general policy discussion during July 1975, 'because of the real danger in the present situation of the lack of incentive to able young graduates to enter and stay in medical research'. The most desirable situation, in giving long-term support to a medical school, would be that it should use the period to redeploy its budget in order to assume responsibility for the initiative. Considering policy three years later, in May 1978, they agreed that for the selected topics of veterinary medicine, mental health, medical ophthalmology, trauma, neurology and infectious diseases 'it would be appropriate to examine the case for the creation of long-term groups at selected centres interested in these fields', groups requiring perhaps a sum of £75,000 per annum.

> The object should be to develop these new groups into continuing centres for research supported by the University.

Here the ideal – in whose realisation the Trustees are so often frustrated – of 'take-over' by a university of a new development begun and proved to be valid by the Trust is stated once more, but the Trustees were now willing to think in terms of giving support to individual scientists not for one or three years only but for ten years or perhaps longer; moreover, the scientists were not necessarily to be pure full-time research workers but rather

> should be required to participate actively in the lecturing and other general activities of [their] Department for, say, one third of their [working] time.

The Trustees were cognizant of the fact that such a proposal entailed the solution of questions about conditions of employment and other administrative problems.

In January of the following year (1979) the Trustees decided to approach this object by means of a new programme of Senior Lectureships tenable in university departments, first advertised five months later. Nominations to these Lectureships would be made by Heads of Departments with the concurrence of the Vice-Chancellor or analogous institutional chief. Each appointment would be for five years, on a 'rolling contract', reviewed every three years. (The sense of this is, that the Trustees would give to each Lecturer two years' notice of an intention to terminate his funding.) Each Wellcome Senior Lecturer in Medical Science would be expected to be active in research, and to have duties *pari passu* with colleagues of similar standing. The hope was – and it has been realised – that, once the scheme was running, vacancies would occur regularly by the promotion of Wellcome Lecturers to more senior and responsible positions. The Trustees set a limit of 50 to the number of awards of this type in being at any one time. (See further p. 205 and Appendix X, p. 453.) In the first four advertised competitions for these Lectureships, 34 appointments were made from some 300 applications, including six women scientists. One of the Wellcome Lecturers, at the London School of Hygiene and Tropical Medicine, is Dr M. A. Miles, whose work in tropical medical parasitology is noted elsewhere (p. 249).

An especially close relationship has developed between the Wellcome Senior Lecturers in Medical Science and the Trust under the direction of the scheme by Dr C. Harold Edwards, formerly Dean of the Medical School of St Mary's Hospital, Paddington, who was invited to join the Trust's staff for this purpose. Since the early summer of 1981 a series of meetings has been held at the Trust Offices at which each Lecturer, in turn, has an opportunity to present his work to the others. Moreover, as in other areas of activity in recent years, members of the Trust's staff responsible for programmes pay regular visits to the departments in which Lecturers and Research Fellows work. A number of auxiliary grants have been made to assist the Lecturers in their researches. They are roughly equally divided between the clinical and basic medical sciences and range from Southampton to Dundee, with 21 of the present 44 appointments being held in London. Four Lecturers have already received a promotion taking them out of the Scheme. (Appendix X lists Wellcome Senior Lecturers to 1985.)

During the last 20 years the Trustees have evolved a three-fold method of promoting medical research in three geographically distinct regions. In the developing countries their main effort has been concentrated upon specific problems of tropical medicine, such as protozoal and nutritional diseases, investigated in Units wholly or chiefly maintained by the Trust for what now seems likely to be an indefinite period (see further Chapter 11). In Europe their principal objective has been the improvement of international co-operation, by making practical working agreements with appropriate organisations (whether private or governmental) in other countries, and by funding exchange visit Fellowship schemes. Finally, in Britain, to which the preponderance of the Trustees' resources is devoted, they have increasingly made it their endeavour to compensate for the deficiencies in university medical and biomedical research introduced by the economic decline of our society and by accompanying intellectual and social shifts.

The Trustees, though by no means unconcerned in the enormous pharmaceutical enterprise owned by the Wellcome Foundation in the United States and regularly playing a part in the research-supporting activities of the Burroughs Wellcome Fund in that country (p. 85), have not felt it necessary to refine a particular policy with regard to the developed world outside Europe. Grants to institutions in the United States and Canada, sometimes of a substantial magnitude, have been made on a purely opportunistic basis. With respect to Australia and New Zealand, however, the Trustees have recently become more conscious of the opportunity for their fruitful intervention in an academic sphere of rapidly increasing maturity which, nevertheless, still values and wishes to profit from its scientific associations with Great Britain.

Undoubtedly during the last two decades the greatest problem continually on the Trustees' agenda has been the risk of a severe decline in the medical research effort of British Universities. To this theme their biennial reports have returned again and again, and many of their special schemes have been aimed at preventing or limiting such a decline. The Trustees' desire to initiate innovation in lines of research has undoubtedly had a very great influence, but the tendency throughout this period has been towards a diminution, rather than an increase, of the universities' ability to 'take over' enterprises begun by outside bodies. In each of the three geographical types of their activity, therefore, the Trustees have of necessity moved in the direction of increasingly long-term commitments – to exchange agreements in Europe, to the research Units in tropical medicine, and to career appointments in British Universities. Though of course the circumstances inducing long-term plans in each have been very different, it is obvious enough that the pursuit of programmes towards defined objectives must necessitate greater continuity and consistency than are required for 'opportunistic' methods of grant-giving. It is wasteful in terms of the intellectual effort and of resources both of the donor and of the recipient if a research project has too short a time base. Moreover, whereas the Trustees surrender responsibility for a building or a piece of equipment once it is handed over to its users, they cannot so easily disclaim responsibility for human lives. They have accepted the fact that there is an indefinable point at which, having invited men and women to embark upon a career of research rather than the safer, established lines of teaching, clinical practice, or administration, the Trust cannot say: 'We will provide no further opportunity for you to practise your skills.' In other words, if the Trustees make the claim to manage a private system of biomedical research buttressing (and in a minor sense rivalling) the state system, rather than merely acting as capricious fairy godfathers, they must behave systematically, thinking far ahead and being willing to continue a productive programme once they have embarked upon it. *Flexibility* was very much the early watchword of the Trustees; *continuity* has come to seem at least equally important.

10

THE LATEST PHASE

The Trust

Since the establishment of the Trust offices in a new and larger building, and the development of its own financial administration, its organisational structure has not greatly altered, though the increase of the Trust's business has necessitated the growth of its staff during the last ten years. One important event of 1981, however, was the acceptance by the Charity Commissioners of a Scheme of Administration for the Trust, published on 5 October and subsequently printed in the *Fourteenth Report*. The point of formulating this Scheme was that, although many Orders of the High Court had been made concerning the interpretation of Sir Henry Wellcome's Will, and authorising various actions by the Trustees or giving them certain powers, no formal step had ever been taken to create an administrative body to which the Trustees might delegate some part of their powers as conferred by the Will and the Orders of the High Court. The Trust was the Trustees, and until the Scheme of Administration came into force no action or decision taken on their behalf was legally binding; in principle, every decision had to be formally authorised by the full body of Trustees before it had any effect.

The Scheme allowed the Trustees to draw up regulations for the management of Wellcome's charities, which might include the appointment of a Director of the Trust, with prescribed powers and duties.

They were also empowered to create a committee structure, the membership of each Committee including at least one Trustee, and, if the Trustees so chose, officers of the Trust as well as other persons. These Committees might be instructed to discharge the day-to-day business of the Trust in such manner as the Trustees might direct, provided that all actions and decisions of such Committees were reported to the Trustees and accepted by them. Regulations for the administration of the Trust were accordingly approved by the Trustees in November 1981. Their purport, in brief, was to the effect that the name 'Wellcome Trust' should designate the Body of the Trustees, and that they should appoint a Director of the Trust who would also be their Secretary. Power of appointment of officers and staff of the Trust was delegated to a Committee including at least one Trustee and the Director; other subject-Committees also appointed by the Trustees (and each including at least one member from their own body) were given restricted powers to consider applications for grants and approve awards. Similarly, each Trustee acting individually and the Director were given powers to authorise awards up to specified limits. All such appointments, decisions and awards – including refused awards – were to be reported to the full body of the Trustees. These arrangements permitted an important streamlining of both the decision-making procedure within the Trust and the administrative processing of applications. They also reduce the burden of detailed consideration of applications by the Trustees, leaving them more time to consider policies and principles, and the really large expenditures of money.

The *Fourteenth Report* observes that:

> These new arrangements could be said to crystallise all that Lord Franks had done for the Trust during his Chairmanship, having created an organisation for the Trust which could be expected to stand it in good stead for many years to come.

Lord Franks's Chairmanship had been extended because of the unfortunate sudden death of Lord Armstrong (p. 152); his last meeting as a Trustee was held on 2 February 1982. Professor Thompson, Deputy Chairman, spoke of the value and enjoyment found by the Trustees in the Chairmanship of Lord Franks. His wise and sympathetic direction of its affairs, and the friendly way in which he had always guided the Trust meant that he would be greatly missed in the future. Lord Franks replied with words expressing his affection for the Trust and its staff, and his delight that his successor was to be Sir David Steel.

Professor Thompson was himself to retire from 31 August 1982 when (as already noted, p. 162) he was succeeded by Dr Helen Muir. He had served as a Trustee for 19 years.

The retirement of Professor Thompson emphasised the need for a biochemist on the staff of the Trust, in view of the increasing activity in this and closely related fields of science. Accordingly, the Trustees in December 1982 selected Dr M. J. Morgan, Senior Lecturer in Biochemistry in the University of Leicester, for a period of two years' secondment to work on their behalf. A parallel appointment in Clinical Science was suggested by the early retirement, for personal reasons, of Dr Edda Hanington, who had kept closely in touch with this side of the Trust's work and brought new vigour and initiative to its various programmes. In this case, the Trustees appointed Dr David Gordon, Senior Lecturer in Medicine at St Mary's Hospital Medical School, to take charge of clinical research on secondment also for two years, from 1 April 1983. In due course both have decided to join the Trust staff as full-time Assistant Directors; Dr Gordon retains an honorary appointment at St Mary's Hospital.

The Trust's financial growth

As already indicated, it was during the 1960s that the Wellcome Trust first became able to operate on a substantial scale, steadily increasing. In the first years of the decade annual grant awards for the first time exceeded £1 million (equivalent to about £3½ million in the money of 1985) while by the end of the decade almost £3 million were being awarded each year. As the *Ninth Report* pointed out, this was an excessively high level of disbursement, made necessary by provision for five-year projects and made possible only by some (nominal) commitment of reserves. Consequently, there was some temporary contraction of funding in the early 1970s, and by 1974 new reserves had been accumulated. The total of grants since the inception of the Trust was by that date some £27½ million.

Figure 39 shows the charitable disbursements of the Trust from 1974 onwards, normalised to 1983 values. The various grants approved by the Trustees are assigned to their various programmes and Fellowship schemes by the Trust officers, which are in turn grouped into three main categories: selected subjects, special Fellowships and Senior Lectureships, and *ad hoc*, to which History of Medicine is additional. There is inevitably an element of the arbitrary in this classification, since for example, some Fellowship awards fall into the *ad hoc* category. In a loose and general sense, the two former categories represent the efforts of the Trustees to attain objectives defined by themselves. The figure shows that *ad hoc* grants are consistently more expensive than either of the other scientific categories, though not than both of these together.

While the curves manifest a steady upward trend in actual year-by-year payments, and maintain roughly the same relationship one to another, it is obvious that considerable fluctuations have occurred, notably the dips in level in 1977 and again in 1981. In 1976 disbursements were already

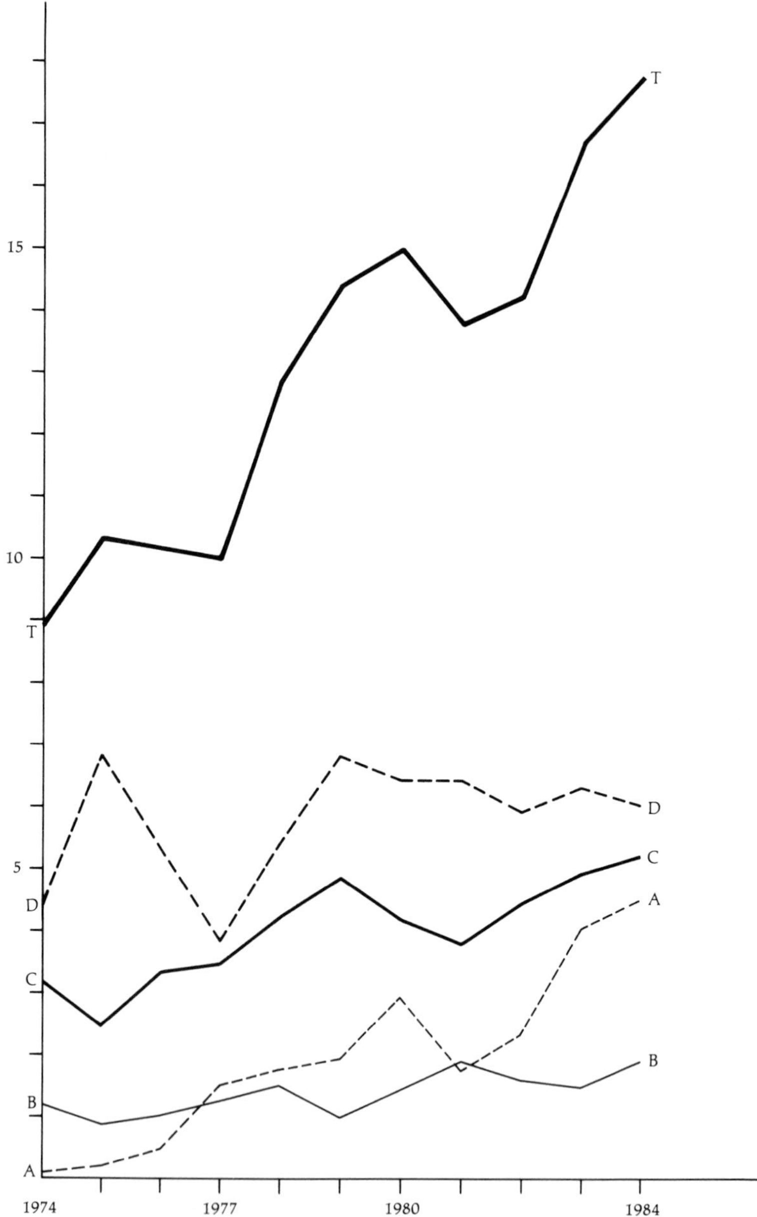

Fig. 39. The distribution of grants, 1974–84. In this graph all figures have been normalised to the values of 1983 and hence all fluctuations shown are real and unaffected by inflation. AA = Special Fellowships and Senior Lectureships; BB = History of Medicine; CC = Selected Subjects; DD = *Ad hoc* grants; TT = Totals.

more than £150,000 *below* the 1975 level and in 1977 there was a further decline of £200,000.

For not easily discernible reasons the *ad hoc* grants payments were markedly lower – a million and a half lower in 1977 than in 1975 – perhaps because of the chance simultaneous cessation of grants – and this fall was not compensated for by an increase in other categories. Thereafter followed a swift increase of total disbursements, from almost £9½ million in 1977 to over £12 million in 1978. Expenditure was greater in all categories, but especially in the *ad hoc* grants. In subsequent years the most notable variation has been in the category of special Fellowships and Lectureships, rising to a maximum approaching £3 million in 1980, and then, after a dip, up again to over £4½ million in 1984. The effect of the Trustees' increasing confidence in this type of support for medical research is clearly evident from the curve of disbursements, rising steadily from a mere £119,000 in 1974. The marked dip in 1981 was occasioned by the relative lack of demand for Fellowships in Clinical Epidemiology and Veterinary Medicine, as compared with earlier years (together, £1.3 million down as compared with 1980).

Among the selected subjects, a temporary slackening of demand for grants in Mental Health and Veterinary Medicine brought about a decline in disbursements in 1980 and 1981, from which some recovery has since been made, although this is concealed to some extent in the curve by the steady growth of Tropical Medicine.

The relative flatness of expenditure on History of Medicine is a consequence of the Trustees' policy of stability in this area, the rise to 1981 being the result of expenditure on the process of Museum transfer and the development of the Wellcome Galleries in the Science Museum.

It perhaps goes without saying that the summation of grant expenditure into four groups conceals much variation in the individual categories of awards, of which there were 41 during the period of 11 years. However, only 12 of the categories are applicable to every year. The rest relate to programmes offered for a lesser number of years, sometimes only for one year. The pattern in which a new category opens with a considerable expenditure, then declines to zero, is not uncommon. The most successful categories tend to show a steady rise in the volume of grants.

Grants programme

In order to provide an assimilable picture of the Trustee's activity in the 1980s, the larger grants (that is, those exceeding £45,000 in individual value) have been extracted and listed in Appendix IV. This list covers the five years from 1 January 1980 to 31 December 1984, the total so awarded being £27 million, a figure to be compared with a total expenditure on all grants, awards and programmes of some £52 million during the same period. Thus the large grants (as defined above) account for some 52 per cent of the whole research-supporting expenditure of the Trust; obviously the number of grants for sums below £45,000 much exceeds the number of large grants. In fact, the average value of a grant rose from about £16,000 in 1980 to £22,000 in 1985, another measure of inflation.

It is obvious too that the choice of a lower limit in order to restrict the number of grants for consideration, which may then be considered as denoting the major projects, is quite arbitrary, moreover, in determining the size of a grant its duration is of very great significance: no grant is likely to exceed £45,000 in value if given for a less time than two years, and many large grants were spread over five years. However, the willingness of the Trustees to support a project for a long period of time is itself a measure of the originality and importance they have attached to it.

It is interesting to compare the pattern of grant-making, as divided into categories by the Trust Office:

	Large grants 1980–84	*All grants* 1974–84
	£	£
Tropical Medicine	3,207,000	16,438,000
Basic Sciences	3,158,000	20,431,000
Mental Health	2,032,000	7,200,000
Clinical Sciences	1,774,000	11,475,000
Veterinary Medicine	1,308,000	7,222,000

The combined weight of the smaller grants is sufficient to alter the 'pecking-order' apparent in the large grants taken by themselves. At the opposite extreme from these large figures, only two large grants were made in Ophthalmology during the five years 1980–84, and the total expended on all grants during the time of its choice as a 'selected subject' (1979–83) was only £726,000.

Considering the recent large grants, the total of awards for research and technical assistance and expenses of research, at about £14 million, was only slightly larger than the sum expended on Lectureships and Fellowships. Taking the ten-year totals (1974–83) of all grants, however, the picture is very different: somewhat over £16 million were expended on Lectureships and Fellowships while other grants (that is, the total of 'selected subjects' and '*ad hoc*' grants) was over £72 million. A more refined computation might enlarge the former group somewhat and diminish the latter, but (that being said) it is clear that among the grants under £45,000 the great preponderance were given in aid of research directly, and relatively few for personal support. To complete the picture of the ten-year totals it should be added that inflation (making supplementation of earlier awards necessary if their purchasing-power were to be maintained) cost the Trustees about £13¾ million over the decade, while overseas awards and commitments cost nearly six million pounds. Thus the grand total of grants in aid of medical research for the ten years was £107.8 million, to which should be added just over £12 million devoted to Museums and Libraries (chiefly, the Wellcome Institute for the History of Medicine).

If we ask why, let us say, £2 million were spent in large grants for research bearing on Mental Health, and only one-quarter of that sum on Toxicology, with but one-tenth of *that* again on Ophthalmology, the answer is to be found in a combination of policy and circumstance. The Trustees would certainly assign a higher priority to Mental Health than to Toxicology without necessarily placing Ophthalmology lower still. But circumstances – the pattern of research in medical science, the structure and direction of its institutions – also determine expenditure: the Trustees would be pleased to devote larger sums to certain branches of medical science, if sufficiently meritorious proposals came to them in greater quantity. The fact is that those fields of research that receive smaller sums year by year do so in part because the small numbers engaged in them are unable to absorb more financial fertiliser effectively, a fact that the Trustees must necessarily consider in making their awards or proposing topics for competitive awards.

Similar considerations apply to the institutional distribution of grants. Analysis of a relatively long period (1970–84) covering *all* grants shows the following table of descending magnitudes of total sums received:

Grant totals, 1970–84

	£
Oxford University	6,633,000
London School of Hygiene and Tropical Medicine	4,368,000
Cambridge University	4,056,000
Royal Postgraduate Medical School	3,883,000
University College London and U.C.L. Medical School	3,576,000
Glasgow University	3,026,000
St Mary's Hospital Medical School	2,962,000
Edinburgh University	2,874,000
Bristol University	2,450,000
Newcastle University	2,390,000

In this list, the ratio between the awards made to institutions in London and those in the rest of Britain is as two to three, but the ratio would shift nearer to equality if all grants made were considered, because of the very considerable sums under £2 million awarded to London institutions not enumerated above. Inevitably London, together with four of the ancient universities of Britain, absorbs a very large share of the Trustees' generosity. Again, it is a truism that those institutions that are best equipped by their ethos, facilities and equipment to undertake research are those most likely to receive awards from bodies like the Wellcome Trust which permit them to multiply their research effort. Where a subject receives research attention at few centres and in them, perhaps, only on a small scale it is difficult to bring about a rapid increase of activity. In Veterinary Medicine, for example, despite the Trust's efforts over many years and the strenuous efforts of the officer concerned, Dr Sinclair (p. 269), expenditure in 1983 was only £866,000, though it had passed the £1 million mark in 1978. In this instance the Trust was fighting against the effect of governmental policy which has tended to reduce the interest in research on animal medicine.

Analysis shows that there is a good deal of variation, year by year, in the success rate of *'ad hoc'* applications for grants: it has been as high as 74 per cent (1974–5) or as low as 40 per cent (1980–1). The trend seems to be slightly downward, and perhaps this is a natural consequence of the tendency for the number of grant applications to grow larger – a total of 577 *'ad hoc'* applications for the four years 1974–8 increasing to 935 for the four years 1978–82. The greater importance of the Trust on the medical scene would account for this increase. The number of applications that were successful increased rather less – from 411 in the first period to 626 in the second. The applications are those actually considered by the Trustees and their advisers; invariably some tentative inquiries about support are eliminated at an earlier stage. Inspection suggests that the success rate among applications for personal awards and specific awards advertised by the Trustees is much less, because these are of high value and arouse wide interest in the profession.

The Trustees' close attachment to the most 'open' end of the medical profession, where students are recruited and taught and where liaison with non-medical biological departments is close, is shown by the fact that during the last five years roughly £25 million – that is, one-third of all grant expenditure – was given by the Trustees to British medical schools, nearly equally divided between London and the non-metropolitan universities. By the same token, after subtracting the £7 million expended upon the history of medicine during the same period, £43 million were expended on medical and veterinary research carried out in the Trust's own Units, overseas (or for the benefit of foreign scientists coming to Britain), in non-medical departments of British universities, or in non-university institutions; that is, more than half the Trustees' total expenditure.

In a broad sense, the Trustees have continued to support the same kinds of investigation in recent years as during the early history of the Trust, but with a more vigorous effort to promote research in particular fields. Certain possible kinds of scientific work they have not supported – for obvious reasons they cannot concern themselves with drug development or testing. They have not financed work that seems to bear (at any rate very directly) on such diseases as cancer or muscular dystrophy because the public supports such work generously in other ways. They have not felt able to respond to general appeals, for the use of any sums thus given would be outside their control, except in the past in support of the Medical Research Council. Although the Trustees have endeavoured to encourage research by surgeons in various ways, they have not made particularly strong contributions to the development of prosthesis techniques, nor of transplant surgery (though they have invested heavily in immunology, a science of great relevance to organ transplantation). The Trustees have no record of any negative attitude to this recent development – but see above p. 98 – one might guess, perhaps, that they felt such surgery involved no new scientific principles, except as regards immunology. Research would have been considered 'applied' rather than 'fundamental'. Some further discussion of these issues will be found below, in Part II of this volume.

The Trust and the Medical Research Council

At this point in the narrative it may not be inappropriate to offer some comparison and contrast between the policies and activities of the Wellcome Trust and those of its greater neighbour across Marylebone Road, the Medical Research Council. At first sight contrasts may seem the more striking. The M.R.C. operates on a far larger scale than the Trust, its relative growth having been much more rapid during the post-war years (a tendency now reversed). By 1972, when the total expenditure of the Trust on medical research and the history of medicine since its inception amounted to some £23 million, the *annual* budget of the M.R.C. had attained very nearly the same figure. Again, the number of direct employees of the Council has always been vastly greater than that of the

Trust – as early as 1970 the Council employed a staff of nearly 4,000, over a quarter of them scientists. Hence the proportion of its budget that the Council devotes to the indirect support of university research is much less than the proportion so devoted by the Trust, since the Trust employs few research staff directly. Another point of difference – implicit in this contrast – is that the Trustees have created few independent research organisations, whereas the Council maintains the large National Institute for Medical Research and many Units which are attached to, but not integral parts of, universities. The M.R.C. has consistently, through its long history, followed the policy of encouraging the investigation of specific areas or problems by identifying a specific director of such research, and then permitting him to assemble an appropriate team to tackle the work, sometimes housed in its own building like a miniature, but impermanent, university department. Often, but by no means invariably, the life of such a Unit has been co-terminous with the service of its first head. In the years 1960–70 the Council created 43 new Units, of which 12 had a life of fewer than 15 years. The Trust has adopted this method of encouraging research only overseas, in the field of Tropical Medicine, and with less swift changes of direction.

Conversely, and particularly during the 25 years following World War II, the Trust has aided university research into biology and medicine by awards not generally made by the Medical Research Council – by grants for new buildings, new apparatus, and new Chairs, none of them tied to particular lines of research. More recently, too, by creating Fellowships, Lectureships and Senior Lectureships outside the established academic hierarchy, yet related to it, the Trustees have sought to provide more research time and greater resources for university staff (by taking off the perennially increasing pressures of teaching and clinical practice) in ways different from the traditional research-project support provided by the M.R.C.

What the Trust has never done (except, perhaps, in some grants made in the past to the M.R.C. itself) is to make 'block' grants to swell the budget of research institutes, thus supporting worthy purposes without, however, possessing effective means of direction and control. As is evident from Sir A. Landsborough Thomson's history of the Council, it has through the years felt it necessary to make such allocations to various institutions while endeavouring always not to forget its own ultimate responsibility to Parliament. The historical development of the Trust, its smaller scale, and its independence have enabled the Trustees to avoid any onus of this kind.

Despite such contrasts, the Trust and the Council have many long associations and deep likenesses. From Dr Green onwards, the Council has supplied senior officers to the Trust's headquarters. Most of the Scientific Trustees have served as members of the Medical Research Council. Relations between the two bodies are close. In terms of general policy there is virtually no difference betwen them, so far as human medicine is concerned (the M.R.C. has no responsibility for veterinary medicine). In its *Report* for 1960–1 the Council redefined its function as follows:

> to watch over the whole fields of medical and related biological research so as to foresee, to the best of their ability, the needs and opportunities [for future research]; to give support to any promising research in these fields irrespective of the agent concerned; to work in partnership with the universities and professions on the one hand, and the various departments of Government on the other, so that new knowledge may be made available as the need arises. It is according to this concept that we, and our predecessors, have devised our organisation and formulated our principles of working.[1]

If one excepts the clause about 'the various departments of Government' the views here expressed, which are indeed very general, are equally applicable to the policies of the Trust, especially since about 1970.

Certain formal differences of aim remain, nevertheless. The Trust has responsibilities for veterinary medicine, for the history of medicine and museums, and perhaps one should add for pharmacology, which the Medical Research Council does not share. It is also – in proportion to its size – more deeply committed to Tropical Medicine: in general, the Trustees are more free to act as they think fit within the Commonwealth and the international community than is the M.R.C. In such ways as these it has always been natural for the Trustees to act independently without looking over their shoulders at the national organisation. Where the Trust and the Medical Research Council seem to be aiming at the same objectives, however, the distinct character of the former emerged more slowly, especially in the days when the Trustees followed an 'opportunistic' policy and made little claim positively to stimulate, rather than passively to assist, medical research. At times, indeed, the view that the most suitable role for the Trust is to serve as a reinforcement to the national research programme has commended itself to the Trustees. On the supposition that the only possible weakness in the M.R.C. is shortage

Fig. 40. A nineteenth century pharmaceutical laboratory – one of the life-sized reconstructions using original materials, in the Wellcome Gallery of the Science Museum.
Courtesy of the Science Museum

Fig. 41. Also in the Science Museum – cases displaying objects associated with the First World War.
Courtesy of the Science Museum

of funds, then to place more at its disposal seems an ideal policy, and it might be supposed that those projects for research that had just failed of M.R.C. support would be the most meritorious of Trust funding. A scientist disappointed in application to the State would have a private court of appeal. If the rationale of such a policy is obvious enough, so are the objections to it. Sir Henry Wellcome, by implication, intended his Trustees to follow independent initiatives, as he had himself; ideally, perhaps, to step in where the State was lacking not in funds but in vision. As a second line of defence on the national front, the Trustees could do good but thereby also deny themselves the possibility of taking an independent view of the course of medical research, of the responsibility of the medical researcher to society, and of the work of particular investigators and programmes.

In these respects the Trust has certainly increased in maturity in the second half of its history. With greater experience and larger resources at its disposal the Trust has developed a concept of its responsibilities as spacious as that of the Medical Research Council, but independent of it. It has tried to attain important research objectives which the Council, for whatever reason, has been unable to pursue, or to pursue with sufficient vigour. The Trust has, however, continued to avoid the major permanent commitments to particular institutes or research organisations of the kind necessarily undertaken by the Medical Research Council, the particular medical charities, and the state Research Councils in general. The element of bureaucracy in the Trust's activity, and the proportion of its expenditure devoted to internal administration, have inevitably increased as the Trustees have involved themselves more intimately in the medical–scientific life of this country (in particular) at the frontiers of research; even Sir Henry Dale could not single-handed manage the day-to-day business of the Trust in 1986. Inevitably, too, the Trustees have had to accept (like the M.R.C.) the necessity to finance research projects for longer periods than a maximum of three years, and to move towards underwriting a higher proportion of the careers of those whom they encourage to devote themselves to medical research. Although the capital potentially locked up in long-term actual or moral commitments of this kind is at present relatively small, and therefore the Trustees continue to enjoy, from year to year, the liberty to consider new policies and new prospects for fruitful research in the knowledge that the preponderant portion of their resources is manoeuvrable, there are signs that, as the Trust's contribution to the cost of medical research in this country grows larger, so the proportion of annual expenditure that is freely disposable will diminish.

At their policy meeting of May 1985 the Trustees agreed to institute a system of awards

> to develop a cadre of full-time research workers who will work individually or in groups within the university framework. Special attention will be given to fundamental research as well as to the careers of scientists in clinical departments. The central purpose of the Trust's overall programme will be to provide support on a long-term basis in both basic and clinical science, neglected problems of developing countries, and certain neglected subjects identified from time to time by the Trustees, and to encourage links between research workers in Britain and other parts of the world.

The obviously novel feature in this manifesto is the recognition of the need for *long-term* support for selected individuals – precisely what brought the many M.R.C. Units into existence. In implementation of this policy, the Trustees have voted £600,000 for a new initiative in Ophthalmology and Vision Research, £900,000 for six senior awards in basic biomedical science tenable for five years, and to make ten new appointments within the Senior Lectureship Scheme at a cost of £1,300,000.

History of medicine

Throughout the decade of the 1980s the structures already in being have continued to work effectively and without radical alterations. A major landmark was the completion in 1982 of the transfer (on loan) to the Science Museum of Sir Henry Wellcome's historical–medical collections, and of the disposal to other museums of the non-medical material. Some of this latter has proved to be of considerable artistic and archaeological importance, giving much satisfaction to the recipient bodies such as the Fitzwilliam Museum in Cambridge, University College, London, the Manchester Museum and many others. The sorting and classifying of these very miscellaneous materials, followed by the choice of appropriate Museums to receive them, was a difficult and time-consuming operation ably managed by Mr R. de Peyer and Miss Georgina Russell.

Meanwhile, the curatorial staff at the Science Museum directed by Dr Brian Bracegirdle had been able to arrange the second Wellcome Gallery at the Science Museum, opened by H.R.H. Princess Alexandra in December 1981. This displays a topically and chronologically arranged selection of instruments and other artefacts illustrating all aspects and epochs of medical history, and is therefore aimed at a more scholarly audience than was the first Gallery. There is now a large team working on these materials; formal cataloguing of them is substantially complete, and new accessions are being acquired at a very considerable rate, so that the Galleries will be able to move forward with the advance of medicine.

Since 1981 the Institute for the History of Medicine and its staff have been fully incorporated with the Trust and are administered by it. Its leadership in its field has been reinforced during the last few years in a variety of different ways; by the acquisition of the principal portions of existing Libraries, such as those of the Medical Society of London (previously deposited on loan)[2] and the British Medical Association, together with arrangements for the transfer of books from the Royal Society of Medicine; by the increase in number of both the library and the academic staff, more than compensating for retirements; by the activity of the former in arranging very valuable exhibitions and drawing attention in print to the historical importance of the Institute's materials, and of the latter in organising varied series of learned meetings in each year. Thus the range and number of people visiting the Institute has largely increased, and the publications issuing from it have emphasised its intellectual significance.

Dr Edwin Clarke resigned as Director of the Institute from 31 December 1979, having set its academic character. Since 1980 the leadership of the Institute has been closely associated with the Trust; for two years its Director, Dr P. O. Williams, served as Honorary Director of the Institute, in which post he was (from October 1983) succeeded by Sir William Paton, F.R.S., a Trustee. The body of Trustees is thus well apprised of Institute concerns; they continue, as before, to receive advice on historical matters from both their own Institute Committee and the History Advisory Panel.

In 1981 the Trustees appointed a Working Party consisting of Panel members joined by Professor M. J. S. Rudwick and Mr M. W. Hill, Director of the Science Reference Library of the British Library. The tasks set to this body were to frame a judgment of the standing of the Wellcome Institute in the world of scholarship, and to prepare a strategic plan for the guidance of the development of the Institute through the following years. Fifteen years had passed since the International Symposium of 1967 (p. 134) which had provided the basis for the Trustees' support of studies in the history of medicine during the interval, and they judged the time to be ripe for a review.

The Working Party's report, submitted in April 1982, was strongly positive. It had satisfied itself that the Library occupied an outstanding position in the esteem of scholars, and that the academic group had won a reputation attracting both scholars and students to the Institute. It recommended that the academic side of the Institute should be strengthened by the appointment of qualified specialists in Islamic and Modern (post-1850) medicine, and by that of a Curator of Western Manuscripts who should also be, if possible, a scholar in his own right in the renaissance period. All these posts have been filled, and an Assistant Curator of the Wellcome Photographic Collection has been added to the staff. These various young scholars represent a potentially major increase of the scholarly productivity of the Institute. The Working Party discerned some weak and over-costly features in the conduct of the Institute which it thought could be amended, and appropriate steps have since been taken. The final cessation of all Museum work has released funds which can now be applied to other purposes. However, one rationalisation of the Library's routine work, approved by the Working Party and the Trustees, certainly effects no financial savings in the short run: this was the adoption of an automated cataloguing system. After careful appraisal and much study by the Librarian and his staff, the Library has become a member of the O.C.L.C. Library Co-operative whose base is at Dublin, Ohio, in the U.S.A. This particular system for combining the cataloguing resources of libraries in such a way that electronic retrieval of bibliographic information is readily effected, promises to be of great academic utility and had already been adopted by a number of other academic libraries in this country.

The end of museum work at the Institute at last released space on Level 1 of the Wellcome Building so that a sizeable Lecture Room and Staff Room could be brought into existence, and space provided for historical exhibitions from the Library and the Iconographic Department in addition to that already available in the Library. Exhibitions of real value and learning have been mounted and rotated every few months, or mounted in connection with particular scholarly functions. It cannot quite yet be written, however, that the physical disposition of the Institute is definitely settled. In 1981, when it became apparent that the Directors of the Wellcome Foundation might wish to relocate their offices outside London, and dispose of the whole or greater part of the Wellcome Building, the Trustees acquired the freehold of the former Cambridge University Press building, Bentley House, directly across Euston Road, with a view to the Institute's occupation of it. Afterwards, however, it was agreed to transfer the ownership of the Wellcome Building from the Foundation to the Trust and the Institute will retain its present accommodation within it. Bentley House has become the seat of the newly-formed Wellcome Tropical Institute, incorporating the Museum of Medical Science. The Institute therefore is very unlikely to suffer in the future from the physical cramping that has so often restricted its activities in the past, and the advantages of its firm administrative incorporation into the body of the Trust are abundantly evident.

Despite new posts and activities, the cost to the Trustees of maintaining their Institute for the History of Medicine (including payments to the Foundation for accommodation and services) declined in 1982 and 1983 from a temporarily high level in 1981, and now somewhat exceeds £1½ million per annum. By comparison, the sum expended by the Trustees on *ad hoc* grants in the history of medicine – some of them tenable at University College London, the Institute, or the Units – has remained fairly steady at roughly £250,000 per annum. The Oxford and Cambridge University Units budget at about £150,000 jointly, although the heads of both have been taken on to the academic staff of the University. Inflation, new activities, and the increasing seniority of staff combine to cause costs to mount; the disproportionate sums required for certain services and for the purchase of new books are not the least factor.

On the academic side the two Units have proved extremely successful. Both are firmly embedded in the structure of the host university. At Cambridge, the Wellcome Unit for the History of Medicine is a constituent element in the Department of History and Philosophy of Science, and teaches candidates in both the Natural Sciences and the Medical Sciences Tripos. At Oxford, the Unit is academically linked with the History Faculty and also with Green College (an exclusively medical institution) and is wholly or partly responsible for instructing candidates sitting a variety of different papers; both Units have research students and the Cambridge Unit runs an M.Phil. course in the history of medicine. The Head of the Oxford Unit has undertaken a personal responsibility for the official history of the National Health Service. The University of Oxford has recently enlarged the accommodation provided by it for the Unit because of the expansion of its activities.

The distribution of *ad hoc* grants in history of medicine is naturally widespread, though there is a growing tendency for the recipients of such grants to be trained scholars or scientists who have developed a firm commitment to the history of medicine in an academic context. At a few university centres, however (notably the Universities of Edinburgh and Manchester, to which, more recently, Leeds, Newcastle-upon-Tyne, and Glasgow might be added), the Trustees without entering into long-term or very costly commitments have sought to encourage research and teaching in the history of medicine, where enthusiasm and leadership can be provided by an established scholar of distinction or a Department. Though the evolution of these initiatives are quite unstructured and in particular the insertion of study of the history of medicine into the fabric of teaching remains uncertain, it is obviously to be hoped that viable new foci of interest and information will be created.

The Museum of Medical Science

Over the years, as we have seen in this history, the collecting, scholarly and scientific interests of Sir Henry Wellcome, for whose continuation he provided in his Will, have tended to pass from the province of the Foundation to that of the Trust, not least for the reason that these are public and charitable interests, recognised as such by the legal authorities, which consort more naturally with the Trustees' other charitable concerns than they do with the fundamentally business character of the Foundation. The latest, and perhaps the last, of these transitions was

Fig. 42. The Wellcome Trust has supported the study of the history of medicine in Australia as well as in Britain. This reading-room, opened in 1967, is part of the Historical Museum and Library within the School of Medicine of the University of Melbourne; this project was assisted by a grant of £20,000 from the Trustees in 1964.

accomplished in 1983, when the Wellcome Museum of Medical Science was transferred from the Foundation to the Trust, with the willing concurrence of both parties, and renamed the Wellcome Tropical Institute Museum.

When Andrew Balfour returned from the Sudan in 1913 he established a 'graphic museum of tropical medicine and hygiene' in London as part of the Wellcome Bureau of Scientific Research. He had already undertaken exhibitions in Dresden and Ghent and the displays formed a nucleus for the Wellcome Museum of Tropical Medicine and Hygiene which was set up at 10 Henrietta Street (now Henrietta Place) in 1914.

Balfour and his staff continued to collect materials when they travelled overseas during the War and the Museum moved to Vere Street in 1919, being chiefly concerned with the causes, transmission and prevention of tropical disease. H. S. Daukes, who had shown outstanding ability for visual teaching at the Leeds School of Army Hygiene, was appointed Director and continued to develop and expand the collection for the next 27 years.

After more moves, the exhibition finally took its present place in the Euston Road building in 1932. It became a centre not only for tropical disease but for medicine in general. It was closed during the Second World War and dismantled during the bombing of London in 1941. It reopened in 1946; C. J. Hackett, who succeeded Daukes as Director, further developed the display techniques. Further refinement and expansion, to include developments in genetics, microbiology, immunology and molecular biology steadily took place under the succeeding Directors, R. Y. Dunlop, C. A. Bozman, A. J. Duggan and the attendances rose to some 17,000 a year in 1983.

It became traditional for the Museum to contribute to medical exhibitions in many parts of the world, modifying display techniques to suit various types of audience. Displays were provided for the Wembley Exhibition in 1924 and to exhibitions in Dunedin, Antwerp, Buenos Aires, Dresden, Paris and Chicago. After the War, contributions were provided for the Congresses of Tropical Medicine and Malaria in Lisbon and Rio de Janiero, and to many other exhibitions.

When Sir Henry Wellcome died in 1936 the Wellcome Foundation took the responsibility of maintaining the museum, being 'proud to support an activity which is of acknowledged importance to both academic learning and the welfare of tropical peoples' (Sir Michael Perrin in the Preface to 'The Wellcome Museum of Medical Science, 1914–1964'). Since the Museum became the responsibility of the Wellcome Trust in 1983 it has been incorporated within a new centre for tropical medicine in London, called the Wellcome Tropical Institute, for which the Trustees have approved an initial budget of £600,000 per annum. The Institute is directed by Dr. E. H. O. Parry, formerly Professor and Dean of the Medical School at the University of Science and Technology, Kumasi, Ghana. Its offices and extensive library – both historical and scientific – are situated conveniently opposite the Wellcome Building in Euston Road (see p. 20 above). The new historical library of tropical medicine has been generously aided by related institutions. The Trustees have nominated a Board of Management for their Tropical Institute including two of their own number (Dr Gordon Smith and Mr Gibbs) and two experts from the academic world, and also a Scientific Advisory Committee.

Distance teaching methods using film, video and slide-tape techniques are being introduced and there are plans for sending more permanent displays overseas so that the great resources of the collection can be shared by people in the tropics without the need of travelling to London.

The Senior Lectureships (by Dr Harold C. Edwards)

As already described (p. 182) this scheme was devised by the Trustees in response to the threat to the biological sciences from economies imposed on the universities. It was an idea novel to the Trust. The novelty lay in three features: the support would be to nourish a whole department, not only one of its members; to achieve this the lecturer would take a proper share of all departmental duties; the term of the funding would be much longer than for other grants in the Trust's calendar.

There have been six, separately announced, rounds of awards, spread evenly over as many years. The product, so far, is a total of 50 appointments. Six of these have been promoted out of the ranks, to senior posts within, or outside, their own university. A further one has been elevated to Readership in his own department. The present policy is to maintain the number at 45, posts being filled when they become vacant, in a manner yet to be decided.

The long-term future of the scheme will depend on two imponderables: its success and the continued need for it. The first will be difficult to measure in a more objective way than by watching the career of the subjects; their success as deemed by those outside the Trust. The need for it is unfortunately easier to forecast; financial constrain on the universities is likely to continue for a long time.

The kernel of the scheme in the future will presumably remain as it is now, a tripartite aim: to encourage individual research talent; to nourish particular work of likely benefit to human and animal health; to bring additional academic hands to all aspects of a department's duty. These objects, together reflect the need for the scheme, seen by the Trustees six years ago. However, the arithmetic of university finance will not be the only yardstick by which the continued need for the scheme will be measured. For instance, the depth of the government's responsibility towards medical research is relevant. Having set a scene to entice the 'private sector' to participate more, the government's will to reverse that trend is likely to be infirm. Previously, having supplied an icing for an institution's university cake, so to speak, the Trust by this scheme is supplying an ingredient. The search for so-called 'soft money' is said to be invigorating to a scientist, but the receipt of such alms should be a tonic to complement adequate self-sufficiency. The Senior Lectureship scheme is a possible additional means of diluting a government's duty, for they subsidise undergraduate education, albeit to a small amount. Thus if at present it constitutes a very thin edge, nevertheless its insertion into the Trustees' pattern of grant-giving may, in time, cause it to act as a wedge.

However, integral virtues of the awards might persuade the Trustees to continue with them for other reasons than as a life-line. The length of the support is such as to allow more scenes of the individual career drama to unfold. The guardianship over this longer time enables the Trustees to contribute to a more finished scientific product, so to speak, than is the case with other grants. The Lecturers form a growing and now mature body, with an identity satisfying to themselves and to the Trust, and create an image that might encourage young biological scientists to an academic career, at a time when the call is one of several, and less immediately beguiling than some. The scheme is attractively versatile. It is open to all the clinical disciplines as well as the sciences that form the foundations and the buttresses of medicine. Moreover, it is an ideal vehicle to carry men and women to bridge between those various parts, a much sought-after object of the Trustees and one difficult to achieve. The awards are amenable to changes in scientific emphasis and thrusts of discovery. It is hoped that they will in due time become recognised as one reliable road to a career in the biological sciences, one that the Trustees may be loath to close.

New Panels

As a consequence of the redeployment of their endowment noted below (p. 209) the Trustees hope to have considerably greater sums available for disbursement in the coming years. Accordingly, they plan various measures to make the manner and objectives of their support for medical scientific research better known, and to stimulate a wider demand for it. The success of these measures will, in turn, increase the load of processing of applications falling upon the Scientific Officers and the Trustees themselves. The Trustees therefore resolved in June 1985 to introduce new administrative procedures with respect to Basic and Clinical Sciences, which will not only ease the burden upon the Trustees in particular, but will have two further advantages: they will increase the homogeneity of the office system, and they will increase also the element of peer 'judgment' in deciding the fate of applications.

For many years, as we have seen, Advisory Panels have functioned in some branches of special interest to the Trust, and perhaps of special difficulty also: namely, the Panels for Mental Health, History of Medicine, Veterinary Medicine and Tropical Medicine with Infectious Diseases. The Panels have proved themselves to possess undoubtable professional value, and they have greatly reduced the burden of detailed evaluation falling upon the whole body of Trustees and especially the group of Scientific Trustees. The new arrangements extend the same procedure of advice and evaluation across the board. New Panels are to be established to consider grants in the basic and clinical sciences: the 'molecular sciences' (biochemistry, genetics, cell biology); the physiological sciences and pharmacology; and the clinical sciences. Each Panel will have a Trustee as Chairman and a Scientific Officer of the Trust as Secretary. The Panels will, it is envisaged, advise the whole body of Trustees on matters of general policy and scientific strategy besides evaluating grant proposals. The object of creating them is, above all, to enlarge the opportunities for medical research, and to fit these opportunities to the creative energy within the scientific profession. At the same time the Trustees will have greater leisure to consider the strategy of their support for medical research, and to consider its deeper problems in greater detail than at present.

The Trust and the Foundation

Relations between the Trust and the Foundation have for many years followed an amicable routine. The necessary business is transacted from time to time by the Trustees in their capacities as Shareholders of the Foundation. They have, in recent years, paid regular visits to the Foundation's manufacturing establishments at Dartford and elsewhere, and particularly to their research laboratories at Beckenham. The Directors of the Foundation in return visit the Trust offices and are given opportunities to see the nature of the research programmes and the qualities of the individuals that the Trustees are supporting. Both Lord Franks and Sir David Steel have visited establishments of the Wellcome Foundation overseas as have other Trustees, and officers of the Trust. The knowledge and facilities available to the Trustees from these foreign dependencies have often proved very valuable. When Sir Michael Perrin retired in 1971 he was succeeded by Mr A. A. Gray, who had been a Director of the Wellcome Foundation Limited since 1954 and Deputy Chairman since 1967. In turn, his place as Chairman of the Foundation was filled in 1977 by Mr A. J. Shepperd, who was trained in economics and had already acquired a considerable business experience before joining the Board of the Foundation in 1972. Mr Shepperd is still in office, having presided over the Centenary Celebrations of the Burroughs Wellcome Company in 1980. The Trustees and many others associated with the Trust were his guests at a Guildhall Banquet where H.R.H. Princess Alexandra was guest of honour. Another function of this celebratory year was a symposium describing the contributions to scientific research made by the Company.

The Trustees have, moreover, maintained their interest in the research programme of Burroughs Wellcome (USA) Inc. at Research Triangle Park in North Carolina, the Director and one or more Trustees usually combining an annual visit there with the business of the Burroughs Wellcome Fund (p. 85). On the research side of the Foundation, the award of the 1982 Nobel Prize for Medicine to Dr (now Sir) John Vane, its Director of Research, jointly with Swedish scientists, was a very great source of satisfaction to the Trustees.

The business side of the Foundation has prospered with the consequence that the dividends paid to the Trustees have increased, year by year, and correspondingly the grants made for research by the Trustees have become much larger, as their *Reports* have shown. Nevertheless, the Trustees had, by the mid-1980s, become increasingly conscious of the fact that they could not properly fulfil the same dual role that Sir Henry Wellcome had fulfilled in his lifetime. Through the years they had found it necessary to separate his philanthropic from his business interests, for instance by taking responsibility for his Museum and Library. The pursuit of philanthropy and the pursuit of business have very different motivations; to mix them is helpful to neither. In the business world the central motive must be financial profit from efficiency and productivity; in philanthropy any profit gained is in the intellectual or social sphere and upon a long-term, not to say speculative, basis. Wellcome's assignment of his historical collections, educational museums and fundamental research laboratories to a manufacturing business produced an impossible situation, which the Trustees have gradually sought to correct.

Conversely, it may be argued that the private ownership of an important company by the Trustees of a charity may lead to reduced business efficiency, because the pressure towards profitability may be less, and the normal shareholder interest is weakened.

Diversification and the Flotation

It had also long been a matter of concern to the Trustees that the Trust assets comprised almost totally a holding of shares in a single company.

During the 1970s the experience of the Nuffield Foundation (page 115) and the philosophy of the Trustee Investment Act 1961 ensured that the importance of diversification of investments was never far from the minds of the Trustees. In the 1980s the appointment of a new Chairman and of a new Trustee, each experienced in the world of business and finance (Sir David Steel and Mr Roger Gibbs) created an opportunity for further reconsideration of the nature of the Trust's investments. At the end of 1984 the Trustees unanimously agreed that the time had arrived when urgent consideration should be given to the ways and means of diversifying the Trust's assets.

After taking leading Counsel's opinion Sir David Steel and Dr Williams made an approach to the Chief Charity Commissioner. This met with a favourable response. The Trustees selected Robert Fleming & Co. Limited to act as financial advisers to the Trust and instructed the Trust's solicitors Cameron Markby (led by Russell Denoon Duncan) to deal with the legal aspects.

Following discussions with the Foundation, whose co-operation would be an important element in a successful exercise, proposals for sale of part of the Trust's holding were announced in May 1985 and, in July 1985, the Charity Commissioners' Scheme was sealed. The Scheme permitted the Trustees, with the consent of the Charity Commission, to dispose of part of its interest in the Foundation provided that the Trustees retained control.

In announcing the proposals Sir David Steel said:

> The Trustees have for some time been concerned about the wisdom of having all their eggs in one basket notwithstanding the excellence of that basket. They have taken professional advice and have now decided on this course of action. This will

> enable the Trust to diversify its investments and increase its aid to medical research at a time when funds are badly needed. At the same time the integrity and independence of The Foundation will be preserved and the close links between the Trusts and The Foundation will be maintained. Those who work in The Foundation have, over the generations, built a fine and substantial business of which they are rightly proud, and I am glad to say that it is the intention of the Trustees to retain control of this enterprise. The Trust's primary duty is to pursue its charitable objects but it is also mindful of the welfare of the Foundation's employees and of The Foundation's long-established traditions.

The flotation was planned for early 1986 and was to comprise an offer for sale by the Trustees to the public of just over twenty per cent of the share capital of the Foundation and in addition a direct issue to the public by the Foundation of a further five per cent of its share capital. The flotation involved a great deal of detailed technical work. The Trust was advised by Robert Fleming & Co. Limited and the brokers to the issue, Hoare Govett. The Foundation was advised by its merchant bankers S. G. Warburg & Co. Limited and Baring Brothers & Co. Limited as well as its brokers Rowe & Pitman and Cazenove & Co.

As part of the arrangements for the flotation a new holding company, Wellcome plc, was incorporated and it was the shares of this company that were listed on the Stock Exchange – the Wellcome Foundation Limited continuing to be the main operating company.

After a careful review by the financial advisers a price of 120 pence per share was fixed, valuing the Company at just over £1 billion, the offer for sale closing on 7th February 1986. The issue, the largest ever made by a private company in the United Kingdom, was exceptionally will received, applications exceeding the number of shares on offer by 18 times. More than 430,000 applications for shares were received, that number itself almost a record, totalling some £4.5 billion in value.

The proceeds of the sale payable to the Trust were of the order of £200 million and the Trust has been able to diversify its investments accordingly, under the management of four leading financial institutions. There were other advantages to the flotation. The proceeds of the issue by the Company amounted to some £50 million and the Company was able to introduce share schemes for the benefit of its employees as well as having available a certain amount of unissued share capital for the future development of its business.

The flotation could not have been successfully achieved without the willing help at all times of the Charity Commission and the co-operation both of the Company and of the professional advisers upon whom so much work devolved.

These events have been narrated in some detail not only because of their public interest and their special relevance to the medical profession in this country, but also because they stamp such singular significance on the conclusion of the first half century of the Trust's existence. The sum at the Trustees' disposal for university research will, it is expected, be approximately equal to that at the disposal of the Medical Research Council. Hence the Trust ends the first 50 years of its history on a very high note, with the prospect of enhanced income and therefore the opportunity to expand and to innovate in its endowment of medical research.

At the same time, space for the deployment of a variety of activities has been available as never before (above, p. 201). In addition to its purchase of the former Bentley House, the Trustees in February 1986 bought from the Foundation the Wellcome Building in Euston Road, surely the logical final step in the transfer of the non-commercial sections of the Foundation to the ownership of the Trust. The Company has for some time planned to transfer its Head Office from the Wellcome Building to a location outside London. This move should be accomplished by the late 1980s. For the first time, virtually, since the death of Sir Henry Wellcome it will now be possible to return his splendid building to the uses for which he designed it: the housing of his collections, scholarship, medical education and perhaps scientific research also. The Trust will embark upon its second half-century with a complete and distinct identity of its own, and enlarged to such a size that it will be a powerful force in the science and scholarship of medicine. Perhaps in 50 years' time another historian will chronicle the use made by present Trustees and their successors of the new powers for good that lie in their hands.

Part II

THE IMPACT OF THE WELLCOME TRUST ON MEDICAL SCIENCE

INTRODUCTION

The following chapters seek to present a somewhat fuller picture of the Trust's activity in various fields of medical research than has been provided in the former part of this history. Over 50 years, the Trustees have expended some £150 million on thousands of separate grants, listed in 15 biennial reports, most of them in aid of investigations of precise problems defined in technical terms.[1] The preponderance of these awards fall only in the loosest sense into the pigeon-holes of schemes, projects and programmes; to generalise about their common features would be as hazardous as to attempt to measure their overall success would be presumptuous. Remembering Thomas S. Kuhn's distinction between 'revolutionary' and 'normal' science – investigations of the latter class by definition far outnumbering the former – it is easy to see that financial support for an individual or group outstanding or fortunate enough to have achieved 'revolutionary' results may be readily identified and readily praised, whereas selection for merit-awards among the far more numerous investigators in the 'normal' class would be certainly capricious and perhaps impossible. The history of the Nobel laureates indicates plainly enough how difficult, not to say paradoxical, year-by-year identification of exceptional merit may be. How much more hopeless is the task of evaluating, after the event, the justice of awards made by the Wellcome Trustees to many thousands of applicants over many years. For the present writer at least, a discussion of whether it would have been preferable for the Trustees to adopt dentistry (say) as a 'neglected subject' in place of dermatology is certainly *ultra vires*.

Such a discussion would only have meaning if it were possible to show that dental research had suffered more damage through lack of finance, than dermatological research had acquired advantage from receiving it.

To prove such a negative proposition would require a delicate exercise in re-writing history as 'it might have been'. Similarly, if the Trustees' award to Professor Jones or Dr Robinson is to be criticised as founded on misplaced confidence, it has to be shown that *better* objects for the bestowal of their research charity were available to them, and passed over. For the mere *withholding* of grants that could be made is of no merit to the potential donor, nor of any advantage to science. It can rarely be argued that to impede a piece of research would be a positive good; more plausibly it can be argued that any encouragement of 'normal' scientific activity must, in the long run, be beneficial. The 'revolutionary' advances in science are little likely to occur with frequency if 'normal' science be reduced to a trickle. Up to a point, the greater the volume of 'normal' scientific activity going on in our universities and institutes, the stronger our hopes for 'revolutionary' discoveries. Most analysts of scientific progress agree that it is impossible to enjoy the pâté de foie gras without plenty of bread and butter.

Identifying the source of the pâté is in any case a lottery. The British development in molecular biology, a spectacular feature of the scientific progress of the last 30 years, owed much to the enthusiasm of such physical scientists as Bragg, Bernal and Randall, and the work was done in their laboratories. Are the biological scientists to be accused of imperception of a promising line? By no means: the work was supported by the M.R.C. (and the Wellcome Trust). But, as with horse-races, the winner's overwhelming merit is only evident when the prize has been won; until then, the usual aids to picking a winner (horse or scientist) such as lineage, stable and form are more likely to lead to favourites than to dark horses. In science, as in racing, the favourite does not always win. Moreover, the Trustees (like punters) have to make multivariable choices: especially, they have to choose a man (or woman), a project and a place. The finest, most creative results will follow only if all these three (at least) are right. It can only rather rarely happen that all three are so perfectly matched that a 'revolutionary' advance rather than good 'normal' science is the product. There is no way of predicting when this explosive combination will occur.

Large capital donations facilitating the ordinary life of science such as the endowment of new laboratories or of new Chairs are normally asked for by the recipient bodies and because expensive must be infrequent. The total capital now invested in scientific research in this country alone is so vast than an addition of £10 million to it would make little qualitative difference. Grants of far less magnitude injected into a limited field over a period of years, to promote problem-solving, may return more obviously beneficial results. When wishing to further work on particular problems of medicine, it is clear that research financiers such as the national Research Councils or the Wellcome Trust have either to identify recipients of support for themselves or, in a variety of possible ways, invite applications from would-be recipients. In practice the two processes may run together. In the last resort, it is the quality of these would-be recipients and of the research programmes for which they seek support that determines the importance of the work that is done in return for the support received.

Obviously, the extent to which the Wellcome Trust may be asked to finance promising investigations in major institutions depends on the reputation of the Trust within the medical–scientific community, the relations between its staff and active leaders in research, the nature of the proposed research and the ease (or otherwise) of winning support for it (the larger the problem, the more costly the means required to tackle it, the more likely the director of research is to seek support from more than one source, for example) and the efficiency and appropriateness of the staff in their dealings with the scientific community. To be of maximum utility, support for research must be offered in the right kind of way, decisions must be seen to be fair and just, and decisions must be speedy.

Since it is impossible for a Research Council or a foundation to be omniscient, such bodies can only function by appealing for the advice of appropriate teams of senior experts in each field: Advisory Panels. Rotation should ensure their representative character. Scientific research is a changing continuum: only those borne along in the stream of knowledge know the manner and direction of its flow, and only they can suggest how financial support of the right type at the right time may guide and hasten this flow. Like the Trustees, like the officers of the Trust also, Advisory Panels can both stimulate the search for innovation and assist it: stimulate by positive suggestion, assist by critical evaluation of the suggestions of others. The Trust's aim is that Advisory Panels should be reflections in miniature of sections of the scientific community as a whole and it may fairly be said, therefore, that if the Trustees have chosen their Panels well, the quality of the Panels is the quality of that section of the scientific community, and their decisions those that are likely to be approved by the community. The Trust, like other bodies fulfilling a cognate function, operates 'democratically' by the process of peer-judgment; if referees, assessors, Panel members, officers of the Trust and Trustees themselves are all appropriately chosen individuals, then the most that men can do to make fair and just grants to scientists has been done.

Whether the choice of a man or woman to serve at any level in the Trust's machinery of grant-making has been 'right' or not is an unanswerable question, for the reason already given that critical comparisons cannot be made. Nor, turning to tactical decisions or procedure, is it possible confidently to determine whether or not, over the years, the Trustees have supported research groups of the right size, or have defined their various offers of support to the scientific community (for example, research assistance, travel grants, Fellowships of various kinds, Lectureships) in the best terms. Should it have financed more professors, or alternatively more research students? There seems little profit in trying to answer such a question, since there is no way of testing the answer's accuracy. What the historian can say is that the Trustees have offered a great *variety* of support, indeed, they have always been willing to consider any plausible proposition. They have put their resources at the disposal of the academic community, spreading them in many ways over a very large number of individuals, for extremely varied ends, and in many institutions. On general principles it is difficult to fault this practice of spreading the jam pretty evenly, with local concentrations here and there as has seemed most useful from time to time. Focussing of greater effort on the attainment of a single or a very limited number of objectives, besides contravening Sir Henry Wellcome's intentions, would not necessarily or even probably have been of greater benefit to medicine.

In what follows, therefore, it must not be supposed that the mention of some personal names and of some research projects implies the lower ranking of others unmentioned. No man could 'mark' the fruitfulness and importance of awards on a scale of nought to ten. The object is rather to exemplify, selection being usually from among those grants to which the Trustees assigned large sums of money. The result is necessarily impressionistic, even anecdotal, for it has not seemed to those preparing this history that very minute statistical tables derived from the biennial *Reports* and the Trust's files would be of interest to readers or of value to future Trustees.

In fine, the significant conclusion is that the Trust from small beginnings and restricted fields of activity of a somewhat passive type has gone on to win the confidence of many segments of the medical scientific community, wherein it has formed numerous personal bonds of different kinds. Without such bonds the possession of knowledge and influence is impossible. The role played by the Wellcome Trust in furthering research is now very widely known, and the prestige of a Wellcome award has become a significant factor in the choice of the Trust by applicants for research support and programme development. Although the volume of business at the Trust offices is in some measure a response to the Trust's own efforts to make its potential as a grant-giving body better known, it is also a strong indication that its programmes and practices are approved by the scientific community. Like the Research Councils, the Trust does not seek to identify Nobel laureates of the future, but rather the professors and senior clinicians of the future, to hasten their development and advance their researches. The Trust has not gambled on the possibility that this or that award might lead to spectacular innovations. Nor has the Trust believed in the policy 'publish or perish', nor sought to measure its success by the sheer weight of resultant publications. The true evaluation of the success of such an organisation as the Wellcome Trust can only be by answering unquantifiable questions, such as: Has the Trust caused the health and vigour of the medical–scientific community (in Britain especially) to be more flourishing than, but for the Trust, it would have been?

11

THE TRUST AND THE TROPICS[1]

Introduction

Henry Wellcome's interest in the tropics probably began when, in 1879 as a 26-year-old employee of McKesson and Robbins, he travelled to Ecuador and Peru to explore the cinchona forests. He was a friend of Sir Henry Morton Stanley and other explorers of tropical Africa, for whom he made medicine chests. His visit, by Nile barge, to Khartoum (p. 11) after its recapture by Kitchener revealed to him the desperate need for the improvement of hygiene and the control of disease. He offered the Sudan Government a fully equipped and staffed research laboratory and the Wellcome Tropical Research Laboratories were opened in Khartoum in 1902. The director, Andrew Balfour, appointed by Wellcome himself, rapidly organised an efficient sanitary service and a productive research programme. In 1907 Wellcome provided a floating laboratory, the 'Culex', to carry research to the river settlements. Balfour was brought home in 1913 to head the Wellcome Bureau of Scientific Research, which Wellcome created to co-ordinate his institutions and laboratories, to carry out research in tropical medicine and to act as a source of information to doctors, visiting scientists, administrators and others concerned with tropical health.

The Bureau, together with the Wellcome Museum of Medical Science (which began life in Henrietta Street as the Wellcome Museum of Tropical Medicine and Hygiene) formed an integral part of the Wellcome Research Institution in Euston Road, built by Wellcome to house his collections and research interests and opened in 1932. When reorganisation took place after World War II, the Bureau and the Wellcome Chemical Research Laboratories were combined as the Wellcome Laboratories of Tropical Medicine and, with the Museum of Medical Science, were administered by the Wellcome Foundation.

Their founder's interest in the neglected diseases of man and his domesticated animals within the tropics has been maintained by the Trustees, among whom have been specialists in this field such as Sir John Boyd and Dr C. E. Gordon Smith. By one of their first actions, in giving support to the League of Nations and Mr Henry Foy (p. 41) the Trustees created, as it were, a model for other small, independent teams in the tropics, with clearly-defined research programmes, later established at Vellore in South India, Belém in Brazil, at Addis Ababa, and at Bangkok.

It is therefore not surprising that in drawing up lists of their research priorities the Trustees have always included tropical medicine along with pharmacology, veterinary medicine and the medical sciences. They accepted a particular responsibility for the former as early as 1943, according to a memoir written by Professor Elliott some years later, when (in discussions with the Nuffield Foundation on the demarcation of their fields of interest) the Wellcome Trustees agreed that 'Tropical Medicine would be the main department for clinical research' under their auspices. In this they hoped for the positive co-operation of the Colonial Office. At that time, the Trustees evidently thought fit to leave support of clinical research in Britain to the Medical Research Council and the Nuffield Foundation; new possibilities would open up at a later time, however.

The Trustees have also supported research in the British Schools of Tropical Medicine in London (where a Research Professorship of Clinical Tropical Medicine was endowed in 1945, p. 62) and in Liverpool. Joint programmes of work involving Units in the tropics and the Royal Postgraduate Medical School, or the London School of Hygiene and Tropical Medicine, have been financed. Later, a programme linking this School and the Department of Tropical Public Health at Harvard School of Public Health with workers in the field was set up by the Trustees – the 'London–Harvard Scheme'. These enterprises and others have required new laboratory buildings as well as extensions to existing scientific institutions in the tropics, and the provision of clinical wards for the investigations of patients; in Kenya a complete institute was created for the study of foot-and-mouth disease in African cattle, to be operated by the Kenyan Veterinary Department.

During the past quarter-century three major factors have influenced the support given by the Trust to tropical medicine. First, the acquisition of independence by countries of the old British Colonial Empire caused a reduction in opportunities for citizens of the United Kingdom to make careers in medicine in tropical countries. The newly independent nations have, quite properly, filled the posts left vacant by the Colonial regime with their own nationals and, although expatriate teachers and research workers are welcomed in many countries, permanent appointments for them have steadily decreased in numbers.

As a result, and especially perhaps between 1964 and 1966 in the time of transition from Lord Piercy to Lord Franks, it became clear to the Trustees that further work in the developing countries could hardly be embarked upon without a change in existing attitudes. The Trustees were not without contacts with their various medical scenes and needs; for example, in the autumn of 1965 they invited to meet them in London, at their expense, Professor Choksi of the Tata Trust in India, in order to discuss possibilities of co-operation. Obviously the old 'colonial' attitude to research on tropical medicine was out of date: the work must be done in the countries concerned, largely or wholly by their own citizens. (But correspondingly the work was the more essential because the former colonial powers were reducing their interest in the tropical field, while the developing countries lacked both means and expertise to take on the full burden unaided.) If the Trust intervened in these countries, it could only do so after careful scrutiny of the local needs and resources, and with some promise of continuity. It might be necessary, almost inescapable, to enter upon those long-term, indefinite commitments which some of the Trustees so much feared as destructive of flexibility; perhaps, as had been done in Nairobi, to create the Trust's own research institutions. (At this time, nearly four-fifths of each year's income – over £1½ million – was freely disposable and only one-fifth bespoken, chiefly in respect of the Museum and Library.) Obviously, too, though everyone expected the great preponderance of grants to continue to be spent in Britain, a serious effort in the developing countries would enforce some shift of balance.

That the situation merited such a change in the distribution of the Trustees' resources was suggested by the decline in input from other quarters, such as the developing tropical countries themselves, the British Ministry of Overseas Development and the Medical Research Council, a decline caused by changing political policies as well as economic pressures, enforcing economies.

A month-long tour which Dr Williams made early in 1964, extending from East Africa through India as far east as Sarawak and Singapore, was important for future policy and the increase of the Trustees' involvement in tropical medical research. In East Africa, especially at Nairobi and Makerere University, he found excellent centres of research, with great potential for development. Laboratories were in general well equipped and with plenty of scope for further workers, if these could be introduced.

The long-established team of Drs Foy and Kondi was highly productive, though the former was officially due to retire in 1965. As a result of the visit, Professor L. C. Beadle of Makerere was awarded a Wellcome Research Professorship in Zoology to enable him to complete and publish his studies on the disease-bearing fauna of the Ugandan swamps; Dr Williams had noted that in Africa medical scientists tended to be overloaded by teaching duties to the detriment of their research. Another problem was political instability, which tended to discourage long-term commitment by white scientists to research in black Africa.

Possibilities for co-operation with Indian scientists, especially via the Tata Institute in Bombay were also explored. The Trust had long supported clinical research at Vellore, near Madras (p. 235).

A visit to West Africa somewhat later was less encouraging, largely because of the damage done by inter-tribal feelings and consequential political uncertainties. For such reasons it was impossible to develop the full potentiality of such institutions as the University of Ibadan in Nigeria, to which the Trustees had supplied research equipment. One promising prospect was for joint research into the toxic and especially neuropathological effects of cyanide manifest among populations feeding chiefly on cassava (manioc), who were also likely to be sufferers from the malnutritional condition kwashiorkor, to the investigation of which the Trustees also gave support. A committee under the Chairmanship of Professor Thompson was set up in 1965 to co-odinate this work at several centres (in Jamaica, Ibadan, Lagos and London) with a grant of £15,000 spread over three years. Enough had been done to permit a Symposium on this subject to be held in 1969, which was attended by some 70 medical scientists. However, attention of the research workers later turned to the effects of the vitamin B_{12} deficiency associated with a cassava diet, a condition it proved possible to reproduce in baboons. This work was transferred to Nairobi, where it was finally closed down, after a satisfactory accumulation of results, in 1973.

Besides these studies of nutritional and metabolic disorders, continued over many years down to the present, the Trustees have developed important programmes in tropical parasitology and its medical implications. Here a major international role has been played by the Wellcome Parasitology Unit No. 1, stationed at Belém near the mouth of the Amazon in northern Brazil. Begun with a grant from the Trust of £43,000 to the London School of Hygiene and Tropical Medicine, in 1964, the Unit under Professor Lainson F.R.S. and his colleague of many years standing, ing, Dr J. J. Shaw, has in 20 years largely solved the mysteries of the transmission of leishmania parasites in the Amazonian region. (Named after Sir William Leishman, 1865–1926, the diverse species and strains of these protozoa cause a very varied and sometimes mortal range of disease manifestations in man.) A parallel research was carried out by Doctor R. S. Bray at the Haile Selassie I University in Addis Ababa (where a species of hyrax – Abyssinian rock-cony – was incriminated as the animal host) while linked programmes of immunological investigation were carried out in London and Lausanne. Further, the response of the parasites to chemotherapeutic agents was investigated by Professor W. Peters at the School of Tropical Medicine in Liverpool. Thus, by 1970, the Trust was engaged in a considerable programme of research, wide-ranging as to topic and as to geography, all related to these protozoal parasites.

The Trustees have approved a great number of other grants contributing to the study of leishmaniasis and other tropical diseases. The availability at Nairobi of baboons as experimental animals after the cessation of nutritional studies in 1973 encouraged the beginning there of the investigation of the immunology of schistosomiasis, a group of diseases caused by trematodes ('blood flukes'), occurring in eastern Asia, the Caribbean and South America as well as in Africa. This project was proposed by Professor V. Houba with the support of the World Health Organization, whose interest in the medical problems of the developing countries began to increase considerably about this time. In 1975 it was to establish, in collaboration with the World Bank and the United Nations Development Programme, its Special Programme for Research and Training in Tropical Diseases, in order to attract scientists from many disciplines in the developed world to study the problems of disease in the tropics, to train citizens of tropical countries in scientific expertise and to strengthen research institutions in developing countries. This in turn had considerable impact on the activities of the Trust which has made grants to assist the W.H.O. programme.

The Trustees have naturally drawn heavily on the scientific knowledge and experience of experts in tropical medicine. In February 1966 there was a useful dinner-discussion on the Trustees' policy options in this field with Sir Harold Himsworth of the M.R.C., Professor Brian Maegraith of the School of Tropical Medicine at Liverpool, and Professor E. T. C. Spooner, then head of the similar London School.

During March 1971 the Trust organised in conjunction with the Royal Society of Tropical Medicine and Hygiene, at Ditchley Park in Oxfordshire, a conference on 'Medical Education, Research and Medical Care in Developing Countries' at which representatives of donor agencies in the developed countries met with those sent by the health service and medical research establishments of the tropics, together with the heads of the London and Liverpool Schools and other British experts, to define the best and most acceptable ways of providing effective aid to the tropical countries. The published report notes that the annual British contribution towards the solution of their medical problems exceeded £1½ million, and contains the following reference to the Trust's intervention at that time:

> The Wellcome Trust endeavours to identify medical and veterinary problems on which research is needed, but which have not so far been adequately supported by Government funds. It has a special role as an initiator of research work and for this reason maintains a large proportion of its funds free from long-term commitment. During the past 10 years the Trust has contributed more than £2m towards research on tropical diseases of man and domestic animals. At present, up to £0.5m will be available annually for research in tropical medicine. The Wellcome Trust has recently introduced the London–Harvard scheme to enable young research workers, based on the London School of Hygiene and Tropical Medicine and the Harvard School of Public Health, to work in the tropics. It also supports projects in E. Africa, the Sudan, Brazil, Ethiopia, India and elsewhere.[2]

Further consideration was given to the problem of assisting medical research within the tropical countries at a meeting held jointly by the Trust and the Rockefeller Foundation at their Conference Centre in Bellagio, Italy, in October 1974, this time in the light of the known commitment of the W.H.O. to this field. (Dr Williams was a member of the W.H.O. planning group.) The Bellagio meeting re-affirmed the obligation and the necessity of the developed countries making continued efforts to reinforce the scientific communities of the Third World, using W.H.O. facilities, and for collaboration between Europe and North America in the task. The Trustees' *Tenth Report*, after summarising these events, restates the Trustees' policy 'to continue to support scientists of the highest quality, no matter what their nationality, to work on topics of importance and to encourage integration of the activities of the centres in the developed world and between these centres and those in the tropics'.

The useful link between the Trust and the Rockefeller Foundation has continued since 1974.

In October 1976 the Trustees created a Tropical Medicine Advisory Panel, with Dr C. E. Gordon Smith as its Chairman,[3] to assist with the evaluation of applications for grants and special Tropical Training Fellowships were introduced to give scientists who had already demonstrated their potential, opportunities to develop their skills. In 1977 Competitive Awards were advertised for which applications were invited for research programmes within selected, specified areas of investigation in which progress was badly needed (p. 176). Further, in the summer of the following year, posts were advertised for Lecturers and Senior Lecturers in British Universities, who would spend most of their research time overseas, studying disease as it affects people of various ethnic groups and nutritional states in different environments.

For the year 1980–1 £2.3 million (11 per cent of expenditure) was allocated by the Trustees to research in tropical medicine. In the previous year Dr Bridget M. Ogilvie had been appointed (at first, half-time) to take charge of the Trust's programme in this field, Dr B. E. C. Hopwood having resigned in April 1978 in order to undertake advisory work for the Commonwealth Secretariat and other bodies, after nine years' service with the Trust. Dr Ogilvie, whose scientific interests are indicated by her co-editorship of the Journal *Parasite Immunology*, was born and took her first degree in Australia before moving to Cambridge. During the first two years of her association with the Trust Dr Ogilvie was on secondment from the Medical Research Council's Institute for Medical Research, whose research staff she had joined in 1963, initially with a Wellcome Animal Health Trust Research Fellowship.

Before this, at their policy meeting in May 1977, the Trustees had agreed in principle to fund a third research unit, in the East (in addition, that is, to those already existing at Belém and at Vellore in India, p. 235). A decision was postponed until after a tour of exploration made by Drs Gordon Smith and Williams; an agreement of understanding for such a unit at the Mahidol University, Bangkok, was signed in March 1979.

Transport on the Gambia River and in Uganda

A benefaction, which would have appealed strongly to Sir Henry Wellcome himself, derived from an appeal directed to the Trustees by a Secretary of the Medical Research Council, Sir Landsborough Thomson, in August 1956. The Council at this time maintained research laboratories

Fig. 43. A current postage-stamp from The Gambia depicting the *Lady Dale*.

at Fajara, nine miles from Bathurst (now Banjul), the principal port in still-colonial Gambia. However, much important work was also done in a subsidiary laboratory at Keneba, about 100 miles up-river from Fajara, to which place travel by road was both difficult and insecure. Thomson asked whether the Trustees could provide a launch for the use of his people in Gambia, under the direction of Dr I. A. McGregor, as the river passage was easy but cadging lifts from others neither convenient nor dignified. Further, if the launch were big enough, it would be possible for a couple of scientists to live aboard it and do simple scientific laboratory work at a place called Bansang, 200 miles further up the river beyond Keneba, where there was a 'hospital centre, with interesting clinical material'. As it was evidently thought impossible for Europeans to live and work at this remote 'hospital', even briefly, it must have been indeed primitive!

The M.R.C. people in Gambia had originally asked only for some £5,000 to buy a locally-built boat, about 40 ft long by 13 ft beam, with space to accommodate two Europeans and six Africans. What they actually received after consultation between Dale and the Trustees in London was far grander – a vessel 60 ft long, built at Brightlingsea in Essex of African mahogany sheeted with copper and fitted with twin diesel engines. This handsome and well-fitted craft, launched with the name *Lady Dale* in September 1958, cost somewhat under £26,000 (including transport to the Gambia), and was received with acclamation there. She put in nearly 15 years valuable service for the M.R.C. until she was sold to the United Nations for £5,000 in May 1973.

A little later, the Trustees gave to Professor Cecil Luck at the Makerere

Medical College, Kampala, Uganda, a truck fitted out as a mobile laboratory for use in making physiological studies of the larger African animals. It was also used for anaesthetising wild animals and transporting them to suitable reservations. The grant of £12,500 also included the building of animal houses at Kampala, one of them a pool for a hippopotamus. The truck was appropriately (if ambiguously) named 'Sir Henry' and its attendant Land-Rover 'Henrietta'.

Salonika and Nairobi

The investigations of malaria, blackwater fever and nutritional anaemias in Salonika by Henry Foy and Athena Kondi were suddenly terminated by the German invasion of 1941 (p. 42). After their flight the two scientists placed themselves and the equipment they had been able to salvage at the disposal of G.H.Q. Middle East in Cairo who, after attaching them briefly to the British Military Mission in Turkey, despatched them to Johannesburg and the South African Institute for Medical Research, where they worked profitably, still on the Trustees' books, for a number of years.

The approaching victorious end to the war encouraged Foy and Kondi to return to Cairo in 1944, and then under the auspices of the United Nations Reconstruction Relief Administration to Salonika. For a variety of reasons – political unrest, the wartime damage to the laboratory, population movement and changes in the incidence of malaria in Greece – the Thessaloniki laboratory did not settle down to work effectively as it had before the war. The *First Report* of the Trustees states that Foy and Kondi 'identified the sickle-cell trait and sickle-cell anaemia for the first time in Greece' during these years, without listing a publication on this topic. Certainly during the three post-war years they spent much time in England, in part to modernise their laboratory technique. In 1949, finally, Foy decided not to return to Salonika for the time being, but to go back to Johannesburg. *En route* from London he paused at Mombasa and made a trip inland to Nairobi, where he was warmly pressed to prosecute his researches and offered every facility, including baboons and other experimental animals. Nairobi was, he wrote to Dale, 'just the place we needed':

> Malaria is abundant here . . .. There is a wide spread sickle-cell trait that varies in degree . . . abundance of material for all kinds of work . . . we can do better here. . . .

So began the long association of the Wellcome Trust with research in

Kenya. The Trustees acceded to Foy's wish, and soon a stream of papers on sickle-cell and megaloblastic anaemias began to appear. The Trustees' Minutes record, in a quite exceptional way, that on the 19 February 1951 'Sir Henry Dale reported that Mr Henry Foy had made a very important discovery about the treatment of megaloblastic anaemias, including pregnancy anaemia, with penicillin . . .'

Foy was reluctant to accept the idea that he would never again settle down to work in Salonika, and that most of the rest of his working life would be spent among Africans. He spoke of his stay in Nairobi as 'temporary', and indeed he (with Dr Kondi) made a long excursion by invitation into Assam, followed by other research trips to the Seychelles and Mauritius. For a while also he scouted the idea that malaria and blackwater fever were now almost unknown in Greece, writing (in 1950):

> we did not leave our laboratories [in Salonika] on account of the disappearance of malaria due to D.D.T. but on account of the chaos that was reigning in Northern Greece at the time, which prevented us from getting into the hospital of Salonika.

By 1953, however, after another brief visit to Greece, Foy conceded that it was pointless to go back to his work there: macrocytic anaemias had disappeared from Greece; meanwhile, the laboratories had been lent to an Inter-governmental Committee for European Migration of W.H.O. who handled Greek migrants there and incidentally caused some embarrassment to the Greek medical authorities.

Of the research into anaemia and other blood disorders carried out by Foy and Kondi the Trustees' *First Report*, no doubt from the pen of Sir Henry Dale, remarks 'the Trustees have every reason to be gratified by the importance and the distinction of the results which have accrued from this, the first medical research enterprise to which they agreed to give financial support in any form'; the *Report* then goes on to state that the Thessaloniki Laboratories had been a unique effort, and that

> the acceptance, in other instances, of similar direct responsibility on a long-term basis, for the staffing, equipment and working expenses of a research unit does not at present form part of their plans for the further allotment of their funds.

Times change, however, and the direct maintenance of laboratories was to be embarked upon again by the Trustees.

Throughout all this troubled period the understanding and support given to Foy by Sir Henry Dale were crucial. Despite his great press of

Fig. 44. Drs Foy and Kondi on a field trip in Kenya, *c.* 1960.

business in Britain and elsewhere Dale found time to write long letters of encouragement (and occasional reprimand) to Foy, and firmly backed Foy's modest requests for money to maintain his various enterprises:

> Such a policy of adjustment would obviously have been impossible without the unfailing courage, determination and resourcefulness with which Dr. Foy has faced all these unusual difficulties

wrote Dale in the Trustees' *First Report, 1937–56*. Foy had no doubts at all of the advantages of his Unit and the way it was run with remarkable flexibility, its members

> doing work on an individualistic basis with close and informal contact between workers in the field and London, the operation of which requires minimal administration and where activities were not hindered and handicapped by red tape. . . . Such an organisation is in sharp contrast to the vast impersonal machines that seem to be gaining control in almost every scientific field, and whose operation requires armies of clerks, large sums of money and in which the top-heavy administrative machinery results in a rigidity that is frustrating to the field worker and penalises him in favour of the administrator . . .

In 1961 an agreement was drawn up with the Kenya government

concerning the laboratory, and at Nairobi work was centred on the anaemias of children suffering from marasmus and kwashiorkor. Foy did not find his young patients easy to deal with.

In 1962 a joint study was made, based in London, Vellore, Singapore and Nairobi, of megaloblastic anaemias and sprue, a diarrhoeal condition common in Asia, but not in East Africa (see below).

From his excursion to the Seychelles – not then a tourist centre – Foy found that the main cause of anaemia there was iron deficiency exacerbated by the prevailing hookworm infection. This led him to attempt to infect various species of monkeys with hookworms, and stimulated his interest in baboons as subjects for the study of nutritional anaemia. With the help of a catching team sent out by the American South West Foundation, he established a laboratory colony of these animals that has remained as a focus of research in the unit until very recently. New quarters were built to accommodate 150 baboons, including a breeding nucleus.

Foy and Kondi retired in 1970 but received continuing grant support to finish their work for a further four years; Dr Foy is still working (1986)!

The Wellcome Trust Research Laboratory, Nairobi

This new name for the group directed by Dr Henry Foy was introduced during the early 1960s. His official retirement affected neither the Trustees' support for his work nor his own vigour. Nutritional disorders continued to be at the centre of the group's activity, especially in relation to kwashiorkor, marasmus and liver diseases. A particularity of technique was experimentation on a large colony of baboons in which, for example, the effects of diets free from riboflavin or pyridoxine were studied. Deficiency of riboflavin gave rise to biochemical and haematological changes similar to those of marasmus and kwashiorkor in African children on low protein diets.[4] Pyridoxine deficiency led to changes in liver histology and the excretion of α-fetoprotein and, with Dr T. Gillman of the Agricultural Research Council Institute of Animal Physiology, Babraham, the suggestion was made that the high incidence of primary liver carcinoma in Africans might be linked with the consumption of pyridoxine-deficient or aflatoxin-contaminated diets.

Upon Dr Foy's 'retirement' the overall supervision of the unit was entrusted to the Zoological Society of London. Nutritional studies were continued, with special reference to Vitamin B_{12} and folate deficiencies and the part played by the aerobic and anaerobic bacterial flora of the

Fig. 45. Dr Kondi working in the Wellcome library of the Medical Research Institute in Nairobi, *c.* 1960.

intestinal tract. Dr G. D. Gatenby Davies acted as local director and the research work was carried out by Drs R. Siddons, Z. H. M. Verjee and Mrs P. Uphill.

In the late 1960s, however, the Trustees decided because of the shortage of research workers in the tropical field to concentrate their efforts on Vellore and Belém, together with the London–Harvard Scheme (see below); thus they intended to close the laboratory in Nairobi in due time (*Ninth Report*, p. 79). The event was somewhat different. The baboon programme on nutrition at Nairobi and the connection with the Zoological Society were indeed terminated in 1973 but a new research into the immunology of schistosomiasis was begun, using the same experimental animals, at the suggestion of Professor V. Houba and with the encouragement of the World Health Organization at Geneva. Dr Houba, Director of the W.H.O. Research Centre in Immunology and also holder of a visiting appointment at Nairobi University, took charge of the work; Dr A. E. Butterworth was seconded from Cambridge to study immune responses while Dr R. F. Sturrock of the London School of Hygiene and Tropical Medicine went out to continue investigation of the parasitology of schistosomiasis. He established a breeding colony of snails and carried out experiments to induce protective immunity in baboons, e.g. by vaccination with irradiated cercariae. Dr Butterworth studied cellular immunity in infected baboons and his detailed, elegant work gave a new insight into the role of eosinophils in damaging invading schistosmulae in animals with circulating antibody to schistosomes. Dr Sturrock assumed direction of the Laboratory from the end of 1978, Dr Butterworth having gone to Harvard, while Dr B. Cottrell of the Middlesex Hospital Medical School came out to join the group.

None of these scientists wished to follow Dr Foy's example in making Kenya his home. On Sturrock's resignation in 1980, after several fruitful years of work, Dr B. E. C. Hopwood (p. 154) returned to the Trust's service as Programme Director in Nairobi. A new change of direction, more suitable to the needs of modern Kenya perhaps, was already taking place towards clinical research which was approved by the Trustees in March 1979 after a visit to Nairobi by Professor Peart, Professor Sidney Cohen and Dr Williams. With the concurrency of the Kenya Medical Research Institute in Nairobi (Professor M. Mugambi) and the Medical School of the University of Nairobi, gained during 1979–80, a project for the study of hypertension in rural and urban communities in Kenya and of cardiovascular and renal disease was worked out. It was affiliated with the Medical Unit at St Mary's Hospital, Paddington (Professor W. S. Peart and Dr C. Harold Edwards).

Professor Peart and Professor Mugambi were the Honorary Directors of this programme, with Dr N. R. Poulter of St Mary's in charge of the epidemiological part of the work, supported by Dr J. E. Sanderson, holder of a Trust Tropical Lectureship. Students from St Mary's regularly went to help with the blood pressure measurements. Schistosomiasis work still continued, partly maintained by other funds, and part of the Kenyan Clinical Research Centre was also housed in the Laboratory. The St Mary's scheme ended in 1985; later activities in Kenya are noted below (p. 258).

The history of the Nairobi unit from its beginnings in Salonika has been dealt with in some detail because the experience gained over the years enabled the Trustees to plan other activities in tropical countries. The principle that productive, cost-effective work can be carried out in a suitable host environment overseas by a small expert team with a good leader and a clear objective seldom fails. Experience also showed that such a team must have a 'home base' to which it can refer and return, and adequate financial backing and security (usually for at least five years) for a sensible programme of work to be planned and executed.

Fig. 46. The Foot-and-Mouth Disease Institute at Nairobi.

Foot-and-mouth disease in Kenya

Perhaps because of the known interest of the Trustees in East Africa, and the manufacturing activities of the Foundation, approaches were made to both Boards during the 1950s, for the provision of capital costs for the local manufacture of a vaccine against the foot-and-mouth disease in cattle – a vaccine not employed in British veterinary practice. After early negotiations the newest Trustee, Brigadier John Boyd (p. 75), paid a visit to Nairobi in company with Dr R. F. Montgomerie, Veterinary Research Officer in the Wellcome Foundation, during October and November 1956. The visitors were entertained in the highest style and there was clearly great enthusiasm for the project on the part of the Minister for Agriculture, Mr (now Sir Michael) Blundell, and the white farmers generally, whose cattle might be expected to receive protection. Particularly they examined the proposed sites for the Trustees had in mind the possibility of locating there in addition a Wellcome Research Laboratory for East Africa. The satisfactory reports from Kenya induced the Trustees to provide £80,000 of capital for the foot-and-mouth research station, under the direction of Mr J. W. Macaulay, whose running costs were to be wholly borne by the Kenya government. Later, a further £20,000 had to be provided for the construction of a special plant for the treatment of effluents and waste from the laboratory.

After the granting of Kenyan independence in 1963 the laboratory was, in effect, nationalised and so passed out of the Trustees' domain. Mr Macaulay took a post elsewhere.

The Wellcome Trust Research Unit, Vellore, South India

The involvement of the Trustees in medical work in South India, which has lasted to the present day, came about in a strange way. By 1952 it was clear that the course of politics in China precluded the continued activity of missionary-dominated western-style universities in that country, and that (in consequence) the Trustees grant formerly made to aid students of pharmacy at the West China Union University, Chengtu, could no longer be effective. In fact, a balance of £893 remained untransferred. Sir Henry Dale suggested to the committee in London concerned with medical missions in Asia that this sum be devoted to some other appropriate cause in that continent. The late Dr Clement C. Chesterman strongly commended to him the Christian Medical College at Vellore, not far from Madras, and affiliated to the University in that city. Of this college and the cognate institution at Ludhiana in northern India he wrote to Dale:

> These two institutions remain [after Independence] as permanent links between Western Medicine and India, and help to carry on the long tradition of the Indian Medical Service and British leadership in the medical service of the sub-continent.

The Trustees could not, of course, support the teaching programme of the Vellore College, but they accepted Dr Chesterman's proposal that the outstanding £893 be used to help finance a pilot study of the development of medical methods useful in remote and poor rural areas; notably, the medical men at Vellore wished to plan and test an elementary type of 'village hospital' utilising the simplest and cheapest equipment, in order to improve health care at a level and in a style that peasant communities could afford.

In 1956 Dr Chesterman, as Chairman of the 'Friends of Vellore' in Britain, again approached the Trustees for assistance in developing a research project there. After the opinion of Dr A. C. Frazer, Professor of Pharmacology at Birmingham University, had been obtained the Trustees awarded the 'Friends' £10,000 over five years in January 1957. This was to help finance a research unit to investigate tropical sprue, to be set up by two altruistic Australian doctors working in South India, Drs Selwyn Baker and I. A. Hansen: the sum was required for buildings, equipment, and the provision of special diets for patients. The very modest salaries of the investigators were paid by the Vellore Hospital, maintained by the Christian College. Tropical sprue is an enigmatic diarrhoeal disease, typified by the defective absorption of food, especially fat, in the intestine; it can rise to epidemic proportions and is frequently fatal to young children. At this time it was not clear whether the symptoms were caused by an enzyme defect, infection, or the characteristics of the diet. The intention at Vellore was to institute a rigorously scientific examination of the metabolism of sprue sufferers.

When this grant ran out, rather before time, the Trustees sought the advice of Henry Foy, who visited Vellore and wrote enthusiastically of what he found there (January 1961). Dr Selwyn Baker he judged 'keen, industrious, and wrapped up in his work'. Vellore was 'generally regarded as one of the best [medical] schools in India, [drawing] students from all over the Far East. Its hospital is also one of the best in India and patients go to it from all parts of India'. There was also an American-supported research group there working on marasmus and kwashiorkor. Baker's research unit met with Mr Foy's full approval. There were excellent and well equipped laboratories, a good animal house, 'very good technical facilities for keeping his electronic equipment in order, very important in the tropics . . .', the wards for some dozen patients were under the charge of a clinician and nursing staff. 'The whole unit forms a first class research centre, the value of which could be greatly increased by visiting workers to share the material and investigate special problems. [All in all,] the whole place with its 900 or so bed hospital, well-equipped laboratories and staff, etc. forms an ideal centre for all kinds of tropical research.'

At about the same time, Dr Baker wrote to the Trust about the return of Dr Hansen to Australia through ill-health, and the need for increased finance due to the loss of other support; he asked for £5,000 per annum, the Trustees thus to assume the whole cost of the Sprue unit. They found that Dr Farrer-Brown of the Nuffield Foundation thought highly of the work at Vellore, as did Dr David Mollin of the Royal Postgraduate Medical School (with whom Dr Baker had been trained), later Professor of Haematology at St Bartholomew's Hospital Medical College, who was initiating with Baker a joint study of vitamin B_{12} and folic acid deficiency in sprue sufferers.

The Trustees made the requested grant of £25,000 for five years,

Fig. 47. (*top*) A laboratory in the Sprue Research Institute at Vellore, S. India, *c*. 1957; (*below*) Dr Minnie Mathan demonstrates the electron microscope given to the Institute by the Trustees in 1979.

together with £15,000 for the purchase of X-ray equipment. Shortly after the abortive offer by the Trustees of a Fellowship to Dr K. N. Jeejeebhoy to work at Vellore (1962), Dr Baker recruited Dr A. N. Radhakrishnan as Professor of Biochemistry for whom a good deal of new equipment and material was provided. Others who worked there at this time were Professor Prema Bhat (Microbiology) and Dr Ernie Boulter (Virology), who was supported by the Trust for two years.

At the meeting of July 1961 when the Trustees voted a more generous support for the sprue work at Vellore, they also agreed to finance a collaborative study of tropical metabolic disorders to be carried out at four centres – besides Vellore and Nairobi (by Foy and Kondi), these were Singapore (where investigations were being made by physicians of the Royal Army Medical Corps) and the Royal Postgraduate Medical School at Hammersmith. At the last-named School repatriated patients affected by such disorders were seen; Dr Mollin (with whom Baker had worked) first suggested the value of such a wide study, in which the different manifestations of 'sprue' might be distinguished and defined. Six meetings of the participants took place over the years, each centre working independently meanwhile. The Trust staff was active in co-ordinating and financing the programme, and in publishing its results, ultimately including an investigation of sprue in Haiti (by Dr F. A. Klipstein). In the course of his long tour of the East, made early in 1964, Dr Williams visited Vellore and attended a meeting at Singapore of Dr Selwyn Baker, Mr Henry Foy, and the Army doctors there ('outstandingly able systematic workers who have done a beautiful job'). He advised the Trustees in his report that when they saw the final publication of all the excellent work done at these various centres, they would 'have no doubt that this has been one of their most successful positive efforts at sponsoring medical research'. The book finally appeared in 1972.[5]

Following Dr Williams' recommendation and that of Sir John McMichael and Professor Thompson, who visited Vellore in 1965, the Sprue Unit was again financed (from 1966) by a grant of £16,000 per annum for seven years, thus giving its work a more permanent footing. The Unit was also affiliated to the World Health Organization. A further grant of £75,500 was made in 1972 (including £29,900 for equipment) and since then the Trust has continued to support the work at Vellore down to the present day. Dr Baker continued to direct the Unit until his resignation in 1976, when he was succeeded by Dr V. I. Mathan, who originally joined the Unit as its clinician and is a graduate of Vellore.[6] He is now Professor of Gastroenterology at Vellore. Since 1980, when the Unit was reorganised, the direction has been shared by his wife, Professor M. Mathan of the Pathology Department. The contributions of the Sprue Unit to our knowledge of the aetiology of this disease, and of the associated disorders of intestinal absorption and haematology, have had an international impact. Dr Selwyn Baker's influence as a teacher and counsellor have played an important part in the development of the Vellore medical school as an internationally recognised centre of excellence in India.

Today, the Unit is staffed by a team of young Indian doctors and scientists who are studying sprue from epidemiological, biochemical, microbiological, virological and pathological aspects, in association with the M.R.C. Clinical Research Centre, Northwick Park.

The clauses of sprue are still uncertain and are probably multiple. It seems possible that the syndrome is initiated by a vector-borne virus or viruses that cause fever before becoming localised in the cells of the jejunal crypts, where they cause lasting damage.

The Wellcome Parasitology Unit No. 1, Belém, Para, Brazil (1965 onwards)

In the spring of 1964 Dr Williams was approached by two members of the staff of the Department of Parasitology in the London School of Hygiene and Tropical Medicine, seeking support for a research project of considerable scientific interest and of great potential benefit to the lives of people in tropical countries. Dr Ralph Lainson had recently spent three years in British Honduras directing an epidemiological study of the parasite *Leishmania mexicana*; Dr J. J. Shaw had studied with the Trustees' support the epidemiology of *Endotrypanum* in Panama. They now wished to investigate jointly the transmission of cutaneous leishmaniasis (*espundia*) in Brazil.

Various disease manifestations arise in humans from infection by species of the small intracellular parasite, *Leishmania*. They are in the main – as the Belém work was to prove – zoonoses, that is, the main reservoirs of infection are in wild or domestic animals; in the New World they are rural diseases, afflicting those who penetrate into the forests, especially when the population of sand-fly vectors becomes large in relation to the available animal hosts.

Kala-azar is a well-known visceral condition found in the New World and the old, and in Africa, if untreated, its mortality rate is high and it kills fairly rapidly. It is transmitted to man by the bite of sand-flies of the genus

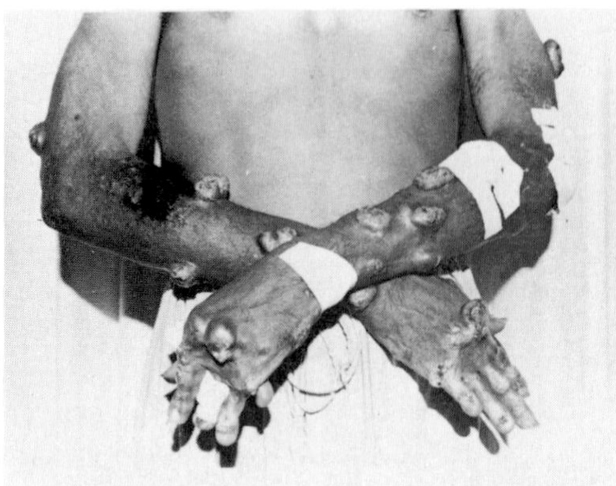
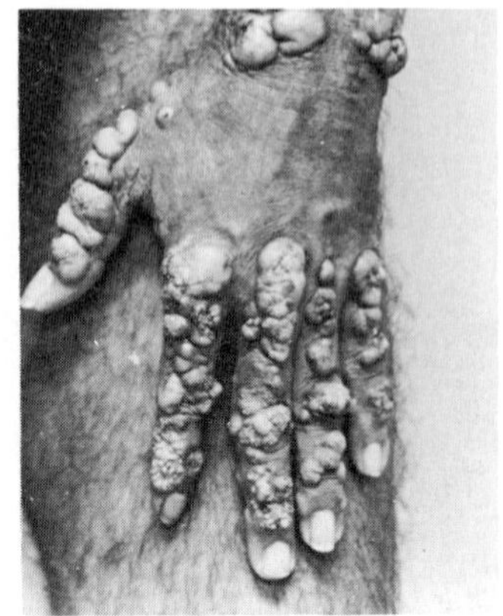

Fig. 48. Cutaneous leishmaniasis affecting the hands.

Phlebotomus, and the reservoir of infection is known to include wild dogs, foxes and rodents as well as man himself. Mucocutaneous leishmaniasis is a disease of Central and South America, whose precise vectors and reservoirs of infection were, in 1964, still unknown, though sand-flies and forest rodents were suspect. Leishmaniasis is far from uncommon in the afforested regions of Brazil, and produces effects varying from single ulceration to widespread lesions and destruction of the nasal cartilage (see figure 48). The sufferers, often condemned to many years of physical and mental agony, are usually people in remote country districts.

Drs Lainson and Shaw proposed to take as their base the laboratories of the Instituto Evandro Chagas at Belém in the Brazilian state of Para, whence they would embark on field trips. (Years later, the British Council scientific representative in Brazil reported that, if consulted, he would have argued against this choice.) Their object would be to discover which species of *Phlebotomus* were infected with leishmania parasites, and to trace further those species of animals which, in the area of endemic disease, served as hosts for the parasites. The transmission of infection by flies from animal to animal would also be studied in the laboratory. The two scientists estimated the cost of this study, for three years, at a little over £43,000.

The Trustees were immediately attracted to this proposal – though Sir John Boyd at least was aware of the local difficulties – and a grant of the sum requested was authorised in July 1964, increased (as other things had to be allowed for) by £4,500 in the following February. The business of getting even a small scientific unit off the ground proved (as Dr Williams noted) 'quite a complicated exercise'. However, the head of the Instituto

Fig. 49. View of the laboratories of the Instituto Evandro Chagas at Belém, Brazil, in 1965.

Evandro Chagas, Dr Orlando Costa, agreed to take them in, the Professor of Tropical Medicine at the University of Brazil, Professor Rodrigues da Silva, signified approval and so (though informally) did the Brazilian Ministry of Health. Such goodwill could not altogether compensate for the inadequacy of transport systems and other difficulties, inflation not least, causing some prices to double annually. The World Health Organization generously undertook to despatch equipment and supplies to Belém, while the London School agreed to continue to manage the salaries of the two scientists, who were still nominally under the direction of its Professor of Parasitology, Professor P. C. C. Garnham. None of this worked well in the first few years, for the personal allowances due to Drs Lainson and Shaw were not clearly defined nor accurately computed, money drafts often failed to get through in time, and supplies of glassware and chemicals suffered even more. Lainson made a first exploratory visit to Belém in July 1965, and both scientists were there with their families by October, after an anxious final flight from Trinidad with the Lainson's Great Dane (concealed by a blanket) as a *sub rosa* cabin passenger. On arrival in Belém they found a two-week fiesta in progress – 'fireworks here can only be compared with TNT'. Not surprisingly, repairs to the Unit's vehicle, half-wrecked *en route* from Rio, took far too long. Meanwhile, they were tortured by *Culex fatigans* until window screening had been installed. The laboratories were first class, but terribly weak in equipment, and the Unit's own microscopes, glassware and chemicals only began to trickle in after Easter 1966. Some large pieces of laboratory equipment disappeared without trace between Rio and Belém, and had to be replaced like others broken in transit. Nevertheless, field-work began in 1966 with the study of insects and the trapping of animals.

Amid a good deal of administrative chaos – as Dr Shaw wrote once 'the financial side of the Unit is sometimes more of a headache than the scientific investigations' – occasioned by the number of interested parties and the difficulty of communication, and only remedied after Dr Hopwood took over the management of the Unit in 1970 (p. 154), it became clear that three years was far too short a time to allow for the Unit's work. By January 1968 the Trustees had voted £93,000 for its support (of which £64,300 had already been expended); 18 months later the Unit's life was again prolonged to 1975 with a further grant of £175,000. On the scientific side it was agreed to appoint a specialist entomologist to the team, for which post Mr R. D. Ward of the London School was chosen, on the administrative side Dr Williams approached Dr A. S. de Almeida, Superintendent of the Fundacão Servico Especial de Saude Publica of Brazil with a view to negotiating an official standing for the Unit in Brazil (whose members had found that they could not legally sell a worn-out truck)!

In these early years, a good start was made in examining animals (for example, about half the rat-like *Oryzomys* trapped in the forest showed signs of *Leishmania* infection), in identifying the various species of sand-fly (one of the new discoveries was named after Sir Henry Wellcome), and in typing the *Leishmania* cultures. It soon became clear to Lainson and Shaw that they had to unravel the parasites and vectors of a whole complex of diseases.

By 1972 the Unit consisted of four scientific staff – Dr Habib Fraisha had indeed been seconded to it by the Instituto Evandro Chagas for some time – and 11 technicians, some of whom were also paid by the Instituto. An examination of 250 strains of *Leishmania* parasites had permitted the conclusion that three types caused the cutaneous form of the disease in man:

(1) *L.mexicana amazonesis* was widely found in animals. Its vector, *Lutzomyia flaviscutella*, preferred animal hosts but was capable of infecting man in certain circumstances;

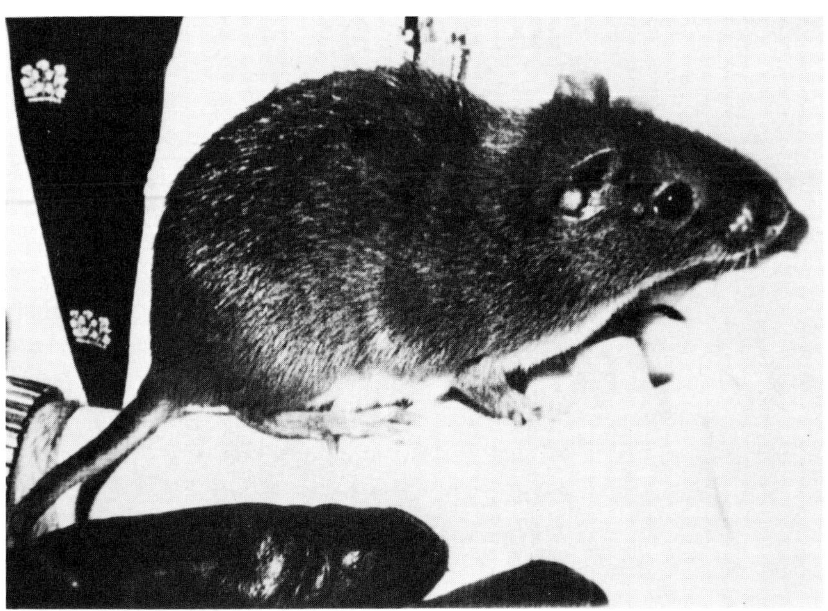

Fig. 50. Two animal hosts of leishmania parasites – (*below*), the cricetid rodent *Otolyomys phyllotis* (*L. mexicana mexicana*) and (*above*) the echimyid rodent *Proechymis* spp. (*L. mexicana amazonensis*).

Fig. 51. The ecology of cutaneous leishmaniasis in the primary forest of the Amazon basin. The animal hosts – sloths and anteaters – infect the sandflies which congregate during the early part of the day on the tree-trunks, biting man when disturbed.
By courtesy of the Royal Society of Tropical Medicine and Hygiene

(2) *L.braziliensis guyanensis*, producing 'pian-bois', carried by sand-flies readily attracted to man;
(3) *L.braziliensis braziliensis*, producing the mucocutaneous *espundia*, and thought to be disseminated by sand-flies of the genus *Psychodopygus*, in specimens of which it had been found. For example, the new species *Ps. Wellcomei* Fraiha readily fed off both man and rodents. But the animal host of this parasite was as yet untraced.

Much work was being done on the life-cycle, habits, and ecology of the insect vectors showing, for instance, that *Ps.wellcomei* was very ready to fly and feed in the daytime and was able to infect forest workers.

In October 1973, as their five-year grant approached its term, the Trustees arranged a meeting at Cambridge to consider leishmaniasis generally, attended by Lainson and Shaw, after which they minuted their recognition of the importance of the Belém Unit as the sole co-ordinated group of scientists working towards the control of a disease of such importance to mankind. They noted also that:

1. Leishmaniasis also provides a useful model for the study of other

Fig. 52. The ecology of visceral leishmaniasis caused by *L. donovani chagasi* in the Amazon region. Chickens, dogs and foxes are among possible hosts of the parasite, distributed by *Lutzomyia longipalpis*. By courtesy of the Royal Society of Tropical Medicine and Hygiene

intracellular protozoa, and a vehicle for the development of immunological techniques.

2. Its complicated epidemiology as a human disease with zoonotic origins necessitates long-term study.
3. The Wellcome Parasitology Unit at Belém provides the basis for all the other research programmes and is essential to them.

Consequently, they agreed that the Unit should continue for a further five years (until 1980) though, because of monetary instabilities, finance was put on a one-year basis. The budget for calendar 1973 had been set at £47,000, which meant that funds would be exhausted by mid-1974; the Trustees voted £60,000 to keep the Unit going for the year up to 31 May 1975. In all, the cost of the research at Belém has amounted to about £1 million over the ten years 1975–84.

Some changes have taken place in the team. Mr Ward left Brazil in 1974 in order to complete his Ph.D. thesis in England; Dr P. Ready of the London School took his place, continuing the study of the habits of sand-flies with the objective of planning practicable methods for their control. In 1978 the team was joined by Dr M. Miles, one of the first London–

Harvard Fellows to work in Brazil, who has studied the isoenzyme patterns of the leishmania parasite, and who has also conducted an investigation of the epidemiology of Chagas' Disease and the nature of the *Trypanosoma cruzi* parasites that cause it in different regions. Animal hosts for these parasites had already been identified at Belém. These researches are still continuing. Dr Lainson's unique contribution to the unravelling of the leishmania complex was recognised both by the Royal Society of London, which elected him to the Fellowship in 1982, and by the Royal Society of Tropical Medicine and Hygiene, which has awarded him the Manson Medal.

Not surprisingly, a thorough review of the work of the Belém Unit in 1978, carried out by Professor (now Sir Richard) Southwood, Dr L. G. Goodwin and Dr Hopwood, came out strongly in its favour and recommended that the Trustees' maintenance of it should be extended for a further five years. This period was again extended in 1983. The Trustees did, however, note the advisability of negotiating a new formal agreement concerning the status of the Unit with the Health Authorities in Brazil, and of involving more Brazilian scientists in the research there. They were also anxious that the risk of infection with leishmaniasis, through the bite of sand-flies, for the workers on the disease should be minimised as far as possible.

A comprehensive monograph on the ecology and epidemiology of the American leishmaniases – extending from Peru and Brazil to Venezuela, through Central America and the Caribbean area to southern Texas – was published by Dr Lainson in 1983, in which he outlined studies (by the Belém Unit and other investigators) of eight sub-species of *L.mexicana* (of which six at least infect man) and five sub-species of *L.braziliensis* affecting man.[7] By this time the association of the many leishmania species with particular sand-fly vectors, some only recently typified, and of these in turn with wild animal reservoir hosts, was much clearer than before.

An interesting lesson of the research is the close specificity of the chain in each case: thus *Leishmania Braziliensis guyanensis* ('pian-bois') carried by *Lutzomyia umbratilis* is restricted in nature to the edentates while *Leishmania donovani chagasi* (causing visceral leishmaniasis in these regions) carried by *Lutzomyia longipalpis* affects dogs and foxes. The animal hosts which include sloths and anteaters appear not to suffer severely from parasitisation; man, severely affected, appears to be so as it were by accident and to play no normal part in the ecological relations of the various species. Another significant feature of the investigation is the importance of biochemical and immunological tests, both for taxonomic and clinical purposes. The existence of the Belém Unit's meticulously documented reference collection of parasites is playing an important role in advances in molecular parasitology. Monoclonal antibodies prepared at Harvard University now help to identify the parasites involved in clinical cases of leishmaniasis at an early stage of infection.

Wellcome Parasitology Unit No. 2, Addis Ababa, Ethiopia

In February 1968 Dr P. C. C. Garnham, Professor of Parasitology at the London School of Hygiene and Tropical Medicine and already associated with the Trust over Belém and other matters, noting the increased interest in leishmaniasis that was developing, suggested to the Trust that there might be formed in London a headquarters staff under a scientist of stature co-ordinating the work of several outstations in Brazil, Africa and India. The Trustees, while not pursuing the suggestion, were conscious of the value of a sustained attack on leishmaniasis, Sir John Boyd writing

> I consider that if any one subject is to be selected for special study, leishmaniasis is the most suitable. In different circumstances I would have chosen trypanosomiasis, but there were good reasons why, at present, this would not be a good choice.

The 'good reasons' were presumably political.

The Trustees were, then, receptive to the idea of there being a second Unit for the study of leishmaniasis when a specific proposal for one was received from a member of Professor Garnham's department, Dr R. S. Bray,[8] with which he soon linked a specialist in immunology at the Kennedy Institute of Rheumatology in Hammersmith, Dr D. C. Dumonde, these two having already collaborated in research. Bray proposed to form the Parasitology Unit No. 2 in Addis Ababa, profiting from the experience already gained by Lainson in Belém. He had already obtained promises of facilities and scientific assistance from the Haile Selassie I University. The objects of investigation would be the widely prevalent 'oriental sore', cutaneous leishmaniasis diffusa, and kala-azar (on the Sudan border). Dr Bray's purpose was to define and characterise the vectors involved in these zoonotic diseases, and to study their immunology: this latter section of the work would be the special responsibility of Dr Dumonde:

> The central position will be that resistance to clinical and experimental infection is largely governed by cell-mediated immunological mechanisms.

Fig. 53. Wellcome Parasitology Unit No. 2 in the field in Ethiopia.

In October 1968 the Trustees agreed to set aside up to £102,000 for the joint programme outlined by Drs Bray and Dumonde, subject to a satisfactory examination of the local position by Dr Bray and Dr Williams. Their visit to Addis Ababa took place in December.

In spite of the cordial support of the President of the Haile Selassie University and of the head of the Pathobiological Institute, Dr Akilu Lemma (who had first invited Dr Bray to Ethiopia), the start of the new Unit was slow and awkward. Dr Bray was not able to leave for Ethiopia with his colleague Dr R. Ashford till July 1969, and scientific work began only at the end of the year. As often, actual costs for equipment, transport, customs dues, etc. were higher than estimated, and there were problems over the admission of goods to Ethiopia. The administration of money matters through the London School proved cumbersome. There were personal difficulties, and the flow of ideas between Belém and Addis Ababa were perhaps less copious than had been anticipated. Nevertheless, there were quick gains after field-work began, while at the end of April 1970 the Unit took '2 days off to climb Magdela 102 years and 10 days after Napier'. In the following winter *Phlebotomus longipes* sand-flies were observed to feed on rock hyrax, and in one of these animals

(*Procavia* spp.) leishmania infection was found. Injecting himself with matter from the lesions Bray developed the typical 'oriental sore', which was removed by surgery to reveal leishmania. Later, man-infecting parasites were found in the sand-flies also. The immunological work ramified considerably; a connection was made with Trust-supported work by the W.H.O. at Geneva, and the Trust also financed a sand-fly colony set up at Silwood Park Research Station (Imperial College), directed by Professor Southwood, a leading member of the Tropical Medicine Panel. All this besides the work of Dr Dumonde and his colleagues.

After the closing down of the Second Parasitology Unit in 1973, when its chief work was done, Dr Bray took charge of the M.R.C. team in The Gambia, to which the *Lady Dale* had been presented long before (though she was not now in service). Dr Ashford, who went to the Liverpool School of Tropical Medicine, has been awarded the Chalmers Medal of the Royal Society of Tropical Medicine and Hygiene.

The London–Harvard scheme

The trend of the 1960s was towards reduced recruitment and opportunities for medical work in the newly independent countries of the tropics, which were short particularly of funds for continued research and not always sufficiently aware of its importance. Among those who shared concern not only because of this trend, but because of the lessening input of the developed countries into tropical medicine, were Dr John C. Snyder (Dean of the Harvard School of Public Health) and Dr Thomas Weller (a Professor in the same School) whom Dr Williams met in Jamaica in 1968. Dr E. T. C. Spooner, Dean of the London School of Hygiene and Tropical Medicine, was ready to co-operate in a joint scheme with Harvard. Accordingly, in February 1969 the Trustees resolved to devote £1 million spread over ten years, to be divided between the two Schools, in order to provide opportunities for young scientists to enter the field of tropical medicine as a career by familiarising themselves with the typical diseases in the field and working in the institutions of the developing countries. Each School was to choose young physicians and scientists to be sent, after any necessary further training, to appropriate laboratories where they would find facilities and colleagues. An announcement of the new programme was made in 1970, but its implementation took longer. The London School was first to act, sending Dr A. Fenwick to work on schistosomiasis in the Sudan, and Dr M. A. Miles to join a group working on Chagas' Disease at Sao Felipe, Bahia, Brazil. This group, already financed by the Trust for the specific investigation of trypanosomiasis and especially *T.cruzi*, consisted of Dr and Mrs D. M. Minter and Dr P. Marsden, all from the London School. The tenure of the first Harvard Fellows commenced on 1 January 1973; Dr M. H. Boyer and Dr J. S. Lehmann were to investigate schistosomiasis, while Dr K. E. Mott was to continue previous studies of Chagas' Disease. These three Fellows were all to be established at another laboratory at Salvador, and in close conjunction with the University of Bahia. Aid was also given to these developments in Brazil by the Pan-American Health Organization – itself a body in receipt of a grant from the Wellcome Trust – and by Brazilian governmental health agencies. However, as Dr Boyer never took up his post at Salvador, his place as project leader was taken by Dr Mott (1973–7) and subsequently by Dr Rodney Hoff (1977–9). Drs J. Maguire and J. Piesman have directed the American research team in more recent years.

In the Bahia investigations which ended in 1975, the Americans recorded the incidence and effects of Chagas' Disease at a field-centre in Castro Alves while the British group concentrated on the parasite, *Trypanosoma cruzi*. They have built up a more complete picture of the ecology of this parasite and of its interactions with its wild animal reservoir hosts and with man, living in bug-infested houses, in various parts of South America. In particular, several different races of the parasite have been identified differing in isoenzyme characteristics and in their distribution through different regions of the South American continent; possibly they also differ in their effects on the human host. Dr Miles presented a thorough review of the epidemiology of trypanosomiasis there to the Royal Society of Tropical Medicine and Hygiene in June 1982.[9]

In 1950 the U.S. National Institutes of Health took over the American work on Chagas' Disease on a five-year contract, after the return of Dr Hoff to the U.S.A. The remainder of that part of the Wellcome grant was used to start a new study of tick-borne diseases in Bahia.

In Khartoum, where the London School carried on a collaborative study of schistosomiasis in the Gezira area of the Sudan with the Ministry of Health and the University of the Sudan, Dr Fenwick studied over a number of years the biology of the snails serving as intermediate hosts of the parasite and the effectiveness of various techniques for applying molluscicides to control them.

Since 1974 the Scheme also financed Dr M. H. N. Golden from the London School who went to the M.R.C.'s Tropical Metabolism Research

Fig. 54. Housing in Brazil – comfortable lodging is also provided for the vectors of Chagas' Disease.

Unit in Jamaica to work on the protein turnover in malnourished children. He has since made a special study of trace element deficiencies in relation to malnutrition in the tropics, as a Wellcome Trust Senior Lecturer. A Research Group under his direction was founded in 1982 with the Trustees' support and within the Tropical Metabolism Research Unit, now under Dr A. A. Jackson, which has itself been assisted since 1980 by the Trust, at a time of exceptional political and economic difficulties.

Most of the scientists recruited by the London–Harvard scheme have maintained their interest in tropical medicine and several are still working overseas.

Bangkok

It appears from the Trustees' interest in the Vellore programme that they were long conscious of the need for the other research centres in the East, where other medical problems could be tackled in a different setting. An early recommendation by the Tropical Medicine Panel was for the setting up of a third Research Unit, and this was endorsed by the Trustees.

Towards the end of 1977 they received a submission from Dr David A.

Warrell, then employed by the Oxfordshire Health Authority, suggesting an investigation of the pathophysiology of infectious diseases and of snake-bite in the Far East. Dr Warrell had already been a Wellcome Research Fellow at the Royal Postgraduate Medical School, and had had experience at the Ahmadu Bello University in Northern Nigeria. His wife, who would join him in the work, was then Senior Registrar in Clinical Virology at the Churchill Hospital, Oxford. After discussion of their plans with the Trustees, the Drs Warrell made a tour of Malaysia, Thailand and Sri Lanka in June 1978, from which they decided that Bangkok would provide their most suitable base. A formal proposal in detail was accepted by the Trustees in December, and negotiated with the Mahidol University, Bangkok, by Professor D. J. Weatherall of Oxford, Dr Williams, and Dr D. A. Warrell in January 1979. The Trustees, the Mahidol University (represented by Dr Chamlong Harinasuta the Dean of tropical medicine) and the University of Oxford (represented by Professor Weatherall, head of the Nuffield Department of Clinical Medicine) signed a 'Memorandum of Understanding' providing for the Warrell's work in Bangkok for at least five years, in February 1979.

The scheme was arranged as follows: Grants to the University of Oxford provided for the salaries of Dr D. A. Warrell in the Department of Clinical Medicine, as Lecturer in Tropical Medicine, and of Dr Mary Warrell in the Sir William Dunn School of Pathology, as Research Fellow. Another grant of £133,000 was provided for the expenses of the Unit, more than half this sum being required for equipment during the first year. After some initial hiccoughs, Oxford University agreed to administer these grants. The Warrells were expected to spend a short part of each year in Oxford, to keep in touch with scientific colleagues. Professor Harinasuta provided local scientific collaboration (notably, in the persons of Dr Danai Bunnag and Dr Khunying Tranackchit, laboratory space, and administrative support).

There was a great rush of preparation in getting material together, but the Warrells were able to reach Bangkok before the end of the year, where they were soon visited by Dr Williams and Dr B. M. Ogilvie, the head of the Trust's tropical section (January 1980). The first few months were occupied in studying the Thai language, modifying laboratories and installing equipment, recruiting Thai assistance, visiting hospitals and patients and making scientific contacts. By summer the Warrells had decided to give first priority in their work to studies of the pathophysiology and clinical management of complicated falciparum malaria, the rapid diagnosis of rabies and trials of antirabies vaccines, and the immunodiagnosis of snake-bite and trials of antivenom preparations. In the first of these investigations they were joined by Dr Nicholas White, who (with the Trustees' support) went out to Bangkok in September 1980. Lord and Lady Franks visited the Unit in December 1980 during a tour of the Far East. A number of Thai scientists soon became associated with the project; besides Dr Bunnag (Director of the Tropical Hospital), its firm friend, there were Dr Santasiri Sornmani (who succeeded Professor Harinasuta on his retirement), Dr Sornchai Looareesuwan who joined in the cerebral malaria work at the Chantaburi Hospital directed by Dr Chaisit, 'a wonderful chap', and Dr Pornthep Chanthawanich.

Many of these had already worked in England. The Trustees made two grants at this time to two Thais, Dr Sornchai and Dr Sasithon Pukrittayakamee, to enable them to undertake research training in the Nuffield Department of Clinical Medicine at Oxford.

The work on severe falciparum malaria infections is bearing fruit – a matter of great importance in Thailand where strains of malaria parasite resistant to the standard antimalarial drug treatment are common. Methods of management of patients with cerebral malaria have been successfully developed, and Quinidine has been shown to be at least as effective as Quinine in its speed and potency of action in severe malaria.

Jamaica

The foundation of the University College of the West Indies in 1946 offered new possibilities for the investigation of health problems in the tropics. In the last colonial phase Jamaica was an island of nearly two million people, preponderantly of African origin, with a public expenditure of £20 million per annum, about one-eighth of it on health. The economy was one of primary production and tourism; poverty, malnutrition, and the diseases associated with malnutrition and poor living standard were commonplace.

In 1955 Dr J. C. Waterlow received support from the Medical Research Council to establish at Kingston, Jamaica, a Tropical Metabolism Research Unit which he directed for a number of years. He in turn was in collaboration with Dr E. K. Cruickshank, Professor of Medicine in the University College (which is now the University of the West Indies). In June 1957 he encouraged Professor Cruickshank to seek from Sir Henry Dale financial support for research into diabetes among the Jamaican population. Encouragement also came from Dr C. M. Best of Toronto, one of the co-discoverers of insulin; Dr Waterlow was able to offer both laboratory facilities and bed spaces for the special study patients. In writing to Dale, Cruickshank pointed out that at that time diabetes was the single most common cause of admission to the medical wards of the University College Hospital in Kingston, and that the disease and the treatment presented many interesting indigenous features, not least in the possibility of studying the connection between malnutrition and diabetes. The Trustees made an initial grant of £1,000 to start an investigation which ran from January 1958 to September 1959.

Through the years, the Trustees made a number of small grants to the Tropical Metabolism Research Unit to aid the work of Dr Waterlow and his immediate successor, Dr D. M. Picou. Among the more important was the provision in 1960 of a mass spectrometer which (in the words of the Unit's present head) elevated the Unit to the position of being the only centre in the developing world with the equipment and expertise to carry out biomedical mass spectrometry, as it still is. But such studies are expensive: the examination of some 2,000 specimens per annum costs about $40,000.

After the M.R.C. ended its support of the Tropical Metabolism Research Unit in 1978, Dr A. A. Jackson (Director from February 1981, but a staff member since 1973) continued its work, in a period of exceptionally troublesome economic and political circumstances, in association with the University of the West Indies. Adaptation of the Unit to the post-colonial era was first aided by the Overseas Development Administration (cf. p. 269) and subsequently by the Wellcome Trust. The Unit has received since 1980 an annual grant of £25,000 towards the cost of materials, medical journals and special diets for patients.

While the Trustees have felt unable to undertake a very large-scale commitment to Dr Jackson's Unit, which now concentrated upon investigation of the metabolism of nitrogen and protein, especially in relation to the adaptive phenomena taking place in men and animals when the diet is reduced to a marginal level, it has (from 1982) consolidated in a Trace Element Research Group the work begun by Dr M. H. N. Golden in 1974 (p. 250). This Group directed by him functions within the T.M.R.U. Dr Golden himself is currently a Wellcome Senior Lecturer in the Department of Medicine of the University of Aberdeen and works in conjunction with the Rowett Institute.

Meanwhile, in May 1967 the Trustees had approved a grant of £17,000 to support an extensive clinical and pathological investigation of sickle-cell anaemia over the whole island of Jamaica. Some 800 cases of the disease had been diagnosed at the University College Hospital during the previous nine years, and it was estimated that there might be five times as many affected persons among the whole population. Extensive field-work was therefore necessary and a mobile laboratory was provided to make it possible. With field-work clinical studies and haematological investigations were to be combined. Professor Cruickshank was in charge of the whole project, the work being carried out by his former Senior Registrar, Dr G. R. Serjeant, who in turn was supported by the Senior Lecturer and Consultant in Haematology, Dr P. F. A. Milner. Both men had a thorough knowledge of the disease.

Important results were achieved during the first two years. Professor H. Lehmann, head of the M.R.C.'s Abnormal Haemoglobin Research Unit at Cambridge, wrote enthusiastically about the project in July 1969, saying that 'there is at the moment nothing to equal the group in the West Indies . . . there is nowhere else an opportunity for assessing a population with homozygous sickle cell disease, who have been under continuous surveillance for so many years'. The team wanted to do more through collaborative studies with the W.H.O., and to develop new lines of research into such topics as red cell biochemistry and iron metabolism. The Trustees awarded a further £22,500 spread over three years in order to continue the work. In 1970 they assisted Mr P. I. Condon, of Lambeth Hospital to make a short study of ocular complications of the haemoglobinopathies in the West Indies, in conjunction with Dr Serjeant, at the latter's request.

Dr Serjeant joined Professor Lehmann's Unit at Cambridge in mid-1971, having studied a total of about 560 cases of haemoglobin disease in Jamaica. In 1974 Dr Serjeant published a monograph on *The Clinical Features of Sickle Cell Disease* which has become a standard authority. He transferred back from Cambridge to Jamaica to direct the M.R.C.'s Epidemiological Research Unit there, now known simply at the M.R.C. Laboratories (Jamaica). A grant for these laboratories, with associated housing for the staff, had been given by the Trustees to the M.R.C. in 1960 (figure 55). They opened in 1962, under the direction of Dr W. E. Miall, and have made long-term studies of pulmonary and cardiovascular diseases among the population of the Caribbean, and also of child development.

Health in the tropics, a continuing concern

The concern felt by the Trustees about the health of populations living in the tropics, and for the level of hygienic, nutritional and medical practice

Fig. 55. In June 1960 the Trustees granted the M.R.C. £61,000 for this building on behalf of the Epidemiological Research Unit established in Jamaica and first directed by Dr W. E. Miall. The buildings were completed in 1962.

available to them, could not but increase as the decade of the seventies ended. Statistical measurement allowed no complacency. In the mid-1970s infant mortality could still range from 150 to 200 per 1,000 live births in African republics (the rate for Sweden being 8, for Britain 16). Similarly, life expectancy at birth might be as low as 41 years (in Sweden 75 years, in Britain 73). The figures for per capita expenditure from public sources in such poor countries on health – two or three dollars per year – equally speak for themselves.

By contrast, in some islands of the West Indies where expenditure upon health amounted to about 50 dollars per head (Sweden, $550, the U.K. $204), the infant mortality rate had been brought below 50 per 1,000 live births. There was no reason to suppose that in the poorest countries the situation was likely to improve.

In Britain especially, official withdrawal of finance and facilities from tropical medicine went on apace. Between 1976 and 1979 Britain's total aid to the developing countries had increased by about one-fifth to £795 million; from 1979 to 1983, it was planned, it should decrease again to almost the previous figure, despite the eroding effect of inflation meanwhile. The effective provision for medical work was necessarily reduced along with other activities. At the same time, the support formerly given by the Royal Army Medical Corps to the study of disease in the tropics was curtailed, as a result of the withdrawal of forces from those regions; the Queen Alexandra Military Hospital at Millbank, London, was closed.

Both the London and the Liverpool Schools of Tropical Medicine have been under great pressure from 1980 onwards, as the effects of the government's policy of reducing the U.G.C. grants, while raising foreign student's fees to a level of nearly £9,000 per annum (1985), came to be realised.

These problems, and many others, were considered in a special *Supplement* to the *Transactions of the Royal Society of Tropical Medicine and Hygiene* published in September 1981 which was stimulated and financed by the Wellcome Trust, and in part prepared by its officers. This drew attention to the importance of the British contribution to the development of tropical medicine, to the illusory (and selfish) nature of the belief that, in a post-colonial world, Britain need no longer make such contributions or concern itself in any way with health matters peculiar to the tropics, and insisted that the destruction 'of the collected talent and facilities in the U.K. would be disastrous'. No strong signs have emerged that the evidence and arguments contained in this *Supplement* influenced governmental policy in the least, but it did have an encouraging sequel in that the Wolfson Trust generously offered (in November 1981) to furnish £1 million a year, for three years, for studies in tropical medicine. Dr P. O. Williams and a representative of the Medical Research Council were invited to devise for the Wolfson Trustees a scheme for the use of this generous gift.[10]

The present position in tropical medicine and infectious diseases by Dr B. M. Ogilvie

The Trust has a broad view of tropical medicine and has always supported research that concerns not only infections and conditions confined to tropical areas but also those medical problems of universal occurrence which have a different manifestation in tropical countries because of genetic or environmental factors characteristic of that environment. Infectious disease became part of the programme in 1983 to stimulate interest in the clinical side of infectious diseases research in Britain and promote a better career structure for medical graduates with this interest. Whilst the majority of the funds available for tropical medicine research is awarded for projects carried out wholly or largely in laboratories in Britain, considerable efforts have been and are made to devise ways of enabling research to be done in tropical countries. To achieve this it has been found necessary to establish five small research Units wholly funded by the Trust in tropical countries.

About one-quarter of the sum allotted for the tropical programme is used to support the Units and they will continue to receive enthusiastic support from the Trustees. The Units in India and Brazil, and that at Bangkok, have reached a steady state in their development and little change is foreseen in their structure or activity. The ending of the current programme investigating hypertension in rural versus city dwellers has led to the possible establishment of a new group on the coast of Kenya. The Kenya Medical Research Institute has invited the Trust to investigate the feasibility of establishing a Unit at Kilifi to investigate the many health problems of the local population with the main emphasis likely to be on malaria. Dr S. J. Oppenheimer went to Kenya in May 1985 to direct Phase I, while Dr W. and Mrs H. Watkins have directed the Trust's laboratories in Nairobi after the retirement of Dr B. E. C. Hopwood in September 1985.

The Trust has had a long-standing interest in the Tropical Metabolism Research Unit (T.M.R.U.) in Jamaica, and supported its founding Director, Professor J. Waterlow before his work was funded by the Medical Research Council. In the past five years, the Trust has provided a subsidy to enable the T.M.R.U. to continue to function under Dr A. Jackson, and has set up a Trace Element Research Group within the T.M.R.U. under Dr M. N. H. Golden in 1982. The future of the Trust's support of the important work of this laboratory is unclear as both Dr Jackson and Dr Golden will shortly return to Britain. The Trust has also had a long-standing interest in the work of the M.R.C. Sickle Cell Unit directed by Dr Serjeant in Jamaica, and early in 1985 gave further support to it by contributing £40,000 for a new 'Wellcome Laboratory' for studies of ophthalmological problems associated with sickle-cell diseases.

A major function of these Units is to provide research training for locally qualified graduates who work in the Units. The Trust is keen to provide training Fellowships for such staff to obtain further experience in the U.K. Frequent awards have been made to young Thai and Indian graduates working in the Units, but sadly for a variety of reasons, it has not yet been possible to identify suitable local graduates in the other Units for advanced training.

Apart from the intrinsic interest of the research undertaken in the Units, they provide a base in which British trained graduates can work. Various career development awards have been designed to encourage young graduates who wish to work in the tropics. There is no dearth of interest, but in order to ensure that those who work abroad are readily able to re-establish themselves on the British academic scene, an important feature of all the Trust's tropical career development awards is a guaranteed year's support on their return to their British base.

The main thrust of the Trustees' interest in infectious diseases is to train clinicians to be equally at home at the bedside and in the microbiological laboratory. Because infectious diseases are such an important aspect of medicine in the tropics, it is felt that a period working abroad is an excellent but not essential experience for such trainees. Awards in infectious diseases are made at the Fellowship, Lectureship and Senior Lectureship levels and some of those appointed will spend a period of time in the tropics. The Trust is especially interested to get the strengths of various clinical sciences applied to a wide range of tropical disease problems. Clinical science is an aspect of research for which British Universities have a high reputation and the tropics offer many neglected opportunities for deepening our understanding of the pathogenesis of disease, both cosmopolitan and tropical, infectious and non-infectious.

At the present time, however, there is particular concern at the Trust about the number of posts available to clinicians both in tropical medicine and the speciality of infectious diseases within the university and medical system and the Trustees are joining with other interested parties to develop methods of overcoming this problem.

Career development awards take up about one-fifth of the funds available for tropical medicine and infectious diseases. In order to accelerate the rate at which the techniques of modern biology are introduced into this programme, the Advanced Training Fellowship Scheme was initiated in 1982 with the object of enabling young scientists, both clinical and non-clinical, who have already had several years' experience in any field of tropical medicine and have shown promise during their post-doctoral work, to extend their training. They are given the opportunity to work in the tropics, or in a discipline that differs from their previous experience, for at least six months and up to two years, in a laboratory anywhere in the world. At the end of the training period, the trainee is promised a final year of support at his or her home base in Britain. This scheme is particularly valuable because support is difficult to find for scientists who wish to change or enlarge their fields of work, especially if this requires them to work abroad to acquire experience or skills not available in Britain. The first recipients of these awards have now completed their training. They have benefited enormously both scientifically and in their

Tropical medical science project grants
Percentage distribution (excluding Wellcome Units)

Years	1971–5		1976–80		1981–4	
Location	U.K. %	Tropics %	U.K. %	Tropics %	U.K. %	Tropics %
Protozoal diseases	31	4	28	9	33	10
Helminth diseases	3	12	20	0	26	20
Bacterial and viral	6	19	16	17	19	30
Insect vectors	13	8	12	4	12	0
Cardiac, renal and respiratory	3	12	4	22	0	10
Nutrition	16	26	10	22	4	10
Miscellaneous	28	19	10	26	6	20
TOTAL	100	100	100	100	100	100
Number of projects	32	26	69	23	68	10

personal development, and it is clear that the departments to which they have returned will benefit greatly from their experience.

Over half the budget is dispersed in the form of project grants and interest in the subject has increased progressively in recent years. In order to promote the subject, major awards for work in a nominated subject over a five-year period are advertised from time to time. The intention of these awards is to stimulate interdisciplinary approaches to neglected subjects to encourage new research of pressing urgency. Themes chosen in the past have included studies of the virulence of infection, gastroenterological, respiratory and renal disease in the tropics, and collaborative studies between the basic sciences and tropical medicine. One of these awards, given for the study of malaria at the University of Oxford, led indirectly to the creation of the Wellcome Trust Research Unit at Bangkok.

In the immediate future, it is thought that there is a sufficiently large number of young scientists engaged in parasitological aspects of tropical medicine to maintain the momentum in basic sciences. This is illustrated by awards in 1983–4 to three universities to enable them to appoint scientists between the ages of 30–32 to their staff under the University Award scheme of the Trust. The British University system may be expected to demonstrate sustained research interest in both areas: at present, the demand for support in the study of infectious diseases is increasing sharply while the demand for tropical medicine awards remains steady. Some 60 per cent of awards (by value) in Tropical

Medicine goes to institutions other than the two Schools of Tropical Medicine in London and Liverpool, indicating that appropriate research interest is widespread.

An analysis of the subjects supported by project grants in British Laboratories and in tropical countries shows an interesting pattern (see the table). Since 1971 about one-third of all grants to scientists in Britain was given for work on protozoal diseases, especially malaria, trypanosomiasis and leishmaniasis research. Interest in helminthic disease increased over the years from 3 per cent of the total in 1971–5 to 26 per cent in 1981–4. In contrast, grants given to workers in the tropics in 1971–80 were largely concerned with nutrition (about $\frac{1}{4}$) and with cardiac, renal and respiratory disease. Since 1980 there has been a change of emphasis in tropical areas, with about one-half of the total in support of research on helminthic, bacterial and viral diseases. It is unfortunate that while the number of projects funded has increased in the U.K. since 1975, the number of projects funded in the tropical countries themselves has steadily diminished.

12

THE HEALTH OF ANIMALS[1]

Although the Trustees' activity in this field before the adoption of the new policy in 1966 was opportunistic and without a settled plan, it was far from inconsiderable. In the 12 years 1956–68 (when the new policy began to affect this field) about £600,000 had been spent on *ad hoc* awards in the veterinary field. Rather more than two-thirds of this sum had been devoted to buildings, including £100,000 for the Foot-and-Mouth Disease Institute in Kenya (p. 234), £141,000 on behalf of the University of Glasgow for its Small Animals Research Institute at Garscube, and £62,500 for the Virus Research Institute at Pirbright, Surrey. In the spirit of 1966, the Trustees now believed that the comparable sum of £52,000 spent on Fellowships – mostly on behalf of the Animal Health Trust (p. 64) – was far too small: nearly as much had been found for equipment. They were, before long, willing to double their investment as well as shifting its balance.

In June 1966 Dr Williams' attention had been particularly drawn to the importance of veterinary research by Professor A. T. Phillipson, Head of Clinical Studies in the Veterinary School at Cambridge. He immediately wrote to Lord Murray:

> I feel that there is a very important area of research in Veterinary Medicine that would not only be valuable to veterinary practice but also to medical practice.
>
> It is an area which the Wellcome Trust could consider stimulating.

Lord Murray responded positively and the Trustees began to consider how they might best do more for animals, as well as people. Early in 1967 the process of planning, listing names of suitable scientists, and sounding out views was much assisted by Mr S. L. Hignett C.B.E. of the Wellcome Foundation's Veterinary Research Station at Frant, who was for a number of years associated with the Trust's veterinary programme. Mr Hignett, after a brief academic career, had joined the Foundation becoming Group Director of Veterinary Research. Besides serving as President of both the British Veterinary Association and the Royal College of Veterinary Surgeons, he has been active on governmental bodies and is a practical farmer too.

On 19 June 1967 a dinner-discussion of veterinary research took place with Lord Murray in the Chair (as Lord Franks was unable to be present) between the Scientific Trustees and Dr Williams, and their guests Sir John Ritchie (Principal of the Royal Veterinary College in London), Sir William Weipers (Professor of Veterinary Surgery at Glasgow), Professor Phillipson, and Mr Hignett. A number of useful negative points emerged: it was agreed that the number of qualifying veterinarians was small and that in their eyes academic research must appear less attractive as a career than practice; that as the Agricultural Research Council financed research in its own extra-University Institutes it did not give much support to University veterinary research; and that there was a need for more senior posts for research workers. But though the Trust received encouragement to press on, nothing like a strategic programme emerged from this meeting.

Accordingly, the Trustees' first resolutions in July and November 1967 in favour of giving more funds to veterinary research – up to a further sum of £100,000 per annum – were made in the absence of such a programme. To help formulate it, they in fact asked Professor Thompson to take charge of development. He was authorised to obtain advice on needs and policy from a Symposium of experts, which met at the Wellcome Institute for the History of Medicine on 21 February 1968. Thirteen scientists attended in addition to the Trust staff; they were invited:

> To make recommendations to the Wellcome Trustees on how best to assist veterinary research with emphasis on work in somewhat neglected fields, especially those which might yield information of value to human medicine. Attention will also be paid to collaborative efforts involving investigations in the UK and abroad into problems of economic importance to overseas countries.

The Symposium discussion was wide-ranging and diffuse, but at least a clearer picture emerged for the Trustees: that the veterinary profession would think useful the advertisement of personal support awards for research training and research; that certain aspects of veterinary medicine (including provision for the hospitalisation of animals) ought to be singled out for promotion; and that, especially, a standing Panel should be created to advise the Trustees generally and especially on the evaluation of applications for grants.

The Trustees accepted all of these recommendations but it was not possible to arrange a first meeting of the Veterinary Advisory Panel before October 1968. The members of this first panel, appointed for five years, with Professor Thompson as Chairman, were Professors R. A. Coombs of Cambridge, C. S. G. Grunsell of Bristol and W. F. H. Jarrett of Glasgow; Mr S. L. Hignett and Mr I. H. Pattison, of the A.R.C. Institute for Research on Animal Diseases, Compton, with Dr Hanington as Secretary. This group believed that it was impractical to attach high priority to such specially important research topics as parasitology, cancer, pre- and post-natal studies, nutrition and metabolism (defined by the symposium), but proceeded to recommend the Trustees to award eight Research Training Scholarships to encourage students to go in for research, and the same number of Research Fellowships (including the two awarded in association with the Animal Health Trust). The Panel also noted that because of the special interest of the A.R.C. in farm animals, there was a tendency to neglect others such as horses, dogs and cats.

Thus the Trustees were able, in their *Seventh Report* (1966–8) to draw attention to the larger programme of personal encouragement to research (consisting of Fellowships and Scholarships) that was on offer, as well as the Trustees' intention to provide aid for new buildings and new equipment. Through subsequent years the importance of personal support for veterinary scientists, and the development of definite programmes of research, has continued to increase.

The Veterinary Panel, reconstituted and re-appointed from time to time, has continued to advise the Trustees, down to the present. It has from time to time been addressed by outside experts, and has visited various establishments of the Universities, the Animal Health Trust, and the Agricultural Research Council. It was found, as expected, that awards had to be made in an opportunistic way, as before; at this stage it was impossible to guide research in particular directions. One particular disappointment was the failure of a scheme (announced in the *Eighth Report*, 1970) for collaborative research in veterinary matters between Britain and tropical countries to make useful progress. Later, the Trustees decided (temporarily) to reduce their allocation for veterinary science

Fig. 56. Research Laboratories at the Veterinary School of the University of Cambridge, built with the aid of the Trust, 1969.

because those whom they had encouraged and supported in research found it almost impossible to find suitable posts thereafter. Nevertheless, some £430,000 was spent on awards during the two first years of the original panel, and about £½ million during the second two years. Investment in university buildings such as an Experimental Unit to study the metabolic physiology of herbivores at the Cambridge School of Veterinary Medicine, at the Glasgow Veterinary School for work on parasitology and leukaemia, and at the Department of Veterinary Surgery, Bristol, was still comparatively heavy, though the amounts devoted to personal support and research assistance (£234,000 and £162,000 respectively in the years 1970–2) were of course much greater.

A breakdown prepared for the Trustees' Committee that reviewed the work of the first Veterinary Panel in January 1974 and made recommendations for the future indicates that the topics receiving the largest research grants were immunology and parasitology; tropical investigations also received over £100,000. Between £50,000 and £100,000 were allocated to physiology and reproductive physiology, anaesthetics, nutrition and metabolism, and biochemistry.

Sums awarded by the second Advisory Panel totalled £1,526,000 and included one further building grant (to the Glasgow University Veterinary School) and one university award (to the Royal Veterinary College, London). During the whole ten-year period, 1968–78, 155 personal awards had been made, 156 awards providing for the expenses of research, and 19 research equipment grants. (These figures exclude all grants for under £2,000 each.)

As the enthusiasm of applicants increased, the Trustees had showed some tendency to limit the growth of expenditure, or at least to concentrate it upon selected fields, especially as their interest in the tropical aspects of veterinary medicine increased. Already the *Eighth Report* emphasised their wish to support 'work in this field linking centres in Britain with centres in the tropics', especially by means of personal grants to improve the technical skills and extend the experience of researchers in the tropical countries.

The Trustees also helped during these years to finance about a dozen symposia on topics in veterinary medicine. One, a symposium in Aberdeen in July 1969, organised by the International Biological Programme and the European Association for Animal Production, may serve as an example. Its subject was trace element metabolism in animals. It was backed by two veterinary research institutes, by the University of Aberdeen, and by the Royal Society. It was, of course, international. The application submitted by Dr C. F. Mills, Chairman of the Organising Committee, states pertinently the objects of many such meetings:

> The enclosed preliminary programme outlines the main objectives of the symposium and indicates the convictions of the organising committee that the most important limitation to the application of the newer knowledge of the trace element function, metabolism and utilisation in human and veterinary medicine and in agriculture is the *lack of opportunity for discussion of mutual problems* between the research worker, dealing with fundamental aspects of the problem, and those whose task it is to apply their research findings in practice.

A subvention of £500 was made towards the cost of this meeting.

The record of discussions implies that by 1974 the Advisory Panel had become a little restless, hesitant to continue in the present path of making awards without change. As one Minute puts it (June 1971):

> The mere subsidy of institutions or individuals who are inadequately supported to do their job is an insufficient objective unless these institutions or individuals are the instruments for creating change.

The Panel was anxious to give stronger advantages to candidates working in topics considered to be specially deserving of attention, such as dermatology, mycology, toxicology and haematology, and initiate more work in comparative medicine (problems, whose study in animals is of direct relevance to man also). The Panel also wished to encourage more work on 'small animals' rather than cattle and horses, whose economic value is certainly greater. A meeting on the last topic was organised by the Trust in October 1975.

The *Eleventh Report*, noting this, also records that two of the larger grants of the period were made for toxicological studies. Professor E. A. Bell (Department of Botany, King's College, London) was awarded £17,067 for an investigation of the physiologically active amines, cyanogenic glycosides and alkaloids in the seeds of leguminous plants; Dr A. T. Diplock (Department of Biochemistry, Royal Free Hospital) was awarded £20,258 for research into the interaction between the metal selenium and other metals (silver, mercury, cadmium) and also Vitamin E. Neither of these projects was based on a veterinary department, nor do they correspond to the most obvious notion of veterinary research; indeed, much of the work financed by the Trust under the veterinary heading could alternatively have been classified as 'physiology', 'parasitology' and so forth. But the Trustees were not unaware of the need for more research into problems of direct concern to farmers, and the economic importance of the losses caused by animal disease; indeed, this point was made by Sir Michael Swann (as he then was) in a talk to the Trustees on veterinary research in January 1976. Sir Michael, an established zoologist, took over the Chairmanship of the Veterinary Panel from Professor Thompson. He proposed that the Trustees should again review their policy.

During the last ten years, during which more than £7 million has been spent on veterinary–medical research, the expenditure year by year has fluctuated markedly. From 1974 to 1975 there was a sharp fall from £716,000 to £392,000, while from 1977 to 1978 there was an abrupt rise from £462,000 to over one million pounds. However, 1980 saw a decline to £744,000 once more. Certainly some of the variation was due to fluctuations in the number and quality of applications, causing concern to the Trustees.

Competitive awards were advertised in 1977: one, for research on tremorgenic mycotoxins and neurological disorders, was made jointly to biochemists at Imperial College, London, and clinicians at the Royal Veterinary College, London, and a few years later it was possible to announce that good progress had been made in examining the effect of mycotoxins produced *in vitro* on neurotransmitters, which it was hoped would ultimately throw light on such diseases as 'staggers' in cattle and sheep.

The second competitive award, for a study of chronic kidney disease in dogs, was made to the Animal Health Trust's Small Animal Centre, at Newmarket.

In 1979 a third award was made to Professor R. J. Fitzpatrick (Department of Veterinary Clinical Studies, University of Liverpool) to finance investigation of changes in the structure of the *cervix uteri* when birth occurs; this was classed as a grant in Comparative Medicine.

No Major Award – as these five-year grants were now called – was made in 1980, but in 1981 a proposal for the study of the protection against viral infection afforded by the mucous membrane of the respiratory tract put forward by Professor F. J. Bourne (Department of Veterinary Medicine, Bristol University) was supported by the Trustees.

The cost of these four awards together exceeded £492,000.

As in other aspects of medical research, governmental policy in a worsening economic situation has tended to discourage veterinary research or to starve it out of existence, thus increasing the importance of the contribution made by the Wellcome Trust. In particular, the reduction in the finance of the Overseas Development Administration necessarily impaired the research conducted on veterinary medicine in tropical countries. In response, the Trustees on the recommendation of their Advisory Panel created a special fund to encourage British veterinary scientists to work on problems of special relevance to animals in overseas countries; during 1981–2 £114,000 was granted from this fund. Since 1979 the Secretary of this Panel has been Dr K. B. Sinclair, an Assistant Director of the Trust. He was formerly Reader in Animal Physiology and Dean of the Faculty of Science, at the University College of Wales, at Aberystwyth, and thus had experience both of scientific research and of academic administration. Dr Sinclair has been able to visit the chief centres of veterinary research in this country, and is thus able to keep the Trustees thoroughly apprised of developments in this field, and its needs.

As Lord Swann noted in his Weipers' Lecture (1981) the Wellcome Trust has been for many years a major contributor to veterinary research in British universities, providing more than one-half of those funds whose use is free from restriction as to subject. The Trustees' support in this field has tended to reduce the effect of such restrictions and to mitigate certain other inequalities which tend to exist in the public sector of veterinary finance. Although not all the hopes of the Trustees in advertising their awards have been realised, the participation of university representatives in the Panel system has worked well (as it has in the history of medicine also) and has encouraged the extension of this system to other areas of the Trust's intervention. The Trustees are actively monitoring the general provision of funds for veterinary research and the effect of official policies, and are consulting with other agencies concerned with regard to developments in the future.

The present position in veterinary medicine

In the early days, most of the support for veterinary medicine was comprised in grants for laboratories and buildings, and it was not until the establishment of the Veterinary Panel in 1968 that a real policy emerged. It seems that, from the beginning, the intention was that all the schemes introduced by the Trust for the support of research in human medicine, would apply equally to veterinary medicine. Moreover, in the early days, there was apparently no discrimination in respect of the provision for research between farm and companion animals. But, by the time that Dr Sinclair joined the staff in 1979, the policy was that applicants whose proposals clearly fell within the special fields of other grant-awarding bodies – such as the Agricultural Research Council and the Horserace Betting Levy Board – should be advised to make their initial approaches to the appropriate body. More recently, however, in accordance with a general easing of the Trust's policy in respect of prior application to 'official' sources of funding, the Panel is now prepared to consider proposals in all fields of veterinary research – provided, of course, that the proposals have scientific merit and promise. It is noteworthy that, although current policy implies no discrimination in the subject or species of animal involved in a research project, the Panel usually takes special cognizance of the lack of alternative sources of funding in consideration of proposals for work on companion and zoo animals.

In consideration of the distribution of their budget, successive Panels have decided to devote substantial resources to the recruitment and training in research of young veterinary graduates. The main avenue for this objective has been the provision of Research Training Scholarships and more than 75 of these awards have now been made. Most of the awards have gone for the support of research training in the United Kingdom Veterinary Schools. But in recent years Dr Sinclair has attempted to persuade veterinary graduates to consider undertaking their research training in medical and pure science departments. The record of the demand for, and the outcome of these awards are both good, and there is no doubt that a Wellcome Veterinary Research Training Scholarship has by now acquired a certain prestige, which is likely to be enhanced in the future.

To complement the promotion of recruitment and training of younger graduates, the Panels have also been keen to encourage the contributions to veterinary research that can be made by more experienced workers. The Veterinary Research Fellowship scheme was introduced for the support of veterinary or post-doctoral biomedical scientists who wished to undertake a period of full-time research. Substantially fewer Fellowships than Scholarships have been awarded, and most have been tenable in the Veterinary Schools; a few shorter-term awards, however, have been tenable in Research Institutes. In the past, the Panel has shown a preference for veterinary graduate applicants for Research Fellowships – probably because they felt that there were adequate alternative resources of funding for post-doctoral scientists. But the current approach is more flexible, and the Panel will certainly be ready to consider Fellowship applications from post-doctoral scientists seeking support for research in Veterinary Schools.

Since 1968, *ad hoc* project grants have been a cornerstone of the veterinary medicine programme. By current standards, the early awards were small and often of short duration. Nowadays, most awards provide for research or technical assistance, consumables, animals, and, perhaps, equipment for a period of up to three years, and involve an expenditure of the order of £30/£40,000. These grants continued to provide an important source of funding for bread-and-butter research in universities and veterinary schools. The recognition of the need for longer-term support in veterinary research came about 1976 or 1977, probably as a spin-off from schemes developed for other programmes of the Trust. Initially, the longer-term support was linked with efforts to promote research in neglected topics and resulted in the launching of the Competitive Awards in Veterinary Medicine scheme in 1978. The intention of this scheme was to provide major grants for the support of research in so-called neglected topics. The list of these topics included dermatology, toxicology, mycology and neurology, and the first award was for research on tremorgenic mycotoxins. The outcome, however, of subsequent attempts to promote research in selected subjects was disappointing and, in more recent years these Major Awards (now renamed Project Development Grants) have been made available on an unrestricted basis. In general, the early response to the Major Award scheme may be judged disappointing but, with the abandonment of the selected subject requirement, the number of good applications increased and a total of five awards – to support research in reproductive physiology, canine renal disease, immunity to respiratory infection, and molecular virology – have been made to date. Other awards will be made.

Finally, three recently introduced schemes reflect the Panel's growing concern about the erosion of staffing and resources in the universities and veterinary schools, the need to promote an interest in research amongst veterinary undergraduates, and the diminishing support available (mainly from the Overseas Development Administration) for research in overseas veterinary medicine. Each of these new schemes has attracted a gratifying response, and there can be no doubt of their value in promoting academic work in veterinary medicine. This trend can be expected to continue in the future.

Zoology: an artist's contribution to the study of animal evolution

The fruition of the largest commitment by the Trustees to pure zoology (as distinct from comparative medicine and veterinary science) has been the occasion of the only visit so far made by a member of the Royal Family to the offices of the Trust.

In 1967 the Trust was approached by Mr Jonathan Kingdon, a Lecturer in Fine Arts at Makerere College, Uganda. He sought assistance with the preparation and publication of a massive study of East African mammals. Mr Kingdon was born in Tanganyika (later Tanzania) and had made some study of zoology as well as art. He had made himself an expert in the vivid depiction of living animals, and had expert collaborators in anatomy. The Trustees approved a grant of £3,000 in June 1967, to which subsequent grants totalling £5,456 were added in 1968 and 1971, in order to enable Mr Kingdon to study animals in the wild. Meanwhile, the first volume of *East African Mammals, An Atlas of Evolution in Africa*, planned as 'a picture of the most impressive spectrum of mammalian evolution remaining in the world today', was prepared for publication. When it appeared in 1971 a reviewer in the *Journal of Anatomy* called it 'a fascinating book and a staggering work of inspiration and dedication', and it was greeted generally by the Press with a chorus of praise. Progress with the next volumes was, however, gravely disturbed by social and political unrest in East Africa: once on safari the author was attacked by brigands and all his materials destroyed. In March 1973 the Trustees made a further award to enable Mr Kingdon to settle at Moshi in Tanzania, with fresh equipment, but even there conditions were not easy and after 18 months Mr Kingdon moved to Oxford, where he was associated with the Zoology Department. There, in October 1975, Mr Kingdon was awarded a Special Fellowship for three years to enable him to make an 'Analysis of the Structure, Function and Evolution of Facial Signal Patterns in a Primate Genus (*Cercopithecus*)',[2] with the strong support of the Oxford zoologists. A paper was published in the *Transactions of the Zoological Society of London* in 1980.

Meanwhile, the second volume of the *Atlas* had been published in 1975, to be followed by the third (likewise in two parts) seven years later. Lord Zuckerman wrote in a review of the whole work that it had 'succeeded in full measure' and that the drawings of animals furnished 'the unique quality of [Mr Kingdon's] *Atlas*, a quality which translates his achievement into one of genius'.

Later, in the same year (1982) the Trustees agreed to finance the

Fig. 57. Reception of H.R.H. the Duke of Edinburgh at the Trust offices. *Left to right*, Lord Zuckerman, Dr P. O. Williams, H.R.H., Mr Kingdon.

publication of all these drawings in a folio edition, issued with an Introduction by Lord Zuckerman. This handsome collection of *African Mammal Drawings* was ready early in 1984, when H.R.H. The Duke of Edinburgh, as President of the World Wildlife Fund International, honoured by his presence and a tribute to the Trust's support of Mr Kingdon's work a reception given by the Trustees to launch the new edition, on 29 February 1984.

Certainly since the publication of the Lachish volumes early in the history of the Trust there has been no other publishing endeavour of comparable importance. However, at the time of earlier awards to Mr Kingdon, grants in aid of scientific publications were far from unusual: in the decade 1960–70, 39 such awards were made, preponderantly to assist the publication of expensive colour plates in illustration of articles or books but sometimes to assist a learned society to print its journal. One of the most interesting of these grants were received by the Royal Society to finance the publication in the *Philosophical Transactions* (B) in 1968 of 50 ophthalmoscopic paintings of the fundi of the eyes of mammals, selected from a total of 160 prepared by Dr George Lindsay Johnson, of Johannesburg. The extraordinary point is that Dr Johnson, who had died in 1943, first published on the comparative anatomy of the mammalian eye, in the same journal, in 1901.

13

CLINICAL AND RELATED SCIENCES

Earlier passages in this history have traced the gradual evolution of the Trustees' interest in aspects of medical research which they judged to be undeservedly neglected, and for that reason susceptible of worthwhile improvement if a strong and properly directed impulse were given to them. As their Statement of Policy in 1966 made plain, they were conscious of the importance of some of the problems to whose solution insufficient attention was being directed, such as those of dermatology, for the quality of human (and animal) life. To direct greater research effort to such topics or problems they employed varied means: schemes to encourage young medical scientists to enter the field in question, or to free older men and women for research; schemes to provide research assistance and expenses for a considerable period to those willing to tackle these matters; schemes to encourage concentrations of workers and resources at particular centres. The programmes seeking to develop the selected subjects were, in general, planned by Panels of expert practitioners and the resources which the Trustees intended to make available were advertised and open to competitive bids from medical or veterinary schools and institutes.

Among the topics considered to merit this special attention and fostering have been Tropical Medicine and Veterinary Medicine (treated in Chapters 11 and 12), Mental Health and Neurology, Dermatology and Ophthalmology. The activities of the Trustees in relation to these latter topics will be discussed in this Chapter.

Mental health by Dr B. A. Bembridge

In 1973, the Director of the Trust, Dr Williams, encouraged Dr Edda Hanington to submit to the Trustees proposals which would justify the allocation annually of a specific sum for research into mental health. A decision to make such an allocation would have been in line with policy which had developed in the previous ten years. The Trustees had said in their *Sixth Report* (1964–6) that they wished to encourage research in medical fields in which funds appeared to be inadequate, although the importance of such research might be considerable if measured in relationship to human welfare – the chief objective set out in the Founder's Will. If such an allocation were made, it would then be a simple matter to administer it through application of the Trustees' policy to encourage the integration of fundamental research into clinical medicine, by designing schemes of support to meet the needs of this specific subject.

Before we try to assess the evidence for the plea that a special allocation should be made for research into mental health, we must understand the definition of mental health and its disturbances which the Trustees used. Disorders leading to disturbed mental health were considered to be those conditions in which recognisable changes in behaviour make a person unable to carry out daily tasks. These disorders may have organic causes such as an excess alcohol intake, or senile cerebral degenerative changes, or may have no demonstrable organic lesion, such as schizophrenia.

The magnitude of the clinical problem was part of the evidence for the need of such a special allocation. The number of people who at some time in their lives suffer from mental disorders justifies the need for research into many clinical problems concerned with treatment and patient care.

In a survey 'Priorities in medical research: indices of burden', published in 1975, Sir Douglas Black and Dr J. D. Pole 'proposed a quantitative assessment of the relative burden imposed on the health service and on the health of the nation by a number of broad categories of illness'. They used a statistical analysis of in-patient days, out-patient referrals, general practitioners' consultations and days of sickness benefit, which gave a high priority to mental illness as a condition for which research was important. They also wrote that 'a clear service need for research cannot be equated with the likelihood of that research being profitable; the problems involved may be clearly insoluble, there may be a lack of skilled workers, there may be stultification of research either by a lack or a superfluity of suitable patients'.

If the Trustees accepted the estimate of the size of the clinical problem, what evidence was there, from their experience of applications to them, that research into mental health was inadequately supported? Was it not equally possible that funds were adequate, but that requests for project grants did not reach the standards expected by the Trustees? Or that requests were frequently for project grants concerned with patient care which the Trustees would not consider as a matter of policy? We shall describe how the Trustees supported studies in mental health before 1973, to see if answers are possible to these questions. The classification of Trust awards before 1973 did not provide mental health as a subject category. For the subject of psychiatry, the Trustees made a single award in their large building and equipment programme of 1946–68. This was in 1958; a contribution of £37,000 towards the building of a department of neuroendocrinology and neuropathology in the Institute of Psychiatry. Between 1962 and 1972, out of 27 awards of senior fellowships in clinical science, one was made to a department of psychiatry.[1] Between 1968 and 1972, out of 16 university awards, none was made for a department of psychiatry. One special research fellowship for a period of five years was awarded in 1970.[2] In the same year, the Trustees made an award to Professor A. N. Davison, to help him establish his department at the Institute of Neurology, to develop biochemical studies of mental retardation and studies of demyelinating diseases and the aged brain.[3]

These awards must be considered in relation to the Trustees' general policy. We have pointed out that when they decided in 1966 to decrease substantially their allocations to buildings and equipment, and increase the allocation for project grants, they wished, if possible, to support projects linking two or more subjects. Many awards were made between 1966 and 1973 for research in neuroanatomy, neurochemistry and neurophysiology, in which the grant holders had no direct links with psychiatrists, or with academic departments of psychiatry.

The evidence showed that there were important clinical problems, but the Trustees had made very few awards for their investigation. Requests for support from academic departments of psychiatry were, in proportion, less frequent than from other departments and were mainly concerned with patient care.

The Trustees reached these conclusions after an assessment of their own activities in supporting research in problems of mental health. Were there, in addition, any background influences which should be understood before deciding that a change of policy might effectively make a contribution to the solution of these problems?

Overriding all other considerations is the sheer complexity of the problem of the form and function of the human brain. Normal neurophysiological mechanisms are far from being fully established and an understanding of such mechanisms is essential for a study of mental disorders. A barrier to investigations of human brain function has been the absence of techniques for studying the living human brain. We should note the enormous advances which have been made in techniques since the Trustees' deliberations in 1973. Computerised axial tomography (C.A.T. scanning) and nuclear magnetic resonance imaging (N.M.R.) have given accurate representations of cross-sections of the brain. Techniques introduced by Sokoloff and others have made it possible to relate functional activity to blood flow. Gene cloning and the production of monoclonal antibodies have led to coding of enzymes of the catecholamine pathway, and to the localisation of specific brain proteins. Studies on neurotransmitter receptor structure and function have been increasingly successful. More recently still, the distribution within the body of radioactive trace molecules has been studied with specialised tomography, to demonstrate, for example, dopamine synthesis in the human brain.

Some of the recent advances in techniques are noted now, because they illustrate another difficulty of research in problems of mental health, a difficulty which is not peculiar to this discipline and will not be easy to rectify. This is the difficulty of finding scientists able both to understand the problems of mental disorders and also to direct investigations with the modern techniques of molecular biology which are becoming increasingly available. In the past, psychiatrists frequently complemented their own clinical work with the use of contemporary anatomical and pathological techniques, or collaborated with anatomists and pathologists. The first pathology department to be established in a lunatic asylum in Great Britain was at Wakefield in 1873. Here David Ferrier, at the invitation of the Director, carried out his experimental work on localisation of cerebral function. Neuroanatomical studies were continued there by Shaw Bolton, Professor of Psychiatry at Leeds, from 1911–34.[4] A Central Pathological Laboratory of the Scottish Asylums was established in Edinburgh in 1896, with Dr W. Ford Robertson as Director. It is worth recalling the objects of the laboratory:[5] '1) to engage in original research on the pathology of insanity; 2) to promote such research in the associated asylums; 3) to afford laboratory instruction to medical officers of the various asylums; 4) to obtain reports on all cases of interest, the material from which should be sent to the pathologist'.

We should note that in 1972 Professor J. A. Corsellis wrote 'it is doubtful whether one brain in fifty deaths in psychiatric hospitals is seen by a neuropathologist, let alone examined histologically'. We cannot now trace the development of neuropathology, but of its state in 1932, Sir David Henderson wrote 'it was difficult to attract a suitably trained man to devote himself entirely to a career in neuropathology. It was rather a blind alley, it did not offer the same chances of promotion as existed in general pathology . . . a dangerous lack of continuity was apt to occur'.

This need for specialist laboratories was recognised by psychiatrists, partly because of the separation of hospitals for the mentally ill from those for general medical and surgical patients. The care of mentally ill patients has always presented problems and psychiatrists from Pinel (1745–1826) onwards have worked towards the application of enlightened methods of treatment. Unfortunately, the separate development of psychiatric hospitals was accompanied also by separation from university departments of medicine. One consequence has been that many medical students of ability have not realised the opportunities to combine clinical duties and research into mental illness. Further, much research relevant to problems of mental health has been carried out by scientists in university departments, or by pharmaceutical firms whose members have had no links with psychiatric colleagues. It is interesting that the first stages of development of psychotropic drugs, the greatest advance in psychiatric therapy in the past 50 years, were initiated by pharmaceutical firms. In the early 1950s, studies of antihistamines led to the eventual introduction of the first major tranquilliser, chlorpromazine. Observations on the side effects of isoniazid led to studies of monoamine oxidase inhibitors and their use in psychiatric medicine.

This brief account of some aspects of research into problems of mental health and its disorders provides a background against which the Trustees considered their policy towards such research when they met in 1973.

The Trustees decided that they should make awards to foster closer collaboration between the basic sciences of biochemistry, physiology and pharmacology and clinical studies of the central nervous system. They selected two fields of study, neuropsycho-pharmacology and neurochemistry, in which they would take a particular interest. They wished to examine methods of encouraging recruits to neuropathology, and to enable trained scientists who were already working in these fields of interest to the Trustees to be relieved of some of their routine service work, or to be able to take research leave.

Awards totalling nearly £6¾ million have been made in the first 12 years of the Trustees' programme for supporting research into problems of mental health.

The allocations have been:

1972–4	1974–6	1976–8	1978–80	1980–2	1982–4
£41,000	£301,000	£1,117,000	£1,481,000	£1,565,000	£2,116,000

We must now describe policy during this period and also record modifications which resulted from the Trustees' closer involvement with the problems with which they were concerned. An early decision was to support investigations into one specific mental disorder. The Trustees were aware of the interests of the Nuffield Foundation in clinico–social studies of schizophrenia, and in 1975 arranged a meeting with the Nuffield Trustees and a group of scientists actively engaged in research. The purpose of the meeting was to identify specific areas of research on schizophrenia, and methods of encouraging research, for which additional financial support appeared essential.

It was clear that the study of schizophrenia was an important activity of several units of the Medical Research Council, but that research was disproportionate to the medical and social importance of the disease. The Trustees decided that they wished to continue encouraging research in neuropsychopharmacology and neurochemistry, with special emphasis on studies related to schizophrenia. They maintained their interest in methods of attracting recruits to the basic sciences relevant to studies of mental disorders, and agreed to consider making joint appointments between departments of basic science and clinical psychiatry. They emphasised the importance of developing departments of psychiatry in undergraduate medical schools, where medical students might be influenced at an early stage in their career.

These policy decisions were implemented as soon as possible.

In January 1976, the Trustees advertised a competitive award for research into mental disorders, totalling £100,000 over five years. They stated that priority would be given to proposals for research into schizophrenia. The policy of making such awards has continued. The subjects of investigation and the holders are listed in Appendix III, p. 418. Support of studies in neuropathology was given through a lecturer post in the Department of Psychological Medicine in the University of Newcastle-upon-Tyne, then under the direction of Sir Martin Roth. The Trustees made an award to Professor Gerald Russell to enable him to undertake a scheme to train medical students in methods of psychiatric research which are derived from the basic sciences.

Having made the initial decisions concerning their policy towards mental health studies, the Trustees appointed a Panel of advisers, to consider applications for grants, make recommendations on awards and to make periodic reviews of policy for consideration by the Trustees. The Chairman of the first Panel was Professor (now Sir) W. S. Peart and the first scientific secretary was Dr Edda Hanington. The members of the Panel were Dr D. Broadbent, Professor D. Grahame-Smith, Dr L. Iversen, Professor M. Sheppherd and Dr D. Watt.[6]

In addition to carrying out policy decisions already made, the Panel recommended that the Trustees should award three fellowships annually at senior registrar level in order to train individuals who would link the clinical and basic science aspects of mental health research. Academic development in an undergraduate medical school was supported through the Department of Psychiatry, Cambridge University Medical School (Departmental Head, Sir Martin Roth), which was provided with funds for two lectureships for a period of five years from 1977. At Oxford University, the Trustees supported a rotating research training scheme initiated by Professor Gelder, for registrars undergoing their training in clinical psychiatry. At the University of Newcastle-upon-Tyne (Departmental Head, Professor D. E. Eccleston) the Trustees made an award for support of a senior lecturer for five years, for studies on patients with affective disorders.

The Trustees continued to follow the four main policy lines which have been described above:

1. Recruitment of research workers through the provision of training fellowships and scholarships.
   21 training fellowships, and 6 scholarships have been awarded 1976–84, at a total cost of £826,000.
2. Selection and support of centres in which schemes for academic development would be available.
3. Advertisements for major awards for research in specific topics.
   18 awards have been made 1974–84, at a total cost of £1,808,000. They are listed in Appendix II.
4. To maintain a special interest in promoting research in schizophrenia.
   18 awards have been made 1973–84, at a total cost of £520,000. They are listed in Appendix III.

After Dr Hanington's retirement from the Trust in 1982, the Trustees asked for a comprehensive review of their support for studies in mental health. Dr David Gordon carried out the review, after extensive discussions with many experts in the fields of psychiatry and related subjects.

The independent assessment of the Trustees' policy and the scientific results of projects supported through the various schemes can be summarised.

Mental health fellowships

Awards were made on the same basis as other fellowships and the scheme had been fruitful, for many recipients of awards had remained in research in psychiatry.

Academic development

a) An extensive programme of support for the Department of Psychiatry at Cambridge had come to an end and results of work published. The outcome of Trust support has been of uncertain value, mainly because local circumstances have not made it possible for those supported by the Trust to be integrated into the department with whole-time posts. None of the experts consulted suggested that this type of support should be tried again elsewhere in the same manner, without guarantees of continuing support. The Mental Health Panel commented that valuable collaborative work carried out in Cambridge would not have been possible without support from the Wellcome Trust.

b) *Lectureships and senior lectureships.* There was general agreement that this scheme has provided valuable support for a few individuals who will eventually move into established posts in academic departments of psychiatry.

c) *The 'Oxford' scheme.* Professor Gelder has held a grant which allows registrars in the Oxford psychiatry training scheme to be seconded for a period of six months research training. The scheme has been successful, largely because of the careful selection of registrars for training, with suitable projects. This scheme has been extended to the Universities of Edinburgh and Manchester and to the Institute of Psychiatry.

Major awards

Some of these have been highly successful in producing valuable results from investigations carried out by multi-disciplinary groups.

Project grant support; schizophrenia

The referees consulted considered that it was difficult to assess results from such support. In the words of one, 'psychiatry is a long-term problem', and it is too soon to evaluate results of specific investigations.

Ophthalmology by Dr B. A. Bembridge

The eye is involved in many systemic diseases. The best known of these are the retinal manifestations of diabetes and hypertension. Stephen Mackenzie described 'A case of glycosuric retinitis' in 1877,[7] and concluded that 'a point of still greater importance is the existence of aneurisms of the retinal capillaries'! Eventually, Wagener in 1937,[8] and Ballantyne and Loewenstein in 1943,[9] showed that diabetic retinopathy is entirely distinct from hypertensive retinopathy. In the United Kingdom diabetes is the commonest cause of blindness between the ages of 30 and 64. In children, congenital defects with eye involvement are increasing in number. In all age groups inflammation of the iris and choroid, associated with systemic disorders, are frequent causes of defective vision. Disorders of the pituitary and thyroid glands and of the optic nerve in neurological disorders are less common as causes of visual defect. However, all patients with ocular signs of systemic disease may present difficulties in management, because responsibility tends to be divided between ophthalmologists and physicians. We must remember that the foregoing remarks about eye conditions associated with systemic disease apply to European countries. The association is very different in tropical countries where the important manifestations are through nutritional defects such as vitamin A deficiency, and infections such as onchocerciasis and measles.

The use of the techniques of intravenous injection of a fluorescein dye and photography of passage of the dye through retinal vessels greatly enhanced the value of information obtained from observation of the changes in retinal blood vessels which occur in pathological conditions such as hypertension and diabetes mellitus. Retinal photography demonstrated the early vascular changes in disease, their development and modification through treatment. In 1963, the Trustees made an award to Dr (now Professor) C. T. Dollery of the Department of Medicine, Royal Postgraduate Medical School (R.P.M.S.) for the purchase of a retinal camera and accessories, for studies of hypertensive and diabetic retinopathy. Members of the Department of Medicine, R.P.M.S. began co-operative studies with members of the Department of Pathology at the Institute of Ophthalmology and in 1968 the Trustees made the award described below.

Professor N. Ashton, Professor C. T. Dollery and Professor Barrie Jones

In 1968 the Trustees made an award for five years for a collaborative research programme into ophthalmic aspects of systemic disease to be undertaken at the Royal Postgraduate Medical School, Moorfields Eye Hospital, and the Institute of Ophthalmology. The award was renewed for three years in 1973. The success of this award for interdisciplinary research was important in influencing the Trustees' later decision to designate ophthalmology as a subject for support with a special budget allocation.

Diabetes: glucose transport in the retina

Retina and brain have a unique system of endothelial cell junctions in their capillaries. These bind cells tightly together, leaving no intercellular spaces for solutes to pass between. Substances entering these tissues must diffuse across cells or be transported in pinocytotic vesicles. One such substance is glucose. In studies on rats, guinea pigs and rabbits, Professor Dollery and his colleagues have shown that glucose must be actively transported across the retinal endothelial cells before it can enter the retina.

They also investigated *oxygen supply* to the retina from the retinal and choroidal circulation at normal and increased arterial oxygen tension. The retinal vessels are extremely sensitive to changes in arterial oxygen tension. The choroidal circulation supplies the deeper parts of the retina and has a very small arteriovenous differences for oxygen, and a high blood flow. At high arterial oxygen pressures, the choroidal demand for oxygen is satisfied by dissolved oxygen, and when venous haemoglobin is fully saturated, the tissue oxygen tension can rise to a very high level. The choroidal circulation can then satisfy the oxygen requirements of almost the whole thickness of the retina. This explains the vasoconstriction taking place in the retinal circulation at high oxygen pressures.

Retinal blood flow

Professor Dollery devised methods for measuring retinal blood flow, and made measurements in groups of patients with varying degrees of retinopathy. He showed that the blood flow, normal in patients with mild to moderate retinopathy, is reduced in patients with advanced

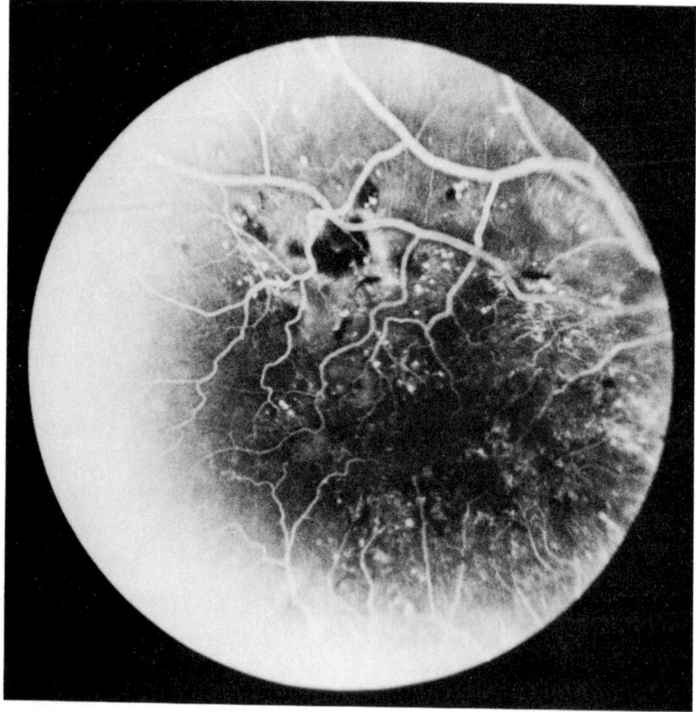

Fig. 58. Fluorescein angiogram of diabetic retinopathy. The dark areas are where laser treatment has been given.

retinopathy. A study of life-cycle of retinal microaneurysms, using fluorescein angiography, showed that damage to the superficial capillary layer is more widespread than previously supposed, early microaneurysm formation being by no means confined to the deep layers from which the veins drain.

Diabetic retinopathy

Dr Eva Kohner had a notable share in the group's contribution to a national trial of photocoagulation treatment of diabetic retinopathy. Patients with maculopathy and proliferative retinopathy were included. The difference between treated and untreated eyes was not significant in the first three years after treatment, but thereafter the results showed that photocoagulation is an effective treatment for this condition.

By means of the electron microscope Professor Ashton showed that diabetic retinopathy is a manifestation of disease of the small blood vessels, the changes there being similar to others elsewhere in the body. The pre-capillary arterioles are thickened in the region of the basement membrane; the resulting closure of the lumen may be responsible for the pathological changes in diabetic retinopathy attributable to ischaemia.

Hypertension

In work carried out before the Trust award, the application of fluorescein techniques to the study of human hypertensive retinopathy demonstrated that there were leaking points on the minute arterioles related to 'cotton wool' spots. The spots themselves appeared not to be perfused. In a search for an animal model for these changes, the investigators first studied retinal changes after embolising vessels of the pig with glass spheres. Emboli caused 'cotton wool' spots, but did not replicate the arterial changes. The next step was to use monkeys with experimental renal hypertension. These animals developed a retinopathy that was almost indistinguishable from human hypertensive retinopathy, both on ophthalmoscopic and fluorescein examination.

Professor Ashton examined many thousands of sections under the electron microscope in an attempt to identify the earliest structural changes responsible for leakage points, previously identified by fluorescein angiography. Points of leakage were precisely located, and ruptures through the vascular endothelium found, while junctions remained intact. Leakage points probably all represent points of endothelial breakdown, with penetration of plasma into the vessel wall.

He also investigated the effects upon the retinal vessel walls of acute and artificial rises of tension induced by repeated forced injections of saline into the carotid. He succeeded in producing focal leakage from retinal vessels, which were shown to be due to endothelial damage. This hypertension could not, however, be maintained, the leaks healed within three days, and no permanent vascular injury resulted.

Malignant hypertension

Professor Ashton's experimental work on hypertension in monkeys demonstrated that it is possible to produce a malignant hypertension, with a retinopathy similar to that in man. The experiments showed that leakage into vessel cells and necrotic changes in smooth muscle cells precede deposition of fibrin. Professor Ashton retired from his post in the Institute of Ophthalmology soon after the termination of this Trust award. He was succeeded by Professor Garner, who has also worked, with Trust support, on hypertensive retinopathy.

The Trustees considered that the results of their support for the collaborative research described above demonstrated, first, the general principle of the feasibility of such productive research when the necessary financial support was available and second, the specific need for support for research in ophthalmology. They therefore decided to set aside annually a specific sum for research in ophthalmology, defined as studies related to the eye, the bony orbit and its contents and the visual pathway. The Trustees decided to carry out their policy through methods which had the purpose of 1) supporting studies on ocular manifestations of systemic disorders and 2) encouraging co-operation between basic and clinical scientists.

In 1977, the Trustees made a major award over five years to Mr A. J. Bron and Dr R. Turner of the University of Oxford for a multidisciplinary study of biochemical indices of diabetic retinopathy.

The Trustees considered that the proposed investigation was important because, in England and Wales, diabetic retinopathy is the major cause of blind registration between the ages of 30 and 65 years and accounts for 800 newly registered blind per year. This is 7 per cent of the total registered. The visual loss is due to microvascular changes in the retina, through macular exudates and macular oedema, but most important through new vessel formation and the resultant retinitis proliferans. The latter accounts for about 5 per cent of all diabetic retinopathy.

The incidence of retinopathy has increased with improved diabetic survival and the overall incidence of retinopathy, including proliferative retinopathy, is known to increase with the duration of diabetes. Although the cause of the retinopathy is not known, it is noteworthy that some patients fail to develop retinopathy even after 40 years of diabetes, that good diabetic control may favourably influence the retinopathy and that proliferative changes may regress after hypophysectomy. This suggests that the retinopathy may be modified by the biochemical milieu and that this is susceptible of investigation.

The results of research carried out by Mr Bron, Dr Turner and their colleagues are described now.

The project examined the relation between diabetic tissue damage and selected biochemical, vascular and haemostatic factors. Patients were recruited from a large retinopathy screening programme. A new technique of quantifying retinopathy was developed. Cross-sectional studies showed that diabetics with retinopathy had high plasma low density lipoprotein (L.D.L.), cholesterol, fibrinogen, fibrinogen turnover, factor VIII procoagulent activity, factor VIII related antigen and *N*-acetyl glucosaminidase compared to those without retinopathy. Their plasminogen turnover was normal, but in response to forearm vein occlusion both plasminogen activator release and reactive hyperaemia were depressed. Although the patients with retinopathy had an altered vascular reactivity and impaired fibrinolytic ability compared with those without, their venous prostacyclin production and plasma 6 keto F1 levels were normal. Diabetic patients had raised corrected blood viscosity, but the degree was small compared with changes in haematocrit and it was felt unlikely to be a major determinant of microvascular damage.

The effects of glycaemic control were examined in various ways: retrospective studies showed a correlation between high mean blood glucose levels and the early onset of background retinopathy, or proliferative retinopathy. In a cross-sectional study in 80 diabetics, asymptomatic nocturnal hypoglycaemia was associated with a lower HbA1 and a decreased prevalence of retinopathy. When these patients were studied in a three-year prospective randomised-controlled trial of a regimen aiming to improve diabetic control, there was a slower progression of peripheral neuropathy, but no difference in the rate of progression of retinopathy. However, genetic factors may have masked an effect of retinopathy, since retinopathy was found more frequently in patients with HLA DR4 and subsequently progressed more rapidly in HLA DR4 positive patients independent of glycaemic control. A genetic factor influencing retinopathy was also suggested by a correlation between complement types and retinopathy.

It is clear that there is always research of a high standard in the basic science subjects related to ophthalmology, in university departments which have no relationships with academic departments of ophthalmology. The Trustees attempted to encourage co-operation between departments by support for collaborative projects (e.g. physiology and neurology at Cambridge) and by fellowship awards, both to established ophthalmologists who wished to carry out laboratory research (e.g. Dr Gillian Clover, for studies of the clinicopathological correlation of blood/retinal barriers in diabetic retinopathy, with Dr John Marshall), or for training in research methods for a physician who wished to become a medical ophthalmologist (e.g. Dr Susan Lightman, training in immunology at the National Institute for Medical Research with Dr Bridget Askonas).

The response to the Trustees' advertisements of the availability of these fellowships had been discouraging and a meeting was therefore held in

1981, with distinguished ophthalmologists, to discuss methods of encouraging research in ophthalmology.

The discussion was mainly concerned with the relationship between clinical ophthalmology and other scientific disciplines; methods for increasing co-operation between ophthalmology and other clinical subjects, and between ophthalmology and the basic sciences; and the training of ophthalmologists.

It appears that both in the Health Service and in university departments, the large clinical service commitment, the overworked laboratory service for basic pathological investigations, and insufficient staff, leave very little time for following up the many unanswered questions in clinical ophthalmology, or for carrying out any research. Difficulties in teaching mean that undergraduates' interests in ophthalmology are unlikely to be fostered.

There was general agreement that links between ophthalmology and other subjects are essential, but that the separation of specialities is much less now than it was 20 years ago. There was, however, some difference of opinion on the nature of the 'bridgeman' between the subjects. Is one man able to receive training for formal recognition in more than one discipline? Is such formal recognition, in any case, essential for a member of an academic department? If the necessary abilities are unlikely to be present in one man, ought he to be a basic scientist co-operating with clinical colleagues? In present financial circumstances the team leader might have to recruit a young graduate who would contribute a special skill, but then have to move on. He would be able to recruit a man of senior lecturer seniority only if the career structure was satisfactory.

It seems that even in times of financial difficulties, a post can be created in the larger departments for an outstanding individual with unusual experience. The negotiations are time-consuming, which means that delays may make it difficult for the scientist to remain at his work. The Trustees are often able to help with short-term financial support in these circumstances. Medical ophthalmology was compared with subjects such as paediatric neurology and clinical neurophysiology. Proper training in a 'double discipline' is very difficult, but the danger of the 'bridge' subject itself becoming a speciality with its own rules and regulations must be appreciated.

Suggestions from the participants about methods of support covered the field from elective periods for undergraduates to Trust support for senior appointments for basic scientists or clinicians and joint appointments between, for example, academic departments of neurology and ophthalmology in selected centres which must not be too small to be effective. The Trustees believe that if suitable centres can be identified, they can be strengthened and become the sources for providing foundations for other departments.

Awards made since 1974 for research in ophthalmology may be summarised by noting that the policy for encouraging research in ocular aspects of systemic disease resulted in a single major award; that the fellowship awards were successful individually, but the small number of applicants had been disappointing; and that there had been many successful applications for project grants, with no clinical component, in basic sciences related to vision. The Trustees decided, nevertheless, to continue their policy of providing a special budgetary allocation for research in ophthalmology and in 1985 they established a vision research working party to co-ordinate and promote all their support for research on the eye and visual pathway. Sir Stanley Peart represents the Trustees and Dr F. W. Campbell agreed to be chairman of the first group of scientists forming the working party, made up by Professors Norman Ashton, A. C. Bird, W. S. Foulds, J. S. Kelly and S. M. Zeki.

Neurology

In their report for 1966–8, the Trustees noted the achievements of British research workers in studies of the physiology of the nervous system, and said that they wished to encourage the application of recently developed techniques of neurophysiology and biochemistry to clinical problems. The Trustees did not carry out their policy by means of any special schemes and support for studies in neurology has not been on a scale similar to other programmes. However, many grants have produced significant results. Two of these awards are now described.

Professor P. K. Thomas

In 1969, the Trustees made an award to Professor P. K. Thomas, of the Royal Free Hospital, London, for conversion of laboratory accommodation, an electron microscope and research assistance for three years, for research on morphological and physiological changes in diseases of the nervous system. The Trustees considered that their award would fulfil their policy of supporting groups with interest both in clinical neurology and basic neurobiology. The results of research supported by this grant encouraged the Trustees to renew it for a further three years in 1972. It is interesting to note that some of the studies were done in collaboration with the Department of Anatomy at St Mary's Hospital, where the electron microscope used was also provided by the Wellcome Trust.

The research unit that was established subsequently became the Department of Neurological Science at the Royal Free Hospital School of Medicine. It currently (1985) houses two research groups. One, headed by Professor P. K. Thomas, is mainly devoted to the study of disorders of the peripheral nervous system; the other, headed by Professor J. Newsom-Davis, is predominantly concerned with the investigation of myasthenia gravis and the Lambert–Eaton myasthenic syndrome.

Previous studies by Professor P. K. Thomas had established that some polyneuropathies are characterised by widespread segmental demyelination in the peripheral nerves and, if this is a continuing process, by concentric Schwann cell proliferation producing a 'hypertrophic neuropathy'. Other generalised polyneuropathies are characterised by predominant axonal degeneration which is often maximal distally. A major interest of the research unit has been in the hereditary neuropathies, combining clinical, genetic, electrophysiological and nerve biopsy studies. One condition investigated was Charcot-Marie-Tooth disease (peroneal muscular atrophy). As was found by P. J. Dyck and his collaborators at the Mayo Clinic, intrafamilial correlations of nerve conduction studies established that Charcot-Marie-Tooth disease is genetically heterogeneous and that the clinical syndrome could be sub-divided into cases of distal spinal muscular atrophy and others with combined motor and sensory involvement. The term hereditary motor and sensory neuropathy (H.M.S.N.) was introduced for the latter category and this designation has now been widely adopted. It was further shown that in some families the disorder was characterised by a diffuse demyelinating neuropathy (type I H.M.S.N.) and others by predominant axonal degeneration (type II H.M.S.N.). Although initially not accepted by all workers, genetic heterogeneity was later confirmed by linkage studies. Some families with H.M.S.N. I are linked to the Duffy blood group locus whereas this was not found for H.M.S.N. II. Other rarer hereditary neuropathies were also investigated, this including the delineation of the morphological features of Tangier disease (hereditary high-density lipoprotein deficiency) and Fabry's disease (alpha-galactosidase A deficiency).

A second major interest of the research unit has been in metabolic neuropathies. During the period of support by the Wellcome Trust, treatment of end-stage renal failure by periodic haemodialysis was introduced. At this stage the recognition of uraemic neuropathy had just been established by A. K. Asbury and others in the U.S.A. In collaboration with the Renal Dialysis Unit at the Royal Free Hospital, the nature of this neuropathy was defined as a distal axonal degeneration with secondary demyelination. Unfortunately, attempts to define its metabolic basis have so far proved unfruitful.

The investigation of diabetic neuropathy by nerve biopsy and the use of morphometric techniques was initiated and this led to the study of animal models of diabetes. These are continuing. The identification of the cause of diabetic neuropathy will be an important advance, as this neuropathy constitutes the commonest form of polyneuropathy in developed countries. Although diabetic neuropathy is likely to have a multifactorial causation, the animal studies have suggested that defective protein synthesis by the cells that contribute axons to the peripheral nerves may be an important mechanism in the generalised sensory polyneuropathy. The third main activity of the research unit has been in idiopathic inflammatory polyneuropathy. During the period of support by the Wellcome Trust, investigations were undertaken on the chronic relapsing and chronic progressive variants of this group of disorders, which includes acute idiopathic inflammatory polyneuropathy (Guillain–Barre syndrome). It was established that, in common with the acute syndrome, the chronic relapsing and chronic progressive forms were characterised by widespread demyelination and the presence of inflammatory infiltrates in peripheral nerve. It was further shown that there are likely to be genetic differences between individuals with the acute and chronic relapsing diseases in that association with certain H.L.A. antigens is demonstrable for the chronic relapsing but not the acute cases. The immunological basis for these disorders is still uncertain but is being actively investigated, including observations on the putative animal model, experimental allergic neuritis.

The other award to be described was for studies in myasthenia gravis.

In 1948, Sir Henry Dale opened a discussion on the physiological basis of neuromuscular disorders in the section of physiology of a meeting of the British Medical Association and said 'Probably the best example of the application of the chemical transmission theory to the elucidation of a morbid neuromuscular defect is afforded by myasthenia gravis.' The disease may be defined as a condition with a severe defect of neuromuscular transmission, without clinical evidence of a motorneurone disease, or a myopathy (J. A. Simpson). Sir Henry recalled that in 1935 Dr Mary Walker had noted the similarity between the effects of curare and the clinical conditions of myasthenia gravis. She had successfully treated the symptoms of myasthenia with injections of prostigmine.

In 1960, Dr J. A. Simpson suggested that the clinically recognised link between functions of the thymus gland and the pathological condition of myasthenia gravis was immunological, mediated by the production of antibodies against acetyl choline receptors at end plates. The thymus is apparently an essential intermediary during the active first stage of the disease, but not later and Simpson has postulated that some aspect of immunological tolerance is broken by whatever is the primary stimulus for myasthenia gravis.

Dr A. I. Weir

In 1980, the Trustees awarded a Senior Fellowship in Clinical Science to Dr Weir, Department of Neurology, University of Glasgow, to study motor end plates of human muscle with Professor J. A. Simpson.

Corticosteroids are employed in the accepted therapy for human myasthenia gravis. During the treatment there may be a severe, but transient, depression of muscle power lasting for a period between five and ten days, followed by a sustained improvement. Dr Weir studied the effects of corticosteroid therapy on neuromuscular transmission in rats suffering from experimentally-induced autoimmune myasthenia gravis. His experiments suggested that the early effects of the steroids upon the disease occurred at the neuromuscular junction rather than by immunosuppression, as had hitherto been commonly supposed.

Dermatology

In April 1967 Dermatology was adopted by the Trustees as a 'neglected subject' in medicine, likely to profit rapidly from the injection of funds to open up vigorous lines of research. By 1969 the sum allocated to this subject had been increased to £150,000 per annum. This policy was pursued with energy during the next ten years, with a particular concentration upon the University of Newcastle-upon-Tyne, where Dr Sam Shuster had been appointed to the Professorship of Dermatology at the early age of 36, in 1964. Professor Shuster quickly explored the possibility of Wellcome research support with Dr Williams; there were, he thought, great opportunities before him in his new post: the University was willing to acquire a house which could be adapted as a laboratory, while both the University Grants Committee and the Medical Research Council were interested. (In fact, the M.R.C. made him a considerable research grant in June 1966.) The action of the sebaceous gland and the aetiology of acne vulgaris – that plague of adolescence – and of psoriasis – a disagreeable,

Fig. 59. Visit to Newcastle-upon-Tyne University, 1970; *left to right,* Lady McMichael, Dr P. O. Williams, Sir John McMichael, Professor Shuster.

disfiguring and resistant condition – were proposed as subjects of research. In 1966 Professor Shuster wrote to Dr Williams:

> I am convinced that the time is now ripe for [the development of basic research in dermatology] and that the application of present day scientific techniques will produce significant answers to the common dermatoses. Moreover a strong academic department would be a major influence towards a scientific dermatology and in the development of a rational approach to its presentation as an undergraduate discipline.

In the July following the Trustees made the University of Newcastle-upon-Tyne a grant of £30,000 for the construction of laboratories for Professor Shuster's department; there was considerable difficulty in getting the work done and it became necessary to add a further £10,000 though other money had been raised elsewhere. Finally, Sir John McMichael opened the Wellcome Laboratories for Research in Skin Diseases at Newcastle in November 1970.

Professor Shuster, who has described himself as a dabbler in both science and medicine, has claimed that 'the recent revival of dermatology is due entirely to its unexpected marriage to biological science'; he has himself been a foremost agent in bringing this marriage about. He believes that 'the quantitative biological approach works in dermatology just as in other fields', whereas years of clinical observation and subjective reporting had produced only an imperceptible forward movement.[10] In his own words an ideas man rather than an experimentalist, Professor Shuster has studied many other processes in the skin such as weal-formation and the treatment of urticaria, and the measurement of itching with the efficacy of suppressant drugs, besides the investigations supported by the Wellcome Trustees. This support began with a massive grant of £112,000 spread over six years, for the study of psoriasis and the physical properties of skin. Other grants made up to 1975 totalled £43,400. In May 1976 the psoriasis programme was taken further with a grant of £20,000 shared by Professor Shuster and his colleague Professor Roger Pain, head of the Department of Physical Biochemistry at Newcastle.

By 1978 interest was concentrating upon the isolation and chemical characterisation of the specific inhibitors of epidermal cell proliferation ('chalones') which some investigators had detected. A conference on this topic, which came to no very clear conclusions, was held at the Trust offices on 23 November 1978.

In the following February the Trustees gave Professor Shuster a grant of £24,300 to wind up this particular research. About this time a new and very promising line appeared: evidence seemed to indicate that psoriasis sufferers might have a reduced activity of the enzyme arylhydrocarbon hydroxylase (A.H.H.) in the skin, even in unaffected areas of skin, and Professor Shuster was inclined to suspect a genetic origin for the abnormality. In 1981 he submitted with Professor M. D. Rawlins (Clinical Pharmacology) a request for support for a considerable investigation of this topic, to which the Trustees allocated £53,000. A fresh researcher, Dr Michael J. Finnen, was recruited to take charge of the work, who reported no abnormality in the A.H.H. levels of the skin of psoriasis sufferers. As it became all too clear that something was amiss with the earlier results, which had been widely reported, a disclaimer was published in the summer of 1982. In January 1984 the Trustees made Professor Shuster a fresh grant of £28,000 to permit further clarification by continuing the investigation.

Altogether, some £332,200 has been devoted by the Trustees to the dermatological researches conducted at Newcastle-upon-Tyne. This University was by no means the sole recipient of funds in aid of such researches, indeed near the beginning of the special programme the Trustees had chosen the Institute of Dermatology in London, in addition to Professor Shuster's department, as a special centre of interest. Twelve other grants have been made in the six years 1976–82 – after dermatology had ceased to be regarded as a 'neglected subject' – to the Institute of Dermatology, to Birkbeck College (Dr Edna Laurence), to the University of Sheffield (Professor F. J. Ebling) and to the University of Oxford. The success of the whole programme, about half way through its development, was thus summarized by Professor Shuster in a report submitted in February 1974:

> The various dermatological projects supported by the Trust have already had a visible effect on the development of dermatology. There are now several strong and developing academic centres, e.g. Cardiff and Bristol, with particularly good groups at St. Mary's, Leeds and Glasgow and there have been developments too in Sheffield and Edinburgh.
>
> The whole climate of work and understanding in the field has now improved enormously and this is also reflected right back at the clinical level. The British Association of Dermatology now has an Investigative Group, which meets regularly and is represented on the Board of the parent society. At its meeting last month in Liverpool there were 150 people and the scientific programme lasted two days. We also have a European Society for Dermatological Research, of a very high standard, and this society now has joint meetings with the Society of Investigative Dermatology of the U.S.A. Finally even the International Society of Dermatology, which organises the monster quinquenial international conferences has asked the E.S.D.R. and S.I.D. to take over the organisation of its next programme. In all these activities the U.K. now plays an important part and has in fact taken the lead in Europe. Much of this development has followed the direct intervention of the Trust in the support of research, the creation of new posts and the training of staff.

What Professor Shuster could not himself say on this occasion is that many of these who carried out work in his Department have gone on to professorships and other senior posts elsewhere.

One of these, Dr M. W. Greaves, was appointed to the Professorship of Dermatology at the Institute of Dermatology in London from 1 January 1975. He at once approached the Trust, with a view to funding at the Institute a new research programme into such topics as the mediators of inflammatory reactions, histamine metabolism, prostaglandin synthesis and drug eruptions. However, further examination of the facilities he was to take over in London at St John's Hospital, Homerton Grove, made improvements to the building of the Institute his first priority.

The Trustees made Professor Greaves a grant of £100,000 in May 1975 so that his Skin Pharmacology Unit could be properly housed, the M.R.C. granting an equal sum for staff and equipment, and the Postgraduate Medical Federation a further £15,000 for equipment. The new laboratories were officially opened on 20 May 1977.

From August 1984 the Institute of Dermatology became a part of the Guy's and St Thomas's Hospital United Medical School, St John's Hospital having been merged with St Thomas's, and it is expected that the Wellcome Trust Laboratories for Skin Pharmacology will be closed in 1986.

In 1973 a University Award of nearly £10,000 was made on behalf of Dr Ronald Marks, so that he could be promoted to a Senior Lectureship in the Welsh National School of Medicine, at Cardiff. This grant was extended later, until in December 1980 Dr Marks was advanced to a personal Professorship of Dermatology at the same School.

Epidemiology

At the Trustees' policy meeting in May 1978 Dr C. E. Gordon Smith presented a paper proposing that a number of five-year training Fellowships should be offered in order to improve recruitment to epidemiological studies. He remarked upon the importance of such studies in tracing the causation and aetiology of disease – Sir Richard Doll's demonstration of the correlation between cigarette smoking and the occurrence of lung cancer might have been a case in point – in ascertaining the effects and dangers of new drugs and vaccines (only to be discovered, again, by careful correlation of cases over a long period of time), and in the investigation of new diseases such as the Acquired Immune Deficiency

Syndrome (A.I.D.S.) and Lassa fever. Further, in well-known diseases such as viral hepatitis there were still many problems capable of being solved by epidemiological methods. Dr Gordon Smith thought the work he had in mind was little favoured by the National Health Service nor by Departments of Community Medicine; there were indeed a few active research centres, but their attitudes and results were not widely disseminated. More specifically, the need for more trained epidemiologists was indicated by posts remaining unfilled, or inappropriately filled, in the National Health Service, the Public Health Laboratory Service, and so on.

In detail, Dr Smith proposed a course of training which should consist of one year spent taking an M.Sc. course at his own Institution, the London School of Hygiene and Tropical Medicine, and four years of directed research. The Trustees agreed to reserve up to £150,000 for a programme of this kind for the following year.

Within the School, Dr Smith asked Professor G. A. Rose of the Department of Medical Statistics and Epidemiology to work out a detailed scheme for the prospective Fellows, and to arrange a meeting of experts to discuss it. The Scheme was publicly announced in April 1979, as aimed to encourage research in the 'interdisciplinary area that lies between the study of disease in individuals and in populations'. Candidates for Fellowships were to be sponsored jointly by Departments of Clinical Medicine and Departments of Epidemiology or Community Medicine.

There was some immediate criticism of the terms of this offer of Fellowships, both as to the restrictive conditions of candidature and the unique link with the London School of Hygiene and Tropical Medicine. Nevertheless, the Trustees decided to continue with the scheme as advertised for an experimental period, and as a result of the first competition three Fellows were appointed, taking as their research topics, respectively, the epidemiological aspects of ophthalmology,[11] prenatal morbidity and mortality, and the health of village populations in developing countries. As a result of further competitions, three more awards were made in 1980, two in 1981, two in 1982 and one in 1983. The number of applications was not great – indeed, only two in all were unsuccessful. This was a disappointing response to a new initiative: after nearly five years (in January 1984) Trust officers met with a number of interested medical scientists to consider the next stage. Evidently there was still little academic interest in epidemiology, Community Medicine seemed to lack purpose and enthusiasm, and these trends were worsening:

> The general feeling was that, although epidemiological studies continued to be attractive to many able young clinicians, the lack of career structure, leading to consultant-grade posts, deterred many would-be candidates. Moreover, the increasingly stringent accreditation requirements of the Faculties had exacerbated the problem of attracting young doctors into research into epidemiology.

The Trustees now accepted the view that their first scheme had been too narrowly and inflexibly formulated, and that a system for awards that was more variable, and perhaps allowed for a shorter commitment, would do more good.

Another competition was held subsequently in 1984, the Trustees having agreed to offer four Fellowships per annum, each for up to three years. However, only five applications were received and all but one of these was successful, two other applicants receiving awards for the same projects from the Medical Research Council and the two others withdrawing. It must be confessed that this does not augur well for the future; perhaps the interest of the M.R.C. in epidemiology has rendered the Trust's support less useful than when Dr Smith urged it in 1978.

Infectious diseases

In 1977 the Trustees decided to embark upon a new programme to encourage research into infectious diseases, a subject which recent reductions in childhood morbidity on the one hand, and withdrawal of British residents from tropical countries on the other, seemed to have rendered unfashionable. Fever hospitals and isolation wards have vanished. Few paediatricians in this country are now interested in the infectious diseases of childhood, now (in principle at least) controlled by inoculations; opportunities for research and advancement were few. Nevertheless, the requirements for specialist knowledge of infections is still real. Post-surgical and intestinal infections of patients in hospital are increasingly troublesome; tourism hastens the transport of disease from regions where it is endemic to unprotected populations; new infectious disease entities appear. As Dr D. A. J. Tyrrell pointed out in a lecture in 1982:

> man will always be living in balance with micro-organisms and from time to time the balance will be disturbed in favour of one invader or another . . . we can assume infectious diseases will

> continue to occur and will require wise management. . . . There is firstly the need to have some individuals with extensive experience in diagnosing and handling patients with a wide variety of proved and suspected infections; secondly, the best practice and research in infectious diseases is based on a foundation of scientific knowledge that includes bacteriology, virology, and epidemiology on the one hand, and immunology and pathogenesis on the other, as well as a detailed understanding of the pharmokinetics, toxicology, and the antimicrobial range of a variety of antibiotics. It requires a substantial effort to build up such a foundation beyond that which is needed for the competent practice of a general physician or other specialist.

Dr Tyrrell noted that the study of childhood infectious disease was taken more seriously in the U.S.A. than here, and concluded:

> Infections no longer plague us the way they did; individual infections may disappear from certain areas but infections as a whole cannot be abolished, they can only be held in check, and over much of the globe they have still to be reduced to a bearable low incidence. There is still much to do.

Considerations of this kind induced the Trustees to encourage clinical studies having as their object the elucidation of the physiological, metabolic and biochemical changes associated with defined infections. They therefore advertised a Competitive Award for research on the metabolic effects of infection, which was given (for four years) to Professor J. C. Waterlow of the London School of Hygiene and Tropical Medicine. The Trustees found the response to their advertisements disappointing as to both quantity and quality, and therefore did not repeat it but chose to look for other ways of gaining their object, such as long-term support.

In fact, the next step was delayed for a few years, partly because of discussions with the Tropical Panel, to which (from May 1983) special responsibility for Infectious Diseases was to be assigned, two additional members being invited to join it for that purpose.

On 2 April 1981 Dr Ogilvie addressed a letter to 18 senior medical scientists known to be interested in infectious disease, soliciting their advice and comment. Her letter stated that the Trustees in particular considered

> that there is a lack of work which aims to throw light on the nature of the physiological metabolic, and biochemical changes that accompany and follow infection, and lead to such effects as coma, shock and fatigue. A good example of the value of such knowledge is the elucidation of the mechanism that underlies fluid loss in patients suffering from cholera.

By contrast, there was no such dearth of work on the microbiological and immunological aspects of infectious disease. The Trustees wished to be advised how best they might stimulate such research, and where it might most fruitfully be encouraged.

Full and carefully argued replies were received from all recipients of this letter, mostly agreeing with the Trustees' analysis as presented by Dr Ogilvie, suggesting likely centres for the work the Trust hoped to encourage, and drawing attention to the absence of a clear career structure for those who might wish to take up infection as a research topic.

Judging that there was a possible 'field', the Trustees decided not to invest in any one centre of their own choice but rather to advertise a Major Award (up to £150,000) for studies aiming to elucidate the physiological, metabolic and biochemical changes that follow infection. There would be a preference for multidisciplinary projects and the clinical approach. Further, they reserved up to £100,000 for three-year training Fellowships for clinicians of Senior Registrar level. In addition, a sum was set aside to assist research by those concerned with the management of cases of rare and dangerous infectious diseases, such as lassa fever, whenever cases might occur.

Two Major Awards were in fact made at the first turn (1982) to the Universities of Birmingham and Oxford (see for details and subsequent awards, Appendix IV, p. 428). Three appointments to training Fellowships were also made in 1982.

In 1984 the Trustees advertised their willingness to support posts at Senior Lecturer or Lecturer level in units within medical schools to be devoted to research into infectious disease. Support would be possible up to ten years, but the school would be expected to manifest a sustained interest in the subject, to provide clinical and laboratory facilities or research, and to offer some prospect of continued interest into the future.

Further awards have been made in 1983 and 1984 (see Appendix IV), but it may be worth remarking that the Trustees have since 1982 included under the broad heading of 'Infectious Diseases' topics falling outside the original conception; for example, the grant to Dr Mary E. Penney (Oxford) relates to microbiology as related to infection, and the awards to Dr I. V. D. Weller and to Dr H. E. Webb to immunology. It is more important, after all, to promote first-class research than to insist pedantically upon rigorous definitions.

Toxicology

Sir William Paton has said that toxicology is that branch of the study of the interaction of chemicals with biological systems which is concerned with adverse reactions, pharmacology being (primarily) concerned with favourable reactions. Throughout the 1970s there was a growing interest in the danger to the health of men (and animals) latent in food and drink prepared or processed in various ways, or in the practice of habits like smoking, or in industrial processes and the emissions or by-products of industry, or simply in air or water. Many substances, like asbestos, were newly recognised as extremely dangerous that had formerly seemed innocent, and it was recognised with alarm that newly-marketed drugs might prove in unforeseen ways horribly perilous. But, as a report to the Royal Society noted, in 1977 there were no established professorships of toxicology in Britain, and only two M.Sc. courses were available to potential students, neither of them based on a firm group of scientists. The great majority of students of medicine and pathology received no coherent guidance in this field.

About this time Professor R. H. S. Thompson perceived a need for the Trust to intervene by identifying aspects of toxicology which it might support, and invoked the expertise of Professor Paton. At their meeting in 1978 the body of Trustees concurred with these two of their number in agreeing to advertise a Major Award (for which up to £500,000 was allocated) whose main object would be to provide funds for prime movers who could set up and co-ordinate an interdisciplinary group or groups.

There was recognition of the difficulty involved in advancing a field lying on the borders of others (biochemistry, pharmacology, pathology, epidemiology, etc.) but this is a feature common to all newly emergent subjects. The advertisement more precisely stated that the award would be for the elucidation of the mechanisms by which some true action or group of actions is produced, while also helping to create within the recipient institution a continuing nucleus of toxicological study. The purpose in giving this direction to the award was to improve the rational basis for the regulatory decisions, affecting the whole community, which are based on toxicology.

Before this was issued, however, a meeting of the outside experts together with three Trustees and Trust staff was held on 24 January 1979. In specific terms – matters wherein the Trust could take action – this meeting commended the interdisciplinary approach, the study of Toxicology not being one that could develop in isolation; links to other key subjects were essential. However, the outside experts thought that a few smaller awards might be more appropriate than a single large award of up to £100,000 p.a. The group agreed that the area specially selected for support should be whole-animal work on mechanisms of cell injury, but no such restriction was announced in the advertisement of the proposed award (24 February 1979).

After interviews of five short-listed applicants the Trustees approved three grants, totalling £181,000 or barely one-third of the sum allocated; to Professor A. M. Breckenridge (University of Liverpool), Professor H. S. A. Sherratt (University of Newcastle-upon-Tyne) and Dr L. J. King (University of Surrey), for toxicological researches relating to synthetic steroids, compounds influencing intermediate metabolism, and the metal cadmium, respectively. Similarly in June 1980 multiple awards were made, this time to four applicants, amounting in all to £200,000; on this round a grant was made to Dr A. E. M. McLean (University College Hospital Medical School) who had been a principal agent in arousing the Trustees' interest in toxicology (see *Thirteenth Report, 1978–80,* 41–2).

The Trustees did not feel that the pattern of applications and awards in these two years quite lived up to the hopes that the Trustees had entertained in starting the scheme. Since some more definite action seemed to be required, they decided early in 1981 to ask one of their number, Professor Thompson, to investigate the setting up of a viable, interdisciplinary academic centre for research on toxicology at Oxford, to find out what work could be done there and inquire into staff, finance and buildings. Meanwhile, a third Competitive Award was to be advertised for a restricted topic:

> studies of the mechanism of action of substances (including drugs) producing toxic manifestations in the central nervous system.

It was expected that projects would involve collaboration between a basic scientist and a clinician. In consequence, in June 1981, four awards were again approved to a total value of £206,000, also less than the £$\frac{1}{4}$ million allocated but, in addition, five separate grants were made to help with research assistance and expenses in the area of toxicity and toxicology.

This was the last open competition. Professor Sir William Paton, himself a Trustee though absent from the earlier discussions relating to Oxford, accepted an invitation from the full Board to bring into existence within his own Department of Pharmacology there a Toxicology Unit, the department having long developed close interdisciplinary links and containing research workers of appropriate experience and interests. It seemed that the Trustees' ideal of a research group could best be realised by building on such a core in this highly fruitful environment. A Unit in Toxicology was established in 1982 with the appointment of Dr David Harvey to a Wellcome Senior Lectureship. Dr Harvey is mainly concerned with the mechanisms of drug toxicity and their study by mass-spectrometry. Soon afterwards, Dr Edith Sim was appointed a second Senior Lecturer. Dr Sim's special interest is the study of drug-induced systemic lupus erythamatosus. The Unit is still evolving within the Department of Pharmacology, under the general guidance of Professor D. Smith, Sir William Paton's successor in the Chair of Pharmacology at Oxford.

14

BUILDINGS AND EQUIPMENT
by Dr B. A. Bembridge

When, after the cessation of international hostilities and the rehabilitation of the Burroughs Wellcome organisation the Trustees were able to devote funds to the support of research, they were faced with a situation in which the lack of new laboratory building for many years and the obsolescence of equipment, combined with rapid technical development in many fields, endangered the proper development of many institutions. They therefore came to the decision to improve the fundamental requirements of medical science. Professor Sydney Brenner has recently said that 'progress in science depends on new techniques, new discoveries and new ideas, probably in that order'.[1] By their decision, the Trustees assisted the great breakthrough in cell biology for 'As with many scientific advances, new tools, not new thoughts, rendered possible the massive invasion of the subcellular world that was launched at that time'.[2]

Because the Trustees followed this policy, grants made for buildings and for equipment constituted a large part of the Trustees' expenditure during the early years of their activity. Their other major interest was in awarding travel grants.

The monetary value of these early grants cannot be judged by today's standards, because of the effects of inflation. Instead, it is instructive to examine figures for grants awards as a proportion of total expenditure. The Trust's total allocation for 1936–70 amounted to approximately £18,300,000. Of this, £4,725,000 was allocated for building, and £2,750,000 for equipment grants. (Appendix V.) Thus, in these years, approximately 38 per cent of the Trustees' budget was expended on buildings and equipment. In the years after 1970, the proportion has rarely exceeded

Fig. 60. Wellcome Research Laboratory in the extension of the Department of Biochemistry, University of Oxford. The grant of £50,000, made in 1954, was one of the early awards made by the Trustees, to facilitate the research of Professor H. A. Krebs and colleagues.

three per cent. Of the sum awarded for equipment, almost one-quarter was for the provision of electron microscopes.

It is impossible to describe the scientific projects related to all such grants. In Appendix VI, the major grants for buildings are listed, with an indication of the scientific programmes for which they were used. In addition, Wellcome Trust grants were awarded for many types of equipment in relation to a wide variety of investigations. These included the use of techniques for studies of fine morphology (electron microscopy); three-dimensional structure (X-ray crystallography); separation of small quantities of substances (chromatography, electrophoresis, ultracentrifugation); tracing movements of substances during metabolic activities (labelled isotopes); and studying metabolic activities in whole human tissue (nuclear magnetic resonance). We shall select for description only four categories. Trust awards were of particular significance for studies with X-ray crystallography, electron microscopy, the ultracentrifuge, and nuclear magnetic resonance. The Trustees accepted the plea that applicants would not obtain from public funds the equipment and buildings essential for the studies described below. The descriptions are mainly in the words of the research workers themselves.

Some dates are given of the main scientific discoveries which led to the introduction of the principal techniques for which the Trustees provided equipment, to enable us to assess the Trustees' recognition of the importance of these techniques for furthering biological research.

X-ray crystallography

The modern techniques used for the study of the three-dimensional structure of proteins are based on fundamental discoveries in physics: X-rays, discovered by Roentgen (1895);[3] and the demonstration by Von Laue of the diffraction patterns which occurred after these rays passed through a crystal (1912). These discoveries formed the basis for work on the analysis of crystal structure by W. L. Bragg. He showed that the diffraction patterns resulted from the structure of the crystal, not from different wave lengths of the X-rays (1915). Bragg must be regarded as the founder of X-ray crystallography studies.

Studies in X-ray crystallography had become of outstanding importance in scientific research when the Trustees began to make grants for buildings and equipment. In those early years, a point of importance was the close personal relationship between Sir Henry Dale, as Chairman of the Trustees, and the secretary of the Medical Research Council. Their relationship influenced decisions on what applications the Trustees could appropriately consider. The importance of this becomes clear when we realise that the leading centres in crystallography in Great Britain were heavily supported by the Medical Research Council in Cambridge and London. If additional support for these centres became necessary, what organisation could be asked to consider providing a grant, if government funds were restricted?

In 1956, Professor J. D. Bernal made such a request to the Wellcome Trust, for a relatively small sum. He wrote:

> I am forwarding to you a request for £1,000 to purchase a precession X-ray camera. This is required in connection with the work of Dr R. E. Franklin and Dr A. Klug in my laboratory for investigations on virus structure.

The Trustees made an award of £1,000 for the purchase of a precession X-ray camera. The research of Professor Bernal and his colleagues on the structure of plant viruses continued, and with the camera, Klug and Franklin were able to get some of the first precession photographs of the crystals of a spherical virus.

The Medical Research Council also turned to the Wellcome Trust when government financial restrictions were hindering the development of the

Council's Unit of Molecular Biology in Cambridge. In 1962, Sir Harold Himsworth, Secretary of the Medical Research Council, wrote to the Trust

> to explore the possibility whether the Wellcome Trust might be able to assist the Council in setting up their Molecular Biology Research Unit in Cambridge. . . .
> I am wondering, therefore, whether in the circumstances your Trust would be able to consider helping us to the order of £70,000.

The Trustees responded to this request by making an award of £70,000, divided into approximately equal amounts for studies in molecular genetics, protein chemistry, protein crystallography and electron microscopy. The Trustees were happy to be associated even indirectly with the activities of such an important research unit, staffed by workers of such high distinction and promise.

Another unit concerned with the fine structure of tissues and cells, their nature and function, had been established in 1947 jointly by the University of London and the Medical Research Council. It was housed in King's College, with Dr J. T. Randall as the University's Wheatstone Professor of Physics and Dr M. H. F. Wilkins as Assistant Director of the Medical Research Council's Biophysics Unit. In 1959 Professor Randall made a formal application to the Trustees for a contribution towards the costs of converting a site in Drury Lane to suitable laboratories for fundamental studies in biophysics (p. 91). In 1960 the Trustees made a grant of £120,000 towards these building costs. When the conversion was completed in 1964, the Department of Biophysics of King's College, and the Biophysics Research Unit of the Medical Research Council, were able to live together in the same building in Drury Lane. It is difficult to assess the results of Wellcome Trust support of this request, because although in financial terms the Trust grant was a major contribution to the building programme, the groups of university workers and Medical Research Council staff became so closely integrated, that their contributions to research must be regarded as a whole. There is no doubt about the high regard in which the research is held internationally.

The grants described above were for equipment and laboratories in which X-ray crystallography was an important method of investigation of biological problems. The Trustees received in 1957 an application of an unusual type for financial assistance towards costs of computer time for work on crystal structure of organic molecules. The request was from

Dame Kathleen Lonsdale,[4] of the Department of Chemistry, University College, London. The Trustees made her an award of £4,000 towards the computational expenses connected with her work on crystal structure of organic molecules. In 1959 she reported to the Trustees that their award had enabled her to make major advances in her studies.

The awards described were all made within the first ten years of the Trustees grant programme, and all were significant in furthering the application of X-ray crystallography to biological problems.

The electron microscope

In 1906, the Nobel Prize for Physics was awarded to J. J. Thomson, 'in recognition of the great merits of his theoretical and experimental investigations into the transmission of electricity through gases'. These experiments led to the discovery of the fundamental particles now known as electrons. Electrons were shown to have wave properties by de Broglie, who published his evidence in papers from 1924 onwards. The behaviour of electrons while moving in an electrostatic and electromagnetic field was studied by Busch, who demonstrated that such fields act as 'lenses', and that electrons can be brought to a focus (1926). These studies in basic physics provided the principles on which Siemens built the first commercial electron transmission microscope in 1939. The importance of the electron microscope in biological research is that it has a very high capability for the production of detail in an image (its resolving power). Magnifications can be up to × 150,000. Important techniques depending on electron microscopy have been the development of the freeze-fracture technique (1957), and of the scanning electron microscope (1965).

At the time of writing this account (1984) it is a reasonable assumption that an electron microscope is available for use in most institutions in which research on structural aspects of biology is undertaken. It is also reasonable to assume that a department of anatomy is a natural home for an electron microscope. We tried to find out, therefore, over what time-span electron microscopes had been installed in departments of anatomy throughout the country, and what part the Wellcome Trust had played in their introduction. We wrote to departmental heads of 27 medical schools in the United Kingdom, and asked two questions: 1) when was an electron microscope first installed in the department; and 2) where the funds for the equipment came from. Twenty-three replies were received. Nine microscopes were installed in the period 1956–60; 11 between 1961

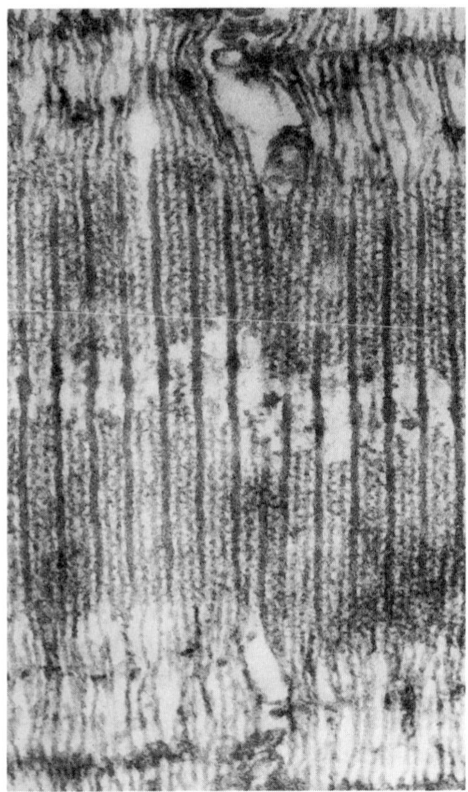

Fig. 61. (*above*) Thin section of muscle, showing the arrays of thick myosin-containing filaments which form the A bands, and the thinner actin-containing filaments which partly overlap them and continue out into the I bands joining up with the Z lines on either end of the sarcomere. × 150,000. (*opposite*) 1005 and 705 ribosome particles from *E. coli*, examined by negative staining techniques. × 160,000.

and 1970; and two after 1970. One department had no electron microscope. Funds for four of the first nine were provided by the Wellcome Trust, and for three of the later ones. This survey of a single type of department would provide only part of the evidence for a statement on time of acquisition of electron microscopes generally; but it seems likely that the Trustees' policy in the early years of their activity, of giving sympathetic consideration to applications for funds for electron microscopes was important in encouraging research using an important new method of direct observation on biological material. Between 1955 and

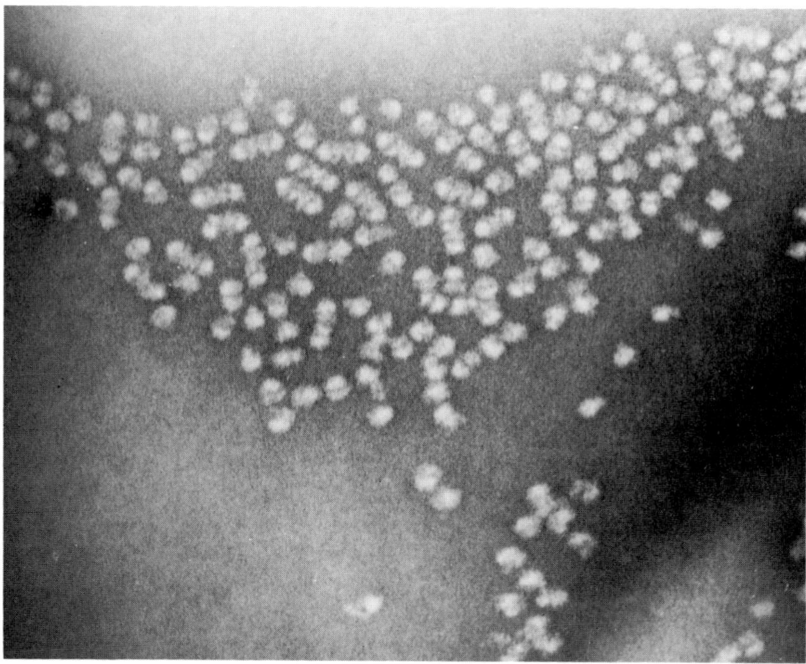

1982, the Trustees made grants for the purchase of 50 electron microscopes, and contributed to the costs of six.

The names of those who received grants for buying electron microscopes, and titles of their scientific projects are given in Appendix VII. A brief account of some of these projects now follows.

1954: *Dr H. E. Huxley, Department of Physiology, University College, London*

With this electron microscope, H. E. Huxley obtained (in 1957 Fig. 61) pictures of very thin sections of striated muscle which demonstrated convincingly that the structure was built up of partially overlapping arrays of two different types of filament (the actin and myosin filaments). Subsequently, he used the microscope to study the structure of separated myosin and actin filaments, and of synthetic ones, and was able to demonstrate their constancy of length and structure and the strict structural polarity with which the molecules are arranged in them, which confirmed beyond all reasonable doubt the reality of the sliding filament mechanism. The microscope was also used in a collaborative study with Professor Bernard Katz and Dr R. I. Birks of motor end-plate structure. Huxley also used the same instrument to develop the negative staining

Fig. 62. Freeze fracture replica of axolemmal E-face in region of node of Ranvier. A, axoplasm; M, myelin; N, nodal axolemma exhibiting nodal particles; P, paranodal axolemma. Rat sciatic nerve × 84,000.

technique, first applied to Tobacco Mosaic Virus (T.M.V.) in 1956, and then, in collaboration with Dr G. Zubay in 1960, used to elucidate the structure of ribosomes (the first such study, Fig. 61) and of Turnip Yellow Mosaic Virus (T.Y.M.V.), which was the first of the small spherical plant viruses to be resolved by this technique. This latter study led directly to the work of Klug and Finch in this field.

1959–81: *Sir Stewart Duke-Elder; Professor C. M. H. Pedler; Professor N. Ashton, Professor A. Garner, Institute of Ophthalmology, University of London*

The study of tissue ultrastructure has been an important aspect of research at the Institute of Ophthalmology since 1961 when the Wellcome Trust provided the first of three transmission electron microscopes. More recently the range of such study has been increased by the provision in 1981 of a scanning electron microscope, with a contribution from the Trust toward the costs.

The basis for the evaluation of diseased tissues is a thorough appreciation of the normal state and, among other studies, a detailed examina-

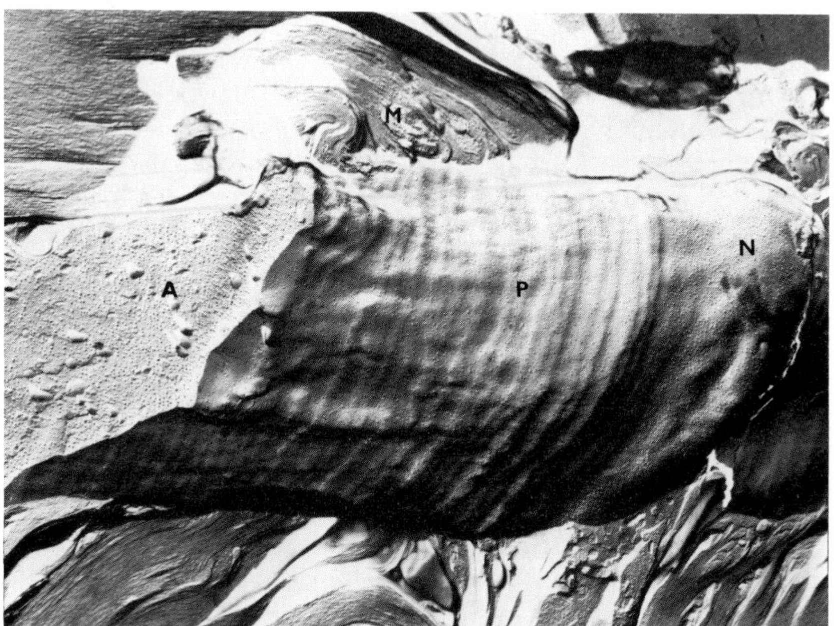

Fig. 63. Freeze fracture replica of axolemmal P-face in region of node of Ranvier. A, axoplasm; M, myelin; P, paranodal axolemma; N, nodal axolemma. Rat sciatic nerve × 34,800.

tion was undertaken of the interneuronal connections of the retina. In part this was achieved by constructing models based on serial electron micrographs using a modified pentograph technique. Latterly an investigation of gap-junctions as a function of developing retinal tissue has been performed.

For many years electron microscopy was used to examine the visual apparatus of deep-sea fishes adapted to minimal illumination and of primitive forms such as the lung-fish and coelacanth in a delineation of retinal phylogeny.

An increasing awareness in the 1970s of the importance of the retinal epithelium in the metabolism of the photoreceptor outer segments prompted a detailed ultrastructural analysis of this cell layer. Electron microscopy explained the blood–retinal barrier function of the pigment epithelium, defects in which were subsequently seen to be involved in the pathogenesis of several retinopathies, and confirmed the phagocytic function of the cells. The latter property has been shown to be defective in certain animal forms of retinitis pigmentosa.

A blood–retinal barrier provided by the endothelial lining of the retinal blood vessels was also demonstrated, the barrier being due, as in the case of the retinal pigment epithelium, to tight encircling junctions between adjacent cells. The nature of cotton-wool spots in the retina, which had long been in doubt, was confirmed by electron microscopy as being due to a large number of swollen, disrupted axons in the nerve-fibre layer and shown to be a consequence of acute ischaemia. An ultrastructural study of experimentally-induced hypertensive retinopathy revealed that the characteristic fibrinous necrosis is preceded by severe arteriolar constriction which later gives way to necrosis and leakage through a damaged endothelium. Although the role of hyperoxia in retrolental fibroplasia was already established, electron microscopy was used to study the mechanism of oxygen toxicity on immature vascular endothelium: lysosomal activation leading to autophagic vacuole formation was demonstrated.

The application of lasers to the treatment of eye diseases has developed and electron microscopy has been invaluable in determining the mechanisms involved. It has been found, for instance, that argon laser emissions are absorbed preferentially by the pigmented cells of the retina whereas those of the krypton laser act chiefly on the red blood cells within the retinal circulation. Other continuing studies are concerned with the genesis and fate of laser-induced holes in the filtration angle in the treatment of glaucoma.

An earlier use of electron microscopy in glaucoma research was to demonstrate the means whereby aqueous humour passes through the trabecular meshwork and across the cell lining of Schlemm's canal. Vacuoles in the endothelium were later shown to be a stage in the formation of pressure-induced channels. Other studies have been helpful in elucidating the nature of hereditary corneal dystrophies and of lens cataracts produced by radiation and by uveitis.

Most recently scanning electron microscopy has been used to study the cellular aggregates on prosthetic intra-ocular lens, changes in the endothelium lining Descemet's membrane of the cornea with age and disease, and the morphology of cells responsible for the formation of vitreal membranes.

1962–80: *Professor F. Goldby; Professor A. S. Breathnach, Department of Anatomy, St Mary's Hospital Medical School, University of London*

The Trustees provided four electron microscopes for use in the Department of Anatomy, St Mary's Hospital Medical School, for work on nervous tissues and skin.

1. *Freeze–fracture replication studies (Figs 62 and 63, pp. 312–3)*

a) Studies on peripheral nerve have been carried out in collaboration with Professor P. K. Thomas of the department of Neurological Science, Royal Free Hospital School of Medicine. The normal freeze–fracture appearances of mammalian peripheral nerve have been established, and symmetrical particle aggregates within the axolemma and periaxonal Schwann cell membrane in the region of the node of Ranvier and at Schmidt–Lantermann incisures have been described. The studies on normal nerve are being used as background for examination of changes in peripheral neuropathies involving demyelination, and animal models are being employed for this purpose. Analysis of numbers and distribution of particles within myelin, axonal, and Schwann cell membranes is a major feature of these studies, and computer techniques are being applied.

b) Freeze–fracture studies of developing intercellular junctional complexes in early chick embryos and tissue culture have been carried out (and are continuing) in collaboration with Professor Ruth Bellairs of the Department of Anatomy and Embryology, University College, London. Assessment of the role of these complexes in early differentiation has been made. In the course of these and the neurological studies mentioned above, refinements and improvements in general freeze–fracture technique and technology were achieved.

c) Pioneer studies on freeze–fracture of skin carried out over the past 15 years have been extended recently to analyses of distribution of specialised contacts, nuclear pores and intramembranous particles within keratocytes of normal, fetal and pathological human epidermis. Replicas are analysed with the assistance of specially designed computer programs and the technique provides for a more objective comparison between replicas than had been previously achievable. The results can be expected to throw new light upon problems of epidermal differentiation, and upon hitherto undefinable properties of epidermis in a variety of abnormal conditions.

2. *Studies on skin pigmentation*

Over the past five years, electron microscopy has been a major technique applied to studies on normal and abnormal skin pigmentation carried out in collaboration with the Istituto Dermatologico S. Gallicano, Rome. These studies are primarily concerned with examining and explaining the beneficial effects of dicarboxylic acids on hyperpigmentary disorders of human skin, including malignant melanoma. The St Mary's contribution to these studies has been concerned with monitoring clinical results by electron microscopy, with observations on straightforward tissue cultures of melanocytes exposed to dicarboxylic acids, and with analytical ultrastructural autoradiography of melanoma cells exposed to radioactive diacids. Results so far have clearly established the beneficial effects of dicarboxylic acids on lentigo maligna, and a positive cytotoxic effect on the malignant human melanocyte. Evidence is accumulating that the cytotoxic effect of dicarboxylic acids is mediated through an anti-mitochondrial activity, and this raises the possibility that they may have a cytotoxic effect on tumours other than malignant melanoma. This possibility is currently being investigated from different standpoints. It has also been established that dicarboxylic acids are effective in the treatment of acne, and electron microscopy is being employed to investigate the mechanism involved.

3. *Identification of nociceptive afferents*

Much of Professor A. D. Hoyes' work on peripheral nerve fibres has been concerned with establishing that a structurally distinct population of axons, which he has identified in the nerve plexuses in structures such as the ureter, cornea, and trachea, are those of primary afferent neurons involved in nociception. By using a combination of quantitative electron microscopical and degeneration techniques, it has been shown that the cell bodies of the axons which terminate in the tracheal epithelium of the rat are located in the nodose ganglion of the vagus.

An *in vitro* technique has been used to study the effect on nociceptive afferents in the ureter of a number of substances. This technique has the major advantage that it allows assessment of the effects of pain-producing substances directly on the axons. It has been shown that histamine produces responses in axons only when it is combined with subthreshold concentrations of acetylcholine. Other work in this area includes analysis of the effects of substances such as bradykinin on the axons and of the extent to which the effects of acetylcholine are modified by analgesic drugs such as aspirin and by morphine. The study of primary nociceptive afferent neurons is currently being extended to an analysis of their capacity for sprouting and regeneration after nerve section and after induction of degeneration with capsaicin.

In addition to work on nociceptive afferents, quantitative ultrastructural, degeneration and immunohistochemical techniques are being used to study the structure and composition of the nerve plexuses in structures such as the ureter and trachea and in the gut. In the gut, this work is providing fundamental new evidence on the identity and mechanisms of uptake of biogenic monoamine by neurons known as monoamine handling neurons. It is also casting a great deal of doubt on current hypotheses about the structure of the endings of neurons which contain regulatory peptides. The presence and distribution of these peptides is one of the major areas of current research on the peripheral nervous system. Using electron microscopical immunocytochemical techniques, it has been possible not only to study the distribution, but also to demonstrate the identity of axons which contain regulatory peptides such as substance P, V.I.P. (vaso-active intestinal peptide), enkephalin and bombesin, both in the gut and in other structures such as the ureter.

In other studies, quantitative ultrastructural techniques have been used to analyse the density and contribution of adrenergic, nociceptive and other types of axon to autonomic nerve plexuses in the muscle of the ureter, trachea and gut, and the perivascular plexuses of arterioles in both the ureter and pancreas.

1970: *Professor T. J. Biscoe, Department of Physiology, University of Bristol*

This grant allowed Professor Biscoe to set up a properly organised, modern electron microscope laboratory for the first time. To start with, the programme was directed towards complementing electrophysiological with structural studies of nerve cells in tissue culture. However, as the experiments evolved it became clear that a more fruitful way forward in the examination of problems of growth and development of the mammalian central nervous system would be to investigate mutant nerve cells. Accordingly the emphasis shifted in the structural work to the investigation of the normal nervous system in the mouse and of the lesions present in a number of mutants. These included:

a) A detailed examination of the lesion of the cerebellum in the *lurcher* mutant. This mutant has a disorder of gait, staggering from side to side and sometimes walking backward. The affected animals were shown to have no Purkinje cells in the cerebellum, and a reduced number of granule cells and inferior olivary cells. The experiments required a comprehensive study of the development of both the normal and mutant cerebellum, of the deep cerebellar nuclei, and of the inferior olivary nucleus. They showed that the primary lesion was in the Purkinje cells and that the other changes were secondary.
b) Definition of the extent of the lesion in the *dystrophic* mutant. This

mutant shows wasting of the skeletal muscles and a failure of myelination in the spinal roots and in those cranial nerves which have Schwann cells. The lesion was especially obvious in the long cranial nerves, e.g. III, IV, VI, XI, but could be demonstrated in the others. Studies of the effects of minor trauma to affected spinal roots in this animal showed that trauma was followed by partial recovery from the lesion. The recovery was demonstrated by electron microscopic study of the roots at various times after the trauma.

c) A quantitative electron microscopic examination of the development of the lesion in the *jimpy* mutant. In this mutant myelination in the central nervous system is deficient and the homozygous animals die at about 30 days of life. The study showed that oligodendroglial proliferation failed to occur. Those oligodendrogliae that did develop underwent a form of sudanophilic degeneration.
d) Studies on the *dystonic* mutant to characterise the lesion in peripheral nerve. This mutant exhibits writhing movements and the peripheral nerves were shown to have swellings which appeared to obstruct normal transport. Grafting experiments showed the lesion to be intrinsic to the mutant. The peripheral changes in receptors and muscle were complex and were not analysed.
e) A detailed quantitative description of the dorsal and ventral roots in the normal mouse and a comparison with some of the roots in the *wobbler* mutant.
f) A quantitative comparison of the structure of the carotid body and its nerve supply in the normal mouse and the *wobbler* mutant combined with physiological experiments. In this mutant many of the endings on the presumed sensory cells degenerate even though the lesion is believed to be predominantly a motor one. The conclusion was that either the endings were not sensory or that only a very small number were required for function to appear normal.
g) An investigation of the dorsal root ganglia in the mouse with respect to properties of different types of ganglion cells. This study showed that two cell types could be distinguished. A more extensive analysis was made at the light microscopic level where cell types were further characterised by the age and size of the cells.

In conclusion, the bulk of this work was concerned with a detailed description of the normal and pathological nervous system in the mouse. It was essential as a basis to Professor Biscoe's present work because it helped to identify those problems in the neurological mutants which might be accessible to solution. It became clear that in many cases they could now reasonably expect to make progress towards understanding the nature of the primary lesion at a fundamental level. Thus their attention was focussed on two problems. In the cerebellar mutants they have now been able to identify a protein that is unique to Purkinje cells and hence absent in *lurcher*, and have an antibody for it. In another mutant, *spastic*, which has muscle rigidity and a tremor, they have shown a defect in the inhibitory amino-acid receptor protein complex and have an antibody for a part of that complex.

These developments into molecular biology have been made possible by the original grant from the Trustees.

The ultracentrifuge

Miescher was the first to succeed in a cell fractionation experiment, when in 1869 he separated nuclei from other constituents of pus cells, and isolated 'nuclein', later shown to be deoxyribonucleic acid. Many techniques were subsequently used to obtain cell fractions. The most important of these developed from the interests of colloid chemists in studies designed to determine the sedimentation boundaries of colloid particles in a solution. Svedberg developed the first analytical ultracentrifuge in 1926, and with this instrument determined the molecular weight of haemoglobin. Important technical modifications were made by Pickels and Beams from 1935 onwards, which led eventually to the modern analytical and preparative ultracentrifuges manufactured by the firm founded by Pickels, Specialised Instruments Inc. (Spinco).

Joseph Fruton has said (1976) 'The aloofness of biochemists towards cytological studies continued through most of the first half of this century. After World War II however, the use of electron microscopy and differential centrifugation erased this separation, and the mode of assembly of the macromolecular components of living cells is now a subject of intense biochemical study.'[5]

We have seen that the Trustees' major equipment awards up to 1970 were for electron microscopes. The Trustees also showed considerable interest in ultracentrifuge studies, for which they made many grants, of which the following is an early example.

1960: *Professor R. R. Porter, Department of Immunology, St Mary's Hospital Medical School, University of London*

The object of the studies to be carried out with the help of the ultracentrifuge was to elucidate the structure of antibodies, the protein molecules

Fig. 64. Spinco analytical ultracentrifuge in the Department of Microbiology, Australian National University. The grant of £10,000 made in 1960, was for use in a programme of research into the fundamental properties and chemistry of viruses, directed by Professor F. J. Fennes.

which bind specifically with antigens. The experiments were to be done in such a way that the ability of the antibodies to bind to antigens was not destroyed. The size and complexity of antibodies is such that detailed structural studies of the whole molecule were very difficult with the methods available at the time of the Trust award to Professor Porter. Attempts had been made to hydrolyse proteins, without destruction of the putative antigen sites and, in 1957, Professor Porter had achieved some success in these attempts by isolating polypeptides of molecular weight of less than 10,000 which retained their ability to bind the antibodies. Antibodies, with a molecular weight of about 150,000 were more difficult to study. Professor Porter had found (1959) that the antibody protein could be split into three fractions, and that all the biological properties of the original molecule appeared to survive the splitting of the antibody. The results suggested that the split corresponded to a natural division in the original molecule. Two fractions (1 and 2) were nearly identical, and retained the antigen combining specificity of the original antibody. The third fraction, which crystallised easily (now known as Fc) appeared to carry the membrane penetrating site, which enables antibodies to cross the placenta.

Professor Porter wished to continue his studies of the structure of antibodies by studying the molecular weights of the fragments, obtained by proteolysis, and by reduction of the disulphide bonds, which cross-link the peptide chains. For part of this work, the ultracentrifuge was essential. He and his colleagues attempted to reduce gamma globulin, and to separate the products in such a manner that they remained soluble and immunologically active. They showed that the major components of gamma globulin were two chains, the major A chain having a higher molecular weight than the B chain.

Subsequent work by Professor Porter, and by G. Edelman in the United States, elucidated the basic structure of all antibody molecules. They showed that they are composed of two identical 'heavy' chains (Professor Porter's A chain) and two identical 'light' chains (Professor Porter's B chain). The heavy chains are about twice the length of the light chains, and are joined by disulphide bridges. Localities of various immunological functions on the chains have been determined.

Nuclear magnetic resonance

Otto Stern, in experiments carried out from 1972 onwards, showed that atomic nuclei, under certain conditions, behave like miniature magnets. Isidor Rabi between 1935 and 1937 devised a method for measuring the magnetic properties of atomic nuclei. The development of nuclear magnetic resonance techniques in analytical chemistry and biology depended on the fundamental work of Stern and Rabi, for which they were each awarded a Nobel Prize in 1943 and 1944; and subsequent work on nuclear induction by Felix Bloch and nuclear magnetism by Edward Purcell. They shared a Nobel Prize in 1952.

The first instruments manufactured commercially became available in 1953. Technical developments during the past 15 years have made it possible to use nuclear magnetic resonance (N.M.R.) for biological and, quite recently, clinical investigations. The applications of N.M.R. to intact animals and humans are of two types:

1. The high intrinsic sensitivity of hydrogen atoms and their high concentration in water and fat make it possible to process the weak magnetic resonances in such a way that they produce an image showing a chosen cross-section of the body.

2. By working at much higher sensitivity, with a corresponding diminution of spatial resolution, it is possible to obtain information about biochemical processes as they actually occur in undisturbed tissues.

The Trustees have made very few awards for equipment for nuclear magnetic resonance studies. It is therefore necessary to explain why these awards are considered to have been significant. We have seen how studies carried out with the types of equipment already described have advanced considerably the knowledge of cell biology, both normal and pathological. In all such studies two main questions concerning their nature have always been asked: how closely do the phenomena observed in cell or tissue preparations of any kind correspond to those of the living cell; and therefore is it possible to explain biological phenomena in terms of physics and chemistry. In his Royal Society Presidential Address of 1885, T. H. Huxley said: 'What an enormous revolution would be made in biology, if physics or chemistry could supply the physiologist with a means of making out the molecular structure of living tissues comparable to that which the spectroscope affords to the inquirer into the nature of the heavenly bodies. At the present moment the constituents of our own bodies are more remote from our ken than those of Sirius, in this respect.'[6] One of the outstanding books on cytology published before World War II was James Gray's *Experimental Cytology* (1931). In an obituary notice of Gray, J. A. Ramsay wrote: 'after writing a notable book, he made up his mind to leave this field; he felt that using living cells, means were not then available to formulate meaningful questions and to obtain clear cut answers – and he was not interested in dead cells'.[7] The physical conditions of living cells interested the physicist Niels Bohr, who at a meeting in Copenhagen in 1933, said 'We should doubtless kill an animal if we tried to carry the investigation of its organs so far that we could describe the role played by single atoms in vital functions. In every experiment on living organisms, there must remain an uncertainty as regards the physical conditions to which they are subjected, and the idea suggests itself that the minimum freedom we must allow the organism in this respect is just large enough to permit it, so to say, to hide its ultimate secrets from us.'[8]

Some biologists also question what is meant by 'living' and 'non-living'. A few years after Bohr's address, N. W. Pirie wrote a paper 'The meaninglessness of the terms life and living'[9] in which he 'examined destructively the various qualities which might be used to define the word life, and found that they are individually inadequate for even an approximate definition'. W. M. Stanley[10] wrote that 'with the realisation that there is no definite boundary between the living and non-living, it becomes possible to blend the atomic theory, the germ theory, and the cell theory into a unified philosophy the essence of which is structure or architecture'.

The time has now come when the behaviour of molecules in living tissues can be studied, as exemplified by phosphorus in muscle, in which intracellular pH can be measured, and the energy state of muscle cells estimated.

Brief accounts of some of the awards given for the purchase of nuclear magnetic resonance (N.M.R.) equipment are now given.

1955: *Sir Alexander Todd, the Chemical Laboratory, University of Cambridge*

At the time of this application, the techniques of N.M.R. had been applied chiefly to inorganic compounds, and a few relatively simple organic molecules. In the words of a scientific referee consulted by the Trustees: 'it requires something of an act of faith to suppose that the method will be equally powerful in its application to the complex compounds in which Alexander Todd is interested. I do not think at the moment that it is possible to predict whether or not this will be so'.

The Trustees realised the potentiality of the technique for chemical and biochemical studies and made the award for research into the molecular structure of substances of biological interest. The instrument was the first of its kind to be installed in the United Kingdom.

The equipment was used for nucleotide and nucleic acid studies, and, together with other methods, provided detailed information about the precise state of the heterocyclic nuclei, and the internucleotide linkages, matters of profound importance in connection with their biological function.

1957: *Professor R. S. Nyholm, Department of Chemistry, University College, London*

1963: *Further award to the same for conversion and modernisation of equipment*

When they considered the first of these requests, the Trustees had essentially two decisions to make:

1. Whether to make a second award for such equipment so soon after the award to the Cambridge University Chemical Laboratory.
2. Whether Professor Nyholm's interests as an inorganic chemist were likely to lead to work of biological importance.

The Trustees decided that Professor Nyholm's research in metal–enzyme chemistry, oxyhaemoglobin, and of the role of phosphate esters in biological systems had been outstanding and that an award should be made. Professor Nyholm died, aged 52, in a motor car accident in 1971. We are grateful to Professor D. P. Craig, F.R.S., of the Australian National University, for this account of the research.

The 40 MHz Varian nuclear magnetic resonance spectrometer, provided to University College, London in the Department of Chemistry was one of a very small number then in Europe. Its purchase followed soon after the introduction of the 40 MHz instrument in late 1956 or early 1957. Professor Nyholm had become aware of the possibilities of N.M.R. in large part through the stimulus of Professor R. G. Gillespie, F.R.S. (now at McMaster University, Hamilton, Ontario) and his student Dr R. F. M. White. He had had his early training in the Sydney metal complex group, particularly coming under the influence of Professors D. P. Mellor and F. P. Dwyer, and was thus alive to the diagnostic value of paramagnetism in the study of metal complexes. He was among the earliest to appreciate the potential for N.M.R. in determinations of structure and bond type in diamagnetic complexes and also, later, in paramagnetics. His initial request was for a multinuclear spectrometer, then something of a rarity, especially in Europe. His first Ph.D. students in this area (Richard Bramley and Garth Kidd), exploiting the multinuclear features of the new spectrometer, worked on ^{13}C, ^{14}N and ^{17}O. They achieved results, without the help of computers and Fourier transform techniques, which now seem remarkable, and were widely noticed and quoted in reviews. These studies were among the very first to make extensive chemical use of the N.M.R. spectra of these elements. The N.M.R. laboratory at University College became well known for its pioneering work. Analysis of the total scientific production from this instrument must include the indirect benefit that followed its wide use for structure confirmation by groups whose primary interest was not in N.M.R.

In 1963 the Wellcome Trust agreed to upgrading the spectrometer to 100 MHz. It was one of the first such conversions. It took the original installation up to the leading standards of the time. Technical problems of the upgrading itself were not trivial. The resulting 100 MHz instrument was for the first period of its use possibly unique in Great Britain, and was widely used by scientists outside University College. Inevitably in the course of time it became one of many similar installations. It continued in use for a long period, at least until late in 1973.

In assessing the total scientific value of this important research support one would have to add to the direct results the effect on scientific thinking within the Department of Chemistry. Scientists were made aware of the great potential of this new instrumental advance and of its application in new areas. For example, it was widely used for the confirmation of molecular structures deduced indirectly from reaction kinetic studies and in other ways. It thus played a part in increasing chemical sophistication and helped to keep the laboratory in a leading position in international research.

1961: *Professor D. H. Barton, Department of Chemistry, Imperial College of Science and Technology, London*

Professor (now Sir) D. H. Barton wrote to the Trustees in 1961 to request funds for the purchase of an N.M.R. spectrometer. Professor Barton was examining the structure, function and photochemical reactions of compounds of potential biological importance and had access to an N.M.R. spectrometer in the Department of Inorganic Chemistry, but found that such use was insufficient for effective prosecution of his own studies.

The Trustees accepted Professor Barton's opinion that N.M.R. spectroscopy would ultimately become one of the most important physical methods employed by the organic chemist, but that considerable developments in the practice and methodology of the technique were necessary. Such developments would be achieved by application of the technique to problems which were simultaneously being investigated by existing physical and chemical methods. The Trustees considered that the problems which Professor Barton was studying were within their field of interests and agreed to make the award.

In 1964, Professor Barton sought an additional grant to modernise the equipment by the addition of a spin decoupling unit. At that time, he wrote:

> The Varian A60 proton magnetic resonance spectrometer is in continuous daily operation. All of the staff and research students now make use of proton resonance spectroscopy routinely in their chemical work. This is because valuable structural information is obtained which mostly could not be got in any other way. Our combined studies of complex simple natural products, compounds involved in biogenetic pathways, products of photochemical reactions, potential drugs, dyes and other synthetic materials are very materially being assisted. Other researches on the aromaticity of hetero-

> cyclic compounds, stereochemistry, enolisation and long-range spin coupling are only possible because we are fortunate enough to have the use of the Wellcome Trust's spectrometer. Our great use of the instrument is amply illustrated by our publications.
>
> Yet, not infrequently, in our mounting experience, the proton resonance spectra from the compounds which we are interested in studying are not capable of full interpretation. The spin decoupling accessory enables more information to be derived from spectra than would otherwise be possible. This is generally vitally important information, giving the proximate relationships and relative stereochemistry of the coupled protons. This accessory would very considerably aid all of the organic chemistry research undertaken here at present and for the foreseeable future. The more complex the compounds investigated the greater proportionately should be the additional benefit.

The Trustees made the additional award requested.

1977: *Professor D. Wilkie, Department of Physiology, University College, London*

Early in 1975, Professor D. Wilkie and Dr Joan Dawson of the Department of Physiology, University College, London, together with Dr D. Gadian, of the Department of Biochemistry, University of Oxford, began collaborative research on problems of muscular contraction, using ^{31}P N.M.R., in conjunction with chemical analysis and other techniques. In 1977, the Trustees made a grant to Professor Wilkie for continuation of these studies.

In 1981 the Trustees made an award to Professor Wilkie, Professor R. H. T. Edwards (Medicine), Professor E. O. Reynolds (Paediatrics), and Mr J. Clifton (Medical Physics) as a contribution to the cost of equipment to carry out topical magnetic resonance studies in human metabolism. Other contributors to the grant were the Muscular Dystrophy Association, and Action Research.

The results of Trust support can be summarised as follows: in 1980, as a result of technical advances, it became possible to extend work on ^{31}P spectroscopy of muscle to studies of limb muscles in normal human subjects and in patients. At the same time, Professor Wilkie and colleagues began very fruitful studies of brain metabolism in normal infants and in infants who have suffered a period of asphyxia during birth or a variety of other disorders. Their results exemplify the kind of basic and clinical information that can be obtained by N.M.R. spectroscopy of living tissues using presently available techniques.

They concentrated mainly on the use of the ^{31}P nucleus because of the relatively large signals obtained and because of the importance of phosphorus containing compounds in cellular energy-exchange reactions. In muscle and brain one observes signals from ATP (the primary fuel for energy-requiring reaction); phosphocreatine (PCr; another 'high-energy' phosphate which serves to buffer the supply of ATP) and inorganic phosphate (Pi). Intracellular concentrations of H^+, ADP and AMP, all thought to have important regulating roles in metabolism, can also be calculated from information contained in the ^{31}P spectrum, as can be the free-energy change for ATP hydrolysis. Thus ^{31}P N.M.R. allows the following:

1. assessment of the energetic status of a tissue,
2. determination of overall rates of flux through particular metabolic pathways (e.g. rate of anaerobic metabolism and/or rate of oxidative phosphorylation),
3. calculation of concentrations of regulatory metabolites.

Skeletal muscle

In basic studies of cellular energetics, experiments must be designed in such a way that tissue function can be related in a meaningful way to the biochemical variables described above. Skeletal muscle is particularly useful in this regard because its mechanical output is easily monitored and because of the large and controllable change in energetic demand when the muscle contracts. ^{31}P N.M.R. has brought about the following advances in our understanding of skeletal muscle biochemistry and physiology:

1. N.M.R. has made it possible to determine more meaningfully than was possible using conventional chemical methods the concentrations of energetically-important P-containing compounds. For example, ADP that is free in the myoplasm is about 50-fold less than that measured in extracts, and AMP is over 1,000-fold less.
2. The mechanical characteristics of fatiguing muscle have been related to biochemical changes and testable theories of the mechanism of fatigues have been proposed.

3. The metabolic response to contraction has been monitored in living muscle.

They, and others, have shown abnormalities in spectra from resting and contracting muscle as a result of various metabolic enzyme defects. In an extensive study of Duchenne Dystrophy, reductions in PCr/ATP and PCr/Pi were found in dystrophic muscle, but ATP, intracellular pH, and ability to breakdown and resynthesise ATP during exercise were normal. Two putative therapeutic agents were tested and found to influence neither the ^{31}P spectrum nor the clinical state.

Uterine smooth muscle

Dr Joan Dawson and Dr Susan Wray, of the Department of Physiology, University College, London, have found that phosphorus metabolites from isolated rat uterus vary with the life stages of the animals. Of particular interest is the fact that PCr/ATP and PCr/Pi are very high in the pregnant uterus immediately before delivery as is a phosphomonoester which may be involved in cellular membrane turnover. These quantities decline substantially during the following period of involution. Results on the time course of these changes and administration of the hormones estrogen and progesterone indicate that concentrations of phosphorus metabolites in uterine smooth muscle are hormonally controlled.

Brain and neurological development

^{31}P Spectra obtained from cerebral tissue in normal infants differ from those obtained in other laboratories using adult subjects. Similar differences are observed in spectra from neonatal and adult rats, so this species was used to investigate the time-course of such changes. PCr/Pi was found to increase with age, perhaps indicating that increased free-energy change for ATP hydrolysis is associated with neurological maturity. The concentration of an unknown phosphomonoester declines with age; the time-course of this decline parallels the loss of resistance to hypoxia in the neonate.

Clinical studies have been carried out on infants who have suffered an episode of asphyxia during delivery. The only abnormalities detected in the asphyxiated infant were inverse changes in PCr and Pi, causing a reduction in PCr/Pi. PCr/Pi was usually in or close to the normal range during the first day of life, but then fell dramatically between the second and ninth days. The minimum PCr/Pi was closely associated with the children's prognosis for survival and early neurodevelopmental outcome. These results encourage the speculation that if the fall in PCr/Pi could be prevented, prognosis would be improved.

15

EUROPEAN AND OVERSEAS STUDIES (non-tropical)

by Dr B. A. Bembridge

The Trustees' aims in their European and overseas programmes have been in accordance with their general policy, that is, to promote medical and veterinary research, and to identify any special problems which Trust funds might help to solve. In pursuing them they have shared the view that:

> In the presence of the pervasive and universal value of truth-seeking, the barriers of exclusive nationalism are strange and anomalous. They stand for folly instead of wisdom. Every nation can profit from the advantage which flows from a free interchange of students and ideas.[1]

The Trustees decided that the encouragement of research by co-operation between European and overseas scientists would best be effected by following four principal methods, travel grants, fellowship awards, special methods for support of inter-laboratory collaboration: and contributions to the costs of symposia. They also identified several special needs, of which one was aid for the scientists of Eastern Europe.

Travel grants

Sir Henry Dale was Chairman of the Trustees, when, in 1955, they started a formal scheme for awards of Wellcome Research Travel Grants (p. 100). It is interesting to recall the experience the Scientific Trustees had of carrying out research in a foreign country. Dale himself had spent only a short period in an overseas laboratory, when he worked for four months (1903–4) in Frankfurt-am-Main, in the laboratory of Paul Ehrlich. Of his experience there, Dale wrote: 'I believe that I came away with my store of ideas, and my repertory of ways of approach to problems greatly enriched. I suspect, for example, that my recognition of the possible significance of the action of histamine, when Laidlaw and I later worked out its details, for an understanding of the curiously different anaphylactic reactions in different species, would have been much less prompt and instinctive if I had not spent those four months in an atmosphere so highly charged with ideas about phenomena of immunity as was that of Ehrlich's Institute.'[2] At that time, when Germany was the Mecca of biological scientists, Dale could not have conceived the later political isolation of that country's scientists, leaving 'no opportunity to compare German research with work abroad', and causing a 'loss of contact while we were studying, and later specialising, very harmful to science in Germany'.[3] Dale all his life was conscious of the internationality of science. When Director of the Wellcome Laboratories, he suggested that special leave should be given to his young colleagues to enable them to attend scientific meetings. The proposals he put to Henry Wellcome were enthusiastically received, but unfortunately never obtained formal approval for proper financial arrangements to be made.[4] The second Scientific Trustee at the time of the inception of the Trust travel grant scheme, was Sir John Boyd, F.R.S., who had been Director of Pathology at the War Office (p. 75). His research had been carried out in laboratories in many parts of the world. It is reasonable to assume therefore, that both Scientific Trustees considered that, if an overseas laboratory could provide scientific advantages for a research worker, means should be provided to facilitate visits to such a laboratory.

When the Trust Travel Grant scheme was started, there were three major aspects of the problem of finance for travel for the purpose of promoting scientific research. First, although there were various funds in the United Kingdom and elsewhere for travelling fellowships which enabled younger scientists to spend a year or so overseas, it was difficult for older, established scientists to obtain funds for a short visit to another country in connection with their research. It was easier to obtain money for a visit for one year, than for one month. The second factor was that many promising young scientists, when offered overseas fellowships, were frequently unable to take up awards which did not include expenses for travel. Finally, funds were necessary to enable research workers to attend scientific meetings abroad.

These were the reasons which the Trustees considered, in 1955, necessitated a special scheme. They have not changed since then; in fact there has been an increasing need for such awards, although the value of travel to large scientific congresses has recently been questioned. Professor H. Gutfreund thought that large international congresses are unnecessary, and perhaps even detrimental to science. He put forward his reasons for this view in a journal which at the same time published the contrary view of Professor P. N. Campbell.[5] The Trustees consider that the experience of attending a scientific meeting abroad can be invaluable to the younger scientist.

In addition to the travel grant scheme described, which made possible journeys between the United Kingdom and laboratories anywhere in the world, the Trustees started two other types of travel grants (as distinct from Travelling Fellowships), for special purposes.

The first was in response to a request from Italy. In 1970 the Director of the Mario Negri Research Institute in Milan, Professor S. Garattini, asked the Trustees to consider making grants to enable Italian research workers in biomedical subjects to make short visits abroad to learn new techniques not yet established in their own country. He said that the few national schemes available were inadequate, and that research workers were often spending time developing a method which was already functioning well in a foreign laboratory. The Trustees decided to help, and made an award to be administered by Professor Garattini and a local committee. The committee set up an adjudication method which made grants available in a very short time. Since the inception of this scheme 65 Italian scientists have been able to arrange visits to laboratories in the United Kingdom for training. The award made in 1970 has been renewed several times, after consultations with heads of laboratories here and in Italy.

The second type of special travel grant awards was started in 1978, when the Trustees decided to institute a scheme for visits between the United Kingdom, New Zealand, Australia, the United States and South Africa. It appeared to the Trustees that there was a need for funds to enable established scientists to make relatively short visits of up to three months to these countries, to work on specific research projects with colleagues in a similar field. Ordinary travel grants are intended to provide a contribution towards costs of travel; under the special scheme, the full costs of travel and subsistence are shared through agreements with organisations in the countries mentioned.[6] It is unfortunate that it was impossible to reach a satisfactory agreement with a Canadian organisation, but the Trustees have, nevertheless, made awards for visits between Canada and the United Kingdom.

Visits to laboratories in all parts of the world have been supported through the Trust's travel grants. It is a condition of the awards that the holder must submit a report to the Trust after returning to his home laboratory. The Trust's scientific staff have made a continuing assessment of all types of travel awards by examination of these reports. It is not feasible in this survey to select for further description any from the hundreds of reports; their scientific quality has been very high, and only occasionally has it been necessary to ask for amplification. It is also clear that on many occasions, the initial contacts made during tenure of a Trust travel grant have grown into long-standing collaborations.

In making an assessment of the Trust's travel grant scheme, we must take account of other public and private funds which are available for travel for the same purposes as those of the Trustees. The Royal Society is the main source of such funding, but otherwise there appear to be very few sources. The Research Councils are willing in certain circumstances to receive applications for travel grants from their own award holders, but there have been many times when the timing of such applications has been difficult. On such occasions, the Trust has sympathetically considered them. Other research charities which award fellowships tenable in the United Kingdom may decline to make additional awards because of financial restraints, rather than because the organisations do not approve of overseas visits by their fellows. The Trust has encouraged scientific co-operation by making awards to such fellows. The aims of the British Council are not comparable with those of the Trust.

The conclusion is justified that the Trustees' travel grant schemes have been extremely valuable to research workers, and highly appreciated. The Trustees' allocations for travel grants for the period 1954–84 are tabulated at the end of this section (p. 340).

Fellowships

It is significant that during the period of the Trustees' first report, 1937–56, out of a total of 21 awards for personal support, 13 were made to overseas scientists. There appears to have been no deliberate policy governing the selection of candidates, but clearly the Trustees very soon decided that use of Trust funds should not be confined to awards in the United Kingdom.

Two main categories of fellowships will be described, those for European countries and those for other overseas countries.

(a) *Europe*

The first formal scheme for European co-operation was started by the Trustees in 1957, through an agreement with the Carlsberg Foundation for an exchange of fellows between Denmark and the United Kingdom (p. 91). The object of the scheme was to enable young scientists from Denmark and the United Kingdom to spend a year extending their investigations in the other country under the guidance of leading experts on their subject. Similar agreements were subsequently made with the Medical Research Council of Sweden, the Jahre Foundation in Norway, and the Sigrid Juselius Foundation in Finland. The foreign foundation submits its choice of fellows to the Trustees for approval; if accepted, the fellow receives a stipend and travel expenses from home and research expenses from the Trust. The agreement works in reverse for the Trust. The original agreement with the Carlsberg Foundation provided for all payments to Danish fellows to be made by the Trust and for British fellows to be paid by the Carlsberg Foundation. This led to many administrative difficulties and the system was changed in 1969.

The administrative details are mentioned, because they are appropriate to a consideration, in general terms, of the usefulness of a formal agreement for the exchange of fellows. There are advantages in such an agreement. It is made with a responsible body, which should be able to make a reliable assessment of candidates. The Trustees' experience has confirmed this. The awards are competitive, because of the fixed number of fellows. The publicity in the European country is probably properly directed. The great disadvantage is the rigidity inherent in any formal agreement, and the Trustees have so far not been inclined to enter afresh into such agreements. They prefer to retain their freedom of choice as far as is practicable.

There has been one important exception to this general principle. In 1971, the Trustees made an exchange agreement with Hungary, through the Hungarian International Cultural Institute, at its request. It has been to the Institute's disadvantage. Before 1971, the Trustees had made a large number of fellowship awards, after considering personal applications from Hungarian nationals sponsored by scientists in the United Kingdom. Under the terms of the agreement, the Hungarian Institute submits for approval by the Trustees a list of fellows selected after competition in Hungary. The agreement provides for British fellows to visit Hungary, but requests for such awards have been negligible. It appears that British scientists have a limited knowledge of scientific opportunities available in the Eastern European countries. In recent years, however, the Trustees have made grants to encourage co-operation between laboratories in the United Kingdom and Hungary. In 1985 an agreement was concluded with the Czechoslovak Soviet Republic very similar to that with Hungary.

The Trustees have made a continuous assessment of fellowship awards, on the basis of interviews and reports from fellows. The conclusion is justified that the European fellowship scheme has made a valuable contribution to research, and that it continues to attract good candidates.

As a result of Trustees' reviews two types of awards were discontinued. In 1968 the Trustees had made an award to Queen's College, Oxford, to provide one Florey memorial studentship annually for five years, for studies in medicine or any closely allied subject, to be undertaken in Oxford by students from Europe. The award was renewed for five years in 1972. There were no suitable candidates in 1977 or 1978, and the Provost of Queen's College wrote 'Medical students in Europe do not seem willing nowadays to take advantage of these awards in Oxford'. The Trustees did not continue this scheme. The other discontinued awards were for fellowship exchanges between European countries, excluding the United Kingdom. The awards were made on recommendations from a committee of the European Society for Clinical Investigation, and eleven fellowships were awarded between 1970 and 1974. The fellowships became very costly, and it also appeared to the Trustees that their own activity in making the awards was too remote.

Fellowship awards for the period 1954–84 are tabulated at the end of this section. It will be seen that there was a marked disparity between the number of awards for fellowships to visit Europe, and those to come to the United Kingdom. National bodies in most Western European countries have exchange agreements with the Royal Society. Fellowships are offered by organisations such as the European Molecular Biology Organization and the Federation of European Biochemical Societies. France has also an agreement with the Medical Research Council. The Trust has therefore offered an alternative means of support for candidates who have been unable to find support from official sources, and has been particularly helpful to scientists who have wished to make arrangements at relatively short notice. It is not clear why there was a reduction in applications to visit Scandinavia. The noticeable increase in applications from Italy was probably a result of the enormous difficulties facing young academics there who wished to carry out research.

In the period 1974–84 the Trustees allocated approximately £2,600,000, to their European programme, mostly through fellowship awards. This compares favourably with their allocation of £2,000,000 for Research Fellowships in the selected subjects of Surgery and Pathology, and £4,600,000 for Senior Research Fellowships in Clinical Science. In the same period, the Royal Society, which draws on a government grant for its science exchange programme, set aside approximately £5 million for fellowships (excluding travel grants) between Great Britain and Europe. This sum was matched by the foreign governments with which the Royal Society had agreement. We should recognise that the biological sciences form only a part of the Royal Society science programme. The Wellcome Trust has thus been a British medical research charity which has used a significant proportion of its funds to provide for international co-operation in active clinical and laboratory based medical research. There is clear evidence from published figures that the activities of the Trustees in this respect have compared very well both with government and independent agencies.

(b) *Other overseas awards*

The Trustees devote a separate programme and budget to the support of research in tropical medicine. These overseas awards are not included in the present account, which therefore concerns Trust policy towards overseas countries other than Europe and the tropics. In the early years of their activities, the Trustees provided grants for buildings and equipment for institutions and fellowships for individuals. The Trustees' policy for buildings and equipment has been considered already. The award of fellowships became the chief method of support for scientists from overseas. Many such awards were made in the 1950s and 1960s, but it is difficult to find evidence of any clear policy concerning overseas applications until 1961. In that year, the Trustees undertook to make a block grant to the Medical Research Council for the awards of up to five research fellowships annually, for candidates of the same status as those receiving research fellowships from the Council. The majority of the fellowships awarded were for visits to laboratories and hospitals in the United States. The scheme was highly successful in attracting good candidates, but in 1976 the Trustees decided not to delegate their responsibilities to the Medical Research Council, and discontinued the allocation. Seventy-one fellowships were awarded between 1961 and 1976. The Trustees decided that Senior Clinical Fellows supported through the Trust should be enabled to spend one year in an overseas laboratory, and that the necessary funds should be available from the grant made hitherto to the Medical Research Council.

The need, at one time, for the delegation of awards is an indication that the administration of schemes for support of overseas scientists can be difficult, unless the administrators have special experience of problems and conditions in the host country. One of the countries with which the Trustees have attempted to make special arrangements has been Australia. In the mid-1960s, conversations between the Director, Dr P. O. Williams, and visiting scientists from Australia, led to the suggestion that a Trust scheme similar to that for Senior Clinical Fellows should be available for candidates from Australia. In 1968, the Trustees agreed that one senior fellowship in clinical science should be available annually for competition between candidates from Australian Universities. This scheme was discontinued in 1972, because of difficulties in the administration. Four fellowships had been awarded for research to be carried out in Australia.

An exchange of fellowships between Australia and the United Kingdom was proposed by the Council of the Royal Society in 1968, as a memorial to Lord Florey, President of the Royal Society from 1960 to 1965. The Trustees made a contribution of £20,000 to the Royal Society fund to help inaugurate this scheme.

More recently, the Trustees have set aside funds for awards to scientists in Australia and New Zealand. They made arrangements, effective initially for three years, for the annual award of two senior fellowships in the medical sciences, each tenable for five years in an Australian University or Institute. Two awards were made in 1985. The Trustees, in conjunction with the New Zealand Medical Research Council, have made funds available for two types of award. First, for a programme grant, and second, for a fellowship tenable for two years in the United Kingdom, followed by a final year in New Zealand.

The difficulties encountered in administering overseas awards, mentioned above, have not occurred to the same extent when schemes have been set up to enable scientists to visit Great Britain. Such a scheme is that for Wellcome–Japanese awards. In 1966, the Director of the Trust received inquiries from Japanese sources about the possibilities of Trust support for Japanese scientists to visit Great Britain. Professor R. H. S. Thompson attended the International Congress of Biochemistry in Tokyo in 1967, and was therefore able to meet Japanese scientists and discuss with them the work and objectives of the Trust. The Trustees decided to award two fellowships annually for Japanese scientists to carry out medical research in Great Britain. The administration of the scheme has been greatly helped by the co-operation of the British Council in Tokyo.

The assessment of the scheme, made by the Trust's scientific staff on the basis of reports and interviews with fellows, is that its scientific value is high. Success in obtaining recognition by Japanese scientists of Trust activities is not so obvious. In 1977, a distinguished member of the Japanese Academy visited the Trust office. He had come to Britain with a delegation which was examining methods of increasing scientific co-operation between Japan and Great Britain, and he had already seen the President and the Foreign Secretary at the Royal Society. He asked if the Wellcome Trust could help in any way, being unaware of the existing Trust scheme. The Trustees have continued the Japanese awards with no contributions from other sources.

In the period 1969–82, 22 Japanese fellowships for a period of one year were awarded. Of these, 12 were extended for one year. The total cost has been approximately £225,000.

Overseas fellowship awards are tabulated at the end of this section. It will be seen that there has been a marked decrease in the award to Commonwealth citizens. This was a result of a Trustees' decision, recorded in their 1970–2 report, to limit such awards, and in recent years the Trustees' policy concerning applications for fellowships from scientists from developed countries has been to consider such requests only from those who are already in the United Kingdom, supported by a fellowship grant, and who wish to extend their stay to complete a research project. Only rarely have awards been made to enable such overseas scientists to visit the United Kingdom to start a research project.

Awards have been made to Indian and Pakistan nationals, outside the specific Tropical Medicine budget, which was first separated from other budgetary items in 1970–2. Fellowship awards have been made since then to scientists whose programme is not considered to be of particular relevance to medicine in the tropics.

European research fellowships

	1954–74			1974–6		1976–8		1978–80		1980–2	
	To	From	Total	To	From	To	From	To	From	To	From
Hungary	1	56	57	–	8	–	6	–	9	–	7
Sweden	36	7	43	1	1	3	3	2	1	1	1
Denmark	14	16	30	2	2	3	2	1	1	–	–
Czechoslovakia	–	29	29	–	5	–	5	–	1	–	4
Poland	1	18	19	–	4	–	5	–	5	–	10
Italy	1	15	16	–	4	–	10	–	8	–	12
Germany E.	–	–	–	–	–	–	–	–	–	–	2
Germany W.	6	7	13	2	1	1	–	2	–	–	1
Greece	–	13	13	–	2	–	3	–	2	–	2
Yugoslavia	–	13	13	–	–	–	–	–	–	–	1
France	3	7	10	1	2	4	3	5	3	3	3
Spain	–	7	7	–	3	–	1	–	6	–	4
Bulgaria	–	5	5	–	3	–	3	–	2	–	5
Norway	1	3	4	–	1	–	–	–	3	–	2
Belgium	–	4	4	–	–	–	–	–	3	–	–
Switzerland	–	1	1	1	1	–	–	–	–	1	–
Finland	–	2	2	–	–	–	1	–	1	–	1
Iceland	–	1	1	–	1	–	–	–	–	–	1
Romania	–	–	–	–	2	–	–	–	–	–	–
The Netherlands	–	–	–	1	1	–	1	1	1	1	1
U.S.S.R.	–	1	1	–	–	–	–	–	–	–	1
Austria	–	1	1	–	–	–	–	–	1	–	–
Malta	–	–	–	–	–	–	1	–	2	–	–
Portugal	–	–	–	–	–	–	–	–	2	–	1

Overseas fellowships

From	1954–74	1974–84
Australia	43	13
United States	40	9
India	34	13
New Zealand	16	2
Canada	14	–
South Africa	13	–
Other countries	43	32

Travel grants

1954–74	£600,000
(Approximately $2\frac{1}{4}$ per cent of budget)	
	£
1974–6	73,500
1976–8	121,750
1978–80	120,000
1980–2	135,000
1982–4	175,000
	625,250
(Approximately $\frac{3}{4}$ per cent of budget)	

These figures do not include Wellcome Italian travel grants, nor the special awards for visits to New Zealand, Australia, South Africa and U.S.A. These amounted to £275,000 for 1974–84.

Interlaboratory collaboration and support of Symposia and Workshops

Many holders of Wellcome Trust Fellowships have returned to their countries, and maintained scientific contacts with laboratories in the United Kingdom. The Trustees have always tried to encourage such continuing collaboration, in addition to supporting new attempts at collaborative ventures.

In 1972, the Trustees decided to make a specific category of award which would enable scientists in the United Kingdom, and other European scientists engaged in related work, to meet regularly, visit and work in each other's laboratories, and exchange materials. Initially, the awards were for relatively small sums of up to £1,000 per annum for two years.

The scheme started well, and the Trustees made 34 awards during the first four years of the scheme's operation. However, the interest of the scientific community was not maintained, and the scheme as a whole has not been so successful as had been hoped. It is interesting to note the success of collaboration with Hungarian scientists. With them, Dr R. A. Dwek of the Department of Biochemistry, University of Oxford, has worked on biochemical problems of complement; and Dr A. D. Smith of the Department of Pharmacology, University of Oxford has studied specific neuronal connections of basal ganglia.

Another scheme, related to inter-laboratory collaboration, but confined to assistance for Polish laboratories, was started in 1972. Returning from a visit to Poland, the Director of the Trust suggested to the Trustees that certain Polish laboratories would benefit considerably if they were able to buy small items of equipment, chemicals and supplies, from United Kingdom sources without the need for permits from Polish authorities for foreign currency. The Trustees agreed to make an award of £3,000 per annum for three years, for two Polish laboratories in Warsaw, and one in Krakow. Three heads of research laboratories in the United Kingdom agreed to administer the awards, and receive the requests for support from Poland. The scheme has been very successful, and the grant has been renewed on several occasions.

In their second report (1956–8) the Trustees paid tribute to the great value of Symposia organised by the Ciba Foundation, and the Council for the International Organization of Medical Sciences (C.I.O.M.S.). In accordance with their general policy of avoiding overlap with the functions of other bodies, the Trustees decided to support international meetings only if the subject fell within their special interests. They agreed also to support small meetings attended by a limited number of experts who wished to discuss research aspects of a particular problem. The Trustees considered that such small meetings were likely to be more effective as aids to research.

Funds allocated for support of symposia have therefore been a very small part of the total budget.

The present European programme by Dr M. J. Morgan

Since 1957 the Trustees have shown an ever-increasing interest in the development of interchange between medical research workers in Europe. Besides general schemes to provide fellowships and travel grants, which facilitate communication, special arrangements have been made with organisations in various European countries.

There is general concern within Europe about the lack of mobility of scientific workers which is as characteristic of the medical sciences as of the physical sciences. No one is entirely certain what the reasons for lack of mobility are, but it is clear that contributory causes are the lack of employment prospects in all European countries, tending to persuade young scientists to remain in their home countries in the hope of permanent employment rather than venture abroad to gain new experience. There appears to be a tendency to marry earlier and start a family with a consequent decrease in a willingness to move to another country for a short period of time. Of course, there is in addition a general lack of funds to finance exchanges. The Trustees, therefore, wish vigorously to pursue and encourage inter-collaborative programmes between investigators in the United Kingdom and those in the rest of Europe. As the cost of scientific research increases, and as the biological sciences become more and more dominated by American and Japanese laboratories, it is evident to many that greater collaboration between European laboratories is essential for the health of European medical research. The Trustees therefore aim to publicise the opportunities that exist for the support of collaborative programmes, and will continue to make fellowships available for young scientists who wish to spend one or two years doing research in a laboratory within a foreign country.

16

THE BASIC SCIENCES AND MEDICINE
by Dr B. A. Bembridge

Sir Henry Wellcome declared that one of his aims was that his funds should be used for the 'advancement of research in medical subjects which have, or may develop, an importance for the improvement of the physical condition of mankind'. The expression 'medical subjects' might of itself seem vague, but elsewhere in the Will, Sir Henry Wellcome expanded his conception further by the words 'medicine, surgery, chemistry, physiology, bacteriology, therapeutics, materia medica, pharmacy and allied subjects' and went on still more broadly to include within his scope 'subjects which may develop in importance for scientific research or which may induce to the improvement of the physical conditions of mankind'. Clearly, Wellcome meant his Trustees to paint his generosity across a broad canvas, and clearly too he was one of those who believe that advances in medicine may spring from discoveries in physics, chemistry and biology, though those basic sciences are far from being the *sole* source of such advances. Wellcome recognised the importance of basic as well as applied research, and the Trustees have continued to give support to projects in the basic sciences. Professor Arthur Kornberg has said 'Advances in medicine spring from discoveries in physics, chemistry and biology. Among key contributions to the diagnosis, treatment and prevention of cardiovascular and pulmonary diseases, a recent analysis shows two thirds to have been basic rather than applied research. Without a firm foundation in basic knowledge innovations perceived as advances prove hollow and collapse.'[1]

Bearing in mind his description of the Trustees' responsibilities, what definition of medical research would fulfil Sir Henry's objectives? It is clear that the terms of the Will were broad enough to include what is generally understood to be basic research (subjects which may develop an importance) as well as clinical research (subjects which have an importance for the improvement of the physical condition of mankind). The research to be described will be, therefore, studies of normal and abnormal biological phenomena; attempts at their explanation in terms of the physical and chemical properties of the substance present in the body of man and other animals; and the efforts to utilise such understanding in the control of disease.

The evolution of the Trustees' policy through changing circumstances has been considered already. They have followed the broad path that Wellcome prescribed, and have not shared the despairing view of Sir Macfarlane Burnet (an early beneficiary of their generosity) that 'the contribution of laboratory science to medicine has virtually come to an end'.[2] They have consistently taken the contrary view that modern basic research in the medical sciences *does* have a 'direct or indirect bearing on the prevention of disease, or on the improvement of medical care'. Up to 1970, as we have seen, this took the form of support predominantly for buildings and equipment. Overseas travel and fellowships were also important, and the value to scientists of these various awards has been assessed. An attempt is now made to assess other methods of support for the basic and clinical sciences.

The Trustees have supported basic and clinical research by several methods. The most important have been:

1. In response to requests for support for project grants for periods of up to three years, the so-called '*ad hoc*' grants.
2. Awards over longer periods for selected subjects; or related to specific policy decisions (e.g. interdisciplinary awards). They were often in response to Trust advertisements.
3. Fellowship awards in selected subjects.

The present account is concerned with the first two of the above categories. The third category is considered in earlier chapters. Figures in Appendix VIII show the allocation of funds for research in the basic and clinical sciences between 1937 and 1984. (These sums do not include awards in special subjects, nor for fellowships. Basic and clinical research studies are also supported through these categories of award.) The figures show the change towards personal support for research assistance and expenses. From 1968, *ad hoc* grants for the basic and clinical sciences varied from 35 per cent to 21 per cent of the Trustees' budget. Of these grants, approximately two-thirds were for the basic sciences, and one-third for the clinical sciences. We shall see that a further change in the allocation of funds was towards support for selected topics of special interest to the Trustees, and for personal support for periods longer than that provided by project grants.

The methods of support for research, outlined above, are not difficult to categorise and describe. The Trustees, in any case, have always been flexible in interpreting their policy. It is more difficult to give an account of the scientific projects supported by such methods. The Trustees have never been responsible for any research units in the United Kingdom, and only in the past 15 years have they made a deliberate effort to encourage research in specific topics in limited fields. It is true that in their second and third reports the Trustees declared that they wished to encourage research in tropical medicine, veterinary medicine, pharmacology and pharmacy, therapeutics, experimental physiology, biochemistry and biophysics. Their statement concerned so many subjects that both exclusion and selection of applications on grounds of policy must have been very difficult. If biomedical research can be classified into such subject headings, then every category has received support at some period of the Trustees' activities. It is clear that they have always set aside a substantial proportion of their budget for support of research other than in specially selected subjects, and that a large number of awards have been for projects in the basic sciences, with no obvious immediate relevance to clinical medicine. Examination of unpublished budgetary figures shows that the subjects of physiology and biochemistry have consistently taken a large proportion of the basic sciences budget; the figures for the clinical sciences are more variable, but gastroenterology and endocrinology have always been well supported.

The figures are:

All awards 1970–84; excluding special subjects, but including special types (University Awards, Senior Lecturers, Senior Fellows). Categorised according to first classification, e.g. *Physiology*; (sub-categories – endocrinology; neurology).

	£	
Physiology and reproductive physiology	7.175	million
Biochemistry	6.9	million
Immunology	3.5	million
Pharmacology	3.35	million
Pathology	3.01	million
Endocrinology	2.55	million
Gastroenterology	2.125	million
Total for ALL subjects	72	million

In the early years covered by the present study, clinical studies became firmly based on a sound understanding of the physiology of organ systems. It is appropriate to record here the great contribution of Sir John McMichael to the integration of physiology with clinical medicine. Sir John was Professor of Medicine at the Royal Postgraduate Medical School from 1946 to 1966, and a Wellcome Trustee from 1960 to 1977. In the early 1940s, he was the pioneer of cardiac catheterisation in this country, and made outstanding contributions to the understanding of the mechanisms of heart failure. In addition, he made valuable studies of disorders of the spleen and liver. In their lectures after receiving Nobel prizes for discoveries concerning cardiac catheterisation and pathological changes in the circulatory system, Werner Forssmann and Dickinson Richards both referred to the work of McMichael. Forssmann referred in particular to the antagonisms which he and McMichael had to overcome in their attempts to introduce cardiac catheterisation into clinical practice.

It is interesting to recall that long before the period of the present study, physiologists were engaged in arguments with chemists about the development of a discipline of biochemistry, or physiological chemistry, independent of classical physiology.[3] The relationship of biochemistry to physiology may seem obvious to us now, and the arguments about this appear to be pointless. Fruton (1976) however, holds the view that tensions between different practitioners of chemistry and biology are 'the principal source of the vitality of biochemistry and are likely to lead to unexpected and exciting novelties in the future, as they have in the past'.[4]

The historic relationship between physiology and biochemistry is stressed now, because in the years after the Second World War, when the Trustees began to be able to use their funds, an understanding of the chemistry of biological systems became increasingly important in clinical medicine. The Trustees have always given strong support to biochemistry and physiology, and we shall show that they have encouraged applications which attempted to relate these sciences to clinical medicine.

At the present time, we see a further stage in the integration of basic science with clinical medicine, the attempt to interpret biological systems at the molecular level. It is relevant to ask the meaning of the term molecular biology, and inquire if the problems studied by molecular biologists lie within the interests of the Trust. Gowland Hopkins in 1927 had already said 'it will be the ultimate privilege of advancing biochemistry to tempt all biologists, including the physician, always to picture mentally the molecular events which underlie the changes of form and visible appearances which interest them'. The phrase molecular biology was first used in 1938 by Warren Weaver, then a Director of the Rockefeller Foundation. He referred to 'a relatively new field, which may be called molecular biology, in which delicate modern techniques are being used to investigate ever more minute details of certain cell processes'.[5] The term was probably brought into general use by Astbury in papers published between 1945 and 1950. Kendrew[6] pointed out that there was no agreement between molecular biologists themselves about the meaning of the term. There were two main schools. The British school, started by Bragg, and continued by Bernal, Astbury and others, was concerned with problems of three-dimensional studies of biological macromolecules. This approach enabled Perutz and Kendrew to elucidate the structure of haemoglobin and myoglobin. The American school, led by Delbrück, began with studies of bacteriophage to attempt to answer the problems of reproduction and transfer of genetic information in micro-organisms. This approach eventually resulted in a full understanding of the function of phage DNA.

The attitude of the Trustees to applications for support of studies which they would classify as molecular biology has changed recently. We have seen that the Trustees gave modest support to the M.R.C. Cambridge Unit in 1968, but for a long period, after molecular biology studies were seen to be flourishing in that unit, the Trustees considered that their funds should not be used for what might be interpreted as a duplication of the M.R.C. efforts. The Trustees have now decided that the time is right for them to promote the application of new developments in cellular and molecular biology to the study of human disease, and in particular to encourage greater use of recombinant DNA technology. We have noted that in the United Kingdom, the Trustees have never provided complete support for research units, in contrast to their policy overseas. However, Trust grants have been significant in starting up research groups; or have given additional support to groups in an early stage of their development, or to groups in financial difficulties. Some projects have made a contribution, over a period, to the development of specific topics, not formally designated to be of particular interest to the Trustees.

We have shown that until the late 1960s, Trust awards were predominantly for buildings and equipment, and we have described some of the projects carried out with Trust grants for major items of equipment. These studies were mainly in the basic sciences. Appendix IV summarises large awards for the period 1980–4 and shows how the Trustees allocated their funds between the basic and clinical sciences. A classification in greater detail of research projects under a single subject discipline (e.g. physiology, biochemistry, gastroenterology, endocrinology) is becoming more difficult to apply because of the multidisciplinary approach to investigations. The selection for description of topics within each discipline is also difficult. Projects classified as 'Physiology' have probably received the greatest proportion of awards by the Trustees, whose interest in such studies is demonstrated in the list of subjects and contributors to the tenth edition (1984) of the publication 'Recent Advances in Physiology'. The chapters of this book summarise important growth areas of the last few years in the physiological sciences. Of the 12 contributors seven have received support from the Trustees for their research. They are: Dr S. G. Cull-Candy, a Wellcome Trust Senior Lecturer (synaptic channels); Dr T. D. Lamb, a Trust Senior Fellow before becoming a Locke Research Fellow of the Royal Society (photo-receptor physiology); Professor S. Zeki (physiology of the visual pathway); Dr A. E. Warner (early development); Dr M. J. Dawson and Professor D. R. Wilkie (N.M.R. studies of muscle and brain metabolism); Dr A. V. Edwards (neuroendocrinology); and Dr R. Smith (bone metabolism). The editor of the book is Professor P. Baker of the Department of Physiology, King's College, London. The Trustees made a substantial grant for building alterations to this department in 1978.

There is good evidence therefore of the Trustees' wide interests in the basic sciences. We shall now describe some of the awards made to encourage the introduction of the basic sciences, especially physiology and biochemistry, into clinical studies. The investigations described are distinct from those which have been supported as a result of the Trust policy of making awards for projects in specially selected subjects. In the main, the following account is concerned with the results of investigations into specific aspects of a problem rather than a summary of what was questioned and attempted over a broad front. It will then show how the Trustees' support for research has contributed to advances in knowledge.

I. **Biochemistry and Endocrinology:** parathyroid and vitamin D

Since the Trust's foundation endocrinology has become 'a vast area of development which has no particular boundaries, since it is rapidly assuming the nature of cell biology, where communications between cells at all levels is the major problem'.[7] In the past 15 years, the Trustees have made 150 awards for studies classified as endocrinology, at an approximate cost of £3.2 million, suggesting that the Trustees have given strong support to investigations in the subject. We select for description those studies in biochemistry and endocrinology in one field of investigation, vitamin D metabolism and the parathyroid, which have contributed to the understanding of the principles of the structure, function and synthesis of peptide and protein hormones and steroids; the mechanism and control of hormone actions; stress the part which the development of techniques has played in the advance of knowledge; and relate these studies to clinical practice. In addition to demonstrating general principles, the assessment will show that studies supported by the Trustees have contributed to specific advances in knowledge of vitamin D metabolism, which have occurred in the past 15 years. First, several metabolites of vitamin D have been identified with greater biological actions than the parent compound. Second, the relationship between vitamin D and parathyroid hormone has been clarified. Third, the long term administration of enzyme-inducing agents (e.g. anti-epileptics) has been shown to alter the rate of vitamin D metabolism.

Professor Russell Fraser and Professor Iain MacIntyre

In 1967, Professor C. C. Booth wrote to the Trustees, asking them to consider setting up a clinical endocrinology unit at the Royal Postgraduate Medical School, to be supported for five years with a view to its incorporation in the University quinquennial budget. He said:

> With the development of more complex techniques in all types of clinical work, successful research has increasingly required effective co-operation of groups of workers drawn from different departments in universities and medical schools . . . there is little doubt that progress depends on a thorough application of modern biochemical knowledge and practice. At present we are lagging behind some other parts of the world in the extent to which biochemistry has been developed in the clinical fields. . . . We believe that the future success of research in many fields depends on integrating clinical medicine and biochemistry as effectively as we can.

The Trustees made a grant over five years to the Royal Postgraduate Medical School, for the purpose of developing a Unit for Clinical Endocrinology, under the direction of Professor Russell Fraser and Professor Iain MacIntyre. The Royal Postgraduate Medical School took over the cost of this support and, the School having promised to take over a second grant if it was awarded, a further grant over five years was made in May

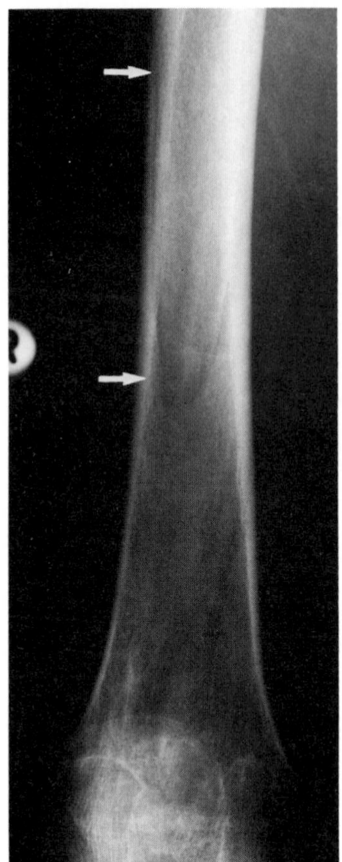

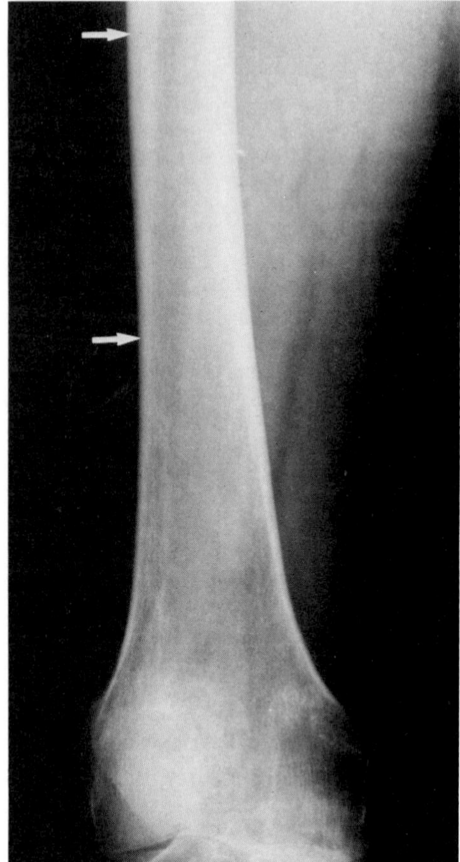

Fig. 65. Paget's disease of the femur. A classical osteolytic lesion (*left*) which shows complete radiological healing (*right*) following three years continuous treatment with synthetic human calcitonin.

1972 to Professor MacIntyre. The most important practical result of the work in the Hammersmith Clinical Endocrinology Unit was the finding that human calcitonin produces a complete clinical, biochemical and histological remission in Paget's disease of bone, with rapid relief of pain. The Unit also evolved a new double isotope calcium absorption test, and defined the importance of vitamin D as a factor in determining whether hyperparathyroidism presents as renal stones or as bone disease.

This group at the Royal Postgraduate Medical School has developed methods for peptide synthesis and for the preparation of limited sequences of hormones and their conjugates. Its development of a very small-scale methods for sequencing proteins, using radioactive tracers, has enabled the group to make metabolic studies *in vivo* and *in vitro* of peptide hormones, using physiological concentrations. The clinical application of these studies is that new compounds may be produced which have a more prolonged therapeutic action.

The work of this Unit has gone on successfully since Trust support ceased, and members of the group are now applying the techniques of molecular biology. Its success is clearly a consequence of initial support by the Wellcome Trust.

Dr R. Smith

Dr Smith was appointed to a Wellcome Senior Fellowship in Clinical Science in 1965. He has studied the effects of vitamin D on bone matrix, the therapeutic usefulness of vitamin D derivatives and the effects of vitamin D on muscle function.

Dr T. C. B. Stamp

In 1970, Professor C. E. Dent of University College Hospital Medical School wrote to the Trustees to say that because of recent cuts in university spending, he was unable to renew an appointment for Dr T. C. B. Stamp. Professor Dent requested support for the continuation of his studies on the analysis of vitamin D and its metabolites by gas chromatography. The Trustees made an award to Dr Stamp and also encouraged him to visit the United States to study techniques. Dr Stamp also received encouragement in his early studies from Dr E. Kodicek in the Strangeways Laboratory, Cambridge.

At the time of the Trustees' first award to Dr Stamp, research in the U.S.A. had shown that the active form of vitamin D was an hydroxylated metabolite, whose exact chemical nature was uncertain. Professor Dent and Dr Stamp proposed to investigate these mechanisms of hydroxylation and find an assay for the products. They also wished to examine the interference with vitamin D metabolism of anticonvulsant drugs such as phenobarbitone and phenytoin. Dr Stamp succeeded in introducing a method of assay for 25 hydroxyvitamin D to Britain and, among other interacting results, showed that (even in Britain) solar radiation is the chief agent of vitamin D nutrition, rather than food.

Subsequent support from the Wellcome Trust allowed Dr Stamp's work to continue from a new base at the Royal National Orthopaedic and the Middlesex Hospitals. Problems of vitamin D deficiency among the elderly population were studied in collaboration with Professor A. N.

Exton-Smith and showed that even non-institutionalised ambulant elderly subjects attending a day centre suffered relative vitamin D deficiency throughout the year. Further studies were made of vitamin D nutrition during pregnancy in different racial groups, all patients being sampled during the February nadir showed a significant deficiency at this time among Asians compared with blacks and whites, while a survey of vitamin D nutrition among Asians in East Africa revealed that newly arrived immigrants from Uganda showed no evidence of vitamin D deficiency.

Studies with Professor Alan Richens confirmed that among epileptic patients their vitamin D deficiency was associated with seasonal variation.

Dr Stamp was awarded the Prix André Lichtwitz in 1973. This French award is made annually by the Institut National de la Santé et de la Recherche Médicale for outstanding research in calcium metabolism. The citation specified Dr Stamp's work on vitamin D nutrition and anti-convulsant osteomalacia.

Dr J. L. O'Riordan

In 1972 the Trustees made an award to Dr J. L. O'Riordan, of the Middlesex Hospital, for his studies on the role of metabolites of vitamin D in man, using protein binding assays. At that time, the Trustees considered that the intricate chemical problem relating to vitamin D, parathyroid hormone, calcitonin and related subjects justified this award in addition to awards they had already made in this area of investigation. The Trust supported Dr O'Riordan from 1972 to 1980, when the Medical Research Council took over funding of the work.

At the start of these studies, there was increasing concern about the occurrence of osteomalacia and rickets in Asian immigrants to this country. The Middlesex group showed that vitamin D deficiency, as reflected by low concentrations of 25-hydroxy-cholecalciferol in plasma, was the cause of the problem and, in collaboration with Drs Dunnigan and Ford in Glasgow, showed the addition of vitamin D to chapatti flour could correct the situation. A radioimmunoassay was developed at the Middlesex by Dr Clemens and colleagues to measure 1,25-dihydroxy-cholecalciferol and it was shown that the concentration was low in vitamin D deficiency (a subject which had previously been controversial). A particularly interesting observation was that once treatment was started, supranormal concentrations were produced and were maintained until the bone disease had healed. In subsequent work, a converse situation was studied in which it was shown that there was resistance to the action of vitamin D and a new form of rickets was characterised; in that, patients have a high concentration of 1,25-dihydroxy-cholecalciferol. Rickets in these patients may be associated with total alopecia. Vitamin D resistance was subsequently shown to be through lack of receptor protein.

Thus, in many ways, this research funded by the Wellcome Trust led to practical advances and a greater understanding of the vitamin D endocrine system and has opened the way to further advances.

Dr John Kanis

The role in renal bone disease of a disturbance in the metabolism of vitamin D was studied by Dr John Kanis, as part of investigations he carried out when he held a Wellcome Senior Clinical Research Fellowship at the Nuffield Orthopaedic Centre between 1976 and 1979. The Oxford Renal Unit was one of the first to evaluate polar derivatives of vitamin D in renal bone disease. Long-term studies showed that these agents were highly effective in reversing many of the features of bone disease including bone pain, myopathy and radiographic abnormalities. The results in children were particularly impressive since progressive deformity could be prevented and linear growth partially restored. Long-term histological studies, however, were disappointing and it became clear that a minority of patients, particularly those maintained on dialysis treatment, showed disappointing histological responses. Moreover, with continued treatment, bone disease recurred in some patients despite the maintenance of serum calcium.

Investigation into the mechanism of action of these compounds suggested that they acted principally to increase calcium absorption and thereby raise plasma calcium, rather than by acting directly on skeletal tissue or the parathyroid gland.

Dr A. W. M. Hay

The Trustees have always been willing to support studies in comparative medicine, and in 1972 they made an award to Dr A. W. M. Hay of the Nuffield Institute of Comparative Medicine, the Zoological Society of London, for an investigation into the comparative aspects of vitamin D transport. The vitamin is transported in the blood bound to a protein, usually a globulin. Dr Hay examined the main groups of vertebrates and showed that the binding protein differs in various families. In 130 species examined there was increasing specificity in the mode of vitamin D transport with evolutionary advance.

Dr S. Edelstein

In 1972 the Trustees awarded a fellowship to Dr S. Edelstein of the Weizmann Institute in Jerusalem to work with Dr E. Kodicek at the Strangeways Institute in Cambridge. They wished to study the action of the vitamin D metabolite 1,25 dihydroxy-cholecalciferol, with particular reference to setting up a sensitive assay to replace the laborious biological assay available at that time, and succeeded in providing a double isotope technique. The Trustees made a further award to Dr Edelstein to continue his studies at his Institute in Jerusalem, where he was investigating receptor mechanisms for vitamin D metabolites.

Dr S. C. Manolagas

In 1976 the Trustees awarded a fellowship to Dr S. C. Manolagas, of Athens, to work with Dr D. C. Anderson of Manchester Royal Infirmary, to work on problems of decalcification. He carried out an exacting experimental study related to the determination of specific receptors for oestrogens and corticosteroids in bone cells, and found specific receptors in bone for corticosteroids. Dr Manolagas has continued his work after this early support from the Trust.

Professor A. G. E. Pearse and endocrine cytochemistry

R. A. Gregory[8] has said that 'since 1962 the isolation and identification of the major gastrointestinal hormones has resulted in a remarkable advance of knowledge in every aspect of this field of study'. An award made by the Trust contributed to this advance.

In 1961, the Trustees made a grant to Professor Everson Pearse of the Royal Postgraduate Medical School for the purchase of an electron microscope for his studies on enzyme histochemistry. In 1969 the Trustees made a second award, for three years, for research assistance and expenses, to enable Professor Pearse to establish endocrine cytochemistry and ultrastructure as the central theme in his department. The award was extended for three years in 1972. They also made a substantial contribution towards the cost of replacing the electron microscope in 1973.

Professor Pearse's studies of endocrine glands from various species had suggested to him that a common metabolic pattern was shared by cells with widely different functions. The single factor linking different cell types was the nature of their principal product, in each case a low molecular weight polypeptide. When it became necessary to trace and identify the cell type responsible for producing calcitonin, a test was provided of Professor Pearse's hypothesis, which it passed successfully.

A great deal more is known today than when these studies began in 1964, but the viability and creativity of the cytochemical concepts introduced by Professor Pearse are still manifest. They continue to provide a stimulus for extensive research, by adherents of many disciplines and sciences and look set to do so well into the foreseeable future.

Support from the Wellcome Trust helped considerably to establish Professor Pearse's strong base for endocrine research.

Dr Stephen Bloom

Professor (now Sir Christopher) Booth, then Director of the Department of Medicine at the Royal Postgraduate Medical School, considered that further advances in the study of intestinal hormones would be possible through an investigation of the physiological and clinical importance of enteroglucagon and vasoactive intestinal peptides. In 1975, he supported an application by Dr Bloom for support for such studies, and the Trustees made an award for three years.

Important fundamental research on the nature of the neurohormonal peptides, vasoactive intestinal peptide (V.I.P.) and enteroglucagon was undertaken. Dr Bloom's group was the first to report that V.I.P. was present in the brain and demonstrated its neuronal distribution in the gut; afterwards they detected its presence in nerves in the islets of Langerhans and also its role in atropine resistant vasodilation of the salivary gland. Although following long after the original grant, a fundamental paper on the nature of enteroglucagon, in collaboration with Dr A. J. Moody, who was the first person to isolate this substance, was published.

The effect of the Trustee's grant to Dr Bloom, newly appointed to the Hammersmith Hospital, was to enable a new group to be developed, which has expanded since.

Professor P. N. Campbell and Dr R. Craig

We have already described the contribution to the knowledge of structure and function of some hormones made by projects supported by the Trust. The award in 1978 to Professor Campbell and Dr Craig of the Department of Biochemistry at the Middlesex Hospital Medical School was for studies on the biosynthesis of human radioactive pituitary hormones *in vitro*. This was the first award made by the Trustees for the application of recombinant DNA technology to an aspect of medical research. The grant provided for the equipment of a Category II biological containment facility, salaries and running expenses. Work on the cloning of human and animal gene sequences was initiated in 1978.

This award proved invaluable as it permitted many other projects to be initiated at the Middlesex Hospital Medical School. Without it the application of recombinant DNA technology to medical and fundamental research at the School might have been delayed by several years, as might the support by the Wellcome Trustees of a technology which, since this particular application was received in 1977, has revolutionized our understanding of human diseases.

II. Biochemistry and gastroenterology: intestinal absorption and coeliac disease

The study of the complex mechanisms of absorption of dietary substances from the gastrointestinal tract provides fundamental information concerning cellular events associated with transport of molecules across membranes, and the relationship of such mechanisms to the varying morphology of the gastrointestinal tract. This basic knowledge of mechanisms is necessary for a proper understanding of a wide range of clinical signs and symptoms which may result from their derangement, and together form a malabsorption syndrome. The clinical manifestations of one of the diseases of malabsorption now known as coeliac disease were first described by Samuel Gee,[9] almost 100 years ago, but it is only within the last 35 years that laboratory and clinical investigations have given results which provided a base on which an understanding of the pathogenesis of coeliac disease is being built. Studies by Dicke in the early 1950s showed that some individuals are sensitive to ingested gluten, a complex protein/carbohydrate constituent of wheat.

Their intolerance of gluten may be the result of a primary abnormality of the intestinal mucosal cells, and a further advance in coeliac disease studies was the demonstration by Paulley in 1954[10] that a diagnostic feature of coeliac disease is a flattening of the mucosa of the jejunum, evident in biopsy specimens.

It is a reasonable claim that the Trustees' awards for studies of coeliac disease have improved our understanding of it.

Professor C. F. McCarthy, Professor B. McNicholl and Professor P. F. Fottrell

In 1970, the Trustees made an award for three years (later extended to six) to these scientists at University College, Galway for a study of small intestinal peptidases in coeliac disease.

At the time of the award it was unusual for the Trustees to make a large grant for a project to be undertaken outside the United Kingdom, but they considered that conditions in Galway where the incidence of coeliac disease was high appeared favourable for such a study.

Many aspects of the physiology, pathology and epidemiology of intestinal disorders were studied, and micromethods for assays of intestinal enzymes developed. The multiple forms of peptidases in the human small intestine were examined without detection of any deficiency occurring in coeliacs. Type 1 and type 2 tissue antigens in the population and in coeliacs have been investigated. Those associated with coeliac disease have a very high incidence in the normal population of Galway. Studies of the distribution of these antigens within families allow the prediction of those relatives most likely to develop coeliac disease.

A register of patients with coeliac disease throughout Ireland has been established and the number now on record approaches 2,000. It is hoped that the long-term study of these patients will allow an answer as to whether a gluten-free diet prevents the development of malignancy, commonly associated with coeliac sufferers.

The initial grant from the Wellcome Trust was of special value in fostering scientific collaboration between two hospital-based clinical departments of University College, Galway, and a non-clinical department of Biochemistry. As a consequence also, two full-time permanent posts were established: a lectureship in Biochemistry and a lectureship in Medicine. After the cessation of the Trust's funding, the Medical Research Council of Ireland formed a Coeliac Research Unit in Galway.

Dr J. F. Woodley

In 1975 the Trustees made an award for three years to Dr Woodley, of the University of Keele, to enable him to study enzymes of the human intestinal epithelial cell membrane, with particular reference to coeliac disease. The purpose of this study was to investigate the possibility that the disease is due to a defect in a membrane-bound digestive enzyme. Dr Woodley achieved two of his major aims, the preparation and purification of the membranes concerned and the identification of a number of peptidase activities in them.

These findings were the basis for continuing work, now supported by funds from other organisations, relating his findings to abnormal conditions. Dr Woodley thought it likely that the hydrolytic function of any one enzyme may be compensated for by others present.

Dr L. Fry

In 1975, the Trustees made an award for three years, to Dr L. Fry, of the Department of Dermatology, St Mary's Hospital, to enable him to study the relationship between dermatitis herpetiformis and coeliac disease.

When this award was made, the association of a coeliac lesion of the small intestine with the skin rash of dermatitis herpetiformis was well known, but the view most widely held by clinicians was that the two lesions were unrelated. Dr Fry and his colleagues, believing that this view was incorrect and that trials of the effect of a gluten-free diet on the skin lesions had been inadequate, carried out a carefully supervised trial of a strict long-term gluten-free diet in patients who had had a full clinical, haematological and intestinal examination, and found that the diet benefited the skin lesion in almost all patients with dermatitis herpetiformis. However, not all patients with coeliac disease respond to gluten-free diet, and it is therefore possible that a proportion of patients with the skin lesion also do not respond to the diet.

Dr A. M. Dawson, Dr M. J. Farthing

In 1976, the Trustees made an award for three years to Dr A. M. Dawson, of St Bartholomew's Hospital to study the relationship between androgen sensitivity and intestinal disease. Dr Dawson and Dr M. J. Farthing investigated gonadal function in patients with coeliac disease, particularly the association of infertility with the condition.

III. Diseases of the Liver

Three specific aspects of the last half-century's advance in knowledge of the liver and its disorders are relevant to what follows: the demonstration of the importance of laboratory research in providing new techniques for that early diagnosis of disease which is essential for effective treatment; the discovery of an infectious agent for a form of hepatitis; and the emergence of organ transplantation as a possible method of treatment for liver disease.

In 1939, Professor J. W. McNee wrote 'we know so little at present about disorders of hepatic function, unassociated with obvious structural changes, that our attempts at therapy are rudimentary – there may be very many serious functional disorders of the liver about which we know nothing'. Forty years later, Professor Sheila Sherlock wrote: 'The definitive therapy of most types of liver disease, particularly if chronic, leaves much to be desired.' Nevertheless, in the interval between those two statements, there has been a greatly increased understanding of the disorders of hepatic function, and the principles of their treatment. This knowledge has resulted from biopsy and serological techniques which have facilitated clinical interpretations and given particularly valuable information about the early stages of lesions which may be reversible with rational therapy. The introduction to this country in 1943 by Professor McMichael (now Sir John) and Dr Sheila Sherlock (now Professor Dame Sheila) of the technique of liver biopsy contributed greatly to the understanding of the pathogenesis of liver disease. They used the technique in a study of the pathology of epidemic hepatitis, one of the major diseases affecting servicemen during the Second World War.

The probability that this disease is of viral origin became apparent between 1936 and 1946. G. M. Findlay working at the Wellcome Laboratory of Tropical Medicine carried out much of the early experimental work on infective hepatitis: he and others suggested that it had a viral origin. Virologists are now satisfied on the basis of epidemiological, immunological, biochemical and ultrastructural evidence and studies by molecular biology techniques, that hepatitis B is caused by a virus. At the time of writing (1984) it has not been possible to culture the virus, although specific antigenic sub-units of the virus have been identified for use as vaccines.

The Trustees have supported many projects designed to elucidate biochemical mechanisms associated with liver disorder. We shall describe a project concerned with the study of fundamental properties of liver tissue: the functional reserve of the organ, and the immense capacity of liver cells for regeneration. This project was carried out by the combined use of techniques of surgery and physiology for the study of liver blood flow measurements, which are essential if investigators wish to quantify the biochemical process occurring in the liver during the response to various forms of injury.

Professor L. H. Blumgart and Dr A. M. Harper

Professor Blumgart of the Department of Surgery, and Dr Murray Harper of the Wellcome Surgical Institute, both in the University of Glasgow, devised an experimental method for the study in the dog of the effects of partial hepatectomy and the influence of local or general hypoxia on the ability of the liver to regenerate following the surgical procedure. They employed new methods for venous injection and hepatic venous blood portal sampling. They decided that their studies would be more effective if accompanied by measurements of liver blood flow, and applied to the Trust for a grant to enable them to develop an experimental method to do so, while the liver was experiencing a variety of disorders.

The Trustees decided that the proposal for a physiologist and a surgeon to combine in a research team was sound, and in 1975 they made an award for three years, extended to six in 1978. Dr R. Mathie also joined the group. A further award for three years was made in 1981, to enable work to continue after Professor Blumgart's move in 1979 to the Royal Postgraduate Medical School.

In order to measure liver blood flow, the investigators injected radioactive isotopes of the inert gases krypton or xenon into the portal vein, and the transit of the gas was monitored by a detector placed over the liver. Detailed studies of the hepatic arterial injection of inert gas generated the important conclusion that blood from the hepatic artery and the portal vein mix uniformly in the normal liver. A similar method of portal venous injection of xenon via the splenic pulp, after trials on the dog, was extended to man allowing pre-operative flow measurements to be made at the time of splenoportography.

The application of these techniques provided important information about liver regeneration and resection, haemorrhagic hypotension and the choice of procedures in liver surgery.

In the laboratory investigations mentioned above, immunological techniques have been of great importance in the study of a wide range of disorders of liver function. Immunological studies have also been of great significance in the specific problems associated with liver transplantation. In the past 20 years it has been shown that liver transplantation is feasible in patients with end-stage cirrhosis, in some patients with tumours of the liver and in patients with inborn errors of metabolism.

The first attempt at human liver transplantation was made by T. Starzl at the University of Colorado in 1963. Up to 1984, more than 1,000 such operations have been carried out throughout the world, and in North America of 568 patients who have received a transplant, 269 are still active. The use of immunosuppressive drugs has improved the prognosis for patients; and their survival has in turn provided information about immunological reactions in general, and specifically about the pathogenesis of metabolic disorders of the liver. The possibility of viral infection of the liver remains a serious problem. The ethical problem of the quality of life enjoyed by patients who have received a liver transplant will be answered only by continuing research into fundamental problems of liver function. In this country, Professor R. Y. Calne, of Cambridge University performed the first transplant operation in 1968 and is the pioneer in this form of treatment. He has collaborated in this work with Professor R. Williams of King's College Hospital. We have noted in an earlier chapter that the establishment of the Chair of Surgery in Cambridge was made possible by a contribution from the Trust.

Professor R. Williams

In 1970 the Trustees made an award to King's College Hospital Medical School, as a contribution towards the costs of providing research accommodation for studies of diseases of the liver. The research group, directed by Dr R. Williams was concerned primarily with problems of liver failure, and transplantation.

The grant awarded from the Wellcome Trust in 1970 represented a most important step forward in the development of liver research at King's. In the new laboratories that were built, the group of clinicians, biochemists, immunologists and bioengineers that had been gathered together during the previous few years, were brought together for the first time into an open-plan laboratory area purpose designed for the long-term interdisciplinary work proposed. Since the award there has been a gradual increase in the number of research staff.

Early work was concerned with the development of an immunological test for the specific diagnosis of rejection. Similar *in vitro* tests were used to explore the role of cell-mediated immunity in the pathogenesis of two forms of possible auto-immune liver disease – chronic active hepatitis and primary biliary cirrhosis. More recently the mechanism of hepatocyte damage in chronic hepatitis due to hepatitis B virus infection has been shown to be the consequence of a direct T-lymphocyte attack on hepatitis B virus antigens expressed on the cell surface in addition to the auto-immune reaction referred to above.

Viral hepatitis, a major public health problem throughout the world, is caused by several different viruses. Hepatitis B is particularly important in view of its propensity to lead to the carrier state, chronic liver disease (including chronic active hepatitis) and cirrhosis. There are at least 200 million carriers of hepatitis B worldwide. In addition, there is now compelling evidence of a causal association between hepatitis B and hepatocellular carcinoma, one of the 10 most common cancers in the world with over 250,000 new cases annually.

The Wellcome Trust has made several grants to fund investigations of this virus.

Dr H. C. Thomas

In 1978 the Trustees awarded a fellowship to Dr Thomas at the Royal Free Hospital, London for studies on the mechanisms of elimination of viruses in patients with chronic active hepatitis. Dr Thomas now holds a personal Professorship of Medicine at that Medical School.

The hepatitis B virus infects chimpanzees and man, and in 10 per cent of cases produces a chronic infection which may terminate in cirrhosis and hepatocellular carcinoma. The virus is not cytopathic and it is possible that immunological mechanisms are responsible for the lysis of the infected cells during the course of acute and chronic hepatitis.

Dr Thomas, with colleagues, studied the replication of the viruses in samples of liver tissue taken from chimpanzees and human patients. With another collaborator he ascertained the interaction of antigens and proteins at or near the membranes of liver cells in which virus replication is occurring, finding certain changes that may be capable of undergoing malignant transformation.

Trials were made in patients of the effectiveness of three substances (adenine arabinoside, adenine arabinoside monophosphate, and lymphoblastoid interferon) in preventing the replication of the virus. Success in one-third to one-quarter of patients indicated a significant effect; but the success rate (up to 60 per cent) was much greater in heterosexual patients than in homosexuals, suggesting an impaired immune response in the latter.

Hepatitis B Micelle Vaccines: Professor A. J. Zuckerman

In 1975, the Trustees made an award for three years to Professor Zuckerman, of the London School of Hygiene and Tropical Medicine, for his studies on sub-unit hepatitis B vaccines. In 1978, the Trustees thought that the progress made in this difficult subject warranted an extension of the award for a further three years.

Several studies have shown that individual high molecular weight polypeptides obtained from the protein coat of the hepatitis B virus, when purified, are effective antigens. To obtain quantities of these substances, Professor Zuckerman's group dissolved the protein coat in a detergent, and then removed the solvent to obtain water-soluble protein micelles

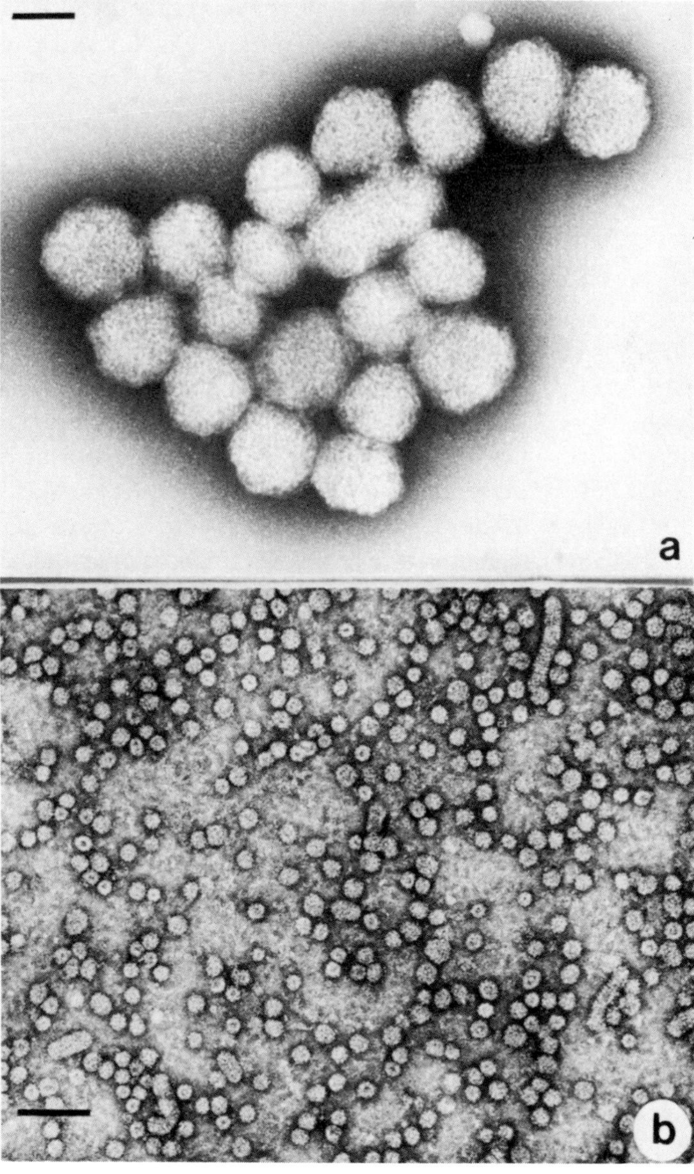

Fig. 66. Electron micrographs of negatively stained hepatitis B polypeptide micelles showing (a) the surface morphology and the variable size (the bar = 100 nm). The intact spherical 22 nm hepatitis B surface antigen particles are shown at (b) for comparison. Courtesy of Professor Arie J. Zuckerman

(that is, aggregates of polypeptides so arranged that the hydrophilic regions are on the outside of the particle, rendering them water soluble). Assayed in mice, a vaccine prepared from these micelles gave a more vigorous antibody response than did intact particles. After tests of safety and efficacy had been made in primate animals, clinical trials were begun and are still in progress.

IV. Perinatal studies; developmental neurobiology

Prematurity of the infant may be associated with respiratory distress and cerebral haemorrhage, two of the most important causes of neonatal and perinatal mortality. In 1963, Professor L. B. Strang wrote that five of every 1,000 children born alive in Britain died from respiratory failure within the first ten days of life; and of all babies affected in this manner, only about 10 per cent were in full-term infants. There was then no really effective therapy for respiratory distress. Only 12 years later Professor E. O. R. Reynolds could write that probably very few infants born at a gestational age of 30 weeks or more would die from respiratory distress. Major advances had been made as a result of 1) studies of the structure of the developing lung and related biochemical phenomena, and 2) the application of new methods for the management of the condition.

Research, described below, supported by awards from the Trust, has contributed to the understanding of prematurity of the infant and associated conditions of respiratory distress and cerebral haemorrhage. The award to Professor Tizard also shows how joint efforts of the medical charities have maintained an important research unit.

Professor L. B. Strang and Professor E. O. R. Reynolds

One of Britain's leading centres for research into diseases of the newly born is the Department of Paediatrics at University College, London. This academic department was started in 1963 with Professor L. B. Strang as its director. Trust support for studies there on respiratory failure began in 1966, when a grant was made for the provision of additional laboratory space. Professor Strang wrote to the Trustees in 1968 to say that the department faced a crisis in staffing with the possibility of losing a key member of his team, Dr E. O. R. Reynolds. The Trustees agreed to help, and made an award for five years which enabled University College to retain Dr Reynolds as a senior lecturer. Since then, Professor Reynolds (as he now is) has been continually active in the development of perinatal and neonatal services in the United Kingdom. In addition to his research and clinical duties he has served on government committees inquiring into such services.

He assisted Professor Strang to carry out studies on the permeability of the pulmonary capillaries and alveolar epithelium in fetal and newborn lambs. These studies provided new information about the permeability characteristics of the lung, and about the changes which occur at birth. Observations on lambs also provided the clue to the demonstration by Professor Reynolds and his colleagues that the serious illness known as massive pulmonary haemorrhage in newborn infants was usually attributable to increased pulmonary capillary pressure leading to overwhelming haemorrhagic pulmonary oedema. At the same time, Professor Reynolds gained new insights into the mechanisms of hypoxaemia in respiratory distress when surfactant returned to the lungs during the first days of life. Professor Reynolds went on to develop new methods of managing the care of infants with serious respiratory illness, to be put into practice in the expanding neonatal intensive care unit at University College Hospital. New ways were devised for the mechanical ventilation of infants with respiratory failure, which resulted in a large increase in the chances of survival for these infants, due mainly to a reduction in the incidence of bronchopulmonary dysplasia. Together with colleagues at the Medical Physics Department at University College Hospital, methods for monitoring breathing were developed and also sensors for continuously recording blood oxygen levels. A system for transporting infants with respiratory failure from outlying hospitals to the neonatal intensive care unit was developed. A long-term follow-up study of infants treated in the Unit was the first to make the important observation that very premature infants, whose lives were saved by intensive care, usually proved later to be normally healthy children.

Professor P. Tizard and Professor V. Dubowitz

The Neonatal Department of the Institute of Child Health is located in the Royal Postgraduate Medical School. In 1961, a research unit was established in the Department, by a generous grant from the Nuffield Foundation, on the understanding that eventual responsibility for the Unit would be assumed by the University of London. This proved to be impossible because of the University's financial difficulties. The Nuffield Foundation extended their support for a period longer than that guaranteed, but was unwilling to go beyond six years. In 1968 Professor Tizard, Director of the Unit explained the difficulties to the Trustees and asked for help. The Trustees decided that the Unit had achieved considerable success in the previous six years, and that its disbandment would be a severe setback to neonatal research in this country. They therefore made a grant for five years to enable the Unit to continue its work. After this award, the National Fund for Research into Crippling Diseases made a substantial grant for a joint Obstetric and Neonatal Paediatric building.

The Trustees continued their support for the paediatric research unit when Professor Dubowitz succeeded Professor Tizard in 1973. Professor Dubowitz wished to study new techniques of monitoring cardiovascular variables, and improved methods for making respiratory measurements in the newborn infant. In his view the great advances made during the previous five years in the investigation and treatment of neonates with severe respiratory or metabolic disorders, could be extended further by the improvement of techniques for intensive care. In 1974 the Trustees made an award, for five years, to finance his researches, which proved successful in several areas. Dr Simon Godfrey's contribution was particularly noteworthy.

1. *Development and application of new techniques for evaluation of neonatal lung function*

   Apparatus which allows accurate measurements of lung function was developed. The most significant advance was the design of elaborate valves as part of a heated re-breathing circuit, through which the sleeping infant could breathe, while lung function was being measured in a whole-body plethysmograph. This has made possible the precise measurement of lung function in infants.

2. *Development of techniques for measurement of pulsatile capillary blood flow*

   This required the design and production of an entirely novel miniaturised three-way valve and re-breathing circuit, a project assisted by the Royal Postgraduate Medical School Computer Unit. It provided normal values for effective pulmonary capillary blood flow in pre-term infants. Plethysmography was used in a novel, standardised and non-invasive technique of measuring neonatal cardiac output, by means of trans-thoracic impedance.

3. *Servo-control of arterial oxygen tension in newborn babies*

   The successful development of a microprocessor unit automatically to control oxygen tension in newborn babies over long periods was a major success. This had not been achieved previously, and represented a significant advance in the use of microprocessors, and in the application of servo-control systems in neonatal care.

Many practical difficulties, however, rendered the system unsuitable for general clinical use.

These fundamental physiological studies contributed to the solution of problems associated with the intensive care of premature newborn babies, the understanding of the aetiology of bronchopulmonary dysplasia, the pulmonary effects of congenital muscle disorders and the factors affecting pulmonary blood flow.

Cerebral haemorrhage

The most important single cause of death in premature infants is now probably haemorrhage in the brain. In the country as a whole, the number of deaths from this cause is not accurately known, but probably amounts to many hundreds each year.

The haemorrhage nearly always originates in the germinal layer, a specially vulnerable area of brain substance adjacent to the normal cavities of the brain. The initial bleeding may spread into the cavities (sometimes causing hydrocephalus) or widely into brain tissue. If haemorrhage occurs, it usually takes place within three days of birth.

Investigators have examined:

1. the effect on blood-vessels of varying degrees of asphyxia;
2. the effect of raising pressure within the vessels;
3. the vulnerability of the vessels to stress at various stages of development;
4. the effect on the permeability of developing blood vessels of changes in the composition of the blood.

Clinical and experimental evidence suggests that the combination of impaired respiratory gas exchange, and its haemodynamic consequence of increased cerebral intravascular pressure and blood flow, is the major cause of bleeding. Non-invasive methods such as ultrasound and N.M.R. spectroscopy have provided valuable information about this phenomenon, while new methods of clinical management have reduced the risks of its occurrence.

Studies of development neurobiology are clearly important if the pathogenesis of intraventricular haemorrhage and ischaemic brain injury in the premature infant is to be understood. The Trustees encouraged such studies by an award to the Departments of Physiology and Paediatrics at University College, London and University College Hospital. The Trustees considered that these studies would provide information about the influence of the internal environment of the brain on its development, and enable the effect of abnormalities possibly related to cerebral haemorrhage to be tested.

Dr N. R. Saunders and Professor E. O. R. Reynolds

In 1975 the Trustees made an award for five years to these scientists for studies in developmental neurobiology. Significant advances in the understanding of the pathogenesis of intracerebral haemorrhage in premature infants resulted from their development of an animal experimental model, the first of its kind related to this condition. Improved understanding of the pathogenesis of intraventricular haemorrhage had a direct bearing on the formation of hypotheses about prevention.

For the experimental work, unborn lambs, pigs, and rats were used as well as human subjects. Topics investigated were the histology of blood vessels in the brain, the experimental induction of haemorrhage, the protein composition of the cerebrospinal fluid and their derivation from the blood, the movement of these proteins within the brain, and the penetration of other substances into the brain and cerebrospinal fluid.

Dr Saunders and Professor Reynolds extended the collaboration between their two departments to include other laboratories especially the Department of Medical Anatomy at the University of Copenhagen.

These studies opened up two entirely new research topics, the development of the blood–brain barrier and the protein composition of the cerebrospinal fluid. In 1980 Dr Saunders was awarded an extension of this grant. Another distinguished investigator in the field of fetal physiology was Professor A. St G. Huggett of St Mary's Hospital Medical School. In 1960 the Trustees made an award for five years to Professor Huggett for his studies on growth and development in various mammals before birth. Professor K. W. Cross had been a colleague of Professor Huggett. His studies on the physiology of the newborn were supported by a building grant to the London Hospital Medical College for laboratory accommodation. In 1975, Professor Cross received a major award for his studies with Dr Stothers on heat production in the infant brain. They have estimated that in the adult brain heat production is 18 per cent of total metabolism, whereas in the infant it is 70 per cent of the whole. These studies have provided valuable information relating to thermal responses of the newborn infant.

Studies carried out in North America must also be noted. In 1961, the Trustees awarded a senior research fellowship for five years to Dr Karlis Adamsons, tenable at Columbia University. The research programme was directed towards various aspects of fetal and neonatal physiology, the importance of body and environmental temperature to the newborn, and the effects of different thermal environments upon the recovery process from birth asphyxia.

V. Perinatal studies: parturition

We began this account of neonatal studies with the statement that premature birth of the infant is the most important single cause of perinatal mortality. Describing the relationship of respiratory distress and cerebral haemorrhage to prematurity, we have shown that a better understanding of fetal physiology may make these conditions preventable, and that the Trustees' awards have contributed to this. We have made no mention of studies on the mechanisms which initiate labour. If these problems of physiology were better understood, it would be possible to render the pathological conditions which we have discussed considerably less common. Why does the uterine smooth muscle, which has been gradually stretching, begin its contraction after nine months? Are the initiating pharmacological mechanisms in the uterus itself, elsewhere in the mother, or in the fetus? In 1967, the Trustees made an award to Dr C. G. Liggins, a New Zealand scientist who wished to investigate the problem of the initiation of labour. Trust awards continued until 1977 for Dr Liggins' studies on endocrine factors in labour. He provided strong evidence that the fetus determines the time of onset of labour, through the interaction between the hypothalamus, pituitary and adrenal. Dr Liggins showed that in the sheep, foetal hypophysectomy results in a prolonged pregnancy. The Trustees have continued to make awards for the study of the physiology and biochemistry of uterine muscle, but it cannot yet be said that the mechanisms of the control of uterine contractility are fully understood.

Congenital abnormalities

In his Nuffield Provincial Hospitals Trust Lecture for 1982 Professor D. J. Weatherall said that it has been estimated that, in the developed countries, congenital conditions account for as much as one-third of admissions to paediatric wards and for about one-half of all childhood deaths. These conditions are therefore of great medical interest. They comprise three main groups: single gene disorders (e.g. thalassaemia); chromosome disorders (e.g. Down's syndrome) and congenital disorders due to environmental factors (e.g. rubella cataract). Professor Weatherall also estimated that of all congenital diseases, the genetically determined disorders of haemoglobin synthesis are probably the commonest disorders of a single gene, and are responsible for much ill-health in the world population. These genetic conditions are also of considerable theoretical interest and a brief account of studies on haemoglobin and the genetic factors concerned in the heritable disorders of human haemoglobin will show the reason for this.

VI. Haemoglobin and the haemoglobinopathies

Studies of haemoglobin are of great significance because of its vital function in oxygen transport through tissues; moreover, the studies which have explained this function have demonstrated fundamental principles of protein structure and synthesis.

Haemoglobin was the first protein to be crystallised, by Reichert, who published the results of his experiments in 1849. He examined blood from a guinea pig and described his findings as 'observations on an albuminous substance in the form of crystals'. Four years later, Teichman showed that iron is present in these crystals and in 1864 Hoppe Seyler gave the name haemoglobin to the colouring substance of blood. From the mid-1850s, until well into the 20th century, the nature of the substances we now know as protein, remained in doubt: were they defined chemical entities, which could be obtained in a crystalline state? During this time proteins were considered as colloids, that is, substances unable to penetrate certain membranes, diffusing slowly, and incapable of crystallisation. Research on colloids led to considerable advances in knowledge of the properties of solutions of substances of high molecular weight and of surface chemistry, although theories founded on the concept of colloids were antagonistic to the idea that proteins could exist as very large molecules. When Hermann Staudinger, in the early 1920s, provided evidence for the existence of large molecules, his arguments met with considerable opposition. Support for him came from the experiments by Gilbert Adair in Cambridge and Theodor Svedberg in Uppsala to determine the molecular weight of haemoglobin, published between 1924 and 1926, and attributing to haemoglobin a molecular weight of 67,000. It was after this that biochemists realised that an understanding of the structure of macromolecules would be essential for understanding cellular metabolism. Dr M. F. Perutz began his lifelong crystallographic studies of the structure of the haemoglobin molecule in 1937, at a time when (he has recalled): 'the most complex organic substance whose structure had yet been determined by X-ray analysis was the molecule of the dye phthalocyanine, which contains 58 atoms'. Twenty-two years later, Perutz demonstrated the structural arrangement of the four polypeptide chains (2 α chains; 2 β chains) and the four groups containing iron and the oxygen combining sites, which combine to form adult haemoglobin. The binding of the haem and globin groups provide the physical environment necessary for the function of the molecule, its ability to combine reversibly with oxygen and act as a 'molecular lung' – Perutz's descriptive phrase. The sequences of the amino acids in the chains were demonstrated subsequently and it has also been shown that fetal haemoglobin differs from adult haemoglobin, having α chains combined with γ chains, rather than with β chains.

The foregoing remarks illustrate only a few of the fascinating aspects of the history of studies on haemoglobin, and their relationship to advances in knowledge of protein biochemistry. The study of the transmission of the genetic code during maturation of red blood cells is another aspect of haemoglobin studies and serves as an example of the advances in the understanding of the biochemistry of genetics. It may be remembered that O. Avery had confirmed in 1944 the earlier experimental transformation of one type of pneumococcus into another by Griffith and showed that the transformation was caused not by a protein, nor by an enzyme, but by a substance he proved to be DNA. These experiments, suggested that DNA might be the substance responsible for carrying genetic information, but there was much argument between biochemists before this proposition was accepted. In 1953, Watson and Crick proposed a structure for DNA. They concluded 'it has not escaped our notice that the specific pairing we have postulated immediately suggests a possible copying mechanism for the genetic material'. It was subsequently shown that the synthesis of cytoplasmic proteins was determined by nuclear DNA and the linear arrangement of DNA. The amino acids which constitute any protein depend on instructions from DNA. F. Sanger's discoveries made possible the reading of amino acid sequences in proteins, and then the sequences of nucleotide bases on a strand of DNA. That accomplishment made possible the mapping of genes.

Returning to Professor Weatherall's statement concerning the frequency of the haemoglobinopathies, the most important of these are sickle-cell anaemia and thalassaemia (first described in 1925). The fundamental discoveries in molecular biology made it possible for these diseases to be defined as conditions due to molecular variations in human haemoglobin, resulting from a specific abnormality in the genetic code. In sickle-cell anaemia, there has been a mutation in the gene for the formation of adult β globin, which has resulted in the single substitution of an amino acid. Such a mutation gives rise to a variation which is heritable and is an essential factor in Darwinian natural selection. How have human beings survived a mutation causing a harmful abnormality? The answer is that the mutation has also conferred on the subject a protection against a more severe disease – malaria. The mechanism is not fully understood. Such protection is useful to black Africans in areas where sickle cell anaemia and malaria are present together, but of no value to those of African descent living in countries where malaria does not exist.

The explanation of sickle-cell anaemia as a molecular disease resulted from investigations by several scientists. In 1949, Linus Pauling showed different electrophoretic patterns between normal haemoglobin and sickle-cell haemoglobin. In the same year, J. V. Neel provided epidemiological evidence to prove that sickle-cell anaemia is due to a mutant gene.

Perutz found that sickling of red cells occurred when they were not carrying oxygen, the solubility of haemoglobin changed, and it precipitated into elongated aggregates. He published the results of his experiments in 1950. V. M. Ingram published in 1956 his paper on a specific chemical difference between the globins of normal human and sickle-cell anaemia haemoglobin.

The heritable molecular variants of haemoglobin associated with the clinical condition known as thalassaemia are more complicated than those of sickle-cell anaemia, in which the β globin chain alone is affected. In the thalassaemias, methods of gene analysis, brought into use in the past few years, have demonstrated the wide variety of abnormal heritable patterns in the synthesis of α and β globins. These abnormalities result from mutations which have caused nuclear DNA to transmit a faulty message, but the fault may differ from one family group to another. The clinical condition known as β-thalassaemia major can result in death at an early age, unless treated by repeated blood transfusions. This form of treatment may be accompanied by important clinical complications, because of the effects of overloading the tissues with iron, which may reach four times the value of normal adult iron stores. Death may result from cardiac arrhythmias and cardiac failure. Endocrine glands may also be affected, with disturbances in growth, failure of puberty, diabetes and other endocrine deficiencies. Patients may therefore be treated simultaneously with blood transfusions and iron chelating agents such as desferrioxamine to reduce the excess iron in the tissues. Prevention of thalassaemia is attainable only through population screening, fetal diagnosis and termination of affected pregnancies. At present, diagnosis is only possible after 18 weeks' gestation. Haemoglobin studies are carried out on fetal blood samples obtained by fetoscopy. The haemoglobin estimations take up to a week to complete, which delays further the possibility of the termination of pregnancy. In future, diagnosis may be possible at an earlier date, by biopsy of chorionic villi, and by restriction endonuclease mapping of DNA of fetal tissue.

We turn now to some awards made by the Trustees for projects on haemoglobin and the thalassaemias. The Trustees' support for studies on sickle-cell anaemia has been described on page 228.

Professor D. Weatherall and Dr J. B. Clegg

In 1968, Professor C. A. Clarke, of the Department of Medicine, University of Liverpool, asked the Trustees for an award which would enable Dr J. B. Clegg to continue studies, with Professor D. J. Weatherall, on basic problems of haemoglobin synthesis. The Trustees were satisfied that the University was unable to fund developments of these important projects, concerned with the genetic control of human protein, and made an award for five years at senior lecturer level, to support Dr Clegg. When Professor Weatherall moved to Oxford to become Nuffield Professor, Dr Clegg accompanied him and now holds a permanent post in the Molecular Haematology Unit of the Medical Research Council at the John Radcliffe Hospital.

Study of thalassaemia as a genetic disorder was still, in the early 1960s, hampered by lack of experimental evidence, though it had been postulated that impaired production of the α and β chains of normal haemoglobin might account for many of the observed phenotypes.

In 1965, while working in the U.S.A., Drs J. B. Clegg, M.A. Naughton and D. J. Weatherall devised a method for *quantitatively* separating the individual peptide chains of normal human haemoglobins and subsequently went on to show that this method could be used accurately to measure the rates of globin chain synthesis in red cell precursors. Their first experiments quickly verified the suggestions that impaired synthesis of globin chains was responsible for the common types of thalassaemia, in particular it was clear that there were two general classes of disorders, α and β thalassaemia, depending on which particular globin chain was affected. Later work, following the award of a Wellcome Trust grant in 1967, enabled a much more detailed dissection of the molecular basis of the more common thalassaemias to be carried out. It was clear by the early

1970s that the majority of thalassaemias were caused by defects in globin messenger RNA structure or synthesis. However, two notable exceptions to this general pattern were caused by structurally abnormal haemoglobins.

By the expiration of the Wellcome grant in 1974 the thalassaemia field had moved from the first crude insights into the biochemical mechanisms involved to a detailed understanding at the molecular level of many of the common types of the disease. This was nicely illustrated by the demonstration in 1974 by the Liverpool group in collaboration with a group at the Beatson Institute, and independently in the U.S.A., that a common form of thalassaemia in which α-chain synthesis was abolished, was due to the deletion (i.e. complete loss) of the α genes from the human genome – the first example reported of a gene deletion causing a human disease.

Professor D. L. Mollin and Dr Barbara Anderson

In 1970, the Trustees made an award to Professor D. L. Mollin, of St Bartholomew's Hospital, London, for an investigation of the metabolism of 'pyridoxine responsive' anaemia and other sideroblastic anaemias. During the course of these studies Professor Mollin and his colleagues found abnormalities in the vitamin B_6 metabolism in the red cells of patients with thalassaemia. In 1973 he asked the Trustees for an extension of their support for investigation of these, and other abnormalities. The Trustees decided that the finding of a reduced rate of red cell conversion of pyridoxine to pyridoxal in the majority of individuals carrying the trait for β thalassaemia was important and may have clinical implications. The work was covering new ground in an area in which information was extremely sparse and could be a model for studies of other vitamin–vitamin interactions. The Trustees therefore extended the award for three years.

Professor Mollin's group first observed in 1969 that the red cell is an active site for the metabolism of vitamin B_6. Pyridoxine is first converted to the physiological form pyridoxal phosphate and there is a large genetic variation in the rate of this conversion in different individuals. In the thalassaemic red cell, they found a high incidence of a slow rate of conversion, in turn due to the low activities of certain enzymes. The biochemistry of this phenomenon was investigated in detail.

Most of the work on thalassaemia heterozygotes was done on short visits to Ferrara, in the Po Valley of Northern Italy where there is a high incidence of thalassaemia, and where family studies could be made. Dr

Anderson and her colleagues confirmed their earlier findings that red cell metabolism of riboflavin was low not only in thalassaemic heterozygotes, but that such low metabolism could also be present in and inherited by normal relatives.

Several of these subjects with heterozygous β thalassaemia had signs of abnormal liver function (possibly precipitated by alcohol consumption), which Professor Vullo has found to be common in several series of β thalassaemia heterozygotes studied from the Ferrara region. A preliminary finding in many of the heterozygotes was a high red cell ferritin level (measured by Professor Jacob's team in Cardiff). This may be related to the metabolic abnormality of the thalassaemic cell or to the liver disease, though plasma ferritin was often not raised. However, it is worth considering a connection with the red cell flavin mononucleotide (FMN) deficiency, as the enzyme thought to cleave iron from ferritin is FMN dependent. These findings have led to a study of the relationship of abnormal liver function to heterozygous thalassaemia in the Ferrara region, involving investigation of the enzymes concerned.

Dr Bernadette Modell

The Trustees made their first award to Dr Modell, of the Department of Obstetrics and Gynaecology, University College Hospital, London, in 1974 for her studies of excess tissue iron arising from blood transfusions during the treatment of thalassaemia major. The Trustees made further awards to enable these studies to continue, and additional awards for investigations of the problems of antenatal diagnosis of the haemoglobinopathies.

Dr Modell's work started in 1965 with the objective of improving the clinical management of thalassaemia major. It was felt that England was an ideal place for such a study, because the small number of patients (about 300) would make possible a study of the natural history of the disease in their entire population. The first step was to develop simple guidelines for standardising the treatment by regular blood transfusion. The second was to study the natural history of the excess iron in children. The third was to confirm the original work of Sefton-Smith at Great Ormond Street, suggesting that regular daily injection of the iron chelating agent Desferal might reduce the excess of iron. This form of treatment has now progressed to regular sub-cutaneous infusion. This first clinical phase culminated in the definition of optimal basic management that provided a background for evaluating further developments.

As infant mortality from infection and malnutrition is falling worldwide, thalassaemic children are beginning to be diagnosed in significant numbers in more centres and attempts must be made to treat them. Regular transfusion is usually possible, but because Desferal is expensive, unless an alternative iron chelator can be found these patients will die of excess transfusional iron by about 20 years of age. Dr Modell and her colleagues recently re-investigated the old and cheap iron-chelating agent diethylene triamine pentacetic acid (DTPA) which had previously been abandoned because of toxic side-effects. It now seems that these were mainly due to zinc depletion, so it may be possible to treat iron overload in developing countries with sub-cutaneous DTPA plus oral zinc supplements, until a better approach is available. A clinical trial is likely to start in Asia this year (1985).

In 1973 it became apparent that thalassaemia might be prevented by fetal diagnosis and subsequent termination of pregnancy. As progress was made with treatment, emphasis gradually shifted to prevention. First Dr Modell and colleagues collaborated with American workers to show that the diagnosis of thalassaemia major could be made *in utero*. They then standardised the laboratory analysis of fetal blood samples, finding that nearly 100 per cent of Mediterranean women liable to bear thalassaemia offspring made use of fetal diagnosis, so that the method has the potential for near-eradication of the disease. Many trainees from the Mediterranean region after time spent in their laboratory have applied the method effectively so that thalassaemia is well on the way to coming under control in the Mediterranean area. There is now a World Health Organization haemoglobinopathy control programme, which is stimulating the spread of prevention to less developed areas.

Another development has been that of a simple catheter which is now used world-wide to obtain chorionic villus samples for first trimester fetal diagnosis. This is recognised as an important advance in the prevention of genetic disease and it seems that it will prove acceptable to Muslim populations. The main problems of controlling thalassaemia may have been solved in principle, but there is still an enormous amount of work to do to solve the clinical problems of thalassaemic patients, to improve existing methods of prevention, to meet the needs of different countries and to identify the complex social implications of providing genetic services on a large scale.

VII. Enzyme abnormalities

Congenital familiar conditions had, of course, been recognised clinically long before their explanation was possible in biochemical terms. A. E. Garrod was one of the earliest physicians to be interested in conditions which he named 'inborn errors of metabolism'. He knew, for example, that the blackening of urine in the condition called alcaptonuria is due to the abnormal presence of homogentisic acid, and postulated that this resulted from absence of an enzyme which normally would split the benzene ring of the acid. It was not until the late 1950s, 50 years after Garrod's suggestions, that the lack of a specific oxidase was proved in patients with alcaptonuria. The clinical state is recognised by pigmentary disturbances in connective tissue and arthritis, but does not appear to decrease life expectancy. We shall describe below a Trust award for research into another heritable metabolic disorder of connective tissue which, in its severe form, can lead to death within 15 years.

Another type of variation in enzyme activity explains variabilities in different human individuals in their response to certain drugs. For example, Carson and others showed in 1956 an enzyme deficiency in erythrocytes which caused a haemolytic anaemia in some patients treated for malaria with primaquine. The explanation is the absence in the individual of an enzyme necessary for normal red cell metabolism. Another example is the variation in response to the muscle relaxant drug, succinyl choline, due to a variant of circulating cholinesterase. A small proportion only of the population may have genetic characteristics causing an unusual response to a drug, but the increasing use of drugs in therapeutics is an important practical reason for research into the genetic regulation of pharmacological responses. Research within the past 30 years into these genetic mechanisms has led to results which have affected clinical practice.

The Trustees have made a number of awards for studies of congenital abnormalities resulting from the inherited defective function of enzymes.

Dr D. A. Price-Evans

In 1964, the Trustees made an award to Dr Price-Evans, Lecturer in Medicine in the University of Liverpool, for the purchase of a spectrophotometer, to enable him to continue his studies on the genetic control of isoniazid metabolism in man.

After the introduction of isoniazid therapy for tuberculosis in 1952, a large variation in the metabolism of the drug was found to exist among patients: some metabolised the drug quickly so that after a given period of time, relatively little remained in the blood; others metabolised the drug slowly and maintained a high concentration in the body for a relatively long period. Research carried out between 1958 and 1960 suggested that the different metabolic rates might be genetically determined. Dr Price-Evans wished to study further how the patients' reaction affected the response to treatment with isoniazid and its relationship to the development of complications in isoniazid therapy, perhaps resulting from retention of the drug within tissues.

The Trustees agreed that the spectrophotometer requested by Dr Price-Evans would enable him speedily to plot the absorption spectra of large numbers of samples, and made the award for this purpose.

The award contributed to the development of pharmacogenetics as a special subject within the Department of Medicine in Liverpool University in which department Dr Price-Evans became a titular Professor in 1968. The Trustees made further awards in 1968 and 1972 for research assistance and expenses for his studies.

Professor Price-Evans and his colleagues studied many aspects of the genetic control of drug metabolism, particularly the mechanisms of hydroxylation associated with a number of drugs, including insulin.

Professor R. L. Smith

In 1979, the Trustees made an award for three years to Professor R. L. Smith of the Department of Biochemical Pharmacology at St Mary's Hospital Medical School, to enable him to carry out studies of polymorphisms of drug oxidation in man and their significance. The contributions of Professor Smith's research group include:

a) identification of a new human gene which regulates the oxidation of a number of drugs;
b) demonstration that individuals who are homozygous for the variant of this gene metabolise drugs poorly;
c) discovery that distribution of the gene abnormality varies racially (1–2 per cent among Asians, up to 12 per cent for West Africans, about 9 per cent in the U.K.);
d) a method of testing for the abnormality by use of the drug debrisoquinine;
e) identification of the poor metabolisers of these drugs as a group in danger of suffering from untoward and exaggerated effects upon administration of the drugs, which may include toxic effects leading to damage to the liver or to the nervous system.

In the course of animal experiments it was found that certain female rats displayed a deficiency of drug oxidation analogous to that found in man. Hence it was possible to follow further lines of investigation impossible in the human patient, suggesting that a defect or absence of a particular enzyme (mono-oxygenase) is responsible for many drug oxidations.

When the award terminated, Professor Smith applied for its extension, to permit further studies of genetic regulation of human drug oxidation and its implications. The Trustees considered that the group directed by Professor Smith had made important contributions in the field of drug oxidation. The discovery of the debrisoquine oxidation genetic polymorphism by Professor Smith and Dr J. Idle was an important development in pharmacogenetics, because it controls the metabolism of many drugs in common use. The Trustees made the award, which will terminate in 1986.

Dr P. F. Benson and Dr Helen Muir

The mucopolysaccharidoses are a well-characterised group of single lysosomal enzyme deficiency diseases. These diseases contribute significantly to severe mental retardation and physical deformity and are almost always fatal. The defect in each type of mucopolysaccharidosis is known to be in one of a group of hydrolases necessary for complete catabolism of connective tissue glycosaminoglycans (GAG). A deficency of any one of the hydrolases leads to a systemic accumulation of partially degraded GAG, particularly within the cells of the visceral organs and central nervous system.

Dr P. F. Benson, Dr J. F. Mowbray and Dr Helen Muir foresaw that it might be possible to provide long-term supplementation of deficient enzymes by implantation of normal fibroblasts in a selected group of patients not previously treated in this way. Their preliminary investigations in patients with Hunter's syndrome had shown that implantation of histocompatible fibroblasts could provide sufficient enzymes to induce significant changes in GAG metabolism. In 1976 these workers therefore asked the Trustees to consider making an award for studies in enzyme replacement therapy by fibroblast implants.

The Trustees' assessment of their proposals turned on the points that the diseases are rare, that the clinical evaluation of their progress would be protracted, that the immunological problems would be considerable, and that uncertainty about the amount of enzymes would be great. However, the investigations were to be undertaken through collaboration between a physician with considerable clinical experience of the condition (Dr Benson); a biochemist with detailed knowledge of the mucopolysaccharidoses (Dr Helen Muir); and an expert immunopathologist (Dr Mowbray). The Trustees therefore made an award in 1976, which was renewed in 1978 and 1981.

Although the treatment failed clinically interesting data resulted. The main technical problem was to implant enough cells, grown *in vitro* and then injected subcutaneously. There was no evidence that there was any immunological reaction; however, it is unlikely that the fibroblasts proliferated *in situ*.

The scientific questions which arose from this work prompted a new discovery. Dr Helen Muir and her colleagues Dr I. Olsen and Dr M. F. Dean at the Kennedy Institute of Rheumatology wished to know how cells could exchange enzymes and utilize normal enzyme. They discovered that through an unknown mechanism, normal lymphocytes can transfer enzyme by direct contact to deficient fibroblasts or even heterozygous fibroblasts which are low in the normal enzyme. The discovery was entirely unexpected since it did not operate through the well known mechanism of receptor-mediated endocytosis. Its clinical relevance is also concerned with the mechanism of treatment with bone marrow transplants, some of which have been reasonably successful.

We may reasonably conclude that although the immediate object of the award by the Trustees was not attained, new ideas resulted from investigations in what may be a developing area of therapeutics for a small, but disabling group of heritable disorders and may also have some bearing on molecular mechanisms in inflammation.

VIII. Congenital disease due to environmental factors

We have previously noted that congenital abnormalities constitute one of the most important groups of childhood disease at the present time, as a result of a decline of communicable disease in childhood. Approximately 20,000 children with major malformations are born each year in England and Wales. It may be estimated that 20 per cent are affected by genetic or chromosomal abnormalities and 10 per cent by purely environmental factors. Although infectious diseases have been increasingly brought under control, their relationship to congenital disease is important for two reasons. First, because the damage they cause is often extensive and severe and second, because an infectious cause of a congenital disease (if identified) is potentially preventable.

It is interesting to recall that the first observations of the relationship between German measles and congenital cataract, and the frequency of an accompanying heart lesion, were made by the ophthalmologist Dr (later Sir) N. M. Gregg who in 1941 noted the appearance of an unusual number of congenital cataracts in Sydney. Careful investigation showed that in the mothers' clinical history 'the early period of pregnancy corresponded with the period of maximum intensity of the very wide-spread and severe epidemic in 1940 of the so-called German measles'.

Professor J. A. Dudgeon and Dr W. C. Marshall

In 1971, the Trustees made an award for five years to Professor Dudgeon and Dr Marshall for studies on the pathogenesis of intra-uterine virus infections and the mechanisms responsible for fetal damage. Professor Dudgeon held the view that not all the manifestations of fetal damage could be attributed to the direct action of virus upon the cell. He considered that such a view did not take into account the effect of virus upon the placenta, nor could a single pathological process explain the diversity of the clinical manifestations. In congenital rubella, for example, there was evidence of damage to blood vessels by the cytolytic effect of virus, and also of immunopathological effects. He and Dr Marshall wished to study the way in which virus spreads to and within the fetus; the response of the fetus to infection; and the mechanisms of production of abnormalities.

Rubella

Clinical observation of large numbers of congenital rubella children seen at, or referred to, the Hospital for Sick Children, Great Ormond Street, London clearly demonstrated that the clinical spectrum of effects of the virus is extremely broad. The clinical disorders comprised permanent structural defects such as congenital heart disease and eye abnormalities, and transient disorders of the neonatal period especially those involving blood-forming organs, liver and bones. Complete recovery of the latter manifestations often occurred but as there was evidence of an active inflammatory process in the central nervous system in some children, it seemed reasonable to conclude that some disorders involving the brain and other tissue may develop or become manifest at intervals after birth. A severe form of pneumonitis and a chronic generalised macular rash in congenital rubella children aged 3–9 months was another *'late onset' manifestation* of this infection; a descriptive term first introduced by Dr Marshall. It was shown that the usually fatal lung disorder responded to corticosteroids and the rash was associated with a chronic virus infection of the skin suggesting the hypothesis that these manifestations were mediated by an immunopathological process. Hence, the number of known or presumed mechanisms of damage by the virus was increased and it became clear that the damage was multifactorial.

Further clinical observations and subsequent laboratory studies led to the discovery of another of what might be termed the endocrine disorders of congenital rubella – that of *growth hormone deficiency* and diabetes mellitus. Although a number of cases of diabetes have been seen in congenital rubella patients in Australia and the U.S.A., only one has been observed in the United Kingdom.

Virological studies on fetal materials received in the laboratory have shown that infection was almost always widespread. Examination by immuno-electrophoresis indicated that a feature of this infection may be an inhibition of synthesis of A.F.P. (α feto protein). The significance of this is not clear, but there is a need to investigate enzymatic, biochemical or hormonal effects of the infection.

Little is known about rubella virus as a possible cause of spontaneous abortion. When fetal materials from 200 spontaneous abortions were studied (in collaboration with the Department of Paediatric Research, Guy's Hospital) there was a complete failure to detect viral infections. Other findings also indicate that virus infections probably do not play a significant role in the causation of spontaneous abortion in man. In addition, the particular agents mentioned above do not contribute to the frequent chromosome abnormalities found in these fetal materials by the group at Guy's Hospital.

Since it has often been supposed that the fetus is damaged by a specific inhibitor produced by rubella infected cells, experiments were carried out to detect the presence of such a substance. Extracts from human cells infected both *in vitro* and *in vivo* by the virus were examined by means of their effect on cell numbers and DNA synthesis, but no evidence for specificity could be demonstrated; extracts from uninfected cells were found to produce an identical inhibitory effect. In the retrospective serological diagnosis of congenital rubella, it was demonstrated that rubella antibody could be detected well into the second six months of life. This fact should eliminate the need for taking repeated blood samples from children under 12 months who are presented for diagnosis beyond the third month of life.

This study was carried out at the beginning of the national rubella vaccination campaign. It monitored a steady increase in the history of rubella vaccination amongst the student nurses of the Great Ormond

Street Hospital, which in 1977 reached 82 per cent, as well as a change in the prevalence of HI antibody which increased from 78 per cent in 1972 to 94 per cent in 1977, and to 98 per cent in 1983.

Cytomegalovirus

A greatly increasing attention has been paid to cytomegalovirus (CMV) as a cause of fetal infection and damage. Early reports on the incidence of fetal infection indicated that it was by far the commonest virus infection of the human fetus, occurring at a rate of 3 to 4 per 1,000 live births. Although clinical disease was observed in considerably fewer newborn infants, there was evidence that (as with rubella virus) damage could occur or become manifest weeks or even years after birth. Older estimates that upwards of 6,000 to 8,000 children might be infected *in utero* and 10–20 per cent of these (600–1,600) suffer damage, frequently involving the central nervous system and leading to mental retardation, have been revised to indicate that no more than 200 infants per annum are likely to suffer mental retardation due to CMV, that is, between one and five per cent.

Investigation of cytomegalovirus is perplexed by several difficulties: the striking absence of any significant clinical illness in almost all adults, preventing clinical recognition of infection during pregnancy, the absence of diagnostic clinical features from affected infants as well as the high 'sub-clinical' attack rate which requires the use of labortory tests for diagnosis. There are also doubts about the available serological tests.

The strain of CMV, a member of the herpes viruses, that affects man is specific to him and therefore the results of animal experiments cannot necessarily be extrapolated to man. Initially *sero-epidemiological* studies of *congenital* CMV were carried out upon 600 cord-blood specimens, which represented as near as possible consecutive deliveries in a London maternity hospital. Testing for antibody levels (IgM, IgA and IgG) by standard immunodiffusion methods revealed an incidence of congenital CMV of 0.74 per cent which was in close agreement with reports from other London populations. None of the infants examined had clinical signs of congenital infection within the first year of life.

Epidemiological studies were continued in older patients to whom there was ready access in large numbers. Of special importance was a group of children with a wide variety of neurological disorders undergoing extensive investigations into the cause. Three other groups of children were investigated by means of tests for the presence of virus in urine. They were children with deafness and related disorders, infants of birth weight less than 1,500 g undergoing prospective developmental and neurological assessment and normal children of a similar age range (six months to four years). Since this work was completed it has been realised that the only way to make an accurate diagnosis is by virological tests carried out within seven days of birth and the careful follow-up of virus excretors for some years thereafter.

Of the 750 deaf children 8 per cent were found to be excreting virus, but this percentage was significantly greater in those with no family history of deafness (10.4 per cent) than in children with conductive deafness (2 per cent) and children with no abnormality. Similarly, 8½ per cent of infants born with a birth weight of less than 1,500 g, when tested during the first three years of life, were excreting virus. Virus was found in only 2.5 per cent of normal children.

The virus resisted antiviral drugs and so it was decided to attempt an immunological remedy. Three children with congenital CMV were treated with transfer factor (T.F.), a dialysate obtained from lymphocytes from healthy blood donors who had experienced CMV infection previously. A temporary suppression of virus excretion was observed in these patients and other immunological responses indicated that the T.F. had induced a change in the immune status of these children, but the effect was only temporary. No adverse side-effects from this treatment were observed.

These summary accounts of investigations supported by the Trust show how the Trustees have carried out, mainly through project grants, their policy of integrating the clinical sciences with the basic sciences, physiology and biochemistry in particular. Many other projects have been successfully completed. As long ago as 1975, at the opening of the new offices of the Trust, nearly 30 such projects were chosen to illustrate the Trust's work in a public exhibition. Within the past few years, the balance of support has shifted from the more established aspects of biochemistry and physiology to the newer investigations of immunology and molecular biology but the Trustees have continued to adhere to the main lines of policy adumbrated above.

Future prospects in the biological sciences by Dr M. J. Morgan

The Trustees' policy of supporting basic research in the biomedical sciences by means of a scheme of project grant awards has resulted over the years in the support of outstanding pieces of basic research (as related elsewhere in this book). This policy of supporting unsolicited, good science will be maintained, but in addition the new financial climate will lead to a significant increase in publicity to ensure that more research groups become aware of the possibility of support.

New grants are usually initiated by a personal approach from a prospective applicant to one of the Scientific Officers of the Trust, followed by the submission of an outline of the proposed research. The proposal is given careful evaluation, and, where appropriate, the applicant is invited to submit a formal application. Applications are then sent out for peer review and considered at a meeting of the Scientific Trustees. Support usually includes salaries, running expenses and the cost of equipment, and is normally provided for three years.

The principles of this procedure will be preserved but the expansion of activity will necessitate different administrative arrangements in the future. In particular, the Trustees will themselves no longer be able to consider each and every application for support. As noted elsewhere (p. 206) new Advisory Panels are to be established of which two are relevant here: there will be Panels to consider applications in the 'molecular sciences' (biochemistry, genetics and cell biology) and in the physiological sciences and pharmacology.

It is also clear that the increased range of scientific expertise now available at the Trust's headquarters will lead to the closer involvement of the Trust officers with the scientific activities funded by the Trustees. One way of bringing this about is by the series of special, informal, meetings at which grant holders are invited to come to the Trust in order to speak to the Trustees and their officers on the projects which the Trustees have been supporting. An example of this was the meeting held in the autumn of 1984, on the topic 'New approaches to the study of membranes and calcium'. At the morning meeting the Chair was taken by Professor D. Chapman, Department of Biochemistry and Chemistry, Royal Free Hospital School of Medicine. Professor P. Garland, Unilever Research, presented his studies on the mobility of membrane proteins using laser microscopy and fluorescent photobleaching. Dr A. G. Lee, Department of Biochemistry, University of Southampton, described how electron-spin resonance can be used to study membranes and membrane proteins. Dr N. Woods, Department of Zoology, University of Liverpool, described his work in Dr Cobbold's laboratory on the use of aequorin to study calcium in single mammalian cells. Professor T. B. Bolton, Department of

Pharmacology, St George's Hospital Medical School, showed how patch clamp techniques can be applied to study the electrophysiology of single muscle cells.

In the afternoon, with Professor P. F. Baker, Department of Physiology, King's College London, in the Chair, Dr M. J. Whitaker, Department of Physiology, University College, London, described his investigation of the changes in intra-cellular calcium following fertilisation of sea urchin eggs. Dr Bastien Gomperts, Department of Experimental Pathology, University College School of Medicine, described how guanine nucleotides are involved in the regulation of stimulus-secretion coupling. Finally, Dr Alan Drummond, Department of Pharmacology, School of Pharmacy, London, presented his work on the regulation of phospholipid metabolism in cultured cells. Sufficient time was given to enable a very lively discussion to follow each contribution. All of the contributors were, or had been, funded by the Trustees, each, however, funded independently of the others. The meeting thus gave an opportunity for the Trustees to review their support to a specified area of research, which had developed in an *ad hoc* fashion. It also gave the grant holders an opportunity to meet one another, exchange ideas, and present their latest findings to an interested audience. A number of participants remarked that it was an extremely healthy development for research support agencies to ask their grant holders to report directly on their research activities! It is an exercise which the Trust will wish to repeat.

The Trustees have also expressed an interest in the possibility of creating another interaction between the Trust and academic science in the form of 'Wellcome Summer Schools' to be focussed on particular topics with the object of putting on courses of instruction serving to introduce scientists to the latest research techniques.

A deeper look into the future necessarily becomes highly conjectural and in the present situation any prediction is likely to be falsified. Nevertheless, it is expected that the Trustees will continue, from time to time, to identify areas of special need which they wish to encourage. One such potential development lies in the application of molecular biology to clinical medicine, a field receiving major awards in 1985. The standard of applications then received was so high that the Trustees have decided to continue the scheme for another year, and have earmarked £700,000 for it. Further, in recognition of the continuing lack of research opportunities within the basic sciences, the Trustees have announced a new scheme for Basic Science Fellowships. The intention of this scheme is to attract younger scientists who aspire to a career in research, and who will eventually be strong contenders for senior academic positions. These fellowships will normally be tenable for five years, with an extension for a further three years, subject to satisfactory review. In all likelihood, this will be part of an overall programme of support for outstanding individuals which will develop into Wellcome Trust career awards, whereby outstanding scientists might be supported from the time they graduate until the time they retire. This policy is clearly in its infancy and needs to be fully worked out before implementation.

All in all the prospects for the next 50 years are ones of immediate excitement and unprecedented opportunities.

17

PAST AND FUTURE
by Dr P. O. Williams

The past: The Trust before 1965

What I am going to write can only be a personal impression of the evolution of the Wellcome Trust during the time I have worked with it. I have learned from the historians with whom I have been associated during these years that it is impossible to get real history written by someone who has participated in the events to be analysed. Such history is inevitably biased by selective memory of the events that do the author credit and omission of those that do not. But equally well the 'true' history is usually not recorded in memoranda and minutes of meetings, such papers being but the distillate from ages of preparation and negotiation. What I therefore hope to do is to describe the Trust as I have seen it evolve and to see if I can draw any conclusions from this analysis.

I came to the Trust from the staff of the Medical Research Council where I had been for the previous five years. My recruitment was a result of the departure from the Assistant Scientific Secretaryship of Dr Edwin Clarke (see later) to take up a fellowship in the History of Medicine at the Johns Hopkins University. My qualifications were my medical background and five years' experience running the grant programme of the M.R.C. and being responsible for the Head Office end of the tropical research of that Council.

But above all, I suppose I was recruited because Sir Henry Dale (Chairman) and Dr Frank Green (Scientific Secretary) were old M.R.C. men and had a high regard for the Council. I am not altogether sure why I was recruited, however, as there was very little for the new Assistant Scientific Secretary to do. Sir Henry Dale was still a Trustee at 84, and Frank Green and he could very well have managed the load of work that came to the Trust. However, I supposed they had envisaged the growth that would take place during the coming years and wanted a 'young man' to get into the saddle for the future. Nevertheless, there was very little to do other than respond to the enquiries for travel grants and help process the other requests that came to the Trust. The routine of the office was very straightforward. The post arrived, was taken to Dr Green who took it in to Sir Henry to discuss with him, and then replies were written. I think I would have remained doing the travel grants if I had not suggested to Dr Green's secretary that the letters should come to me instead. I then dealt with them and the others found that I began to receive the letters and so they did not have to be bothered with them.

The Trustees met once a month with Sir Henry Dale in the chair; they formed a body by now well advanced in years: Martin Price (Accountant), Claude Bullock (Lawyer), Lord Piercy, Sir John Boyd and Sir Henry Dale with their secretary Jack Clarke. Dale dominated the group. Dale and Boyd with Green and I met about once a week to look over any matters of scientific importance that had come up during the previous week and Dale, Green and I had lunch every day at the R.S.M. Casual visitors often had an interview from the whole group.

The first significant change from this situation was the 'retirement' of Sir Henry Dale from the chairmanship and his appointment as Chief Scientific Adviser. I think he made this change for two reasons. The first was to persuade Mr Bullock that he too should resign because he was also 85 and the other was because he felt the Courts might not agree to a further extension of his term. But the resignation had very little effect on the workings of the Trust because Dale still kept his office and came to it every day and Lord Piercy, who took over, was given very little rope as Dale sat on the right hand of the chairman at meetings and effectively saw to it that the pattern of activities did not change. So in a way Lord Piercy's chairmanship was almost a continuation of Dale's under a different name. Dale stayed at the office until he was 90 when, as a result of a broken hip, he went into hospital and later retired with Lady Dale to a nursing home in Cambridge.

By this time, I had taken over from Frank Green and part of my job was to visit Dale in Cambridge and go through the papers with him. He continued to give his opinion on all applications until the day before his death even though disabled by a pulmonary embolus. During the seven years or so that I worked with Dale I came to admire the incredible way in which his scientific judgment had been preserved by constant discussion and refurbishment. He was still open to new scientific ideas and I remember him being fascinated by Levi–Montalcini's Nerve Growth Factor but I doubt whether he would have accepted new plans for the organisation and management of the Trust. He had made it that way and it suited him well to sit at its head and help the many people he had known to develop their work. And, in fact, as long as the Trust was operating at its then scale and putting one half of its income into buildings and equipment the system worked very well. The papers for meetings were typed (with carbons) twice as no other copying machinery was available until later when a cyclostyle was introduced.

New policies after 1965

A series of events of great significance to the future of the Trust then happened over the next few years. In the first place, Henry Dale had retired from the scene and Lord Piercy had been replaced by Lord Franks. Sir John Boyd and Martin Price had also retired and, although the former continued as scientific adviser in the Trust's office for a few years, the age of the Scientific Trustees had been reduced by the introduction of Professor (later Sir) John McMichael and Professor R. H. S. Thompson. Mr R. M. Nesbitt replaced Claude Bullock as Legal Trustee and Lord Murray replaced Martin Price.

The first major change of policy was to curtail the programme of building grants and this immediately released considerable funds for fellowships, project grants, etc. The volume of work of the office immediately increased as procedures had to be developed to assess and monitor the much larger flow of smaller applications. The chairman was no longer 'in residence' and he was in any event non-scientific so arrangements had to be made to build up the staff of the Trust to handle the load. The Trustees decided, on the recommendation of Lord Franks, that the secretaryship to the Trust should be taken over by me (by then the Scientific Secretary) so that all the affairs, except the payment of grants, could be undertaken from the main office. Mr Jack Clarke therefore became Financial Secretary. His role during the first 25 years of the Trust had been very significant as its affairs had at that stage been concerned with setting up the Trust and supervising the Company. The shift in emphasis towards the scientific role made a change of administrative leadership an obvious step and Jack Clarke in any case also had a busy practice now as senior partner in a leading firm of city accountants (Viney, Price and Goodyear, now Viney Merretts).

The Trust was therefore launched into a new era with a totally new board and administration and a policy that gave much more room for innovative action. That situation has continued since it was initiated, mainly under the Chairmanship of Lord Franks, but with a changing board of Trustees, both scientific and non-scientific. An important factor was the introduction of a retirement age of 70 for Scientific Trustees, later to be extended to all Trustees. This change created a Board of Trustees possessing a varied background of professional knowledge which was available for developing policy and assessing scientific proposals. A little later, the number of Trustees was expanded from five to seven to increase the scientific coverage. Thus, the Board of Trustees had altered from consisting of a lawyer, an accountant, a man of business and two scientists to an academic ambassador–administrator, a lawyer, a university administrator and four scientists. The staff had changed no less; from being simply an accountant and a scientific administrator whose business was to respond to applications it had developed into a scientifically interested group trying to see what it could do to promote research in a variety of neglected areas of medicine. It was at this time that the office of the Trust expanded scientifically by the addition of Dr Edda Hanington and later Dr B. A. Bembridge and Dr B. E. C. Hopwood, who between them looked after clinical, basic science and tropical aspects of the Trust's work. The initiative that they showed led to the development of Mental Health, Veterinary, Ophthalmological and Tropical programmes of the Trust. They have now retired and been succeeded by a younger group which has further developed the areas already pioneered and penetrated into areas where even more initiative can be shown by the use of the increased income available to the Trustees.

The core strength of the Trust lies in the regular involvement of the Trustees and scientific staff in the development of new programmes. The Trustees are involved in some aspect of the Trust's activities almost daily and apart from the monthly meetings either as a group of scientists or as the full board, chair the specialist panels, assessment meetings and exploratory seminars. There is thus a multi-disciplinary team of the highest calibre in close touch with the scientific and medical community promoting different methods to support research. A flexible, relaxed, helpful body is of great importance to those who seek funds.

The Trust's activities

During the past 25 years the Trust has evolved in a context of governmental support of medical research showing a phase of growth, followed by a levelling off and gradual decline in government funding. All through the biennial reports of the Trust the same theme recurs: Government is cutting back – what should the Trust do? It would be easy simply to try and make good the deficiency but our funds are inadequate for this purpose and so a more specific view has to be taken.

My description of the support for research can be divided into two departments: (1) support for subject fields and (2) the development of methods of support. By approaching from both these angles a policy has evolved which now encourages a fairly full range of methods and which has been concentrated on a few subjects. Subjects have been selected by the Trust for special attention for various reasons. Often these have included a personal interest on the part of one of the Trustees or a member of staff. The Tropical Medicine programme arose directly from Sir Henry Wellcome's interest in the subject and his reference to it in his Will. But more than anything it grew from Sir John Boyd's personal experience in India and subsequent activities in the Army, the Wellcome Foundation and on committees and societies. Because of Sir John Boyd I was recruited because I had had a tropical birth and upbringing, and experience at the M.R.C. The opportunities to make an impact in this field are immense and the Trust has developed a more and more significant role as decolonisation has proceeded. Dr Gordon Smith followed Sir John Boyd as a Trustee with special interest and experience in this field and Dr Hopwood, followed by Dr Ogilvie, have each given their own particular imprint to the programmes. Today this is our largest field of interest and our Units in various parts of the world are doing important work. The future of this field for the Trust has been greatly expanded since the take-over of the teaching role undertaken by the Wellcome Museum for Medical Science and the plans that are afoot, together with the Commonwealth Secretariat and the Schools of Tropical Medicine, to develop 'distance learning' for this subject.

The support given by the Trust to the basic sciences of medicine has always been very significant. It stemmed from Sir Henry Dale himself and his support for the subjects which he had played such a large part in fostering all his life. The support was maintained by the continuity of Trustee appointments in the basic sciences – Robert Thompson (Biochemist), Henry Barcroft (Physiologist), William Paton (Pharmacologist), Helen Muir (Biochemist). In fact, the Trust has always been heavily weighted towards the basic sciences, having only had three clinically experienced Trustees (in series) Elliott, McMichael and Peart, all of whom had a strong basis in physiology and other laboratory sciences.

Despite this leaning towards the basic sciences the Trust has never, until recently, shown any real interest in the promotion of particular topics, being content to support a wide variety of subjects as they arrived on its doorstep.

The Veterinary programme arose because Sir Henry Wellcome's business had always encompassed the animal as well as the human aspects and he had included the health of animals in his Will. But a major force in bringing it to programme status and in the creation of a Veterinary Panel was the advice of Mr Sam Hignett, Director of Veterinary Research at the Wellcome Foundation Ltd. He advised the Trust for many years and, together with Dr Hanington, developed the Trust's programme. More recently the significance of this field led to the appointment of Dr Keith Sinclair, a veterinary surgeon, to the staff of the Trust. Professor Thompson, and more recently Lord Swann, have chaired a very active and changing panel of advisers from the veterinary field. It is difficult to assess what our efforts have achieved. Certainly many projects have been supported and numerous fellows and scholars have had an opportunity to undertake research. Nevertheless, the organisation of research in the veterinary field has until recently been so biased towards the Institutes of the Agricultural Research Council (which the Trust could not support) and so neglected by the universities that the opportunities to foster research in the University Veterinary Schools have proved less numerous than the Trustees would wish.

The Mental Health programme grew from an acknowledgement of the backwardness of this branch of medicine as compared with the importance of mental illness in the health pattern of Britain. The feeling was also very strong that psychiatry had become separated from the mainstream of medical advance by its isolation from the sciences of neuropharmacology, biochemistry, etc. and that it would be helped if stronger links could be created. A Panel including psychiatrists and neurobiologists was appointed under Professor Peart with Dr Hanington as its secretary, whom Dr Gordon later succeeded. This panel took considerable pains to foster scientific studies and pioneered the major competitive grants scheme (of which more later) to reinforce links between the basic and clinical aspects of mental disease studies. It also developed major training and fellowship schemes all with the aim of strengthening the scientific input into the field. I think there is evidence that this investment is paying off but as with other neglected fields it takes a long time before the impact of training programmes comes to fruition in an increase of the general strength of the subject. The interaction between the psychiatrists and basic scientists in the discussion of applications has been interesting to observe.

Other smaller programmes have been developed in ophthalmic medicine, dermatology, clinical pharmacology and infectious diseases. In all cases the subjects had been isolated from the mainstream of medical advance and had not had applied to them the degree of scientific interest commensurate with their importance as a cause of morbidity. In general, this can also be said of the surgical specialties where the need to gain practical surgical experience has taken up the time that physicians devote to original research. Once a subject becomes designated as surgical it seems to reduce the medical input of research and ophthalmology is a striking example, in which the Trust has especially tried to encourage research.

Clinical pharmacology was a particular case where a new discipline had to be fostered and introduced into the system of training and research, in the context of increasing awareness of the lack of good knowledge of the therapeutic efficacy and true effects of many drugs either in common use or newly entering into use.

Infectious diseases on the other hand had formerly been so universally dangerous that special hospitals were devoted to them, and it may seem surprising that they needed particular attention. This was the case because the discovery of antibiotics had so changed the medical scene that those problems that remained were left in the hands of general physicians. However, infectious diseases' specialists are needed for consultation across all hospital specialties and, in this, their role is similar to that of clinical pharmacologists. Fostering these specialties, and especially research in them, has led to the tackling of problems of hospital organisation that are outside the usual range of the Trust's activities. Dr Bembridge, Dr Hanington and Dr Ogilvie have taken a special interest in these topics.

Special schemes

Turning now to the methods developed by the Trust for the support of research.

Research support can take many forms. In its earliest days the Trust was largely passive, responding to applications made to it by individuals for the requirements that they perceived as necessary for the development of their ideas. While this approach to funding is very important it neglects such broader aspects as the provision of training, and career patterns for research workers, and the problem that some aspects of research may become inactive and starved of attention unless fostered in special ways. The record of the past 25 years shows the way in which the Trust has created new schemes as it has proved necessary to do this in the changing scene.

One of the earliest special schemes was that for Senior Research Fellowships in Clinical Science, suggested by Sir John McMichael (see Appendix IX). This scheme, now 22 years old, has supported 65 individuals and is an illustration of the need to enable highly selected individuals to develop their ideas over a number of years unpressurised by the clinical responsibilities of regular posts. The achievements of these Fellows during their tenure and their subsequent appointments into leading posts have been a significant contribution to the academic research scene in Britain.

At a less senior level the Surgical Fellowship scheme, and a similar one in Pathology started later, gave recruits to these fields an opportunity to train in research as well as routine clinical work. These schemes were necessary because the peculiar patterns of training in surgery and pathology did not make people in these subjects competitive in general research fellowship schemes.

But there are also special needs that are over and above fellowship schemes. Thus, the Trust developed a scheme of linked fellowships to allow non-medical graduates to retain a position in their basic discipline while working in a clinical department. There continues to be a need for ways to ensure that medicine can benefit from its basic sciences.

Another scheme called 'research leave' was initiated to allow active research workers in university posts who had become overwhelmed with routine duties to work full-time at research within their own departments, their routine duties being performed by a replacement.

During the past 20 years there has been a repeated worry about the 'brain drain'. In an attempt to encourage the return of our best graduates who had gone abroad the Trust initiated the University Award Scheme which provided a stipend for a university post on condition that the university would guarantee to take it over after a few years. This scheme enabled jobs to be offered to people overseas as they were ready to return and gave time to fit them into the normal university establishment. This scheme has lost its usefulness now that the universities cannot make future guarantees.

More recently, the Trust introduced a Senior Lectureship scheme with a five-year rolling contract aimed at bolstering the staffing of active departments not only to help the individuals themselves but to release other members of the department for research. (See Appendix X.) Some

50 of these senior lecturers have been appointed and it is hoped to keep up the number as they get appointment elsewhere. Lectureships were also introduced later – some 35 of these being made available.

One other major scheme of the Trust that has been used extensively to promote various subjects was the Competitive Awards Scheme, now the Major Awards Scheme. Until this was introduced there was a general view that the best procedure for supporting research was to await applications from the research workers themselves. Such a limited approach in fact does little for subjects that are already at a low ebb.

The idea of the Major Awards Scheme was to offer a substantial sum, say £150,000 to £200,000, for the support of a research project in a particular field of interest to the Trust. The wording of the advertisement might be general or more specific or aim at linking separate disciplines. Some 34 such competitions have now taken place and I believe they have introduced a new way to encourage neglected topics.

The Trust has tried to stimulate research developments in a variety of other ways. Thus European Co-operative Grants, European Fellowship Schemes, Commonwealth Fellowship Schemes and Travel Grants have all aimed at encouraging international co-operation.

Similarly Career Development Awards and Advanced Training Fellowships have been established to encourage the most efficient and effective training of research workers.

The general objective is to make these various programmes appropriate to help promising people and their ideas. It is with this in mind that the Trust has an active staff of scientists who are ever ready to discuss projects with intending applicants and who spend a lot of time making visits all over the country and in many parts of the world to keep in touch with progress of research supported and to make plans for the future.

Administration

To make all these developments possible the premises of the Trust had to be expanded and so new offices were built behind the Regency facade at Park Square West. This led to a new outlook and the opportunity for consultative meetings on many topics in the Franks Room.

Behind all these developments of a scientific nature lies an administrative structure. In this structure three individuals have been especially significant. Mr M. A. F. Barren has been responsible for the buildings and staff of the Trust, and Mr D. G. Metcalfe has been in charge of Grants

Administration. Each has developed a system of administration that has greatly simplified the scientific management.

On the financial side, during the last ten years a very efficient finance department under the direction of Mr K. C. Stephenson has been developed to take over from the accountants Viney Merretts supervised by Jack Clarke. The financial aspects of the Trust's activities are now on a considerable scale with distributions of £18,000,000 per annum and payments and investments take a great deal of time and management.

Mr Stephenson and Mr Barren retired in 1985 and a new Deputy Director (Finance and Administration), Mr Ian Macgregor, has now taken over joint responsibility for these fields of interest and will see the Trust into its next phase.

The history of medicine

Sir Henry Wellcome was enormously interested in the history of medicine and during his life time he bought large numbers of books and objects illustrating this subject. Despite all his efforts very little had been achieved during his lifetime in the way of the orderly organisation, cataloguing and exhibition of these treasures. He had built the Wellcome Building to house his collection and private laboratories and he had provided in his Will that a museum and library charity should be formed which would be responsible for looking after these collections and funding this field. Unfortunately, however, the ownership of the building and the collections was vested in the Wellcome Foundation Ltd. The building long remained the property of the Foundation though half of the floor space was occupied by his collection. It became obvious once the Company had got on its feet and was providing a respectable dividend to the shareholder Trustees that the responsibility for the museum collections was anomalous. A commercial concern is not the natural organisation to take care of a major historical museum and library. These latter cannot compete for funds against the requirements of capital and developmental funds needed for business activities. Furthermore, the Trustees who were responsible under his Will for Wellcome's collection were excluded from helping to develop them because their charitable funds could not be used to help the commercial enterprise. The Trustees found themselves in the position where the natural development of the History of Medicine would be by exploiting Sir Henry Wellcome's collections but they were excluded from doing this. The decision was therefore taken that the historical museum and library should be transferred to the Trust and this having been done a joint committee of the Trust and Foundation was set up to supervise the future management. That committee was chaired in turn by Sir John Boyd, Mr Nesbitt, Lord Franks and now Sir David Steel. I was its secretary from the beginning for its first 20 years when Professor Rupert Hall took it over.

At first the Museum and Library continued as before under the general administration of the Foundation acting as agents for the Trustees and two directors of the Foundation were members of the management committee. In due course the Foundation reduced its involvement until eventually the staff were transferred to the payroll of the Trust.

At the time of the takeover the Museum and Library were directed by Dr E. Ashworth Underwood, a dour Scotsman with a deep interest in the History of Medicine. His colleague, Dr F. N. L. Poynter, was a scholar–librarian who had worked prodigiously to organise and develop the Library collection. The Library had received priority under the Foundation but had never been properly housed. The Museum was not on exhibition being largely in unsatisfactory stores at Dartford. The task of the Trust was to see that the Library developed and became available to scholars and that the Museum material was sorted, catalogued and exhibited. Plans were made but little could be done to implement these until more space could be made available in the Wellcome Building. In due course this was arranged and the Library and Museum were properly accommodated in excellent and pleasing premises. This did not come about until after Dr Underwood's retirement and was principally the result of the imaginative organisation of Dr Noel Poynter. By the time he retired in 1973 the Library had been excellently organised and housed, a comprehensive card catalogue was available and the printed catalogue was well in hand. Poynter had also created an excellent exhibition from the collection and the whole enterprise that he had created was renamed the Wellcome Institute for the History of Medicine. Despite these efforts the Trustees still considered that they had not done justice to the collection and Sir Henry Wellcome's ideas for the History of Medicine. They therefore formed a Panel under the chairmanship of Lord Cohen of Birkenhead to advise them on the future. The Panel's initial task was to advise on the future of the Museum and Library and the Trust's activities in the History of Medicine generally.

The decision was taken that the Trust should concentrate on the support of the History of Medicine as an academic discipline rather than as a public spectacle since to aim at both objectives would be excessively costly. It was therefore decided to commence negotiations with the Science Museum for the creation of a national collection of History of Medicine artefacts as a department of the Science Museum based on the permanent loan of Wellcome's collection and for the Trust to emphasise the Library and the development of academic Units both in the Institute and in universities around the country.

On Dr Poynter's retirement Dr Edwin Clarke became Director. His principal task was to develop the academic activities of the Institute and by the time he in turn came to retire he had recruited a strong staff which was able to launch an academic programme. He also had responsibility for seeing to the transfer of the collection to the Science Museum. This came about after prolonged delays due to legal niceties which greatly inhibited the development of the academic activities of the Institute. Eventually the Museum was taken under the wing of the Science Museum and the Trustees made major grants to that institution to get the collection sorted, catalogued and transferred. This task which took some four years was directed by Dr Brian Bracegirdle, the Keeper at the Science Museum responsible for the collection.

Much material came to light that was not relevant to the history of medicine and this was donated to many appropriate museums around the country. Now that the transfer has been completed there is an excellent exhibition in the Science Museum of Sir Henry Wellcome's historical materials, justifying the Trustees' policy, and the considerable effort made by the Museum staff.

The Institute meanwhile began to expand its academic activities and I was very fortunate to become its Honorary Director for two years at just the stage when it was ready to launch a full programme of seminars etc. A working party made a comprehensive report in 1982 and one of its main recommendations was that the Institute should increase its interest in the history of 20th century medicine.

The original History of Medicine Panel had recommended that Units of the History of Medicine should be created in universities and that a grants programme should be established. This recommendation led to the founding of Units in Oxford (Director: Dr Charles Webster); Cambridge (Director: Dr Roger French) and University College, London (Dr Edwin Clarke and at present Dr W. F. Bynum). Other regular support was provided in Edinburgh and grants were given to many individuals. These Units have been significant in spreading interest in and teaching of the subject and the staff have undertaken important original work. The institutions concerned have also become responsible for the stipend of

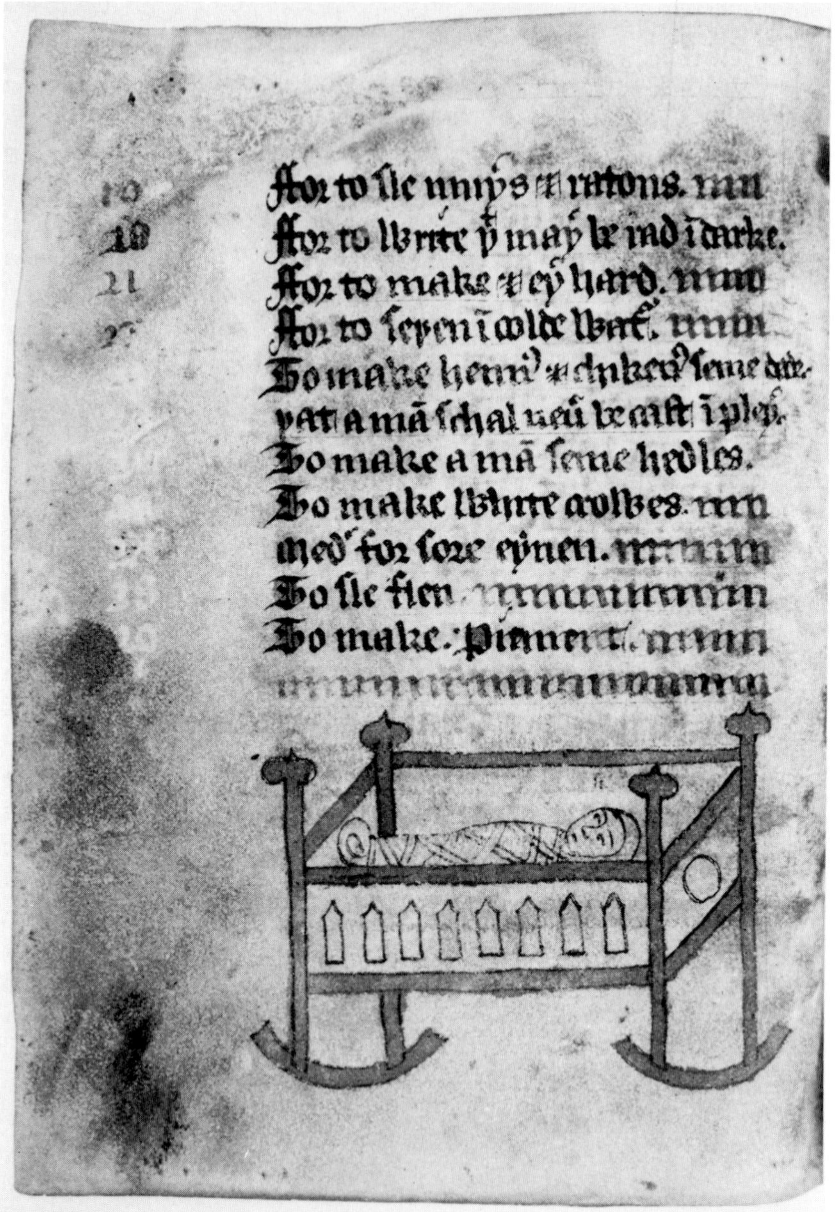

Fig. 67. A page from Western MSS.5252, recently acquired with the aid of a special grant from the Trustees. This is a late fifteenth-century collection of over 200 medical recipes and charms, written in Middle English. There are four full-page drawings in colour and smaller illustrations: at the foot of this page, a swaddled baby in a rocking cradle.

the director but the Trustees continue to provide each with an annual grant.

Over the past 25 years I have been involved in the development of the Trust's participation in the History of Medicine from an uncatalogued Museum and Library only marginally available to the public to the creation of an excellent and elegant Library of the History of Medicine, a magnificent exhibition in the Science Museum, and the growth of scholarship in the Institute for the History of Medicine as well as the Wellcome Units in the universities. We believe that we have done more than fulfil Sir Henry Wellcome's wishes. We cannot foresee finance for this subject being available from other sources on a very large scale and so it is likely to remain a major responsibility of the Trustees for the foreseeable future. In promoting this subject the Trustees have taken a major initiative and displayed great interest by their provision of support.

The Wellcome Tropical Institute

The Wellcome Museum of Medical Science has only recently become the responsibility of the Trustees. It was not taken over from the Foundation at the time of the transfer of the historical collection because it was a teaching, rather than a research museum, and was thought to be of commercial significance to the Company. More recently, however, as plans were being evolved for the housing of the Foundation outside London and the future use of the Wellcome building it was considered that this Museum would fit more snugly with the Trustees' interests. The Trust has therefore assumed responsibility for it and is examining ways in which it can be modernised and used as a basis for 'distance learning' in the Tropics. It is also planned to link its activities with a new Library for the History of Tropical Medicine and with the research programme of the Trust in this field. The recently formed Institute (p. 205) will be an important new element in the Trust's portfolio of interests.

The future

I have attempted in this account to sketch the way in which I have seen the Wellcome Trust evolve from a small grant-giving Trust with very few staff into a major organisation with its own Museum and Library and an extensive programme of research both in this country and overseas. I believe that it has developed new methods for the support of medical research and an appropriate style of medical research administration. It has made a special impact at various times in a variety of branches of medicine; it is a very significant organisation on an international scale in Tropical Medicine and the History of Medicine, and on a national scale in Mental Health and Veterinary Medicine.

During the first 50 years of the Trust's history its provision of support to the universities for medical research both in the basic and clinical sciences has been a significant element in maintaining Britain's competitiveness in these fields. This support has been given in accord with policies slowly formulated by the Trustees in implementation of the widely-drawn terms of Sir Henry Wellcome's Will. What were the factors that have affected the evolution of their policy? Obviously, internally, the increasing profitability of the Foundation. Then, externally, the changing health-experience of humanity and the autogenous development of medical science. But the history of the Trust also illustrates the way in which policy has developed against the background of the political, financial and social climate of Britain and especially its universities. Hence, any look to the future requires a crystal ball in which to spy out many events that are outside the control of a medical research funding organisation.

Nevertheless, it is possible to forecast how the Trust might be expected to react to various events and trends. Moreover, the Trust is not solely a reactive organisation: it has shown itself to be innovative and experimental in leading the support of medical research.

The income of the Trust

The Trust receives the bulk of its income from its ownership of the Wellcome Foundation Limited. It was Sir Henry Wellcome's intention that his Trustees should retain the ownership of the Company and that the purposes of his Will should be carried out within the Commercial Company, directed by the Trustees, which would provide the income to the Trust for distribution to look after his collections or to support medical research the results of which he hoped might be of benefit to the Company. The creation of a separate Board for the Company and charitable status for the Trust, led to the consequent separation of the two organisations. Nevertheless, the Trustees have to safeguard their source of income and therefore exert an element of control over the Company and also ensure that their investment (the Company) is the best one for the well-being of the Charity (the Wellcome Trust). The new situation arising from the sale of 20 per cent of the Trustees' shareholding in the newly formed Wellcome plc (pp. 209–11) was discussed at a meeting of

Trustees and their staff in March 1986; the main conclusion reached was that the Trust should provide more senior appointments, and longer-term programme support. The retention of a majority shareholding means that, besides managing their new investments outside the Foundation, the Trustees will still be responsible for the health of their firm, and have to keep its profitability under constant review. This in turn may be influenced by such unpredictable factors as the future development of the pharmaceutical industry, the success of the Foundation's own research efforts, and national politics.

The scope of the Trust's activities

The Will gives broad scope for the endowment of research within the fields of medical science and medical history, while the ownership and responsibility for Wellcome's historical library and two museums gives the Trust, also, some involvement in certain aspects of medical education.

To the present, medical research has been defined as biomedical research ranging from the basic sciences of medicine to the application as clinical research. This has now been extended into the epidemiological area but there has been no inclination to go further into such fields as social medical research. For a different reason (the existence of other substantial private funds) the Trust has not supported cancer research. There is a danger in spreading the coverage too widely if the funds available are limited because then one acts from a less deeply informed base. While I can see a gradual extension of the research coverage of the Trust, I believe it will tend to stick to its traditional areas of biomedical research as its main priority because it has developed the experience to operate usefully in this area and there will always be new projects that need to be supported. In particular, the exciting advances of modern biotechnology are likely to have a revolutionary effect on two of the Trusts most significant areas – Tropical Medicine and Mental Health. I believe that it will be the task of the Trustees and their staff to keep research under regular scrutiny to see what aspects need special and flexible support and to act appropriately.

The charities and government support

In Britain today the support for medical research is shared between government and private organisations.

The government provides for the Universities and the Research Council Institutes and Units but the funds for the development of new ideas and subject-orientated programmes in the universities come predominantly from private sources. These funds are either for general purposes (e.g. Wellcome Trust) or for specific diseases (e.g. British Heart Foundation, Cancer Research Campaign, Muscular Dystrophy, etc.) Since many of these are individually relatively small in size they mainly provide short-term support in the form of project grants. The overall support of research thus consists of a permanent government core of staff in the universities and institutes whose support is supplemented by a variety of short-term grants for training, temporary research assistance or expenses provided from numerous public and private resources. The private funds therefore tend to be used for the support of new and prospective projects. However, the number of new things that are ready for support at any time are limited and so when a fund is over a certain size then (if it is not to spread itself more widely) it begins to take on longer-term commitments. This is the situation with the Wellcome Trust. It spends up to one-third of its income on long-term support and the balance on short-term.

Long-term and short-term support

The decision on what to choose for long-term support again depends on the state of university finance provided by the government. The decision of the Wellcome Trust to launch a Senior Lectureship Scheme was based on the view that the universities were being reduced below the critical mass level for their most successful functioning. Similarly, the decision to have long-term units in the Tropics arose from our view that tropical research was not getting the right share of research interest for its significance and that short-term funding could not be used to alter the position. Looking to the future the Trust will have to decide whether it has a continuing role in bolstering the universities. It does appear that the present government is trying to reduce the government monopoly and encourage alternative funding. Some universities have moved towards closer links with industry to help maintain their strength. This method has its inherent dangers (as well as its virtues) and so it may be especially useful that some funds are available that are not designated for particular practical ends.

It would seem to me that within the mixed economy of Britain we can always expect there to be a role for private funds for flexible use and that some of these will be needed for longer-term support to enable universities to follow lines of activity that do not attract government funding.

Tropical medicine is a particular example of such a field in which long-term support is needed, and from which government is withdrawing.

The Medical Research Council and the medical charities

One question that is frequently raised is the place of private funds and especially of a single fairly large research Trust working in parallel with a government sponsored organisation such as the Medical Research Council. Several answers have been given. The most frequent is to the effect that it is important for research workers to have an alternative source of support or court of appeal for their programmes of research. This has not so far been a major factor in our experience because the M.R.C. has, on the whole, been so well funded and acts in such a liberal way that all aspects of research are considered for support. The Trust has a certain role as a second line to the M.R.C., though as the Council's mechanism of support and that of the Trust are so similar, wide differences between their judgments are unlikely. This being the case the conclusion might be that the private funds might as well pass over the income to the M.R.C. to administer.

Certainly there is a case for wondering whether the very numerous organisations that have been created to improve the handling of separate diseases may not be a rather cumbersome way of helping research workers. On the other hand, I am sure that the individuals who devote so much of their time to raising funds on a voluntary basis would not do so if their disposal were to be at the whim of some large anonymous body. This is just as true if one thinks of such a body as an amalgamation of numerous Trusts. Apart from providing funds there are other ways in which separate organisations can help to give strength to the research world. Being self-governing (with responsibility to the Charity Commissioners for observance of the terms of their Trust) and free from Civil Service administration, the Trustees are able to think independently and develop policies of their own which are appropriate to the time. Obviously a body like the M.R.C. can do the same but, inevitably, it has to satisfy many interested parties and so new ideas take a long time to develop and are often squashed in the process of development. Private Trusts can take action more quickly and risk the possibility that a new scheme may not have been adequately researched beforehand. Should it fail to work it can always be abandoned without major harm. Should it succeed then it demonstrates a method which can be adopted more easily by the government body. A Trust can also pinpoint an area of neglect and concentrate its mind and resources for a limited time to see if it can increase positive activity in that field. The M.R.C. has to be more careful to ensure a 'fair deal' for a wider range of topics. Effectively the various Charities focussed on particular diseases therefore play a significant role in the medical research arena because each is working for its own particular interest and stimulating more activity to help that subject. A broader and larger Trust can play a similar role on a larger scale but also takes a more significant potential place in the research arena. The M.R.C. is an excellent organisation which is the envy of the world but inevitably since it is government funded it is affected by the policies and opinion of government. There is therefore a role for Trusts to watch the development of government policy and act both defensively and offensively to safeguard the progress of research. Looking to the future it is impossible to judge what specific role the Trusts may have to play but certain trends are ominous. It seems apparent that the universities and the M.R.C. will continue to have less funds available from government. Unlike the former, the M.R.C. cannot as an organisation raise funds elsewhere, although it now allows its staff to seek ancillary support and has certain private funds available for distribution. If therefore the universities need more money for research and the government will not provide it then the role of the private Trusts will become more significant, and if they can increase their input then their policy role will be more important. We can therefore speculate that under a Conservative government there will be a tendency for the role of the Trusts to grow in significance. Under a Socialist regime there is no assurance that the Government will provide more funds directly nor will it encourage the private sector to be more open handed. While Trusts' role will therefore be broadly affected by government policy there will always be smaller and larger things to do that will make the system of research support more pluralistic and therefore more appropriate for this type of activity. All this points to the importance of having an organisation like the Association of Medical Research Charities (of which the Director of the Trust was a co-founder) which keeps these bodies in contact with one another. It also points out the importance of the Trusts' remaining independent and not pooling their funds along with government organisations such as the M.R.C.

Type of support

The Trust has at different periods during its history put an emphasis on the provision of research laboratories, major equipment project grants and university staff. These have been geared to the particular situation prevailing at the time. It is possible to envisage a change of policy if the Trust feels that government stringency or policy is creating needs that cannot be met from government funds.

Selected subject areas

The case for selecting certain subjects for special attention must continue to be a matter for policy attention by the Trust. Many of the Medical Research Charities have been created from a belief that research into certain diseases needs greater impetus than it receives from public sources. This 'will of the people' forms a useful buffer against the egalitarian tendency of government. On the other hand, the people are not entirely fair in their judgment of what is neglected. There is a tendency for funds to be provided for lethal conditions (e.g. cancer) or subjects that cause an emotional reaction – disablement of children, the suffering of the elderly – and for significant aspects of medicine such as mental disorder, skin disease and tropical medicine to be less attractive to those who subscribe to charities. In such cases there is a special reason for a body like the Wellcome Trust to discover whether it should play a special role within such a field. In the past the Wellcome Trustees chose the three subjects mentioned for attention and special awards have been made in other fields to try to promote their development. It can be expected that in the future new initiatives will be taken in other fields still.

Relationship to medical education

The absorption of the Wellcome Museum of Medical Science has revealed an opportunity for the Trust to help with medical education in the Tropics through 'distance learning' techniques. It made us realise that we had a major group of people supported by the Trust who could, if they worked together, form the basis of a teaching programme. Such a spin-off from the Trust's support for research may become significant in other fields in the future. The growth of the Trust carries with it the possibility for a broadening of its impact on medicine by bringing together the people it supports.

The office of the Trust

One special strength of the Trust is the high level of knowledge and experience of research available among the Trustees and the staff of the Trust. This knowledge is used not only for the investigation of research programmes that come forward for consideration but also to promote and develop new areas of science and new methods for the support of research. A number of the schemes, now in being, originated from ideas brought forward by Trustees or staff members. This pattern means that the office staff perform a function that is useful for the future pattern of research because experiments can be undertaken with novel approaches without a long-term commitment. It has been gratifying in the past to find some of these methods have been taken up by others. A flexibly funded and administered organization supporting research within which a scientist can discuss his plans with a scientific administrative colleague has a special role which the Trust plays at present. I hope that in the future, as the various programmes now supported become more firmly consolidated, the office of the Trust will become an even more significant academic resource for medical research.

Tropical medicine

This field which is a special interest of the Trust will, I believe, continue to absorb a large fraction of its effort. Its scope, which so far has been limited to research, with the absorption of the Wellcome Museum of Medical Science will now expand to include 'distance-learning'. The opportunity exists for the Trust to play a more important role by creating a comprehensive exportable service to tropical medicine based on a unique historical archive, and exhibition of present-day knowledge and progress and a teaching and research programme regionalised in different parts of the world. The strength of the research supported by the Trust will form the backbone of the programme. It will be many years before tropical medicine will become the responsibility mainly of tropical countries and in the meanwhile the role of the Wellcome Trust in its survival and development will be a major one, especially in relation to the British contribution from other sources.

Veterinary medicine

Support for this subject by the Trust has been very important during the period in which the Veterinary Schools have lacked funding from the Agricultural Research Council. It appears that a new era is starting for the new A. and F.R.C. and so the role of the Trust in Veterinary Schools may change. Nevertheless, veterinary research is very neglected and I believe the Trust has a special role to play possibly in the tropics and possibly in encouraging the overlap between studies of man and animals, that is, in comparative medical research. Again, a balance has to be struck between innovative support and filling the gaps left by government funding. If veterinary research were to accelerate – as is very possible with new technology – then the demand on the Trust could be much greater and so a greater proportion of funds could be used for this field.

History of medicine

The Trust's unique position in this subject stems from the interest of Sir Henry Wellcome. The significance for the subject of the Library of the Wellcome Institute places on the Trustees a great responsibility not only to maintain it and foster it but to see that it retains its significance by keeping up its position. This is a difficult task because of the explosion of modern publications. The library cannot expect to have *most* of the major publications post-1850 as it has for the period before that date. It must, however, have the most important ones and must know where to get the others. The association that has developed with the Royal Society of Medicine makes one significant source readily available and other associations may develop. The appointment of staff concerned with the history of modern medicine is another step in that direction. In particular, the effort being made to link the history of tropical medicine with the teaching of that subject through the new Wellcome Tropical Institute will, we hope, show a way in which the history of medicine can be integrated into the corpus of knowledge of medicine instead of its present position as an entity somewhat divorced from present-day life.

The development of Units in the history of medicine in some universities will we hope continue to be a significant feature of the Trust's support for the subject and we hope that these too may help to project the subject to a greater range of people than at present. The adoption by the Trust of the policy of ensuring that the history of medicine should rate academically with other aspects of history has been significant, but the achievement of parity cannot be the unique line of progress open to this subject in the future. It is to be hoped that more can be done to see that it becomes part of the medical curriculum probably by interweaving with the ordinary subjects rather than as a formal and separate discipline.

In summary I would take the view that the Wellcome Trust will continue to play an important role in the support of medical research in Britain, Europe, the Commonwealth and the Tropics. This role will be mainly at the biomedical and clinical science end of the medical research spectrum. The Trust will gradually pull together its support for individuals into a more cohesive entity through the scientific ability of the staff of the Trust. This new entity will then play a role as the provider of teaching at the cutting edge of medical research. It is also my hope that the development of the history of modern medicine will be integrated with this new cohesive activity of the Trust.

APPENDIX I

The Trustees' statement of policy, 1966

First printed in the *Sixth Report*, pp. 14–20

The income of the Wellcome Trust has increased in recent years. The Trustees in consequence are now able annually to make allocations and grants on a scale which has significance, particularly in the United Kingdom, for the shape and development of medical research. They have therefore re-examined their policy to ensure that they are using the funds at their disposal to the best advantage.

The Trustees consider that one of the principal aims in the administration of the funds of the Wellcome Trust as a charitable foundation is to give flexibility to the methods by which medical research is financed.

Their intention is to support promising new advances and inadequately supported or inter-disciplinary subjects which offer opportunities for development, until such time as these can be absorbed into regular budgets. They do not consider it to be their function to make up the deficiencies created in regular budgets by inadequate allocations from public funds.

The view of the Trustees on the most effective ways in which they can use the funds at their disposal is set out in the following paragraphs.

Until now the Trust has used most of its funds by way of grants to support projects put forward by individual research workers. Each application has been assessed on its scientific quality and importance, and awards have been made for those projects which were judged most promising by these criteria. The Trustees intend to continue to allocate a large proportion of the funds of the Trust in this way because they believe that the mainspring of new developments will usually be the ideas of individual researchers. The basic and clinical sciences of medicine will continue to receive help as men and projects of high scientific quality can be identified.

In addition the Trustees plan in future to look for investigators of high promise so that more emphasis can be given to certain selected problems. The following spheres of research give an indication of possible directions in which the Trustees could provide support.

I. Inadequately supported subjects. The progress of medical research in different fields is uneven. Some subjects which might on scientific grounds have been expected to advance rapidly have not done so. Furthermore, the emphasis of research does not always reflect the importance of a subject for human welfare, the chief objective of the Trust set out in the Founder's Will. The Trustees therefore will encourage research in fields giving such opportunities for development and, with the aid of qualified advisers, seek ways in which they can increase interest and performance in these fields.

II. Interdisciplinary subjects. The opportunity for new advances of knowledge that can arise from linking two or more disciplines is well known: molecular biology is a current example. Such creative links are often difficult to bring about because increased specialisation reduces the number of researchers with a sufficient knowledge of more than one field. For example, the increasing emphasis of biochemists on pure organic chemistry can weaken its links with clinical medicine. In another field, increased association between ophthalmology and medicine can be of help in tackling many of the unsolved problems of the influence of general diseases on the eye. Recognising the value of such special inter-disciplinary team research, the Trustees will consider opportunities for its promotion, including arrangements for longer-term support where desirable.

III. Established centres and field research overseas. Association between established centres and work in developing countries can increase knowledge. The Trust has already organised two schemes whereby workers in this country have collaborated with colleagues abroad to study problems of mutual interest, the basic laboratory research being done in the United Kingdom and the field research abroad. Such links are leading to advances in knowledge unlikely otherwise to occur.

IV. Endemic tropical diseases. The Trustees have for long had a special interest in the diseases of tropical countries and have supported a number of projects overseas. They still consider that the important problems of health and disease in the tropics are insufficiently studied, largely because they occur in countries which have little money to devote to research. The Trustees hope therefore to devise means by which they can help to develop work on tropical diseases in established laboratories of the United Kingdom and to associate this work with centres overseas where the diseases are endemic and the problems can be studied in patients. In addition to providing grants as at present, they may wish in due course to demonstrate a pattern of study by concentrating efforts on one such disease.

V. Veterinary medicine and animal nutrition. Animals provide most of the protein foods consumed by man. From the standpoint of the welfare of man, study of the nutrition and diseases of animals is important. Work on animals is also relevant because comparative studies yield facts which assist the understanding of similar problems in man. Since veterinary medicine has lagged behind human medicine, advances can be expected from increased application of the principles and methods evolved for the latter. The Trustees therefore intend to foster the development of research in this field, and, in particular, to promote more work on the tropical diseases of animals, since the need for protein foodstuffs is so much greater in the developing countries.

VI. History of medicine. The history of medicine was a special interest of Sir Henry Wellcome which the Trustees will continue to support, believing that doctors and medical researchers should be better informed about the ways in which the great advances in knowledge, especially during the last century, have created the standards of medical practice and research which exist today. Their major expenditure in this field will continue to be on their Museum and Library in Euston Road, and on the recently created Sub-Department of the History of Medicine at University College London. They hope that these centres will be a source of interest and inspiration to others in the development of medical history as a university subject.

VII. Research fellowships. The Trustees at present award about 50 research fellowships each year. Some of these awards are competitive, such as those for clinical and veterinary research and the Sir Henry Wellcome Travelling Research Fellowships. But the majority are provided for graduates from overseas who wish to come to the United Kingdom to extend their research experience. The Trustees believe that at present there is no shortage of fellowships for graduates of the United Kingdom who wish to undertake research in their own country,

The Trustees intend for the future to provide fellowships of the following kinds:

(a) awards to encourage research in inadequately supported fields of medicine;
(b) competitive awards for graduates from a greater number of countries overseas who wish to extend their research experience by working in the United Kingdom. These competitive awards will gradually replace the present *ad hoc* fellowships. Some will be of senior status;
(c) awards to permit research workers in one field to obtain training in a second field and thus acquire interdisciplinary qualifications.

VIII. Communication between research workers in medicine. The Trustees will continue their present policy which is designed to improve communications between research workers. They will therefore go on providing travel grants, support for symposia and small international meetings, and grants to aid publication and illustration. They may also occasionally give help to medical research libraries and museums.

In the past the Trustees have normally allocated most of the funds of the Trust on a short-term basis. In the future they intend to make a large part of the funds available in this way: but to undertake new developments on the lines now proposed it will be necessary sometimes to give longer-term support for projects which they wish to encourage. When the Trustees assume such longer-term responsibilities they will work in close collaboration with the university or other institution concerned so that the project may always be closely linked with the development plans of the institution.

Up to the present, 45 per cent of the funds of the Wellcome Trust have been used to build research accommodation. The need for buildings is not likely to diminish, but the Trustees consider it inappropriate as a policy that so large a proportion of their funds should continue to be used in this way. In order to make funds available to promote the objectives stated earlier the Trustees will in future take a stricter view on requests for the provision of research accommodation and will normally consider them favourably only when a building proposed is to accommodate a programme of research which the Trustees in any case desire to support. They take the view that, in general, laboratory space for research workers paid from public funds should be provided from public funds; its provision should not be dependent on a charitable foundation such as the Wellcome Trust.

In other respects the Trustees will continue to make appropriate type of grants for the research programmes which they think should be supported.

The graph below indicates the effect of the Trustees' new policy between 1964 and 1976. The lines show, on a biennial basis, the percentage of the total sum distributed assigned to each class of award (omitting that of 'Other awards').

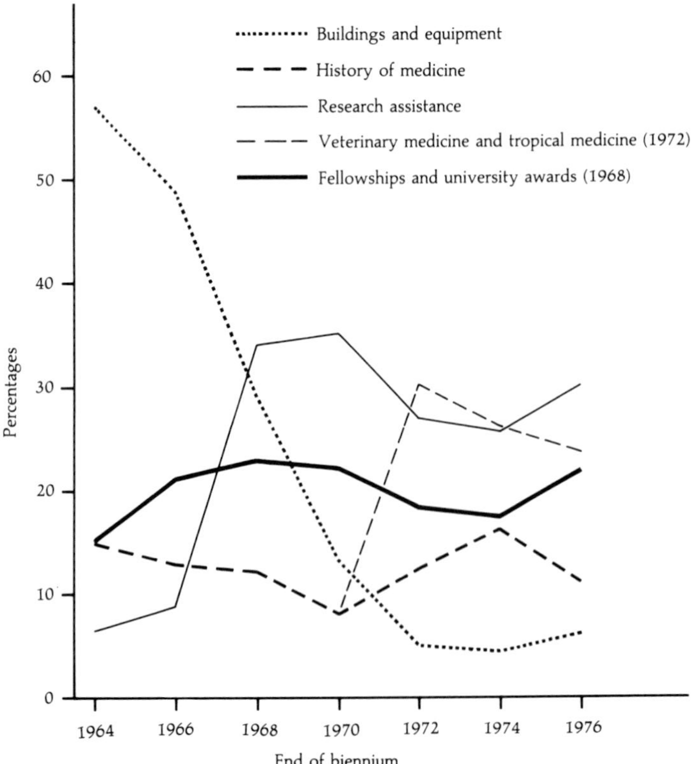

APPENDIX II

Advertised awards in mental health, 1976–84

Total allocation 1976–84 £1,808,000

1974–6

Dr J. A. Edwardson, Senior Lecturer in Physiology, St George's Hospital Medical School, London, and Dr H. R. Morris, Lecturer in Biochemistry, Imperial College of Science and Technology, London, in collaboration with Dr T. J. Crow, Head of the Division of Psychiatry, Clinical Research Centre, Northwick Park, London:

An exploratory study of cerebral peptides in cerebrospinal fluid, blood, urine and post-mortem brain tissue from schizophrenic and control subjects to establish whether there are changes in the functioning of peptidergic systems involving known or novel compounds of this class.

Dr J. L. T. Birley, Dean and Consultant Psychiatrist, Professor C. D. Marsden, Head of the Department of Neurology, and Dr R. Rodnight, Reader in Biochemistry, Institute of Psychiatry, London:

An investigation of the hypothesis that some aspects of psychotic behaviour may be due to abnormal metabolism of indoleamines in the brain with secondary effects on dopaminergic activity.

1976–8

Dr D. F. Roberts, Department of Human Genetics, University of Newcastle-upon-Tyne:

A pilot study on the association of schizophrenia with HL-A and other histocompatibility antigens.

Professor P. H. Venables, Department of Psychology, University of York:

A pilot study of schizophrenia and non-schizophrenic features in the relatives of schizophrenics.

Mr J. S. P. Lumley, Department of Surgery, St Bartholomew's Hospital Medical College, London:

To investigate the assessment and role of surgical management of dementia.

Dr J. L. Crammer, Metabolic Unit, Institute of Psychiatry, London:

A clinical neuroendocrine study of brain function in mental illness.

Professor B. Tomlinson, Department of Pathology, Newcastle-upon-Tyne University Medical School:

An inter-disciplinary study of Alzheimer's disease.

1978–80

Professor A. N. Davison, Department of Neurochemistry, Institute of Neurology, London:

To study genetic transcription in the developing brain, its regulation and possible alterations in mental subnormality, with special reference to Down's syndrome.

Dr E. T. Rolls, Department of Experimental Psychology, University of Oxford:

An analysis of brain mechanisms of eating and drinking in relation to disorders of eating and drinking.

Professor G. F. M. Russell, Department of Psychiatry, Institute of Psychiatry, London:

The use of drugs with effects upon appetite in the investigation and treatment of bulimia nervosa.

Dr T. Silverstone, Academic Unit of Human Psychopharmacology, St Bartholomew's Hospital Medical College, London:

The pharmacology of appetite in normal subjects and in the Prader–Willi syndrome.

1980–2

Professor J. R. M. Copeland, Department of Psychiatry, University of Liverpool:

The early detection, causal factors and outcome of mental illness in elderly subjects living at home, with special reference to depression and dementia.

Professor P. J. Graham, Department of Child Psychiatry, Institute of Child Health, London:

An epidemiological investigation into affective disorders and problems of eating control in late adolescence with Dr Naomi Richman.

Dr G. I. Szmukler, Department of Psychiatry, Institute of Psychiatry, London:

The incidence, early detection and feasibility of some preventive measures in anorexia nervosa.

Professor A. Wakeling, Department of Psychiatry, Royal Free Hospital School of Medicine, London:

An epidemiological enquiry into the onset and prevalence of eating disorders, by means of a retrospective study of hospital patients and a prospective study of schoolgirls, with Dr A. H. Mann.

Professor E. S. Paykel, Department of Psychiatry, St George's Hospital Medical School, London:

Depression, antidepressants and receptor plasticity, with Professor J. S. Kelly and Dr R. W. Horton, Department of Pharmacology.

1982–4

Professor J. A. Gray, Professor P. Lantos, and Professor R. Rodnight, Institute of Psychiatry, and Professor P. M. Rabbitt, University of Manchester:
The neuropsychology of Alzheimer's disease.

Dr T. W. Robbins, Department of Experimental Psychology, University of Cambridge:
The neuropsychology of Parkinson's and Alzheimer's diseases: a comparative study of human subjects and experimental primates, with Dr B. J. Everitt and Dr J. B. Dunnett.

APPENDIX III

Awards for studies of schizophrenia

Total Allocation, 1973–84 £520,000

1972

Dr D. Kelly, Department of Psychology, St George's Hospital Medical School, London:

To study limbic leucotomy and to undertake a further evaluation of its effects in schizophrenia and obsessional neurosis.

1974–8

Dr B. Costall and Dr R. J. Naylor, School of Studies in Pharmacology, University of Bradford:

The aetiology of schizophrenia and a new approach to drug design.

Professor M. Gelder, Department of Psychiatry, University of Oxford:

Clinical, pharmacological and neuroendocrine correlates of response to neuroleptics in schizophrenic patients.

Dr B. Costall, School of Studies in Pharmacology, University of Bradford:

The 'presynaptic' dopamine receptor mechanisms, a key to therapeutic developments in schizophrenia and an understanding of the disease aetiology, with Dr R. J. Naylor.

Professor D. F. Roberts, Department of Human Genetics, University of Newcastle-upon-Tyne:

The association of schizophrenia with HLA and other histocompatibility antigens.

1978–80

Professor Sir Martin Roth, Department of Psychiatry, University of Cambridge:

1) for Dr C. White to assess the significance of longer-term changes in arousal in schizophrenic disorder, and 2) for Dr T. R. E. Barnes to investigate clinical pharmacological endocrinological, neuropathological and neurochemical aspects of tardive dyskinesia.

Professor P. H. Venables, Department of Psychology, University of York:
For a follow-up of a physiological screening procedure for risk of psychiatric illness at the pre-adolescent stage.

Dr D. C. Watt, St John's Hospital, Aylesbury:
To carry out an assessment of the long-term outcome in a defined schizophrenic population.

Dr. D. C. Watt, St John's Hospital, Aylesbury:
For a linkage study of 32 blood genetic markers in the families of schizophrenics.

1980–2

Dr E. S. Johnson, Department of Pharmacology, King's College, London:
The extrapyramidal side-effects of dopamine antagonists used in the treatment of schizophrenia.

Dr G. H. Jones, Department of Psychological Medicine, University of Wales College of Medicine, Cardiff:
The corpus callosum in schizophrenia and the correlation of cerebral dominance with recovery from schizophrenia.

Dr P. B. C. Fenwick, Department of Psychiatry, Institute of Psychiatry:
Pattern-evoked responses in acute schizophrenia.

Dr C. L. E. Katona, Department of Psychiatry, University of Cambridge:
The dexamethasone suppression test in schizo-effective illness.

Professor M. G. Gelder, Department of Psychiatry, University of Oxford:
The reasons for incomplete response of schizophrenic patients to neuroleptic drugs.

1982–4

Dr Janet M. Allen, C.R.C. Division of Psychiatry, Medical Research Council Units, Northwick Park, London:
Abnormalities of neuropeptide in schizophrenia, depression and dementia.

Dr R. Murray, Genetic Section, Institute of Psychiatry, London:
A combined twin and family investigation of biological markers in schizophrenia.

Dr O. T. Phillipson, Department of Anatomy, University of Bristol:
Thalamic control of dopaminergic functions.

Professor G. Burnstock, Department of Anatomy and Embryology, University College, London:
The ultrastructure of the schizophrenic brain.

APPENDIX IV

Major grants (exceeding £45,000), 1980–4

The place is London unless otherwise indicated. Figures to the nearest £1,000. Counter-inflationary increases have often been added subsequently.

Basic sciences

1980

University of Nottingham, to Dr R. J. Mayer to provide research assistance and expenses in studying the topography, turnover and tissue concentration of monoamine oxidase, £50,000.

University of Oxford, to provide an electron microscope for the Department of Human Anatomy, £90,000.

Imperial College, to Professor E. A. Barnard, for research assistance and expenses in studying the primary changes in muscular dystrophy, and their experimental correction, £48,000.

University of Oxford, to Dr W. F. Cook for research assistance and expenses in studying the location and function of peptidase enzymes in the nervous system, £45,000.

University of Cambridge, to Professor C. N. Hales for an extension of research assistance and expenses to undertake immunoradiometric assays on cell-specific proteins in human disease, £70,000.

1981

University of Bristol, to Professor J. R. Clamp for research assistance and expenses in studying the carbohydrate moieties of mucus glycoproteins, £48,000.

University of Oxford, Dr B. D. Ross, to provide a Special Fellowship to enable him to study the clinical application of ^{31}P nuclear magnetic resonance, £72,000.

St Mary's Hospital Medical School, to Professor L. Brent for research assistance and expenses in investigating the parameters affecting the transplantation of allogenic haemopoietic cells to the human fetus, £80,000.

1982

St Mary's Hospital Medical School, to Professor L. Brent for research assistance and expenses in studying the mechanisms of interference by environmental mycobacteria with B.C.G. protection against tuberculosis and leprosy, £60,000.

Middlesex Hospital Medical School to Dr R. K. Craig for a joint study of the human calcitonin gene family, £75,000.

St George's Hospital Medical School, to provide a Lectureship for Dr A. P. Johnstone, to study the molecular basis of eukaryotic cell differentiation, £70,000.

University of Sheffield, for research assistance and expenses to enable Professor Pauline M. Harrison to make immunochemical studies of the isoferritins, £49,000.

University of Cambridge, for research assistance and expenses to enable Professor R. R. A. Coombs to investigate red-cell labelled antibody reagents as the basis for an analytical and diagnostic system of immunoassays, £50,000.

Royal Veterinary College, London, to Dr P. A. Mayes, for research assistance and expenses in studying the metabolism of chylomicron remnants and the lipoprotein precursor of biliary steroids, £57,000.

1983

Institute of Ophthalmology, for Dr Susan Lightman to extend her immunological investigation of ocular inflammation, £46,000.

University of Leicester, for research assistance and expenses to Dr J. W. Almond's development of a new poliovirus type 3 vaccine using recombinant D.N.A. techniques, £50,000.

University College London, for research assistance and expenses to Dr J. C. Foreman, studying the functional relationship in skin of substance P and histamine, and their roles in inflammation, £50,000.

Royal Postgraduate Medical School, for Dr P. J. Barnes, research assistance and expenses in his work on autonomic receptor localisation in human and mammalian lungs, £48,000.

St Mary's Hospital Medical School, for research assistance and expenses incurred in Professor R. L. Smith's research into the genetic regulation of human drug oxidation and its implications, £95,000.

Royal Free Hospital Medical School, for research assistance and expenses to Professor J. A. Lucy, studying molecular mechanisms in the fusion of myoblasts and erythrocytes, £46,000.

University of Manchester, to Dr Jacqueline B. Weiss, providing research assistance and expenses in her work on the isolation and characterisation of angiogenesis inhibitors from the vitreous humour of the eye: their mechanism of action and relationship to ocular disease, £55,000.

University College, London, for research assistance and expenses in Dr Anne E. Warner's investigation of the distribution of small ions during the early development of the mammalian embryo, £49,000.

University of Glasgow, a University Award and research expenses for Dr M. W. Kennedy, to advance his research on parasite specific antigens in protective immunity and serodiagnosis, £91,000.

University of Liverpool, for Dr P. H. Cobbold, research assistance and expenses for his aequorin studies of hormone-induced changes in cytoplasmic free (Ca^{2+}) in mammalian cells, £47,000.

University College, London, to Professor N. A. Mitchison, research assistance and expenses for his study of the development and function of mammalian sensory neurones, £50,000.

London School of Hygiene and Tropical Medicine, for research assistance and expenses in Dr C. R. Howard's research on the development and properties of synthetic viral peptide vaccines, £123,000.

University of Birmingham, to Dr D. R. Stanworth for research assistance and expenses in the development of anti-immunoglobulin peptide antibodies with immunoregulatory and immunodiagnostic potential, £89,000.

Royal Free Hospital Medical School, for research assistance and expenses to aid Professor D. Chapman's research on surface forces and biomembrane molecules using a new technique, £75,000.

University of Leicester, to Dr M. J. Morgan for research assistance and expenses in research on the molecular genetics of carbohydrate metabolism in cultured animal cells, £46,000.

Charing Cross Hospital Medical School, for research assistance to Dr T. N. Palmer in his research on the hepato-muscular axis in branched chain amino-acid metabolism, £50,000.

University of Oxford, to provide technical assistance to Dr A. C. G. Cuello's study of the neuroanatomy of the central nervous system cholinergic neurones, £50,000.

Royal Free Hospital Medical School, to Dr H. C. Thomas, research assistance in order to determine the mechanism of lysis of hepatocytes containing replicating and integrated hepatitis B virus, £81,000.

University of Hull, for research assistance to Professor I. M. L. Donaldson's study of the effects of extraocular and neck muscle proprioceptors on vestibular control of eye and head movements, £48,000.

University of Cambridge, for a Research Fellowship for Dr R. J. L. Hooper and expenses in his isolation and purification of the dopamine D_2 receptor, £59,000.

University of Oxford, for research assistance to Dr J. F. Stein in developing a systems analysis approach to the role of the cerebellum in motor control, in conjunction with Dr R. I. Kitney of the Department of Electrical Engineering, Imperial College, London, £65,000.

1984

Royal Postgraduate Medical School, for research assistance to Dr J. Calam in studying plasma cholecystokinin-like bioactivity, £49,000.

University of Southampton, to Dr H. V. Wheal as Wellcome Senior Lecturer in Medical Sciences, for research assistance and expenses in his experiments on the functional replacement of interneurones and CA3 pyramidal cells in the hippocampus using transplanted and cultured tissue, £48,000.

University College, London, an extension for Dr A. E. Lieberman of his research assistance and expenses in studying the development of the hamster visual system, £52,000.

St George's Hospital Medical School, for Dr J. C. Booth, research assistance and expenses in his investigation of the antigenic structure of human cytomegalovirus using monoclonal antibodies, £53,000.

University of Surrey, research assistance and expenses for Dr I. Kitchen's study of the developmental neurotoxicity of lead, disruption of the opioid system in the brain and its behavioural consequences, £90,000.

University of Edinburgh, to Dr C. R. House for research assistance and expenses in examining the membrane channel current flow during fertilisation of mammalian eggs, £80,000.

University of Birmingham, to Dr S. Salmons for research assistance and expenses in his investigation of the co-ordinated regulation of myosin genes in adult mammalian muscle, £54,000.

City University, London, to Dr J. L. Barbur for research assistance and expenses in studying the function of pupil response in human vision, £58,000.

University of Bristol, to Dr F. Cevero, for research assistance and expenses in electrophysiological studies of the action of biologically active peptides and visceral afferent neurons, £45,000.

Westminster Hospital Medical School, for Dr S. L. Lightman for research assistance and expenses in his investigation of the structure and function of mammalian inter-neuronal vasopressin-like peptide, £51,000.

University College, London, a University Award on behalf of Dr D. Lawson, for the investigation of cytoskeletal structure and function by rapid freezing, antibodies, microinjection and gene cloning, £120,000.

St Bartholomew's Hospital Medical College, to Dr P. J. Lowry for research assistance and expenses in his investigation of corticotropin releasing factor complex using cell culture, £75,000.

University of Sussex, to Dr R. C. Bray, for research assistance and expenses in his study of the structure of the molybdenum co-factor, £60,000.

University of Liverpool, to Professor D. H. Petersen for research assistance and expenses in his study of the control of K^+ conductance in pancreatic acinar cells from pig and man, £52,000.

University of Oxford, to Dr C. D. Stern, for research assistance and expenses in his investigation of the mechanisms of formation of the embryonic axis, £50,000.

University of Liverpool, to Dr S. Marshall-Clarke for research assistance and expenses in his research on the identification and characterisation of B-lymphocyte surface receptors for growth and differentiation factors, £47,000.

Buildings, libraries, etc.

1980

St Mary's Hospital Medical School, for building conversions, £50,000.

1981

Liverpool School of Tropical Medicine and Hygiene, for an Animal House, £50,000.

University of Edinburgh, towards building conversions providing accommodation for studies on the genetics of the eye, £50,000.

1982

Royal College of Physicians, Edinburgh, towards the renovation of its rooms, £50,000.

Royal Society of Medicine, for the development of its Library in closer association with the Wellcome Institute for the History of Medicine, £350,000.

1983

University of Oxford, Laboratory of Physiology, towards the building costs of the Sherrington Memorial Library for the History of Neuroscience, £30,000.

Clinical Sciences

(*see also* Senior Research Fellowships in Clinical Science)

1980

University of Birmingham, to Dr J. E. Fox for research assistance and expenses in undertaking an assessment of brain stem function: a combined clinical and experimental investigation, £50,000.

1981

University of Newcastle-upon-Tyne, to Professor S. Shuster research assistance and expenses for a study of the aryl hydrocarbon hydroxylase activity and the aetiology of psoriasis, £76,000.

Royal Postgraduate Medical School, to Dr I. N. Ferrier, for a Special Fellowship and expenses to study the central nervous system and hypothalamic regulation of gonadatropin secretion in man and psychotic patients employing immuno-histochemical and neuroendocrinal strategies, £72,000.

St Mary's Hospital Medical School, to Dr Pamela W. Ewan, for technical assistance and research expenses in a study of T cell sensitisation to extrinsic allergens in asthma, £47,000.

Institute of Child Health, to Dr D. J. Atherton for personal support and research expenses, part-time, while investigating the pathogenesis treatment and prevention of atopic anaemia, £62,000.

University of Nottingham, to Dr W. G. Reeves for research assistance and expenses in a study of the characterisation of immune complexes in insulin-dependent diabetes and of their clinical significance, £56,000.

University College London, to Professor R. H. T. Edwards, a contribution towards the cost of equipment with which to carry out topical nuclear magnetic resonance studies of problems in human metabolism, £100,000.

1982

Institute of Dermatology, to Dr Jaya L. Naidoo for a Lectureship, assistance and expenses in studying the transfer and maintenance of plasmid genes in skin bacteria, £48,000.

Royal Free Hospital Medical School, for Dr H. C. Thomas as Wellcome Senior Research Fellow for research assistance and expenses in connection with his study of anti-viral compounds for treating hepatitis B virus infections, £50,000.

St Mary's Hospital Medical School, for Dr S. L. Lightman as Wellcome Senior Lecturer, for research assistance and expenses in studying the control by the central nervous system of posterior pituitary secretion, £50,000.

University of Cambridge, for Professor R. Y. Calne to make a study of the clinical relevance of Cyclosporin A in blood levels in transplant recipients, £72,000.

University of Edinburgh, to enable Professor J. J. K. Best to purchase equipment to evaluate proton nuclear magnetic resonance imaging, £100,000.

St Mary's Hospital Medical School, for research assistance and expenses to enable Dr D. J. Jeffries to investigate immunocompromise in homosexuals related to viral infections and drug abuse, £49,000.

1983

Western General Hospital, Edinburgh, to Dr Anne Ferguson for research assistance and expenses in her work on the characterisation of human mast cells and their relevance to intestinal inflammation, £65,000.

London School of Hygiene and Tropical Medicine, to Dr P. M. McKeigne for a Research Training Fellowship to enable him to investigate risk factors for coronary heart disease among different ethnic groups in East London, £77,000.

University of Southampton, to Dr H. V. Wheal, a Wellcome Senior Lecturer, research assistance and expenses for a study of the mechanisms of epileptogenesis in the hippocampus, and their control, £71,000.

Middlesex Hospital Medical School, for research assistance and expenses to Dr G. F. Bottazzo in his study of the relevance of induced HLA-DR and Ia-like molecules expression on endocrine cells to autoimmune disease, £80,000.

Institute of Neurology, to Professor L. Symon for research assistance and expenses to aid his research on the biochemical mechanism of ischaemic cell damage in the brain, £80,000.

Cardiothoracic Institute, for research assistance and expenses in Dr Joan L. Longbottom's immunological investigation of aeroallergens, in relation to laboratory animal allergy, £48,000.

Royal Postgraduate Medical School for a Fellowship and expenses for Dr R. I. Lechler, to undertake functional immune studies following transfection of class II MHC genes, £48,000.

Institute of Psychiatry, an extension of the research assistance to Dr B. S. Meldrum's basic studies in epilepsy, £58,000 (the previous grant was made in 1980).

St Mary's Hospital Medical School, a University Award on behalf of Mr S. T. F. Chan, for an investigation of the factors determining the role of carbohydrate and water-electrolyte repletion in body tonicity and protein conservation following starvation and injury, £45,000.

1984

University of Leicester, to Dr P. H. Williams for research assistance and expenses in investigating the epidemiology and biosynthesis of the hydroxomate siderphore aerobactin by *Escherichia coli* isolated from extra-intestinal infections of man, £47,000.

Royal Postgraduate Medical School, to Dr D. N. S. Kerr for research assistance and expenses in studying the role of leucocytes in the pathogenesis of acute and chronic lung disease, studies using Indium-III-labelled cells, £50,000.

St George's Hospital Medical School, to Professor J. Hermon-Taylor, for research assistance and expenses in order to undertake the chemical synthesis of novel proteinase inhibitors for the specific chemotherapy of acute necrotising pancreatitis, £51,000.

Chelsea College, London, to Professor H. Baum, research assistance and expenses for his study of antimitochondrial antibodies of primary biliary cirrhosis, £57,000.

University of Bristol, to Professor G. M. Stirratt for research assistance and expenses in his study of material immune reactions to the placental villous stroma using pemphigoid gestationis as a model, £47,000.

London Hospital Medical College, to Dr J. K. Stothers for research assistance and expenses in further investigation of the effects of hypoxia on metabolism and ventilation in newborn infants, £58,000.

University College, London, to Dr D. C. Linch for research assistance and expenses in a study of the regulation of erythropoietic progenitor cells, £60,000.

Special fellowships and lectureships

Senior research fellowships in clinical science

1980, three £238,000; 1981, no awards; 1982, six, £807,000; 1983, four plus one extension, £740,000; 1984, three plus two extensions, £690,000.
Total: £2,475,000.

Senior lectureships in medical science

1980, eight, £725,000; 1981, eleven, £1,085,000; 1982, eight, £968,000; 1983, seven plus eleven extensions, £1,674,000; 1984, eleven, £1,244,000.
Total: £5,696,000.

University lectureships

1983, twelve, £900,000; 1984, thirteen plus six extensions and four research grants, £1,925,000.
Total: £2,825,000.

Fellowships in surgery

1980, five, £102,000; 1981, six, £140,000; 1982, no award; 1983, four, £136,000; 1984, one, £32,000.
Total: £410,000.

Fellowships in pathology

1980, four, £151,000; 1983, three, £129,000; 1984, one, £54,000.
Total: £334,000.

Wellcome–Australian senior research fellowships

1984, two, £380,000.

Research training fellowships in clinical epidemiology

1980, three, £171,000; 1981, two, £81,000; 1982, one, £74,000.
Total: £326,000

Lectureships in epidemiology

1984, two, £200,000.

Infectious diseases

1982

University of Oxford, for research assistance and expenses to Professor D. J. Weatherall in his investigation of the pathophysiology of the anaemia of infection, £157,000.

Royal Postgraduate Medical School, to provide a Training Fellowship for Dr J. Cohen, for studies on endotoxin in the immunocompromised host under Professor D. K. Peters, £88,000.

University of Birmingham, for Dr J. Stephen of the Department of Microbiology, to provide research assistance and expenses for his investigation of the pathophysiology of rotavirus and *Salmonella* experimental gastroenteritis in parallel with human clinical studies, with Dr D. C. A. Candy, Department of Paediatrics and Child Health, and Dr M. P. Osborne, Department of Physiology, £150,000.

1983

University of Birmingham, for research assistance and expenses for Professor H. Smith's investigation of the mechanisms of differential production of fever and constitutional effects in ferrets by strains of influenza differing in virulence, £81,000.

University College, London, for research assistance and expenses to Dr A. W. Segal in his study of the factors in the interaction between phagocytes and bacteria that predispose to microbial infection, £80,000.

1984

Royal Free Hospital Medical School, to provide a Lectureship, technical assistance and expenses for Dr A. M. L. Lever, for an investigation of patients with defined acute and chronic viral infections, to determine the role played by interferon in determining the natural history of these conditions, £83,000.

University of Oxford, a Lectureship with research expenses for Dr Mary E. Penney to make a prospective study of duodenal microflora during and following acute infantile gastroenteritis, £69,000.

Middlesex Hospital Medical School, a Senior Lectureship for Dr I. V. D. Weller with technical assistance and expenses in his investigation of the natural history, aetiology and immunology of the prodromal phase of AIDS, £122,000.

St Thomas's Hospital Medical School, for Dr H. E. Webb, research assistance and expenses to investigate the possibility that encephalitogenic budding viruses through their glycolipid coats may produce an autoimmune disturbance in the central nervous system, £45,000.

Major awards

1984

New Zealand
University of Auckland, to Professor J. D. Watson, to assist his research on the molecular biology of lymphokines, £100,000; and to Professor P. D. Gluckman for an *in vivo* investigation of the functional development of the fetal brain, £100,000.

Britain
University of Oxford, to Professor J. A. Gray for research assistance and expenses in the investigation of the neurophysiology of Alzheimer's disease, £155,000.

University of Cambridge, to Dr T. W. Robbins for research assistance and expenses for an investigation of the neuropsychology of Parkinson's and Alzheimer's diseases, a comparative study of human subjects and experimental primates, £137,000.

Mental Health

(*see also* Neurology)

1980

University of Oxford, to Professor M. G. Gelder for research assistance and expenses in investigating schizophrenia, £60,000.

1981

University of Oxford, to Dr A. D. Smith for research assistance and expenses in developing an approach to the identification of synaptic connections involved in drug actions as a basis for the therapy of psychotic disorders, £99,000.

Institute of Child Health, to Professor P. J. Graham for research assistance and expenses in an epidemiological investigation into affective disorders and problems of eating control in late adolescence, £50,000.

Royal Free Hospital School of Medicine, to Professor A. Wakeling for reseach assistance in his epidemiological inquiry into the onset and prevalence of eating disorders by means of a retrospective study of hospital patients and a prospective study of schoolgirls, £50,000.

University of Liverpool, to Professor J. R. M. Copeland, for research assistance and expenses in order to study the early detection, causal factors and outcome of mental illness in elderly subjects living at home with special reference to depression and dementia, £50,000.

St George's Hospital Medical School, to Professor J. S. Jenkins for research assistance and expenses in order to study the localisation and function of neurohypophyseal hormones in the central nervous system, £47,000.

University of Oxford, to the Department of Psychiatry continuing a scheme begun in 1979 for the provision of research training posts and expenses, £68,000.

1982

Charing Cross Hospital Medical School, to Dr Jacqueline de Belleroche providing research assistance and expenses for research on the cholinergic innervations of the cerebral cortex and hippocampus in relation to dementia, £50,000.

St George's Hospital Medical School, to Professor E. S. Paykel for research assistance, and expenses incurred in a study of depression, antidepressant drugs and receptor plasticity made in collaboration with Professor J. S. Kelly and Dr R. W. Horton of the Department of Pharmacology, £187,000.

Institute of Psychiatry, to enable Dr R. M. Murray to make a combined twin and family investigation of biological markers in schizophrenia, £80,000.

Southampton University, to Dr R. S. J. Briggs in the Department of Geriatric Medicine, for research on the regulation of cholinergic receptors in the brain and the role of established and experimental techniques in relation to senile dementia, with Dr G. N. Woodruff and Dr P. J. Roberts, Department of Pharmacology, £97,000 (two grants).

St George's Hospital Medical School, to Dr B. H. Anderton for research assistance and expenses involved in his chemical study of Alzheimer's neurofibrillary tangles, £76,000.

University of Newcastle-upon-Tyne, to Professor D. Eccleston for anatomical and biochemical investigations of serotonin–peptide interactions in the mammalian nervous system, £52,000.

1983

Royal Free Hospital Medical School, for Dr P. D. Griffiths, research assistance and expenses in aid of his inquiry into the factors responsible for childhood mental retardation following intrauterine infection with cytomegalovirus, £56,000.

University of Nottingham, for research assistance and expenses in the investigation by Dr M. Kidd of the biochemistry and immunochemistry of pathological proteins isolated from senile brains, £63,000.

University of Bristol, for research assistance and expenses in Dr O. T. Phillipson's research on thalamic control of dopaminergic functions, £64,000.

Institute of Psychiatry, for a Research Training Fellowship awarded to Dr P. H. Robinson, to work on the failure of mechanisms limiting eating: a study of gastric physiology in bulimia nervosa, £47,000.

Institute of Child Health, to extend research assistance and expenses in Professor P. J. Graham's epidemiological investigation into affective disorders and problems of eating control in late adolescence, £84,000.

University of Oxford, for research assistance and expenses in the study by Professor M. G. Gelder of the effect of female sex steroids on monoamine receptors and moods, £100,000.

University of Oxford for technical assistance to Professor M. G. Gelder on his studies of the neuropharmacology of anxiety and anxiolytic agents, £61,000.

1984

Institute of Psychiatry, to provide a Fellowship for Dr A. C. Angold, to enable him to study depressive symptomatology in children referred to an outpatient child psychiatric unit, £50,000; and similarly a Fellowship for Dr S. R. White to investigate the neuropsychiatric sequelae of subarachnoid haemorrhage, £56,000.

University of Oxford, a Fellowship for Dr Susan A. Iles to research on the psychiatric complications of termination of pregnancy because of fetal abnormality, £50,000.

University of Oxford, to Professor M. G. Gelder, to finance research training posts, with expenses, in the Department of Psychiatry, £85,000.

Institute of Neurology, for Dr L. Lim's investigation of the molecular biology of Down's syndrome: the effects of Trisomyl-21 on the genetics of a specifically affected microtubule-associated protein, £153,000.

University College, Cardiff, research assistance and expenses for Dr K. J. Collard's study of the regulation of 5-hydroxytryptamine synthesis and release in mammalian nerve terminals by tryptophan, £52,000.

University of Oxford, research assistance and expenses for Dr R. E. Passingham's investigation of the influence of the basal ganglia on cortical function, £46,000.

Institute of Psychiatry, research assistance and expenses for Dr S. A. Checkley's neuroendocrine studies of alpha adrenoceptor status in the pathogenesis and treatment of depression, £45,000; and for Professor G. Russell's study of puberty in girls, interaction of physical and psychosocial development; effects of bodyweight on the timing of puberty, £104,000. *See also* Major Awards.

Neurology

(*see also* Mental Health)

1980

Institute of Psychiatry, to Dr B. S. Meldrum for research assistance and expenses in making basic studies of epilepsy: on the causes and prevention of epileptic brain damage and the role of neuro-transmitters in variations of seizure threshold and anticonvulsant drugs, £100,000.

University of Southampton, to Dr H. V. Wheal for research assistance and expenses in investigating the mechanism of epileptogenesis in an *in vitro* mammalian brain preparation, £50,000.

Institute of Neurology, to Dr A. Richens for research assistance and expenses in a multi-disciplinary collaborative study of the role of viruses in the aetiology of epilepsy, £95,000.

Ophthalmology

1984

University of Bristol, to provide a Fellowship, technical assistance and expenses for an investigation by Dr C. M. P. Claoue of the immunology of herpes simplex infection in the eye, £49,000.

University of Leicester, to Mr A. R. Fielder, for research assistance and expenses in his study of premature infant vision, £94,000.

Toxicology

1980

Royal Postgraduate Medical School, to Professor C. T. Dollery, for research assistance and expenses in studying the role of reactive intermediates in cellular and immunological toxicity in man, £65,000.

University College Hospital Medical School, to Dr A. E. M. McLean, for research assistance and expenses for a study of age, nutrition and toxic mechanisms, £50,000.

University of Surrey, Guildford, to Professor J. W. Bridges for research assistance and expenses in an investigation of the mechanisms of chemically-induced renal papillary necrosis, £60,000.

1981

Institute of Psychiatry, to Professor C. D. Marsden for research assistance and expenses in studying the mechanisms of long-term neurotoxicity of dopamine antagonists and agonists used in the treatment of schizophrenia and Parkinson's disease, £100,000.

1983

University of Surrey, extending research assistance and expenses given to Professor J. W. Bridges for research into the mechanisms of chemically-induced renal papillary necrosis (an earlier grant was made in 1980), £61,000.

University of Oxford, for salaries, equipment and running expenses over five years, to enable Sir William Paton, Department of Pharmacology, to establish a

Toxicology Unit for the study of drug-induced systemic lupus erythematosus, £165,000.

1984

University of Oxford, to Dr D. J. Harvey, for technical assistance and expenses as Wellcome Senior Lecturer in investigating mechanisms of drug toxicity and their study by mass spectroscopy, £55,000.

Tropical medicine

1980

Harvard University, to Professor T. Weller, for research assistance and expenses for studies of Chagas' Disease in Brazil, £106,000.

University of Nairobi and St Mary's Hospital Medical School, to Professor A. Kung'u and Professor K. A. Porter for research assistance and expenses in investigating glomerulonephritis and secondary hypertension in Nairobi, Kenya, £70,000.

St Bartholomew's Hospital Medical College, to provide a Tropical Lectureship for Dr M. J. Farthing (tenable in India and South America) to study the pathogenesis of secretory diarrhoea, with special reference to Shiga enterotoxin, £50,000.

London School of Hygiene and Tropical Medicine, to Professor D. J. Bradley for research assistance and expenses in studying the genetics of resistance to infection in mice, in particular with respect to *Leishmania donovani* and *Salmonella typhimurium*, £60,000.

University of Oxford, to provide a Tropical Lectureship for Dr J. N. White to work in the Bangkok Unit on malaria and dengue fevers, £49,000.

Mahidol University, Bangkok, to Dr P. Malasit for research and expenses in a study of immune complexes, complement and reticulo–endothelial function in acute and chronic glomerular diseases in Thailand, £51,000.

1981

London School of Hygiene and Tropical Medicine, to Professor W. Peters for research assistance and expenses in making an antigenic characterisation of *Trypanosoma cruzi* and related biochemical studies, £80,000.

Medical Research Council Centre, to provide a Tropical Lectureship for Dr G. B. Lee to investigate the intestinal immune mechanisms in tropical sprue and non-specific tropical enteropathy, £70,000.

University of Edinburgh, to Dr H. S. Micklem for research assistance and expenses in his analysis of the antigens of the human malaria parasite *P.falciparum*, £62,000.

University of Oxford, to Dr J. E. Sanderson, for a Tropical Lectureship and equipment, in order to investigate hypertension and cardio-myopathy in Africa, £73,000.

London School of Hygiene and Tropical Medicine, to Dr M. J. Doenhoff for research assistance and expenses while Wellcome Senior Lecturer and studying the immunological control of hepatotoxicity and parasite egg excretion in experimental *Schistosoma mansoni* towards a functional definition of schistosome antigens, £45,000.

Universidad Nacional de Cordoba, Argentina, to provide a Tropical Lectureship for Dr C. J. Schofield to study the response of domestic populations of *Triatoma infestans* to treatment with insecticides, £67,000.

Liverpool School of Tropical Medicine and Hygiene, to Professor G. S. Nelson, for research assistance and expenses in developing new immunodiagnostic methods for detecting *Echinococcus* infection in man and animals, with reference to the epidemiology of hydatid disease in Turkana, £50,000.

1982

Tropical Metabolism Research Unit, Kingston, Jamaica, to Dr M. H. N. Golden, a Wellcome Senior Lecturer, for research assistance and expenses in establishing a Trace Element Research Group with Dr A. A. Jackson, £43,000 (see p. 254).

Dundee University, to Dr J. R. Kusel of Glasgow University, for research on the mobility of, and macromolecules in the surface membrane of, *Schistosoma mansoni* and other parasites, £110,000.

London School of Hygiene and Tropical Medicine, to Dr D. A. Broadbent for studies of the pathogenicity of *vibrio cholerae*, £100,000.

Liverpool School of Tropical Medicine and Hygiene, to Dr S. J. Oppenheimer in order to extend the Lectureship enabling him to study anaemia and infection during infancy in Papua New Guinea, in relation to iron deficiency, £52,000.

Salford University, to provide a Tropical Fellowship for Dr L. Ryan, to study the ecology and taxonomy of neotropical sand-flies at Belém with Dr R. Lainson, £51,000 (see p. 244).

University of Oxford, to provide a Tropical Lectureship for Dr R. E. Phillips, to study the pathophysiology of cerebral malaria, £75,000.

London School of Hygiene and Tropical Medicine, research assistance and expenses for Dr E. A. Gould in studying the use of monospecific and monoclonal antibodies (extending a grant made in 1980), £61,000. Secondly, to Dr J. P. Ackers for research assistance in his biochemical studies of invasive and non-invasive zymodemes, £69,000. Thirdly, an extension of the grant for research assistance made in 1981 to Dr G. A. T. Targett, or his reseach on transmission blocking immunity to *Plasmodium falciparum* malaria, £77,000.

1983

Liverpool School of Tropical Medicine and Hygiene, for a Tropical Fellowship to enable Dr A. E. Bianco to investigate the immunology of *Onchocerca* infections in experimental hosts, partly at the Hall Institute in Melbourne, Australia, £56,000. Secondly, for research assistance and expenses enabling Dr R. W. Ashford to study patterns of infection and morbidity in *strongyloides* infection in Papua New Guinea, £70,000.

London School of Hygiene and Tropical Medicine to provide a Tropical Lectureship enabling Dr Patricia M. Graves to investigate the immunity and infectivity of the human population during malaria transmission, partly at Brisbane, Australia, and partly in Papua New Guinea, £74,000. Secondly, to provide research assistance and expenses for Dr Jenefer M. Blackwell, a Wellcome Senior Lecturer investigating immunogenetics and immune regulation of leishmanial infections in mice, £88,000.

London School of Hygiene and Tropical Medicine, to Dr R. J. Hay, for research assistance and expenses in his investigation of subcutaneous fungal infections, £63,000.

Imperial College of Science and Technology, for a University Award to Dr R. M. Maizels and research assistance in his investigation of immunological approaches to the diagnosis and prophylaxis of human filariasis, £102,000.

Tropical Metabolism Research Unit, Jamaica, to enable Dr M. H. N. Golden's Trace Element Research Group to continue, £78,000.

St Bartholomew's Hospital Medical School, for research assistance and expenses to Dr M. J. G. Farthing, in his study of giardiasis; pathogenesis of intestinal disease and the humoral immune response, £71,000.

Imperial College of Science and Technology, to Dr R. E. Sinden for research assistance and expenses in his research on the control of protein synthesis and expression during sexual development in *Plasmodium falciparum*, £75,000.

1984

Liverpool School of Tropical Medicine and Hygiene, for research assistance and expenses in Dr R. E. Howell's research into the nature of resistance antifolate agents in *Plasmodium falciparum* in Kenya, £98,000.

London School of Hygiene and Tropical Medicine, to Dr R. J. Hay for research assistance and expenses in his investigation of the role of bacteria in the pathogenesis of tropical ulcer, £57,000.

University of Oxford, for research assistance and expenses to Dr C. I. Newbold in his study of the mechanisms and consequences of vascular sequestration of erythrocytes infected with malarial shizonts, £45,000.

University of Aberdeen, to continue a Senior Lectureship for Dr M. H. N. Golden, first awarded in 1981, £142,000.

Tropical Metabolism Research Unit, Kingston, Jamaica, for Dr M. H. N. Golden, to continue support of the Trace Element Research Group, £47,000.

London School of Hygiene and Tropical Medicine, to provide for the appointment of Dr K. P. W. J. McAdam to the Wellcome Chair of Clinical Tropical Medicine with research support for his study of the immunopathology of acute phase response and for a University Award to enable Dr A. S. Whitehead to study the molecular control of acute phase protein synthesis, £230,000.

University of Bristol, to Professor F. J. Bourne, in order to support efforts by Dr C. H. Green, to improve traps for tsetse fly control in West Africa, £101,000.

Liverpool School of Tropical Medicine and Hygiene, for research assistance and expenses to Dr R. D. G. Theakston in his investigation of the neutralising activity of antivenom against the venom of *Echis carinatus*, using monoclonal antibodies, £72,000.

East Birmingham Hospital, for research assistance and expenses to Dr T. H. Flewett in his search for an characterisation of new diarrhoea viruses in man, £49,000.

St Andrew's University, a University Award to provide a Lectureship for five years for Dr R. E. Randall, in order to investigate the molecular analysis of paramyxovirus persistence, £126,000.

London School of Hygiene and Tropical Medicine, to Professor G. Webbe, for research assistance and expenses in his study of West African *Simulium damnosum* cytospecies for susceptibility to *Onchocerca volvulus* and for colonisation, £92,000.

Veterinary medicine

1981

University of Bristol, to Professor F. J. Bourne for research assistance and expenses in a study of mucosal protection against viral infection of the respiratory tract, £157,000.

Imperial College, to provide research assistance and expenses for Professor J. D. Smyth to study strain differentiation and the epidemiology of *Echinococcus granulosus* in Kenya and the United Kingdom, £50,000.

1982

University of Edinburgh, for Dr A. Tait, a Wellcome Senior Lecturer, to provide research assistance and expenses for his research on the characterisation of the surface and stage specific proteins of *Theileria annulata* and their role in the immune response of the host, with Mr C. G. D. Brown of the Centre for Tropical Veterinary Medicine, £71,000.

1983

Imperial College of Science and Technology, for research assistance and expenses to Professor Elizabeth U. Canning in her study of the use of hybridoma technology to isolate the antigens associated with immunity against *Babesia divergens*, £71,000.

Animal Health Trust, Newmarket, for research assistance and expenses to Dr C. M. Colles' research on haemorrheology in the horse, £50,000.

Glynn Research Institute, Bodmin, for research assistance and expenses to Dr P. D. Mitchell in his investigation of a spacially realistic biochemistry of respiratory metabolism and oxidative phosphorylation, £150,000.

1984

University of Nottingham, for research assistance and expenses in Professor D. Wakelin's analysis of immunity to coccidial infections (with Dr M. E. Rose, Houghton Poultry Research Station, Cambridge), £67,000.

University of Liverpool, for research assistance and expenses to Dr R. M. Batt, in the investigation of aminopeptidase and alkaline phosphatase activities in the canine intestinal brush border, £45,000; and to Dr D. Bennett for an immunopathological study of inflammatory joint disease in companion animals, £50,000.

University of Glasgow, to Professor W. F. H. Jarrett, research assistance and expenses for a study of the molecular biology and immunology of canine parvovirus infection, £239,000.

University of Edinburgh, to Professor D. W. Brocklesby, research assistance and expenses for an investigation of the molecular structure and metabolism of the surface glycoproteins in *Trypanosoma congolense*, £85,000; and to Dr M. M. H. Sewell for research on the antigens of *Taenia saginata*, with particular reference to serodiagnosis and prophylaxis, £68,000.

University of Cambridge, to Dr R. J. Evans for technical assistance and expenses in studying astrocyte biology in tissue culture in relation to repair and regeneration in the central nervous system, £45,000.

University of Bristol, to Dr D. A. Harbour for research assistance and expenses in studying the structure of the genome of feline herpes virus type 1, £48,000.

University of Bristol, to Professor F. J. Bourne for research assistance and expenses in his immune investigations into Glomerulonephritis in the cat, £56,000.

Imperial College, London, to Dr D. P. McManus for research assistance and expenses in his study of the development of cloned DNA and monoclonal antibody probes for differentiation of the hydatid organism, *Echinococcus granulosus*, £56,000.

APPENDIX V

Grants for buildings and equipment, 1937–76

To nearest £1,000

	£	£	Total £	Budget £
1937–56	322,000	52,000	374,000 = 51% of	740,000
1956–8	544,000	171,000	715,000 = 69% of	1,060,000
1958–60	612,000	163,000	775,000 = 65% of	1,200,000
1960–2	883,000	432,000	1,315,000 = 66% of	2,000,000
1962–4	785,000	428,000	1,213,000 = 61% of	2,000,000
1964–6	946,000	288,000	1,234,000 = 46% of	2,670,000
1966–8	429,000	363,000	792,000 = 28% of	2,780,000
1968–70	406,000	348,000	754,000 = 13% of	5,780,000
1970–2	36,000	206,000	242,000 = 5% of	4,840,000
1972–4	23,000	180,000	203,000 = 4% of	4,479,000
1974–6	138,000	293,000	431,000 = 6% of	7,240,000

After 1976, awards for buildings and equipment ceased to be classified in a separate category in the Trustees' reports.

APPENDIX VI

Major grants for buildings

The department named is that in which the scientific programme was carried out.

Aberdeen University 1966
£50,000 Postgraduate Medical Research Library

Belfast, Queen's University (1964–77)
£ 35,000 Pharmacology
£180,000 Clinical medicine
Total £215,000

Birmingham University (1958–1966)
£95,000 Medicine and Surgery
£36,500 Anatomy
£14,000 Neurocommunications
£20,000 Child health
Total £165,500

Cambridge University (1960–8)
£120,000 Biochemistry
£ 60,000 Radiotherapeutics
£ 50,000 Veterinary studies
£ 22,000 Pathology
£ 60,000 Pharmacology
£ 20,000 Physiology
Total £332,000

Strangeway's Laboratory (1956)
£60,000 Biochemistry

Dublin, Trinity College (1960–6)
£25,000 Experimental surgery
£88,000 Biochemistry
£25,000 Pharmacology
Total £138,000

Dundee University 1975
£15,000 Dermatology

Edinburgh University (1956–81)
£135,000 Genetics and Epigenetics
£ 75,000 Zoology
£ 28,000 Respiratory diseases
£ 50,000 Pharmacology
£ 50,000 Veterinary physiology
£ 19,000 Biochemistry
£ 14,500 Tropical veterinary medicine
Total £371,500

Glasgow University (1956–78)
£ 66,000 Small animal research
£ 60,000 Genetics
£ 35,000 Biochemistry
£131,000 Veterinary medicine, Pathology and Immunology
Total £292,000

Leeds University (1956–64)
£ 10,000 Pharmacology
£105,000 Medical physics and Urology
£ 25,000 Marine Zoology
Total £140,000

Liverpool University 1981
£50,000 Experimental pathology (tropical)

Manchester University 1960
£30,000 Metabolic medicine

Newcastle-upon-Tyne University (1964–6)
£60,000 Medicine
£30,000 Dermatology
Total £90,000

Oxford University (1956–79)
£50,000 Biochemistry
£16,000 Experimental medicine
£30,000 University animal station
£35,000 Anatomy
£44,000 Sir William Dunn School of Pathology
£30,000 Medicine
£20,000 Surgery
£20,000 Psychiatry
Total £245,000

Pirbright, Surrey, Animal Virus Research Station 1964
£65,000 Animal Virus Research

Saint Andrew's University 1956–62
£25,000 Gatty Marine Laboratory

Sheffield, University 1966
£20,000 Physiology

Southampton University 1964
£25,000 Physiology and Biochemistry

London

Medical schools

Charing Cross 1962
£30,500 Obstetrics and Gynaecology and others

King's College Hospital 1962–70
£45,000 Clinical Medicine
£50,000 Liver Diseases
Total £95,000

King's College (1960–78)
£120,000 Biophysics
£108,000 Physiology, Pharmacology and Biochemistry
Total £228,000

Middlesex (1960-8)
£83,000 Pharmacology
£34,500 Otorhinolaryngology
Total £117,500

St Bartholomew's 1962
£55,000 Accommodation for linear accelerator

St George's 1976
£26,000 Biochemistry

St Mary's (1958–80)
£ 70,000 Clinical medicine
£ 25,000 Chemical pathology
£100,000 Experimental pathology
£ 50,000 Clinical medicine
Total £245,000

University College (1962–6)
£40,000 Pharmacology
£20,000 Anatomy
£60,000 Biophysics
£80,000 Pharmacology and Physiology
Total £200,000

Westminster 1962
£22,000 Clinical measurement

Royal Postgraduate (1956–78)
£ 80,000 Experimental surgery
£ 60,000 Research library
£116,000 Virology
£ 58,000 Haematology
£ 58,000 Cardiology
£ 15,000 Clinical pharmacology
£178,000 Clinical medicine
Total £565,000

Institutes

Cancer Research 1956
£40,000 Experimental chemotherapy

Child Health 1962
£50,000 Clinical medicine

Dermatology 1973
£100,000 Pharmacology and Immunology

London School of Hygiene and Tropical Medicine 1962
£4,500 Entomology

Neurology 1971
£21,000 Biochemistry

Orthopaedics 1958
£43,000 Metabolic disorders

Psychiatry 1958
£37,000 Neuropathology

Imperial College 1970
£15,000 Bioengineering

Royal College of Obstetricians and Gynaecologists 1955
£30,000 Research Museum

Royal Society 1964
£103,000 Research meeting rooms

Royal Society of Medicine (1950–82)
£467,350 Research library
Contribution to rebuilding costs

Zoology Society 1962
£60,000 Comparative physiology

Overseas

Australia (1958–66)
Sydney – £17,000 Experimental medicine and surgery
£20,000 Microbiology

Melbourne – £14,000 Surgery
Brisbane – £12,000 Surgery
Total £63,000

Canada (1966–8)
British Columbia – £12,000 Surgery
Montreal – £46,000 Medicine
Toronto – £70,000 Experimental medicine
Total £128,000

India 1958
Vellore – £10,000 Sprue Research Unit

Kenya 1958
£100,000 Foot-and-Mouth Disease Research Unit

New Zealand 1962
Otago – £120,000, Institute of Medical Research

Uganda (1960–8)
Kampala – £125,000 Mobile Field Laboratory
Entebbe – £50,000 Virus Research Labratory
Makerere – £28,000 Clinical medicine
Total £203,000

United States of America (1960–4)
Johns Hopkins University – £35,000 Circulatory studies; Public health
Harvard University – £26,000 Experimental pathology
Yale University – £90,000 Pharmacology
Total £151,000

West Indies (1960–6)
University – £12,000 Physiology
MRC Unit – £61,000 Epidemiology
Total £73,000

APPENDIX VII

Awards for electron microscopes

The titles of the scientific projects are abbreviated. Every project was for ultrastructural studies of the cells or tissues named in the title.

University of Birmingham

1957 Department of Medical Biochemistry
Professor A. C. Frazer
The myelin sheath

1960 Department of Zoology
Professor O. Loewenstein
Comparative anatomy of the sensory cells of the vertebrate ear

University of Bristol

1970 Department of Physiology
Professor T. J. Biscoe
Information processing at synapses

University of Cambridge

1955 The Physiological Laboratory
Professor A. L. Hodgkin and Dr A. F. Huxley
Isolated muscle fibres; the nerve membrane

1965 Department of Veterinary Anatomy
Dr B. A. Cross
Neuroendocrinology and reproduction; especially fine changes induced in hypothalamic neurones by altered hormone levels

A.R.C. Institute of Clinical Physiology, Babraham, Cambridge

1960 Dr J. H. Gaddum
Specific sub-cellular tissue fractions

Strangeways Research Laboratory Cambridge

1965 Dame Honor Fell
The biological effects of membrane active agents

1978 Mr M. Abercrombie
Mechanisms of cellular immunological reactions of schistosomula and other studies in cellular pathology

University of Dundee

1960 Department of Anatomy
Professor R. G. Coupland
Chromaffin tissue and the islets of Langerhans

University of Durham

1960 Department of Pathology
Professor A. G. Heppleston
The ageing lung

University of Edinburgh

1957 Department of Anatomy
Professor G. J. Romanes
Histogenesis in mammalian embryonic tissues

1975 Human articular cartilage; motor nerve fibres of the rat; and cellular mechanisms in human autoimmune disease

Western General Hospital, Edinburgh

1978 Teaching and Research Centre
Dr A. E. Williams
(a contribution from the Trust)
Clinical and vascular endothelium; gall bladder epithelium; the antibody dependent cytotoxic cell

University of Glasgow

1960 Department of Virology
Professor M. G. P. Stoker
Virus/cell interactions and virus growth

1962 Department of Anatomy
Professor G. H. Wyburn
The digestive tract

University of Liverpool

1965 Department of Veterinary Anatomy
Professor A. S. King
The comparative anatomy and physiology of male reproductive organs; and lactational physiology

1968 Department of Bacteriology
Professor K. McCarthy
Simian virus which has close serological relationship to human varicella

1982 Department of Medical Cell Biology
Professor C. R. Hopkins
(a contribution from the Trust)
The use of electron opaque tracers in the study of cellular events

University of Keele

1982 Department of Biology Sciences
Professor C. Arme
(a contribution from the Trust)
Echinococcus granulosus/host parasite reactions in hydatidosis

University of London

1958 King's College, Department of Biophysics
Professor J. T. Randall
Morphogenesis and development in lower animals

University College:

1954 Department of Physiology
Dr H. E. Huxley
Correlation of structure and function of muscle

1962 Department of Anatomy
Professor J. Z. Young
Neurology

1969 Institute of Cardiology
Professor P. Harris
Cellular pathology and physiology of the myocardium

1959 Institute of Ophthalmology
Sir Stewart Duke-Elder
Tissues of the eye, particularly the retina and cornea

1963 Professor N. Ashton
Diseases of the eye

1969 Professor C. M. H. Pedler
The eye; particularly a method for seral reconstructions of neurones and examination of fresh, unfixed non-embedded tissue

1981 Professor A. Garner
(a contribution from the Trust)
The normal primate outflow system

1969 Institute of Orthopaedics
Professor R. G. Burwell
Articular cartilage, bone and synovial joints

London Hospital Medical College

1957 Department of Anatomy, Professor R. J. Harrison
Dept of Dental Pathology, Professor A. E. W. Miles
The placenta; and aspects of dental disease

London School of Hygiene and Tropical Medicine

1958 Sir James Kilpatrick
Arthropod borne viruses; granules of trypanosomiasis; and structure of plasmodium related to movement

The Middlesex Hospital

1967 Bland Sutton Institute of Pathology
Professor G. W. A. Dick
The development of techniques for the identification of viruses

St Mary's Hospital Medical School

1962 Department of Anatomy
Professor F. Goldby
Pigment-forming cells

1970 Professor A. S. Breathnach
Human foetal skin

1977 and 1980 Skin pigmentation; cutaneous innervation and morphology of the Langerhans cell

St Bartholomew's Hospital Medical College

1967 Department of Zoology and Comparative Anatomy
Professor D. Lacy
The mammalian testis

Royal Dental Hospital, London

1963 Professor R. B. Lucas
Dental pathology

Royal Postgraduate Medical School

1961 Department of Pathology
Dr A. G. E. Pearse
Enzyme histochemistry

University of Newcastle-upon-Tyne

1981 Department of Anatomy
Professor J. S. G. Miller
(a contribution from the Trust)
Developmental cell biology

University of Oxford

1955 Department of Anatomy
Professor Sir Wilfrid Le Gros Clark
The relationship of lepra bacilli to axon filaments of cutaneous nerves; mitochondria and other subcellular particles; cellular changes relating to atheroma; meiotic division; olfactory cells

1959 Dr P. Glees
The terminations of fibre tracts in the central nervous system of mammals (instrument transferred to Göttingen, when Dr Glees took up a Professorship there)

1968 Dr A. G. Weddell
Experimental leprosy

1980 Professor C. G. Phillips
Developmental neuroanatomy

1958 Sir William Dunn School of Pathology:
Professor Sir Howard Florey
The properties of endothelium in relation to changes occurring in arteries during the development of atheroma

1967 Professor H. Harris
Changes occurring in bird erythrocyte nucleus when reactivated within cytoplasm of other cells and other studies

1960 Department of Zoology
Dr J. R. Baker
Fixation for electron microscopy, particularly phospholipid membranes

Marine Biology Station, Plymouth

1964 Professor C. F. A. Pantin
The neurohistology of fish; life histories of microscopic marine algae; fine particles of sea-water

University College of Wales, Cardiff

1961 Department of Anatomy
Professor J. D. Lever
Endrocrine tissues

Overseas awards

University of Melbourne, Australia

1964 Department of Medicine
Professor R. Lovell
Human synovial cells

University of Queensland, Brisbane, Australia

1979 Department of Veterinary Anatomy
Professor T. D. Glover
(a contribution from the Trust)
Reproductive biology

McGill University, Montreal, Canada

1959 Department of Physiology
Professor F. G. MacIntosh
Synaptic morphology

University of Colombo, Ceylon

1967 Department of Anatomy and Parasitology
Professor E. O. R. Abhayaratne
Microfilaria and *Echinococcus granulosus*

Christian Medical College Vellore, India

1979 Professor M. Mathan
An investigation of the aetiology of tropical sprue

University of Auckland, New Zealand

1963 Department of Microbiology
Professor R. E. Matthews
Nucleic acids, virus synthesis and virus inhibition

Makere University College, Medical School, Kampala, Uganda

1963 Professor D. Allbrook
Injured primate muscle with special reference to effects of virus infection

APPENDIX VIII

Awards for research assistance and expenses in basic and clinical sciences

To nearest £1,000

	£		£
1937–56	40,000 =	5% of total expenditure of	740,000
1956–8	65,000 =	6% of total expenditure of	1,060,000
1958–60	98,000 =	8% of total expenditure of	1,200,000
1960–2	140,000 =	7% of total expenditure of	2,000,000
1962–4	149,000 =	7% of total expenditure of	2,000,000
1964–6	244,000 =	9% of total expenditure of	2,670,000
1966–8	961,000 =	34% of total expenditure of	2,780,000
1968–70	2,033,000 =	35% of total expenditure of	5,780,000
1970–2	1,307,000 =	27% of total expenditure of	4,844,000
1972–4	1,133,000 =	25% of total expenditure of	4,479,000
1974–6	2,501,000 =	34% of total expenditure of	7,240,000
1976–8	3,183,000 =	26% of total expenditure of	12,369,000
1978–80	5,142,000 =	25% of total expenditure of	20,672,000
1980–2	6,118,000 =	25% of total expenditure of	24,500,000
1982–4	7,671,000 =	21% of total expenditure of	35,842,000
TOTAL	31,000,000 (approx.)		128,000,000

APPENDIX IX

Senior Clinical Fellows, 1979–85

1979	Cox, T. M.	Royal Postgraduate Medical School
	Johnston, D. G.	University of Newcastle
1980	Lane, R. J. M.	University of Liverpool
1981	MacDermot, J.	Royal Postgraduate Medical School
	McGregor, A. M.	University of Wales College of Medicine, Cardiff
	Summerfield, J. A.	Royal Free Hospital School of Medicine
1982	Chu, A. C.	Royal Postgraduate Medical School
	Home, P. D.	University of Newcastle
	Jones, P. W.	Middlesex Hospital Medical School
	Leslie, R. D. G.	King's College Hospital Medical School
	Neuberger, J. M.	King's College Hospital Medical School
	Rubin, P. C.	University of Glasgow
1983	Ciclitira, P. J.	St Thomas's Hospital Medical School
	Francis, G. E.	Royal Free Hospital School of Medicine
	Gardiner, R. M.	University College, London
1984	Gatter, K. C.	University of Oxford
	Gurling, M. M. D.	Institute of Psychiatry
	Pusey, C. D.	Royal Postgraduate Medical School
1985	Nutt, D. J.	University of Oxford
	Stradling, J. R.	University of Oxford
	Unwin, R. J.	St Mary's Hospital Medical School
	Weetman, A. P.	Royal Postgraduate Medical School

Former senior clinical fellows (since 1971)

1971	Ochoa, J.	Institute of Neurology
1972	Campbell, M. J.	University of Newcastle
	Evered, D. C.	University of Newcastle
	Tulloch, B. R.	Royal Postgraduate Medical School
1973	Fraser, K. J.	University of Melbourne, Australia
	Hamilton, D. N. H.	University of Glasgow
	Peters, T. J.	Royal Postgraduate Medical School
1974	Marshall, J. C.	University of Birmingham
	Reid, J. L.	Royal Postgraduate Medical School
	Rickards, A. F.	Cardiothoracic Institute

1975	Fabre, J. W.	University of Oxford
	Greenwood, R. H. P.	Welsh National School of Medicine, Cardiff
	Wilcox, C. S.	St Mary's Hospital Medical School
1976	Kanis, J. A.	University of Oxford
	McMichael, A. J.	University of Oxford
	Tomlinson, S.	University of Sheffield
1977	Belchetz, P. E.	St Bartholomew's Hospital Medical College
	Boylston, A. W.	St Mary's Hospital Medical School
	Selwyn, A. P.	Royal Postgraduate Medical School
1978	Fairclough, P. D.	St Bartholomew's Hospital Medical College
	Rubery, E. D.	University of Cambridge
	Thomas, H. C.	Royal Free Hospital School of Medicine
1979	Horton, M. A.	St Bartholomew's Hospital Medical College
	Lockwood, C. M.	Royal Postgraduate Medical School
	Mathias, C. J.	St Mary's Hospital Medical School
	Rees, W. D. W.	University of Manchester
	Segal, A. W.	University College Hospital Medical School
1980	Taylor, R. H.	Middlesex Hospital Medical School
	Weir, A. I.	University of Glasgow

APPENDIX X

Wellcome Senior Lecturers, 1979–85

The place is London unless otherwise indicated

1979	Devey, Madeleine E.	London School of Hygiene and Tropical Medicine
	Ewing, David J.	University of Edinburgh
	MacGregor, Graham M.	Charing Cross Hospital Medical School
	Silman, Robert E.	St Bartholomew's Hospital Medical College
	Sissons, J. G. Patrick	Royal Postgraduate Medical School
1980	Aronson, Jeffrey, K.	University of Oxford
	Burchell, Brian	University of Dundee
	Doenhoff, Michael J.	London School of Hygiene and Tropical Medicine
	File, Sandra E.	School of Pharmacy, London
	Ward, Richard D.	Liverpool School of Tropical Medicine
1981	Cooke, Anne	Middlesex Hospital Medical School
	Ford, Geoffrey C.	University of Sheffield
	Golden, Michael H. N.	University of Aberdeen
	Marsden, Charles A.	University of Nottingham
	Meech, Robert W.	University of Bristol
	Miles, Michael A.	London School of Hygiene and Tropical Medicine
	Siddle, Kenneth	University of Cambridge
	Tait, Andrew	University of Edinburgh
1982	Blackwell, Jenefer, M.	London School of Hygiene and Tropical Medicine
	Cull-Candy, Stuart G.	University College London
	Dean, Philip M.	University of Cambridge
	Golding, M. Jean	Hospital for Sick Children, Bristol
	Harvey, David J.	University of Oxford
	Hess, Robert F.	University of Cambridge
	Jones, Hazel C.	University of Hull
	Shepphard, Michael C.	University of Birmingham
	Thompson, David G.	London Hospital Medical College
	Wheal, Howard V.	University of Southampton
1983	Farthing, Michael J. G.	St Bartholomew's Hospital Medical College
	Griffin, George E.	St George's Hospital Medical School
	Idle, Jeffrey R.	St Mary's Hospital Medical School
	Park, Brian K.	University of Liverpool
	Sim, Edith	University of Oxford
	Tooke, John E.	Charing Cross Hospital Medical School
	Wilkin, Terence J.	Southampton General Hospital

1984	Candy, David C. A.	University of Birmingham
	Connor, James M.	University of Glasgow
	Fairburn, Christopher G.	University of Oxford
	McBride, Jana S.	University of Edinburgh
	Mathias, Christopher J.	St Mary's Hospital Medical School
	Nye, P. C. G.	University of Oxford
	Pasvol, Geoffrey	University of Oxford
	Shaw, Jeffrey J.	London School of Hygiene and Tropical Medicine
	Woolf, Clifford	University College London
1985	Cox, Tim	Royal Postgraduate Medical School

Former Wellcome Senior Lecturers

1979	Camm, A. J.	St Bartholomew's Hospital Medical College
	Murphy, Gerald M.	Guy's Hospital Medical School
	Rennie, Michael J.	University College Hospital Medical School
	Sillito, Adam M.	University of Birmingham Medical School
1980	Lightman, Stafford L.	St Mary's Hospital Medical School
	Tomlinson, Stephen	Northern General Hospital, Sheffield
	Welsh, I. K.	Royal Postgraduate Medical School

OFFICERS OF THE TRUST 1986

Director

Dr *Peter Orchard Williams* M.B., B. Chir. (Cantab.), F.R.C.P. is an Honorary Fellow of the London School of Hygiene and Tropical Medicine and in 1983 he was awarded the Mary Kingsley Medal of the Liverpool School of Tropical Medicine for services to tropical medicine. He is, or has been, a member of the following bodies: Managing Committee of the Bureau of Hygiene and Tropical Medicine; Royal Society of Tropical Medicine and Hygiene (former Council Member and Vice-President). He is co-founder and sometime chairman of the Association of Medical Research Charities, of the Foundations' Forum, and of The Hague Club. He is the author of numerous articles in medical journals.

Deputy Director: Science

Dr *Bridget M. Ogilvie* Ph.D., Sc.D.(Cantab.) is at present a Visiting Professor at the Imperial College of Science and Technology, London. She was a member of the scientific staff of the Medical Research Council 1966–81, having previously been an Animal Health Research Trust Fellow. She is a member of the following societies: British Society of Parasitology (Vice-President); Royal Society of Tropical Medicine and Hygiene (Council); British Society of Immunology; and the Medical Research Club (Secretary 1980–83). She edits *Parasite Immunology* and serves on the editorial boards of many other journals. She has acted as consultant to the World Health Organization and the British Council. She has published about 100 articles and reviews in journals devoted to immunology and parasitology.

Deputy Director: Finance and Administration

Mr *Ian Macgregor* is a Fellow of the Institute of Chartered Accountants in England and Wales.

Senior Assistant Director

Dr *Keith Beaumont Sinclair,* D.V.Sc. (Liverpool), Ph.D. (Wales) is a Fellow of the Royal College of Veterinary Surgeons, in which College he was formerly a Lecturer, later being appointed Reader at the School of Agricultural Science, University of Wales, Aberystwyth. He served for a time as Dean of the Faculty of Science in this University. He has also been a Research Fellow of the School of Tropical Medicine, Liverpool. He has served on the Council of the British Veterinary Association, British Society for Parasitology, Royal Society of Medicine (section of Comparative Medicine) and other bodies. He has acted as consultant to the Food and Agricultural Organization, to many Local Authorities, and to industry. He has published many papers in veterinary journals and in the *Journal of Comparative Pathology.*

Assistant Directors

Dr *Peter A. J. Ball,* M.D. (Cantab.), F.R.C.P., is Pro-Censor of the Royal College of Physicians of England and a Trustee of the Sir Jules Thorne Charitable Trust. Until last year he was also Civil Consultant on Medicine to the Royal Air Force. For many years a Consultant at the Middlesex Hospital, he has served briefly as Professor of Medicine at Ahmadu Bello University, Nigeria. He has published in the *Lancet,* the *British Medical Journal* and other British and African medical journals.

Dr *David Gordon* M.B., B.Chir. (Cantab.), M.R.C.P., is an Honorary Consultant Physician at St Mary's Hospital, London, and an Honorary Senior Lecturer in the Medical School of the same hospital. He is a member of the Physiological Society, the British Pharmacological Society, the Medical Research Society and other organizations. He has published papers in the *Journal of Physiology, Clinical Science,* the *American Journal of Physiology,* etc.

Dr *Michael James Morgan,* B.A. (Dublin), Ph.D. (Leicester) is an Honorary University Fellow in the Department of Biochemistry, University of Leicester. He has visited the U.S.A. as a Harkness Fellow (1969–71). He is a member of the Biochemistry Society (Committee), the British Society of

Cell Biology, and the Royal Society of Medicine. He is a Governor of the Gateway Sixth Form College, Leicester. He is a joint author of *Human Reproduction* (1980) and of articles in specialist journals.

Chief Administrative Officer

Derek Gordon Metcalfe entered hospital administration at Margate General Hospital in June 1948, transferring as Establishment Officer to the Thanet and District H.M.C. and moving in 1957 to the Medway and Gravesend H.M.C. In 1960 he was appointed to the executive staff of the Medical Research Council, which he left in August 1968 to join the Wellcome Trust as Fellowship Officer, moving to Head of the Grants Administration in 1980.

Head of External Relations and Coordinator of the Programme for the History of Medicine

William Anderson M.A. (Oxon) was, before joining the Trust, the publications manager of the Nuffield science and mathematics projects and also a Research Fellow at the Centre for Educational Studies, King's College, London. He has published three books of verse and several works on medieval architecture and literature. His book *Dante the Maker* (1980) received the International PEN Club award *The Silver Pen*. His most recent book is *The Rise of the Gothic* (1985).

NOTES TO THE TEXT

PART I

Chapter 1

1 In this and other quotations from the Will I have introduced punctuation where it seems to be necessary in accord with ordinary usage.

Chapter 2

1 A. Landsborough Thomson, 1975, *Half a Century of Medical Research,* II. H.M.S.O. 232.
2 The Government's provision for the Medical Research Council in 1938 was almost exactly £200,000.
3 The Trustees have recently granted a much larger sum to the Smithsonian Institution, Washington, in aid of its purchase of the survivors of these models.
4 For comparison, it may be noted that the Foundation charged for the Wellcome Historical Museum and Library, the Wellcome Bureau of Scientific Research and the Wellcome Research Institute a total of £74,000 against gross profits in 1939 (salary costs for 38 staff were £21,000), while the Trustee's outgoings amounted to only £8,000.
5 The 'junior' Directors of the Foundation (aged 52 and 48 respectively in 1938) were Dr S. Smith, Works Manager, and C. G. Oakes, secretary to Mr Pearson (who thought Oakes might, in due time, succeed himself).

Chapter 3

1 Mr Linstead, elder brother of the future Rector of Imperial College, was both a pharmaceutical chemist and a barrister. From 1956 to 1964 he was a member of the M.R.C. For many years he was an active figure in public life.

Chapter 4

1 The change took more than a year to realise, partly because of Lord Piercy's prolonged illness in the summer of 1962.

2 This latter relief was necessary because long before, after the death of Mr Lyall, the Trustees had felt it necessary to seek an Order of the High Court (duly made by Mr Justice Simmonds on 1 May 1939) defining the composition of the Board of five Trustees as being made up of two lawyers, two scientists and an accountant; when Mr Price approached the end of his Trusteeship (at the age of 81) his fellow Trustees took the view that this professional restriction in their choice of his successor was no longer requisite nor prudent.

Chapter 5

1 Dr Green, who was in poor health, had retired on 23 August 1963. He died only in 1977.
2 It is, however, virtually impossible for such a body as the Wellcome Trust to seek redress for the non-payments of 'loans'.

Chapter 6

1 Or Burroughs Wellcome (Overseas).
2 Ronald W. Clark, 1972, *A Biography of the Nuffield Foundation*, 215–16.

Chapter 7

1 J. K. Crellin, 1969, *Medical Ceramics in the Wellcome Institute.*
2 There was some unintended exaggeration in this fraction.

Chapter 8

1 The Trust's original representatives were: Professors G. V. R. Born (then of the Royal College of Surgeons, later of Cambridge), A. C. Dornhurst (St George's Hospital Medical School) and R. A. Gregory (Liverpool University), with Dr Williams. The German group consisted of Professors K. Fleischhauer (Bonn). T. M. Fliedner (Ulm) and G. Meyer-Schwickerath (Essen). There were also two observers from the Deutsche Forschungsgemeinschaft.
2 That is, cercopitheque (African) monkeys.

Chapter 10

1 A. Landsborough Thomson, 1973, *Half a Century of Medical Research*, I, 92.
2 Generous assistance with the purchase of major recent accessions to the Libary has been provided by the National Heritage Fund and the British Library. The Library is increasingly treated by national bodies (and for that matter, national newspapers) as this country's principal resource on matters relating to the History of Medicine.

PART II

Introduction

1 A conspectus of grants is provided in Appendix IV.

Chapter 11

1 The assistance of Dr L. G. Goodwin in preparing this chapter is gratefully acknowledged.
2 *Trans. Roy. Soc. Trop. Med. & Hyg.*, 1971 65(b), 715.
3 The other original members were Dr L. G. Goodwin, Professors Sidney Cohen, T. R. E. Southwood, W. W. Macdonald, and R. Hendrickse, and Dr R. G. Whitehead. The Panel first met on 12 January 1977.
4 See the extract in *Sixth Report, 1964–6*, 32–5.
5 Baker, S. J., Booth, C. C., England, N. W. J., Foy, H., Klipstein, F. A., Kondi, A., Mathan, V. I., Mollin, D. L. and O'Brien, W., *Tropical Sprue and Megaloblastic Anaemia, Wellcome Trust Collaborative Study*, Edinburgh and Baltimore Md., 1972.
6 Dr Selwyn Baker is now at the St Boniface General Hospital, Winnipeg, Canada.
7 *Trans. Roy. Soc. Trop. Med. & Hyg.*, 1983, 77(5), 569–96.
8 Dr Bray was a Wellcome Research Fellow (having returned to London from Baghdad).
9 *Trans. Roy. Soc. Trop. Med. & Hyg.*, 1983, 77(1), 5–23. Chagas' Disease, associated with poverty and poor housing (see figure 54), and its transmission by the triatomine bug, were identified by Carlos Chagas in 1910. His work was undervalued for nearly 30 years.
10 Later, it was agreed to divide equally, between the London and Liverpool Schools, £3,000,000 spread over five years.

Chapter 12

1 The assistance of Dr K. B. Sinclair in the preparation of this Chapter is gratefully acknowledged.

Chapter 13

1 Dr J. Steiner, Institute of Psychiatry, 1967. 'Risk taking as a method of psychological assessment in patients'.
2 Dr R. P. Hullin, Department of Biochemistry, Leeds, 1970, 'The biochemical basis of mental disorders'.
3 In the period 1910–77 the Beit Memorial Trustees awarded 426 fellowships of which 15 were for fellows to work in a department of psychiatry, or on an investigation related to mental health. Three of these were taken up before the Second World War.
4 This Chair of Psychiatry, established in 1908, was the first in Great Britain.
5 Quoted by Henderson, D. K., 1964, *The Evolution of Psychiatry in Scotland*, Edinburgh, p. 124.
6 Later members, after retirements, were Professors G. Russell, G. W. Ashcroft, R. Miledi, J. S. Kelly, J. Wing, M. Gelder, K. Rawnsley, G. Fink and M. L. Rutter.
7 Mackenzie, S., 1877, A case of glycosuric retinitis, with comments. *R.L. Ophth. Hosp. Repts. ix*, 134–57.
8 Wagener, H. P., Dry, T. J. S., & Wilder, R. M. 1934, Retinitis in diabetes. *New Eng. Med. J. 211*, 1131–7.
9 Ballantyne, A. J. & Lowenstein, A., 1943, The pathology of diabetic retinopathy. *Trans. Ophth. Soc. U.K. 63*, 95–115.
10 See his lecture in *Royal Institution Proceedings*, 1981, 53, pp. 136–63.

11 This topic illustrates neatly the problem of classifying some grants; presumably the topic could as well have come under an ophthalmological programme.

Chapter 14

1 Brenner, S., 1980, from a symposium on 'Biology in the 1980s', *Nature, 285,* 358.
2 de Duve, C., Beaufay, H., 1981, A short history of tissue fractionation, *J. Cell Biology, 91,* 293–9.
3 It is interesting to note that Roentgen performed his experiments in November 1895; published his results in December 1895; and English translations of his paper appeared in January and February 1896.
4 Kathleen Lonsdale was one of the first two women to be elected F.R.S., in 1945. This was during the Presidency of Sir Henry Dale (1940–5).
5 Fruton, J. S., 1976, The Emergence of Biochemistry. *Science 192,* 327–34.
6 Huxley, T. H., 1885, *Proc. Roy. Soc., 39,* 294. The relevance of this remark to recent developments in N.M.R. was noticed by Sir Andrew Huxley while preparing his own Presidential Address, which he gave on 1 December, 1980.
7 Ramsay, J. A., 1976, *Nature, 259,* 433.
8 Bohr, N., 1933, *Nature, 131,* 421–3; 457–9.
9 Pirie, N. W., 1937, in *Perspectives in Biochemistry* (ed. J. Needham, D. E. Green), Cambridge.
10 Stanley, W. M., 1940, in *The Cell and Protoplasm.* Publ. of The Amer. Assoc. for the Advance of Science, No. 14.

Chapter 15

1 Walter B. Cannon, 1945, *The Way of an Investigator,* New York, 211.
2 W. S. Feldberg, 1970, *'Henry Hallett Dale', Biographical Memoirs of Fellows of the Royal Society, 16,* 91–2.
3 Werner Forssman, 1975, *Experiments on Myself* (trans. from German), 40.
4 Feldberg, *loc. cit.,* 98.
5 *Trends in Biochemical Sciences,* Sept. 1986, *1,* N198.
6 The Medical Research Council of New Zealand; the Clive and Vera Ramaciotti Foundation of Sydney; the Burroughs Wellcome Fund in U.S.A.; and the Loewenstein Trust in Johannesburg.

Chapter 16

1 Arthur Kornberg, 1976, *New England J. Medicine, 294,* 1212–16.
2 Sir Macfarlane's scepticism was set out in *Genes, Dreams and Realities,* 1971, p. 218.
3 For example, the Department of Biochemistry in University College, London, became independent of the Department of Physiology in 1945, with the establishment of a Chair. There had previously been a Professor of Biochemistry in the Department of Physiology. At the time of the formation of the Wellcome Trust, there were independent established Chairs of Biochemistry in Liverpool (1902); Glasgow (1919); Oxford (1920); Cambridge (1924); Queen's University, Belfast (1924); Middlesex Hospital Medical School (1925); Edinburgh (1926 Chemistry in relation to Medicine); St Bartholomew's Hospital Medical College (1936).

4 Fruton, J. S., 1976, The Emergence of Biochemistry, *Science, 192*, 327–34.
5 Weaver, W., 1970, Molecular Biology: origin of the term, *Science, 170*, 581–2.
6 Kendrew, J., 1967, Review of: Phage and the Origins of Molecular Biology, *Scientific American, 216*, 141.
7 Peart, W. S., 1983, Rebirth of the Professor of Medicine, *Lancet*, 810–12.
8 In *The Pursuit of Nature*, ed. A. Hodgkin, Cambridge, 1977, p. 128.
9 Gee, S., 1888, On the coeliac affection, *St Bartholomew's Hosp. Rep. 24*, 17–20.
10 Paulley, J. W., 1954, *Br.Med.J.* ii, 1318.

INDEX